Factory Daughters

Gender, Household Dynamics, and Rural Industrialization in Java

Diane Lauren Wolf

UNIVERSITY OF CALIFORNIA PRESS
Berkeley · Los Angeles · Oxford

University of California Press
Berkeley and Los Angeles, California

University of California Press, Ltd.
Oxford, England

Library of Congress Cataloging-in-Publication Data

Wolf, Diane L.
Factory daughters : gender, household dynamics, and rural industrialization in Java / Diane Lauren Wolf.
p. cm.
Includes bibliographical references and index.
ISBN 0-520-07072-0 (alk. paper)
1. Women—Employment—Indonesia—Java. 2. Households—Indonesia—Java. 3. Work and family—Indonesia—Java. 4. Rural development—Indonesia—Java. 5. Sex role—Indonesia—Java. I. Title.
HD6194.Z6J388 1992
331.4'09598'2—dc20 91-41844
CIP

Printed in the United States of America

9 8 7 6 5 4 3 2 1

The paper used in this publication meets the minimum requirements of American National Standard for Information Sciences—Permanence of Paper for Printed Library Materials, ANSI Z39.48-1984. ♾

Factory Daughters

für Frank

Die Welt wird immer böser.
Ich brauche siebzehn Erlöser,
und einer davon bist Du,
Winnie the Pooh.

F. W. Bernstein,
"Mein Lieblingserlöser"

Contents

Illustrations

FIGURES

MAP

Tables

Acknowledgments

To me, one of the greatest delusions is the notion that writing is a joy. . . . In fact, some of the greatest writers have suffered agony of the spirit in the process. I may not have the greatness in common with them, but by Jesus, I've got the agony.

Emma Goldman, 26 June 1928

My first and deepest debt is to the young women and their families who shared their stories and their lives with me. They were generous with their patience, warmth, time, and humor, and they made fieldwork a humbling experience. The family of Bapak Hadi Rowadi welcomed me into their home and tolerated what must have seemed my peculiar questions and habits; I am grateful for all of their help and kindness. I could not have completed this project without my research assistants, Enni Caturini, Agnes Yosephine Retno Dwidarsih, and Yustina Retno Yuniatmi, who helped enormously with their hard work, friendship, and humor.

I am indebted to many people who helped me at different stages of this research, from agricultural extension agents and civil servants to local administrators and *warung* owners; it was all done with a level of hospitality I have never experienced elsewhere. I wish to thank the general manager at LamaTex, who allowed me to live in the workers' dormitory and gave me access to the factory.

This research was sponsored by the Lembaga Ilmu Pengatahuan Indonesia (LIPI). I gratefully acknowledge the sponsorship of the Population Studies Center at Gadjah Mada University, Yogyakarta, provided by Dr. Masri Singarimbun and Dr. Sofian Effendi. From 1981 to 1983 this research was funded by a Title XII grant administered through Cornell University, and in 1986 by a University of Washington Faculty Research Grant.

Peter Berman fueled what was to become my deep appreciation of

Indonesia; I thank him for his help and support during fieldwork. *Matur nuwun sangat* to Loekman, Tutti, Pita B., and Nino Soetrisno, who offered a home away from home, and a place where humor served to vent my frustrations. Chris Manning's good advice and many suggestions during the early stages of fieldwork were helpful.

I would like to thank the professors on my doctoral committee at Cornell for their encouragement: E. W. Coward, Milton Barnett, Edward L. Kain, and Barry Edmonston. Fred Buttel, while not on my committee, provided theoretical guidance.

I am truly indebted to those who have taken time to read parts or all of this manuscript and to give me helpful feedback: Fred Block, Carmen Diana Deere, Christine Di Stefano, Nancy Folbre, John R. Hall, Gillian Hart, Daniel Lev, Roger Rouse, Carol A. Smith, Judith Stacey, Anna Lowenhaupt Tsing, and Michael Watts; many of those mentioned double as good friends. I was also aided by the reactions of three anonymous reviewers.

I have benefited from the support and encouragement of my colleagues in the Department of Sociology at the University of California, Davis, for which I am extremely grateful. I especially want to thank the two chairs from whom I have received support and good advice—Gary Hamilton and Lawrence Cohen. Thanks to James Cramer, who supplied me with the newspaper article that helped me end the book. I would also like to acknowledge my students, whose intellectual and political concerns contribute to the richness of my academic life.

In Seattle, Dr. Dorothy Bestor offered extremely helpful editorial guidance and encouragement. At the University of California Press, I have been aided by Naomi Schneider's editorial expertise, Amy Klatzkin's cheerful help through the production process, and Dan Gunter's fastidious copyediting. In Davis, Erica Crowell has been a wonderful and conscientious assistant.

I wish to acknowledge those who were supportive of this project, either directly or indirectly: Carolyn Bynum, Brenda Kahn, Tai, Suzanne, Mary and Peter Katzenstein, all for very different reasons; Guille Libresco, Diane Lye, Marjorie Nathanson, the late Greta Newman, Meryl Rappaport, the late Stephen Risch, and Guenther Roth. The lives and spirits of Jake and Jeannette Geldwert and the late Ahrne Thorne have taught me a great deal. Chana Kronfeld continues to engage in another way of friendship. As always, Bluma Goldstein supplies the best jokes west of the Bronx. Christine Di Stefano's support has been irreplaceable; her humor and her Sicilian superstitions have kept me laughing and safe, respectively (or perhaps vice versa). Joshua and Rachel have engaged me in the delights of aunthood; I also wish to acknowledge the friends, family members, and assorted cousins, young and young at heart alike, who are a part of my life.

My parents died in the midst of their days, leaving an enormous void in my life. It grieves me that they are not here to enjoy the fruits of their labor.

I feel lucky to have had three grandparents in my life—Alice Scheuer, the late Julius Scheuer, and the late Mina Wolf. All of them gave (and continue to give) me a great deal of love and support, in very different ways, ranging from financial help for my education to purple sweaters and thickly knitted, strangely colored socks that kept me warm during Ithaca winters while I was, as my late grandmother would say, "making my doctor." They taught me firsthand about the sweet, sticky, and difficult webs of family obligation.

I am forever grateful to my relatives Hilde and David Burton, who picked up the pieces after my mother died and made me a part of their lives. A special *terima kasih* to Dan and Arlene Lev, who opened their hearts and home to me during the several years I lived in Seattle.

Frank Hirtz gave up his language, his culture, his context, his tenured job, and German bread to live with me in Davis; this book is dedicated to him as but a token of my deep appreciation. His cheerfulness, humor, warmth, strong support, patience, and superb pasta after a bad day have helped anchor me in a calm harbor. Together we continue to perfect the art of making irrational but delightful choices. During the last year of revising this book, we adopted a boxer puppy who now owns us. Adorno (the dog) is not concerned with my work except to interrupt it, and has provided the critical insight that frequent games of keep-away and tug-of-war are soothing for the computer-weary soul.

Introduction

If every event which occurred could be given a name, there would be no need for stories. As things are here, life outstrips our vocabulary.

John Berger, Once in Europa

RINI'S STORY

Rini is a factory daughter. She dropped out of school during the fifth grade, at age twelve, and helped around her parents' house. In 1978, at age fifteen, she looked for a factory job because, as she explained, she was "bored at home," where she spent her time performing household chores, taking care of her younger siblings, gathering fodder for the goat, and occasionally selling vegetables in the market. She had also helped her parents on their small parcels of wet riceland from time to time, but she did not like going to the *sawah* to do farmwork. She sought factory work on her own initiative, without asking her parents' permission. Indeed, her father did not agree to her new job; he "was angry and quiet for one month" before things returned to normal.[1]

I met Rini (a pseudonym) in 1981, when she was twenty-one years old. Lively, funny, friendly, and very outgoing, Rini challenges dominant notions of Javanese females as reticent and shy. While single, she sometimes flirted with the drivers as she went to and from work. And she was known to stand up to the factory manager, a tough, forceful, and intimidating former policeman.

After two and one-half years of spreading cream on sandwich cookies in the biscuit factory, Rini, who was afraid to walk alone into the village after dark, quit because workers were forced to stay overtime to produce cookies for Idul Fitri, the celebration after Ramadan.[2] After she quit her biscuit job, she started working in an export-oriented garment factory, sewing pockets on men's cotton shirts made for the European market. She was paid one-half cent (3.3 rupiah) per pocket and earned about 46 to 77 cents daily, considerably less than the already low daily minimum wage of 625 rupiah, or 96 cents. Work hours and wages fluctuated, depending on production orders from abroad; sometimes workers went home early, and other times they had to work overtime.

Rini lived with her parents and three younger siblings in an agricultural village about five kilometers from the factories. Her parents—open, warm, hospitable, and animated people—enjoyed telling me that this, their "seventh marriage," was fated to stick. This was her father's third marriage and her mother's fourth, and it had lasted over twenty years.

Rini's family was poor by any standards. They owned one-eighth of a hectare of dry land (about one-quarter acre) and one-eighth hectare of wet riceland, half of which they rented out. They also sharecropped one-sixteenth hectare of wet riceland from the *Carik* (village secretary), and they were entitled to half of the harvest (1/32 hectare) from that piece of land. All in all, they received the harvest from only 0.2 hectare of land (less than half an acre), which was not sufficient for subsistence needs. In 1982, they lost their access to the Carik's land when he decided to rent his land to a middleman who would pay him cash.

Their home was of a generous size, made mostly from wood with thatched bamboo walls in the kitchen and a dirt floor. They owned a radio, a pressure lamp, a watch, and one set of store-bought furniture (chairs and a couch) for guests to sit on; the rest of the furniture consisted of the plain and simple sort that poor people buy or make themselves. Their goat, a form of savings, was tethered inside the house. Chickens ran in and out of the house, often interrupting our talks by jumping on the coffee table and pecking at the food the family had offered me—boiled cassava, fried ricecakes, or fresh fruit.

Rini used some of her salary for herself and the rest to help her parents buy rice and pay for her siblings' education. My first income survey showed that in addition to saving one-quarter of her salary (less than $2.00 a week) in a rotating savings association (*arisan*), she gave her parents more than one-third; at the same time, she consistently borrowed money from them to pay for lunch and transportation. During the first survey Rini thus managed to overspend her salary by half.

Some family members had made various attempts to get Rini married before she finally agreed to marry a young man whom her uncle arranged for her to meet. Rini, however, was unhappy after her fairly costly wedding and claimed that she slept alone, leaving her husband to sleep in a brand-new, expensive, store-bought nuptial bed that stood in one corner of her parents' living room. She was distant from her husband, avoiding him whenever possible. Her mother said: "I advised Rini's husband to be patient and quiet. I thought that if he isn't strong, she can marry again later, but the next time, *I'm* going to choose her husband!"

Rini, though, insisted that her husband was lazy: rather than working, he sat around the house all day and even asked her parents for money. She also told me that she was embarrassed to have such a physically unattractive husband.[3] This conflict quickly became primary material for village gossip. The more Rini rejected her husband, the more difficult I found it to interview other villagers, who preferred instead to discuss Rini's most recent reaction or pronouncement and the most recent story about her new husband.

Rini's parents made it clear that they would not mind if Rini wanted a divorce, since they had had five between the two of them, but they disliked her indecisive and angry behavior. Rini's mother was upset that her daughter wasn't fulfilling her wifely duties: Rini didn't sleep with her husband, nor did she take care of him by making him tea or washing his clothes. Out of embarrassment, Rini's mother washed her son-in-law's clothing.

Rini's husband waited for his wife outside the factory every day after work to escort her home. She so disliked seeing him that she stopped going to work a few days a week and instead went to a friend's house or a nearby market. Her already low weekly wage dropped even lower, and she began to ask her parents more frequently for transportation money; but since they were still burdened by wedding debts, they had nothing to spare.

The financial strain mounted, and finally Rini's parents forced her to quit her factory job. Her father began felling logs and sawing them into boards for sale, while Rini took care of household chores and her younger brother. (Until then, her father had taken care of the child.)

Everyone expected Rini's husband to leave her, but he stayed. When I left Java in early 1983, I thought that she would either get pregnant or divorced, or both. When I returned to the village in 1986, Rini and her three-year-old daughter greeted me with "Hallo, Mbak Diane!"

Not long after I had left, there had been a family confrontation, Javanese style. Rini's mother, unable to tolerate the tension and conflict in the family and unwilling to confront it directly, simply picked up and left without saying good-bye.[4] She went to her sister's house in Jakarta. Rini was three months pregnant when her mother left and eight months pregnant when she returned. By then, Rini had decided to "accept her fate," and she and her husband were reconciled.

Rini returned to work in the factory when her child was three years old, and Rini's mother was happy to take care of her granddaughter during the day. Rini's expenditure pattern had changed; she spent little of her wage on herself and instead either contributed to the household purse, bought things for her daughter, or saved money to build her new house. Slowly the young couple was accumulating enough to build their own home. Bricks, boards, and shingles were piled up in a corner of her parents' living room; soon these materials would be used to build a house in what was now her parents' yard. Rini estimated that the house would cost about two hundred dollars, and she was reaching that goal more quickly because of her savings from factory wages. Soon she would be able to start her own nuclear-family household; and, indeed, by 1988 she was living in her own house, although parts of it were unfinished.[5]

MY STORY

When I set off for Java in 1981, I had a highly economistic view of how households operate. The peasant studies literature in which I had been intellectually socialized focused almost exclusively on political and economic conditions—labor, income, and household production and reproduction, particularly the activities of women and children in poor households struggling to survive. Land, labor, income, nutrition, class status, and gender inequalities were quantified, what Clifford Geertz not so fondly refers to as "what you count is what you get" (1984, 522). I left Ithaca, New York, for Indonesia convinced that poor households basically react to structural economic changes, that such behaviors would be mirrored in the lives and work patterns of Javanese women, and that Javanese culture, while interesting, was a luxury that was peripheral to understanding household survival.

I viewed factory work as part of a household survival strategy. Given the poverty of the households I studied, I expected a close relationship between factory daughters' wages and the households' struggles to survive. In other words, I saw factory daughters as Javanese versions of the working daughters in early industrializing Europe depicted by Louise A. Tilly and Joan W. Scott (1978); with this model in mind, I assumed quite naturally that the Javanese daughters, too, were working to help their families.

THINGS FALL APART, THE HOUSEHOLD DOES NOT HOLD

Although factory employment affects the availability of labor and capital within the family economy, I found that Rini and other factory daughters sought it without their parents' encouragement and even without their awareness or approval. Such an entry into the formal labor force did not indicate the daughters' acquiescence to a collective household strategy. Instead, Rini's father resisted and then accommodated his daughter's actions. Her borrowing practices also countered my assumptions about daughters' contribution to the family economy. Once again, the situation I encountered disturbed notions I had had about poor people, particularly the economic behavior of daughters from poor families.

Obviously, Rini's work, her wages, and her marriage were not part of a collectively or parentally conceived household strategy, even though her parents ended up benefiting from some of these decisions. Instead, Rini made her own decisions to which her parents tended to acquiesce, even if they initially resisted. When their debts mounted and Rini added to them rather than helped relieve them, her parents jointly forced her to quit her factory job. In general, however, she did not automatically defer to household needs or to the economic needs of household members; her reaction depended on the situation. In other words, her household-oriented behavior was fluid and could not be conceptualized in a fixed or static manner.

Despite this family's poverty, we find not strategies, but motley and assorted decisions and behaviors to which others respond by resisting, desisting, withdrawing, or accommodating—or some combination thereof. Rini's parents did not guide their dutiful daughter into factory employment and marriage, with continuous access to her income for household survival; rather, Rini withdrew her labor, income, and marriage from parental control as best she could.

The unraveling of factory daughters' stories over time marked the unraveling of my preconceptions as I grappled with understanding what I saw and entered into a dialogue with the household framework and with the peasant studies literature that had guided my questions and assumptions. The approach I had used, Carmen Diana Deere and Alain de Janvry's framework (1979), explained broader patterns but was not very helpful in accounting for the contradictory dynamics I observed within these domestic units.

As Rini's abbreviated life story suggests, my research challenges popular academic notions about how poor households operate and "strategize"; instead, I examine who makes decisions for whom and how such decisions are implemented, contested, or accepted. The actions and reactions of these young women raise important theoretical and conceptual questions about the economic organization of poor households as well as methodological questions about how to study "the household."

To understand the Javanese case more clearly, I increasingly adopted a comparative perspective in my writing to illuminate the mediating role the kinship system may play as Third World women work within the system of industrial and multinational capitalism.[6] A methodological shift is also part of this study's nonlinear evolution and reflects the theoretical shifts just described. While working on my dissertation during the early 1980s, I gathered a considerable amount of quantitative data; during my follow-up visit in 1986, however, I concentrated almost exclusively on qualitative data, soliciting separate stories from parents and daughters in the same family and listening to their accounts of conflictual situations.

I have gratefully taken license from contemporary feminist scholarship (Mani 1989; Kondo 1990; Nielsen 1990; Joan Scott 1988; Stacey 1990) to integrate reflexivity and notions of self (what Kondo [1990] refers to as the "eye/I") into my text. Although self-reflexiveness constitutes a very minor part of this book, occasional references to my own role and reactions as a researcher explicitly acknowledge the subjective nature of research since "any account is partial" (Kondo 1990, 8).

In depicting these intellectual and methodological shifts in my approach as well as some of my personal reactions in the field, I have underscored the processual aspect of research: struggling to consider as "data" individuals who have lives and personalities; attempting to reconcile these data with theory; jockeying between clarity and the depths of utter confusion; discovering and rediscovering; naming and renaming. Fieldwork and writing a book, like the lives of the women I studied, also represent a process of negotiation and renegotiation. Therefore, I include some discussion of this process of reconceptualization so that readers will feel less isolated by these dilemmas than I did.

CHAPTER I

Conceptualizing Poor Women, Household Dynamics, and Industrialization

This book analyzes the complex interrelationships among subsistence agrarian production, industrial capitalist development, factories, young women workers, and their families in rural Java, the most densely populated area on earth (Hart 1986b), where conditions of poverty, inequality, and underemployment prevail.[1] This research, which focuses on the intrahousehold dynamics of crucial economic decisions, challenges certain notions about how poor households "strategize" and organize themselves economically. The lives and voices of factory daughters such as Rini and their parents reveal the contradictions and complexities of industrial capitalist proletarianization, the mechanisms of change, and the meaning of such changes for those involved. The factory daughters whom I studied worked in rural-based factories and were thus able to remain at home with their parents while working in the factories; this particular geographical configuration allows for a better view of the short- and long-term relationships among factories, young female workers, and village households.

Because I examine interactions among Javanese working daughters, their rural families, and new capitalist factories, this study is situated within and between several bodies of literature concerning (1) the effects of industrialization on families, (2) the effects of multinational factories and the new international division of labor on Third World women factory workers, and (3) the economic organization of peasant and rural households in the Third World. This study weds theoretical and methodological issues from the latter literature to questions typically asked in the first two fields of study.

This research complements previous studies conducted in Southeast Asia on households and agrarian change (Hart, Turton, and White 1989; White 1976; Hart 1986; Wong 1984) and on women and global factories (Ong 1987; Mather 1982; Robinson 1988) by offering a rural-based intrahousehold perspective and a comparative focus on kinship. At the same time, it contributes a Southeast Asian case to a burgeoning feminist-inspired literature on gender, internal household dynamics, and economic structural change (Benería and Roldán 1987; Wilk 1989; Carney and Watts 1991).

THIRD WORLD WOMEN, GLOBAL FACTORIES, AND FAMILIES

This study is partially directed by and to the debate concerning the effects of changes in the global economy on Third World women who labor in multinational firms (Fuentes and Ehrenreich 1983; Chapkis and Enloe 1983; Phongpaichit 1988; Christopherson 1982; Fernández-Kelly 1983; Lim 1983a; Lim 1983b; McGee 1984; Safa 1983; Nash and Kelly 1983). Such research has focused upon the expression of patriarchy and the ways in which it easily mates with the relations of domination inherent in capitalism, as both are enacted through the oppression of women within the factory workplace.[2] Global factories engage in the "superexploitation" of workers because wages are too low in some places to cover the workers' daily costs (Elson and Pearson 1981). Although I draw on and contribute to this particular literature, I offer an interactive view of the dynamics among factory daughters, factory employment, and workers' family and household relations.

Although some analysts conclude that Third World women are worse off with factory employment spurred by capitalist development (Robinson 1986; Mather 1982; Chapkis and Enloe 1983), others argue that women are better off in such situations (Lim 1983b; 1990). This study is more compatible with those who have found the effects of such capitalism on women workers' lives highly contradictory (Ong 1987; Safa 1990). Female employment in multinational factories (or other factories feeding global markets) reaps some benefits for female workers in the familial sphere—for instance, more participation in family decisions or the creation of new boundaries that allow longer periods of escape from parental control. These changes in family relations and control do not lessen the level of exploitation in such employment; they do suggest, however, that the effect of factory employment on women in certain cultures is more ambiguous than much of the literature has portrayed (see Lim 1990).

For example, in an attempt to go beyond the limited and culturally constructed dualism of better/worse, Aihwa Ong's *Spirits of Resistance and Capitalist Discipline* (1987) explores the new cultural constructions of female gender and sexuality as lived by female factory workers in Malaysia. Ong emphasizes an important paradox: although factory work brings women workers more freedom from their families in wage earning, consumption, and choosing their own spouses, it is also "the means whereby they are subjected to intense capitalist discipline" (1987, 113). Additionally, factory workers are perceived in this predominantly Moslem society as sexually loose and immoral, a situation that creates sexual identity conflicts for these women, who are caught in the struggle between Islamic patriarchy and "modernity." Ong argues that occasional spirit possessions and hysterical seizures among factory workers are a form of resistance to capitalist work discipline, expressing the "continuing personal and social crisis" (1987, 8) that this specific organization of production creates for workers.

Although the literature on Third World female factory workers has added a much-needed gendered dimension to our understanding of global economic changes, there are several problematic aspects that I will attempt to redress here. First, in many studies of Third World women and industrial capitalism, the women themselves are missing, rendered undifferentiated, homogeneous, faceless, and voiceless by analyses that, according to Ong (1988, 84), attribute much more personality and animation to capital than to the women it exploits.[3] As Lourdes Benería and Martha Roldán (1987, 8) point out, women are portrayed as victims of capital or as part of a puppetlike reserve labor force whose behavioral strings are pulled in the interests of capital; they are not shown as social agents who think about, struggle against, and react to their own conditions and who can also interpret their own situations.

Second, this literature often errs in basing the argument that factory work is worse and marginalizing for women on an implicit comparison with a non- or pre-capitalist past (or present) in which women were ostensibly autonomous, authentic, and unexploited, particularly in the realm of production (Robinson 1988). The comparison, I would argue, is founded on an overly romantic view of rural noncapitalist life and agrarian production. Again, I am not suggesting that factory wages are not exploitative or that workers are not subordinated, but in peasant societies, where "self-exploitation" is considered normal, the long hours of unpaid labor under the eyes of parents or older male relatives can be highly subordinating.[4]

Finally, because many factory workers are migrants in Free Trade Zones far from home, studies have often focused on factory workers without viewing them within the context of their families, households, or communities. The few studies that have incorporated the family/household context have offered a fuller and differentiated view of the daughter-family-factory nexus (Kung 1983; Ong 1987; Salaff 1981).

FAMILIES AND INDUSTRIALIZATION

Previously, family theory posited that industrialization, through its transformation of the economy and the nature of work, would also incur a social transformation of the family and women's position, freeing young women and men from familial and patriarchal controls as they were exposed to a nonfamilial ideology, the capitalist workplace, and as they earned and controlled their own wage (Goode 1963; Shorter 1977). These changes may have occurred in parts of Western Europe and North America (Dublin 1979), but social historians have recently argued that at least for the first generation of factory workers in Europe and the United States, industrialization, instead of exacting radical change, actually perpetuated traditional mores of familism (Tilly and Scott 1978; Hareven 1982).[5]

Although a few studies of contemporary industrialization in the "Third World" suggest that women may gain more autonomy or say in family decisions because of their factory employment and wages (Safa 1990; Ong 1987), a substantial literature on female factory workers and families in newly industrialized East Asia reinforces the view that industrialization need not disrupt cultural norms with regard to women's position in their families (Salaff 1981; Kung 1983; Kim 1991; Amsden 1989; Spencer 1988). Rather, in Taiwan and in Hong Kong, the new international division of labor has facilitated working daughters' attempts to be dutiful and filial and has intensified parents' economic demands on them (Greenhalgh 1985; Niehoff 1987). Industrialization has, at the very least, perpetuated the subordinate position of Taiwanese working daughters and has possibly sharpened their subordination and exploitation within the family (Greenhalgh 1985; Kung 1983; Arrigo 1980).

But in a recent book on the international division of labor, Sharon Stichter and Jane L. Parpart contend that we still know comparatively little about the impact of participation in the labor force on women's "personal lives and their position in the family and household" (1990, 1). My study will attempt to fill part of this gap by exploring more fully the family and household perspective.

RESEARCH QUESTIONS

This study analyzes several questions, decisions, and processes centered on the junction of structures and actors and on the daily practices of rural family life. The first empirical question acknowledges that factory workers constitute a minority of women in the Third World, and in this particular site, a minority of young Javanese women. This question thus centers on the supply of labor: in other words, who seeks factory employment? Answering this question and the others that follow involves comparing factory workers with their nonfactory peers in the village. In the early 1980s, when I conducted the bulk of my field research, this distinction was useful; for reasons elaborated on later in the text, the line between the two groups blurred over time.

The second major empirical question examines factory workers' control over their income and analyzes their contributions to the family economy. The finding that daughters are often less than dutiful leads to an exploration of family dynamics around the issue of income retention and why parents tolerate such conditions.

In 1986, four years after my initial fieldwork, I returned to Java to study two questions about marriage. In 1982 many of the young women I interviewed told me that they hoped to gain more control over marriage choices, particularly whom and when they would marry. Had they been able to do so? How were marriage decisions made? I also reexamined work roles, financial contributions, and the family economy among the women I studied before, most of whom were, by 1986, wives and mothers.

I increasingly turned to the mothers of factory daughters and elicited their life stories about marriage and other decisions. Although comparisons between factory workers and their nonfactory peers indicate more directly how factory employment makes a difference in rural women's lives, a comparison with their mothers speaks to broader sociodemographic and generational changes occurring in Java.

Thus, while I am seeking to understand who works, who benefits from wages, and who chooses their spouses, these questions allow us to analyze the extent to which daughters can control their labor, their economic activities, the fruits of their labor, and significant life decisions, particularly those related to sexuality. Having control over economic events or decisions, however, does not necessarily imply a dramatic change because Javanese women have long been engaged in economic activities on their own account. In a review of the literature on women and work, Henrietta Moore (1988, 109) poses essential questions that I address through the narratives of the women involved: "What kind of difference does this employment make to women themselves? How do they perceive the advantages and disadvantages?"

To move beyond the limitations inherent in a single case study, I compare the decisions and negotiations of these Javanese daughters with those of their counterparts in Taiwan. This contrast helps illuminate the ways in which kinship structures affect family relations and shape the lived experiences and practices of Asian women in two different settings.

GENDER, "HOUSEHOLD STRATEGIES," AND HOUSEHOLD MODELS

My focus on daughters' control over their economic activities, their income, and their marriages directly binds this research with studies of Third World rural household economies. All the decisions studied here directly affect how labor and capital are mobilized and utilized within the family economy. Researchers often assume that these decisions are made at the household level or, at the very least, are guided by parents concerned with household survival (Tilly and Scott 1978).

Usually, any poor Third World person, and especially a Third World woman, who seeks a paying job, earns a wage, or migrates is interpreted as doing so as part of a household strategy (also known as a "family strategy," "household survival strategy," or "household livelihood strategy"). The concept of household strategies is easily and frequently invoked in Third World research both to describe what poor peasants or urban dwellers do and to explain why they do it. Household strategies are thought to be reflected in any number of economic-demographic behaviors, including labor force participation, migration, coresidence, marriage, childbearing, food allocation, and education, particularly as poor households cope and adapt to external structural change (de Janvry 1987; Hareven 1982; Tilly and Scott 1978; Stern 1987; Arizpe 1982; Findley 1987; H. Papanek 1983; Trager 1981; Hart 1986b; Pahl 1984; Abdullah and Zeidenstein 1982; Rosenzweig and Schultz 1982).[6]

In this section I take a detailed look at the concept of household strategies and the ways in which this term has been used in Third World research. Many of my criticisms of the household strategies approach mirror frequent criticisms of Gary Becker's (1981; 1986) "New Household Economics" because both approaches share certain features (Morris 1990, 19). Many, though certainly not all, of these criticisms have been voiced by feminist scholars who have extended them to Marxist approaches to the household as well. Therefore, as I delineate the problems involved in current notions of "household strategies," I link these criticisms to household models—both neoclassical and Marxist—whenever relevant.

The concept of "household strategies" has appealed to a considerable number of researchers using diverse theoretical approaches in great part because it mediates between micro and macro levels of analysis.[7] Conceptually, household strategies are situated between the overly individualistic focus of social-psychological attributes, on the one hand, and structural determinism, which views people as passive victims, on the other (Tilly 1978, 3). The concept of household strategies links individuals as social actors with broader structures and institutions, imbuing them with the possibility of agency.[8]

At the same time, the concept of household strategies reflects a particular swing in the pendulum of approaches to Third World development in a manner that privileges the actions and decisions of poor peasants. Modernization theory has viewed most poor Third World people as laggards and blamed them for their poverty. In the 1970s development researchers began to view farmers as knowledgeable "rational actors" who made sensible "rational" decisions within a given system; they were the "real experts" in farming decisions (Gladwin 1989, 409). This trend meant that researchers no longer questioned what poor people did but assumed that their actions reflected an underlying economic rationality reflected in a broader collective strategy. The peasant, formerly the "bumbling idiot of modernization theory enslaved by tradition," was then "transformed into a hyper-rational strategist, playing the social game according to optimal strategies" (Gupta 1987, 44); the domestic group formerly viewed as passive and "lacking in rationality" suddenly had its qualities reversed (Rouse 1989, 4). The implication of this theoretical swing is that certain behaviors and decisions were not investigated or questioned but assumed to reflect strategic rationality, a problematic assumption at best.

The concept of household strategies shares one of the most frequently criticized assumptions underlying Becker's New Household Economics—that households have a single utility function. Household strategy research usually assumes that each household pursues one overarching collective goal that reflects a common set of interests. This goal is best represented by the phrase "all for one and one for all" (Bartlett 1989a, 271; Davidson 1991, 14).[9] In some sense, Louise A. Tilly and Joan W. Scott's (1978) discussion of "family economy ideology"—that family members work together toward the collective goal of survival—is tinged with similarly problematic assumptions of household unity and consensus in pursuing one collective goal.

Many scholars have attacked this assumption (Ben-Porath 1982; Morris 1990; Selby et al. 1990; Ellis 1988; Davidson 1991; Berk 1985; Hart forthcoming), and here I highlight only the main criticisms. Basically, assigning a single utility function to the household assumes that consensus and cooperation are at the core of household dynamics. This approach completely ignores intrahousehold conflict, inequality, and exploitation and basically views household unity as unproblematic. This flaw is compounded by the assumption that one central and collective goal actually exists and that it automatically takes precedence over other goals.

One of my main criticisms of the ways in which the concept of household strategies has been applied is a corollary of the single household utility function, namely, that the individual and the household are often merged analytically, something I have termed elsewhere the "I am Thou" syndrome (D. Wolf 1990). In household research based on the tenets of either neoclassical or Marxist economics, the individual and the household are perceived as interchangeable, and as Diane Elson (1991, 81) points out, all individuals within households are treated analytically as identical and interchangeable. The household is treated "as an individual by another name" (Folbre 1986, 5) and discussed as a living, animate object with a life, logic, and interests of its own, defined by a combination of Darwinist, Adam Smithian, and benevolent paternalistic principles. At the same time, individuals are treated as households in miniature, driven by a gene dictating the household good such that any behavior exhibited by an individual—from migration to marriage—is de facto interpreted as motivated by household interests.[10] Third World women in particular are portrayed as fully submerged in and inseparable from the household collectivity, an assumption that is repeated in state-level employment and family policies.

Conceptions of decision making for such strategies are also highly problematic. Those who draw on household strategies as an explanation assert that households make decisions or "very precise calculations" about allocating labor and capital (Guest 1989), drawing on the assumption in the New Household Economics that households maximize their utility and make the most efficient use of labor and capital. Households, however, can neither decide, think, nor allocate since analytic constructs are not so empowered. Rather, one or more persons with power make decisions, and those who are less empowered are expected, convinced, or coerced to comply (Morris 1990; Lockwood 1989). Indeed, the language used—that "the household" allocates or decides—obscures the power relations inherent in household-related decisions.

In the New Household Economics, the household decision maker is portrayed as a benevolent dictator in the form of a "wise Solomonian father-judge" who has internalized family members' needs, makes decisions with the collective good in mind, and rules with justice (Hart 1978, 35).[11] Individuals within the household sublimate their own wishes to this larger goal, as "personal autonomy is subsumed under the constraints imposed by family needs" (Fernández-Kelly 1982, 13).[12] Becker's benevolent dictator is benign and altruistic; thus, he embodies the interests and well-being of other household members. Household strategy research has often embodied some of these assumptions, accepting as unproblematic a highly simplified view of decision making.

The flaws that mar the concept of joint household utility also vitiate Becker's notion of household decision making (Davidson 1991, 14; Hart forthcoming; Ellis 1988; Selby et al. 1990, 56; Folbre 1988). The interests of the household head may not be those of less empowered household members, again because of gender and generational differences. It is difficult to imagine a patriarch making a decision in the best interest of his daughter, who has secondary status in the household and already receives less food, less health care, and fewer goods than her male siblings do. The presence of a household altruist "assumes away all domestic conflicts concerning the intrahousehold distribution of costs and benefits, and in the extreme, obliterates the possibility of intrafamily exploitation" (Fapohunda 1988, 145). And as feminist researchers have pointed out from empirical findings in diverse settings, benefits do not accrue equally in most households (Greenhalgh 1985; Roldán 1984; Agarwal 1991).

Additionally, feminist scholars point out that many earlier researchers betray a sexual bias in their portrayals of household operation, for they often assume that the individual orchestrating these decisions is a male (Folbre 1986, 1988; Moore 1988, 56; Elson 1991, 191). Since "father knows best," he calculates and makes policy decisions while managing the family economy and keeping accounts (Findley 1987, 31). For example, in Lutz Berkner and Franklin Mendels's (1978) historical research on rural family demographic change in Western Europe, Clark Sorensen's (1988) work on Korean peasants, and particularly Samuel Popkin's (1979) book on rural rationality, the ubiquitous peasant is a male who is seen as the household decision maker.

Feminists have faulted Marxist models of the household for problems and assumptions similar to those in the New Household Economics approach—avoiding the issue of material inequality within the household (Folbre 1988, 253; Hartmann 1981; Hart forthcoming, 16). Feminist economists have pointed out that while women's unremunerated labor may have been recognized, the power differential behind the sexual division of labor has not been explored in various household studies guided by modes and forms of production or world systems theories. Instead, the focus has been more on the constraints confronting "the household" as a whole, particularly as it confronts capitalism.

The household strategy approach is plagued by another problem found in the New Household Economics and Marxist approaches to the household (Morris 1990, 20)—a romanticized view of altruism among members of poor families. Although Marxist approaches to the household "avoid using the term altruism . . . implicitly . . . they assume that altruism rules, particularly within the working-class family" (Folbre 1988, 253). The peasant or semiproletarian household is assumed to be a "wholly cooperative unit" with its own moral economy (Folbre 1988, 248). Economists from both neoclassical and Marxist backgrounds assume that the competition, struggle, economic self-interest, and exploitation that pervade the capitalist marketplace are left on the doormat. Thus, within Becker's model, people are selfish in the marketplace and selfless at home.[13] Precapitalist norms of mutual voluntary aid and concern for the group's good are thought to persist inside the house even as the cold winds of capitalism whip around its outer walls. According to Nancy Folbre, in peasant economy models and Marxist analyses, the "vision of pure altruism within the family" resembles nothing short of "utopian socialism" (1986, 6; see also Fapohunda 1988; Morris 1990).

These images are often reflected in assumptions about intrahousehold behavior. For example, assumptions about income pooling in households (usually assumed to be part of a household strategy) are common in Third World studies, particularly when referring to women's work (Lim 1990). In studies of labor allocation and value of children in developing countries, researchers often take for granted that household members automatically labor for the household or pool their earned income. Indeed, the Households in the World System research group at the State

University of New York places the assumption of income pooling at the core of their definition of the household, bypassing questions sociologists should be asking about who retains their income or how the household is able to procure income from members at a distance (J. Smith, Wallerstein, and Evers 1984).

These assumptions about household cooperation have important empirical and methodological implications for household research. The image created about households homogenizes the broad range and variety of household interactions and misses entirely relations that include power differentials, conflict, and dissent. This distortion has prevented many researchers from considering (and therefore observing and documenting) that individual members may engage in behaviors that are passive, nonstrategic, overtly resistant, antagonistic, ambivalent, antistrategic, or even multistrategic; these behaviors could be reflected in laziness, greed, selfishness, revenge, or egocentrism, or in "everyday acts of resistance" such as income retention or noncompliance (Wilk 1989; see also Rutz 1989). These reactions are somehow rarely considered in Third World household studies, an approach that would be deemed unacceptably naive in other settings.[14]

Several related methodological problems in the household strategy approach limit the field of empirical vision in research. First, household strategies tend to be read retrospectively into completed actions. By reading retrospectively, particularly from an activity that worked successfully (i.e., the person received a job or some income or had a child), one can impute household strategies where none actually existed.

Reading retrospectively from completed events also means that those who failed, starved, died, or dropped out tend to be missing from the data. We rarely hear about failed strategies since researchers usually do not follow households through time; instead, we hear from those who survived to tell.[15] Also problematic is that strategies are often read into concrete actions that can be measured by demographers or economists—for instance, entering the labor force, having a child, or migrating. Indeed, those who are strategizing may attempt to prevent change by enforcing passivity, inactivity, or submission; these behaviors, which are less visible and therefore harder to count, may contribute to what appears from the outside to be a lack of change. If people or households were followed through time and qualitative data were gathered, there would be more awareness of how inaction may at times be part of a strategy.

Finally, a serious methodological and theoretical problem that is intertwined with these issues is that researchers often impute strategies from behavior without talking with the strategists, the players, enactors, and enablers. One reason why researchers may infer strategies from behavior is because of the belief that household strategies are conceived at a subconscious or unconscious level (Sorenson 1988; Pahl 1984, 20 n. 7; Becker 1986, 112; for further discussion, see Clay and Schwarzweller 1991; Selby et al. 1990, 67) making it empirically slippery to research the decision making and strategic process directly. This slipperiness gives researchers license to extrapolate strategies from observed behaviors and outcomes where, perhaps, strategies did not really exist. Alternatively, researchers may assume those involved don't really understand or cannot explain what they are doing. Sorensen, in his book on rational adaptive household strategies in rural Korea, states that "informants are seldom capable of fully specifying their cultural knowledge, goals, or strategies as such" (1988, 20); in this way, he justifies imputing strategies.[16]

Anthony Giddens finds this exclusion of respondents' motives and explanations common in both functionalist and structuralist approaches: "Put rather forcefully, social actors are often perceived as either 'cultural dopes' or as mere 'bearers of a mode of production' " (1979, 71). Although we can at best represent our subjects only through our interpretations of their lives and narratives, excluding and ignoring such narratives have given researchers a free hand in interpreting behavior in ways that reflect romantic views about Third World family solidarity or family economy ideologies.[17]

Certain types of methodologies seem to encourage reading retrospectively into strategies and imputing strategies. Rouse points out that large-scale surveys using questionnaires reap very different types of data about household behavior than do long-term, intensive, qualitative field studies involving unstructured or loosely structured interviews with a small number of households. Large-scale surveys often interview each household only once and generally direct the questions to the "household head," usually a male.[18] If more than one person is interviewed in such surveys, they tend to be interviewed in the same space rather than separately. Such techniques create brief and "relatively anonymous" encounters (Rouse 1989, 30) and do not provide the kind of atmosphere in which respondents might discuss family problems or conflicts or air the family's dirty linen.

Thus, Roger Rouse (1989, 30) argues, different methodologies do not simply have a different perspective on similar materials; rather, they produce different types of data and therefore different types of interpretations. Because of these differences, large-scale, quantitatively oriented surveys may encourage the belief that strategies are unconscious. By contrast, ethnographic and qualitative techniques involve a long period of interaction, acquaintance, and even friendship with a smaller number of people and allow time and space for separate conversations with various household members; fieldwork of this sort produces much more thickly textured data about how household or family units operate. The contradictions and inconsistencies that Rouse (1989, 9) heard in family stories in Mexico and the conflicts that I heard about in Java would not have been revealed by a one-shot questionnaire. There is, of course, no guarantee that long-term fieldwork will reap such data, for fieldworkers may still not ask certain questions and may themselves impute strategies to their subjects.

Many of my criticisms of the household strategies concept stem from semantics, particularly the use of flawed and inappropriate terminology. The very term *strategies* implies a long-term plan dotted by serial and conscious decision making, calling on some combination of cost-benefit calculating and economic, even militaristic, reasoning. *Strategies*, however, better describes how Coca-Cola, by introducing "New Coke" and thereby provoking enormous public pressure to bring back the old Coke, attempted to lure away Pepsi drinkers and capture a larger portion of the limited soft-drink market. Unlike profits, however, household survival is not a zero-sum situation.

I do not mean to deny that those in the Third World calculate or act purposively, nor am I denying that strategies exist. But assuming that everyone strategizes most of the time severely circumscribes a culturally, ethnically, and economically diverse range of behaviors, obscuring the power dynamics and processes while freezing a highly fluid situation into stasis. Thus, the assumptions of household strategies have prevented some researchers from recognizing that households are a "site of conflict, a locus of contradictions and a field of negotiations without a single decision-making head" (Selby et al. 1990, 65).[19]

Ironically, although researchers have applied the concept of household or survival strategies to the poorest sectors of the population in particular, the poorest may be the *least* able to strategize because of their minimal access to resources and the high degree of uncertainty confronting them (Selby et al. 1990, 70). Those with more resources tend to have more choices; they may also have more information and may be able to tolerate the higher risks associated with strategic decision making. In *The Mexican Urban Household*, Henry Selby and his coauthors (1990, 69) aptly point out that most poor households in the Third World "are not confronting decisions at all: they are being impelled by forces beyond their control like hunger, the threatened loss of shelter, fear, unemployment, crying babies, police repression, domestic violence, and a work day that seems interminable." Under such conditions, which are not at all unusual for the poor, long-term planning and serial decision making, or strategizing, is virtually impossible.[20]

The current usage of *household strategies* in the development literature is so loose that it has rendered the concept meaningless. Household strategy research can answer the question "What is a strategy?" but it cannot answer the question "What *isn't* a strategy?" because everything has been subsumed under the umbrella of a strategy. A strategy is everything a household does, and everything a household does is a strategy. This tautology does not do justice to the complexity of the everyday lives of the poor. Instead, we need a more precise, careful, and sensitive accounting that looks inside the household, one that views cooperation, conflict, acquiescence, resistance, and other dynamics. It would be more useful ultimately to suspend the assumption of household strategies, explore intrahousehold interactions, and then seek a more appropriate descriptor that is less tautological and teleological.

FEMINIST APPROACHES TO THE HOUSEHOLD

Feminists have long pointed to the limitations of aggregating gendered interests and unequal power relations under a unifying notion of the household (Hartmann 1981; Thorne and Yalom 1982; Benería and Roldán 1987; Agarwal 1988; Moore 1988; Roldán 1984; M. Wolf 1972; Yanagisako and Collier 1987; Guyer 1988).[21] Dissatisfied with the way Marxist approaches to the household have ignored important gender inequalities, Marxist feminist approaches to household studies direct attention to the "dual systems of patriarchy and capitalism," pointing to exploitation within the household (Hart forthcoming, 18; see also Benería and Sen 1981; Agarwal 1988; Agarwal 1991; Hartmann 1981).[22]

One problem within the Marxist feminist approach, however, has been a tendency to portray women as passive victims of patriarchy and particularly of capitalism (a point made by Benería and Roldán 1987; see also Hart forthcoming, 20). Some scholars have dealt with this problem by incorporating a bargaining approach to the study of intrahousehold relations within the Marxist feminist paradigm, attending to more dynamic aspects of intrahousehold interactions (Benería and Roldán 1987; Agarwal 1991; Folbre 1988).[23] Attending to women's roles in bargaining and negotiations incorporates "an explicit recognition of agency—and potentially also resistance—by subordinate members" as women negotiate and renegotiate aspects of their conjugal contract (Hart forthcoming, 20).

In what is considered the classic work in this genre, Benería and Roldán (1987) studied couples in Mexico City in which the wife engaged in industrial homework, one of the least protected and lowest paid jobs. They examined how women's work and income affected domestic relations and found contradictory results. Because of the very low wages, this work reinforced the intrahousehold gender hierarchies in that women remained economically dependent on their husbands. However, the women themselves interpreted their situation from a somewhat different perspective. Though their income was small, it gave them some autonomy in consumption and a sense of more control over their lives, thus facilitating the "renegotiation of the terms of interaction within the family" (Roldán 1984, 279). The women gained more decision-making power in some areas although they were unable to bargain for significant change in gender relations within the home. Despite the fact that their income was small and they were in the most subordinate level of the proletariat, these women's sense of self and their willingness to confront men increased.

Intrahousehold studies in different parts of the world have contributed to our understanding of such processes and have contested many of the assumptions underlying New Household Economics and Marxist approaches to the household (Guyer and Peters 1987; Agarwal 1988; Wilk 1989; Rutz 1989; Lockwood 1989). Such studies have critically analyzed "the manner in which some rights, especially those pertaining to labor and land, are naturalized by tradition and embodied in the conjugal contract" (Carney and Watts 1991, 662) and the terms on which husbands and wives exchange income or services (Whitehead 1981, 88). Findings from intrahousehold studies elsewhere have challenged the image of the income-pooling household (Guyer 1988; Fapohunda 1988), injecting a more complex and dynamic view of how men and women manage their budgets in different domestic situations, different seasons, and different life-cycle states.

In an approach that examines the fluid interactions between internal household processes and external changes, Judith Carney and Michael Watts found that the intensification of labor demanded by a rice irrigation scheme in the Gambia created domestic struggle between husbands and wives, shaping the "trajectory of agrarian change itself" with "ambiguous and contradictory consequences for women" (1991, 653). Women resisted intensifying their labor for the project and began to demand payment for their paddy labor, in part because they had lost their traditional property rights. Women's withdrawal of their labor from their households led to the creation of a rural labor market of work gangs composed of those very women who had lost access to riceland. Thus, some of the women lost land and became proletarianized, but through the work gangs they "bid up their daily wage rates" (1991, 677). Carney and Watts argue that through such agrarian change, "the household has been converted into a terrain of intense struggle and negotiation and of limited victories, which have challenged, albeit obliquely, dominant representations of gender and patriarchal power" (1991, 677). (See also Carney and Watts 1990; Schroeder and Watts 1991; Hart 1991; and C. Jones 1986).

My research is situated in this genre, which analyzes internal household dynamics in tandem with political-economic changes, although I am critical of some aspects of the approach. Much of the terminology used by intrahousehold researchers has remained firmly rooted within economistic boundaries, conceptualizing intrahousehold dynamics in terms of contracts, competition, bargaining, contestation, negotiation, and renegotiation (Cheal 1989; Sen 1990; Benería and Roldán 1984; Hart 1991; Sendauer 1990; Agarwal 1988). Economists cannot and should not be faulted for using the tools and terms of their trade; however, the danger remains that an inappropriate terminology from one economic model has been replaced with yet another. Thus, I question the usage of terms such as *bargaining,* which may homogenize certain highly contextual and varied behaviors in the same way that *choice* or *strategy* does. It is important to look closely at processes of interaction to see how "bargaining" or "negotiating" is actually enacted. Furthermore, this terminology may circumscribe our vision so that we neglect noneconomic and nonconflictual aspects of rural family/household life.

We need to throw open the doors of the household more broadly, to capture the textures of household dynamics and to allow for a greater range of possible intrahousehold relations. "It is clear that the nature of household organization and relations cannot be assumed" but must be empirically investigated (Moore 1988, 59). By cracking open the "black box" of the household, research can examine household organization and intrahousehold relations particularly with regard to such decisions as entry into the labor force, income contribution, the timing of marriage, and the selection of a spouse. This focus centers upon the social mechanisms and processes within households that perpetuate domination or engender resistance. This approach will entail analyzing gender ideology and relationships of power within the household and linking these asymmetries and processes with political and economic change. In this study, the term *negotiation* encapsulates both the process of decision making between daughters and parents and the ways in which young women attempt to change some of the rules as they carve and sculpt their life courses, confronting parents, capitalist work discipline, factory managers, and cultural conceptions of femininity. A closer look at these processes of interaction within the household will help us understand what "negotiation" looks like in this particular cultural and economic context.

The literature on intrahousehold relations brings up questions about the appropriate unit of analysis—the household, relations among household members, or individuals within the household. Given that I specifically examine factory employment and its effects on the lives of young women, I focus primarily on the daughters. But because of the particular questions I ask about interactions among daughters, parents, households, and factories, I navigate between these multiple units of analysis and attempt to capture their various interrelationships.

CONCEPTUALIZING WOMEN, THEIR WORK, AND FAMILY RELATIONS

To present and analyze the lives of Javanese factory daughters while situating them within the constraints of their households' poverty, I utilize the notion of *female agency.* Previously, analyzing women's autonomy has been one way feminist sociologists have conceptualized Third World women's position cross-culturally, looking within and beyond the family to the society at large (Blumberg 1984; Chafetz 1980; Mason 1984; Schlegel 1977; Safilios-Rothschild 1982). Female agency is a much less scripted concept than autonomy is and contains fewer preconceived notions of individual and family behavior.[24] Avoiding the extreme images of women either as autonomous individuals or as completely symbiotic with their families, the concept of female agency offers a broader continuum in which to present the contradictions of a situation and provides a subject-focused orientation based on practice rather than attributes.[25]

Agency, as Joan Scott suggests, is "action taken in specific contexts, but not entirely autonomously or without constraint" (quoted in Abelson, Abraham, and Murphy 1989, 51). Individuals are not simply "free"; rather, their agency is conditioned by outside forces and is structured "within the context of their collectivities" (Etzioni 1988, 181). Agency, however, is not synonymous with activity; agency can involve passivity, accommodation, and withdrawal as much as defiance and resistance.

A focus on agency complements Anthony Giddens's theory of structuration, which takes into account the relationships among structure, agency, and power. Giddens views social structures as both "enabling and constraining" (1984, 169). Social actors are affected by structural features of the political economy and in turn affect and reshape those very structures; thus, we turn our focus to the intersection where structures and actors meet.

Central to an "actor-centered practice approach" (Behar 1990, 225) is the assumption that women and men can evaluate their lives (Mani 1989, 215; K. Anderson et al. 1990).

> All human beings are knowledgeable agents. That is to say, all social actors know a great deal about the conditions and consequences of what they do in their day-to-day lives. Such knowledge is not wholly propositional in character, nor is it incidental to their activities. Knowledgeability embedded in practical consciousness exhibits an extraordinary complexity—a complexity that often remains completely unexplored in orthodox sociological approaches, especially those associated with objectivism. (Giddens 1984, 281)

Conceptualizing women's actions, reactions, and nonactions in terms of female agency counters problematic stereotypes of Third World women (Sen 1990, 149). Currently, there is some proclivity to overcompensate for formerly passive and victimized images of Third World people by characterizing most action and inaction as resistance, which is simply the other side of the coin of passivity (Behar 1990, 231). Broadening the focus to female agency counters these swings between complete passivity and hyperresistance by viewing women's actions and motivations as complex, varied, and nuanced, depending on the situation and its constraints and the actors involved.

Finally, taking a broader approach to female agency counters a tendency in the literature on Third World factory women to privilege capital. This approach, which demonstrates that women are not necessarily locked into a daily and constant battle with capital, offers a wider view of the often contradictory forces that can operate simultaneously in different life arenas (Manderson 1983, 2). Indeed, Gillian Hart (1991, 41) stresses the need for a dynamic conceptualization of agency that "recognizes multiple (and possibly contradictory) sources of identity and interest" and a recognition that interests are not fixed, but fluid. Although I analyze how factory work and the structures of industrial capitalism reverberate in the domestic arenas of rural Javanese factory workers, I also focus on how, in turn, factory daughters and their families affect and, to a lesser extent, reshape these structures (Yanagisako and Collier 1987, 43).

Deniz Kandiyoti (1988) points to the need for culturally based studies to refine our monolithic conception of patriarchy in the Third World. This Southeast Asian case refines such conceptualizations of women and families in an Islamic country by bringing the narratives of those who live amid, with, under, and through such structural transformations into the center of analysis and allowing them to redirect our theoretical journeys. Such narratives enrich a political economy perspective as they provide access to some of the reflections and reactions of social actors directly involved in and affected by structural change. These narratives portray the contradictory, dynamic, and asymmetrical aspects of relationships between parents and daughters, workers and owners, and, indirectly, factory owners and rural households while providing some sense of the ways in which young, poor rural Javanese women attempt to shape and maneuver their lives.[26]

The narratives from those involved are meant to complement, not replace, scholarly analysis of how these accounts are constructed, how gender identities are created and negotiated, and how subjects view themselves and their actions, all within a particular cultural, historical, and political-economic setting (Joan Scott, quoted in Abelson, Abraham, and Murphy 1989, 51). Indeed, academic analysis must complement such narratives because women's perceptions (or the perceptions of any oppressed group) may embody highly asymmetrical notions of obligation, appropriate behavior, and legitimate expectations, particularly within highly patriarchal societies (Sen 1990; H. Papanek 1990).[27]

A subject-focused approach must constantly move back and forth between the "raw data"—the subjects—and theory, continuously modifying and confronting the latter in an attempt to understand and contextualize the former. Clearly, as social scientists we are interpreters, not ventriloquists; we have access to our subjects' mediated representations of themselves and can portray only our own mediated understanding and representation of them as best as we can. Despite such problems with mediation, representation, and subjectivity, it is important and useful to engage with such narratives and weave them into our attempts to understand structural transformations.

GENDER, KINSHIP, AND HOUSEHOLDS

The kinship system greatly affects the boundaries of women's actions, behavior, and decisions and mediates the effects that structural change has on women's lives and female agency. Henrietta Moore stipulates that the effects of women's participation in nonagricultural employment are highly varied: "What is clear is that cultural stereotypes about gender, and about the appropriate behavior of women, interact with family and kinship structures in ways which influence the ultimate effects of factors such as level of economic development" or the structure of the economy (1988, 108). The focus on the connections among women's work, family relations, and kinship structures addresses relationships underlying the nexus that joins industrial capitalism, rural households, and an agrarian economy.

A comparative approach illustrates the crucial role the kinship system plays in shaping the extent to which women may gain or lose control over their lives because of such structural transformations.[28] It is generally thought that a woman's access to external resources such as income can affect her status or bargaining position (Sen 1990, 144). The intrahousehold effects of a woman's access to such resources is tempered by the kinship system within which she resides, since access to income may not necessarily indicate control over it (Safilios-Rothschild 1982; Blumberg 1984). In a highly patriarchal system, women may not be able to control those external resources to which they have access and which they bring into the household (H. Papanek 1990; Salaff 1981), whereas in a bilateral kinship system such control is less problematic.

To understand the lives of Javanese factory daughters more clearly, I often compare them with Taiwanese factory daughters, particularly with regard to socialization, work decisions, control over wages, household strategies, and family relations.[29] Family organization and patriarchal power in East and South Asia contrast strikingly with the nuclear and bilateral characteristics of many Southeast Asian family systems (i.e., non-Chinese kinship systems in Indonesia, the Philippines, Thailand, and Malaysia), traits associated with women's ability to engage in extrahousehold economic activities and their control over income. The different manner in which the bilateral Javanese kinship system and the patrilineal Chinese kinship system define women's roles, boundaries, statuses, space for negotiation, and sanctions demonstrates considerable variance in the effects of the international division of labor on Asian women and their ability to alter the domestic arena through factory employment.

East Asia, particularly Taiwan, has provided the "laboratory" for much of the scholarly research that has been done questioning the effects of industrialization on women (Greenhalgh 1985; Kung 1981; Kung 1983; Salaff 1981; Salaff 1990; Arrigo 1980; Diamond 1979; M. Wolf 1972) and on families (Thornton, Chang, and Sun 1984; Hsiung 1988; Poston 1988;

Freedman, Chang, and Sun 1982). In Taiwan, relations between genders and generations within the family greatly resemble those found in social histories of industrialization and family change in the West, where daughters remained in the clutches of the family while working in industrial capitalist production.

Studies of Taiwanese female factory workers argue that industrialization has not disrupted family relations and patriarchal control, in part because of the patrilineal, patrilocal, and patriarchal nature of the Chinese kinship system; conversely, industrialization has actually reinforced and intensified traditional family patterns, particularly parental control over daughters. Parents adapt traditional patriarchal relationships well within the boundaries of the patrilineal kinship system to help govern their factory daughters, whose labor is closely tied to the global economy and state interests. Family demands and the factory system, along with the state, reinforce controls over young women, creating a disciplined, productive, and docile labor force that has greatly benefited economic growth, state and household revenues, and First World consumers.

Taiwanese daughters seem to operate within a family economy ideology that depends on the subordination of daughters who show few signs of breaking free (Thornton, Chang, and Sun 1984). Instead, they postpone their marriages, "sell their youth to the company" (Kung 1983), and exhibit low self-esteem. Indeed, one of the few ways that they gain satisfaction through factory employment is by repaying their "debt" (of birth and upbringing) to their families (Lim 1990, 110; Ong 1991), thereby proving themselves "filial."

The subordinate family position of Taiwanese daughters and the ways in which they submit their needs to the betterment of the family economy reflect certain stereotypes of how daughters' lives remain unchanged by emergent industrial capitalism (e.g., Tilly and Scott 1978). It is important to recognize that the Javanese and Taiwanese cases are not equivalent in many ways: Taiwan is more urbanized and industrialized than the area in Java that I researched. The Javanese households I studied are all poor and rural and have some connection to agriculture; most Taiwanese studies draw on both rural families and urban working-class families who are better off than the Javanese households. Because of these many differences, I use the Taiwanese case to illuminate the uniqueness of the Javanese case. By focusing on intrahousehold relations in these two settings, I show that both the Javanese and Taiwanese cases contest the notion of household strategies, but in very different ways and in very different configurations.

MAP OF THE BOOK

Chapter 2 presents the broader context of Indonesian state policy, agrarian change, and industrial growth. Chapter 3 examines the position of Javanese women and considers how contemporary feminist research in Indonesia questions certain accepted notions of women's status. In chapter 3 I also examine state-supported gender and family ideology (as reflected in the portrayal of women in the state-run village-level women's organizations in Indonesia) and notions of femininity in Java. The research methods, the research site, and rural class structure and household organization in the villages studied are presented in chapter 4.

As Ong (1987) found in another Southeast Asian setting (Malaysia), industrialization has given workers new freedoms in their personal lives, but it has also engendered new types of controls over women in the factories. Chapters 5 and 6 focus on labor recruitment, terms of employment, and the production process in factories in the research site, paying particular attention to the ways in which gender hierarchies and other relationships of inequality are appropriated, reshaped, and practiced during the labor process. Chapter 5 presents information about all factories in the site and discusses the ways in which male and female gender ideologies are appropriated and practiced in the factories with respect to hiring, labor relations during the production process, and wage structure. Chapter 6 is based on my one-month residence in a multinational spinning mill, thus offering greater detail on daily life in a factory compound.

Like the lives of factory daughters, the chapters move back and forth from households and village life to the factories and back home to families again, underscoring how involvement in factory work reshapes intrahousehold relations. Chapters 7 through 10 present the empirical data on factory daughters, employment decisions, family economy, and marriage. Chapter 7, which concerns the determinants of employment, describes and utilizes Carmen Diana Deere and Alain de Janvry's (1979) framework for the analysis of peasant households and goes beyond it by looking within such households. Chapter 8 focuses on factory daughters, their income, and family economy dynamics. Chapters 9 and 10 are based on my third field visit, four years after my initial research. Chapter 9 focuses on marriage, specifically whether factory daughters were granted more leeway in choosing their own spouses than their peers were. Chapter 10 returns to issues of family economy four years later, when the adolescents I studied in 1982 had become wives and mothers.

• • •

In a recent book on women's employment and families in the new international division of labor, Alison Scott points out that studies of kinship, studies of household structures or the survival strategies of the poor, and studies of gender ideology constitute three separate literatures, each with insufficient attention to the other two domains.[30] These domains, when brought together as they are in this research, can illuminate "the interactions between structure and ideology within the family" (A. Scott 1990, 199), particularly the constraints and contradictions within families and between family systems operating under different principles.

This study addresses the particular confluence where state, industrial, and household interests, family and gender ideologies, and household organization come together to affect rural daughters' work and their position within the labor force (Moore 1988; Agarwal 1988). Javanese females do indeed play an important role in certain decisions, but these "options" are framed within the highly constrained boundaries of poverty. A comparative analysis of Javanese and Taiwanese factory daughters demonstrates how, in two Asian settings, the interests of parents, households, the state, and industrial capitalism meet one another at disparate points with very distinct and contradictory effects on the women workers involved.

By including the reactions and explanations of several family members and by comparing the decisions of Javanese with Taiwanese factory daughters, my research actively peels open semiproletarian and proletarian households and thereby contests the concept of household strategies from two different perspectives. Indeed, this research examines the delicate, harsh, and inconsistent orchestration of intrahousehold relations, particularly as children and parents confront changing economic rhythms, attempt to adapt to new melodies, resist them by playing off-key, and negotiate shifting tempos as they struggle with poverty. This demystification of peasant, semiproletarian, and proletarian households carries with it important implications for Third World household research and its guiding models. It compels a reconceptualization of how poor people in households operate, how they coerce, subordinate, and manage their members, if in fact they do manage their members. It also compels a reconceptualization of poor women as social agents who can simultaneously engage in accommodation, passivity, and resistance while involved in essential productive and reproductive activities.

CHAPTER II

Industrial and Agrarian Change in Java

Rural Java can be deceptive. It is easy for a foreigner to wax romantic about the beauty of perfectly manicured tiers of rice terraces, each displaying a different brilliance, from the intense green of young rice shoots to the golden yellow of older stalks. Every possible inch of land is cultivated; trees are laden with papayas, mangoes, and coconuts, and water buffalo plow the fields. The sounds of children playing or herding livestock provide the soundtrack for this breathtaking scene. "Peasant society" seems harmonious and peaceful, with the smiling villagers happily in tune with nature (Critchfield 1983).

But this Javanese idyll bears another, less romantic aspect. Java is currently the "most densely populated rural area on earth" (Hart 1986b, 1), and most villagers, squeezed onto ever-shrinking landholdings, are extraordinarily poor. Only an increasingly small minority can fulfill simple subsistence needs from their land and are well-off in comparison with their neighbors. In this lush environment, poverty has rooted itself deeply, expanding and flourishing in many households.

In this chapter I explore industrial growth, industrial policies, employment, and agrarian change in Java particularly and in Indonesia more broadly; this chapter thus serves as a backdrop for the empirical chapters to come, situating factory daughters, their households and villages, rural poverty, agriculture, and the growth of industrial capitalism in one specific area in rural Java. Although my research details the structural constraints and life chances confronted by these young women and their families, such specific conditions mirror broader structural trends occurring throughout Java. Because I present a multilayered approach to understanding the effects of industrialization, I start with the macro level. Whenever the data permit, the emphasis will be on rural Java.

INDUSTRIALIZATION IN CONTEMPORARY INDONESIA

Java is the most powerful and populous of the thirteen thousand islands in Indonesia's archipelago (see map). The history of Java is a fascinating and complicated one, layered with Buddhist and Hindu kingdoms, the spread of Islam, three and a half centuries of Dutch colonial rule, occupation by the Japanese, a war of liberation from the Dutch, and a postindependence massacre of Communists and alleged Communist sympathizers (see Reid 1988; Ricklefs 1981; Steinberg 1987). Clearly, I cannot do justice here to the history of Java, but it is useful for the non-Asianist reader to have a sense of historical transformations that have particularly affected rural people.

During the nineteenth century the Dutch introduced several different modes of extraction at different times that served to appropriate labor, export-oriented produce, taxes, and land from villages and their rural inhabitants. A land rent of 40 percent, introduced under the colonial administration of Raffles (1811–16), was replaced in 1830 by the *Cultuurstelsel* (Cultivation System), which forced peasants to cultivate export crops on one-fifth of village land or to provide one-fifth of their labor (about seventy days a year) on government estates or other government projects. These practices were instituted in various ways, and Dutch administrators and Javanese regents often abused the system, frequently appropriating more than the designated amount of labor or land.

After the passage of the Agrarian Law in 1870, private enterprises could lease but not purchase native lands, thus guaranteeing the Javanese their customary rights to the land and the possibility of Javanese private ownership. In some areas this law simply led to the compulsory leasing of peasants' land for sugar cultivation (Geertz 1963; Hart 1986b, 23; Koentjaraningrat 1985; Ricklefs 1981; White 1983). All of these highly exploitative measures left poor Javanese cultivators poorer and powerless while the colonial system maintained the position of the Javanese elite (*priyayi*). Thus, state intrusion into and control over the lives and earnings of poor rural people is not a recent phenomenon in Java.

Because of the extractive nature of the colonial economy, manufacturing did not proliferate, though there were railway workshops in Semarang and small-scale batik and cigarette production (Steinberg 1987,

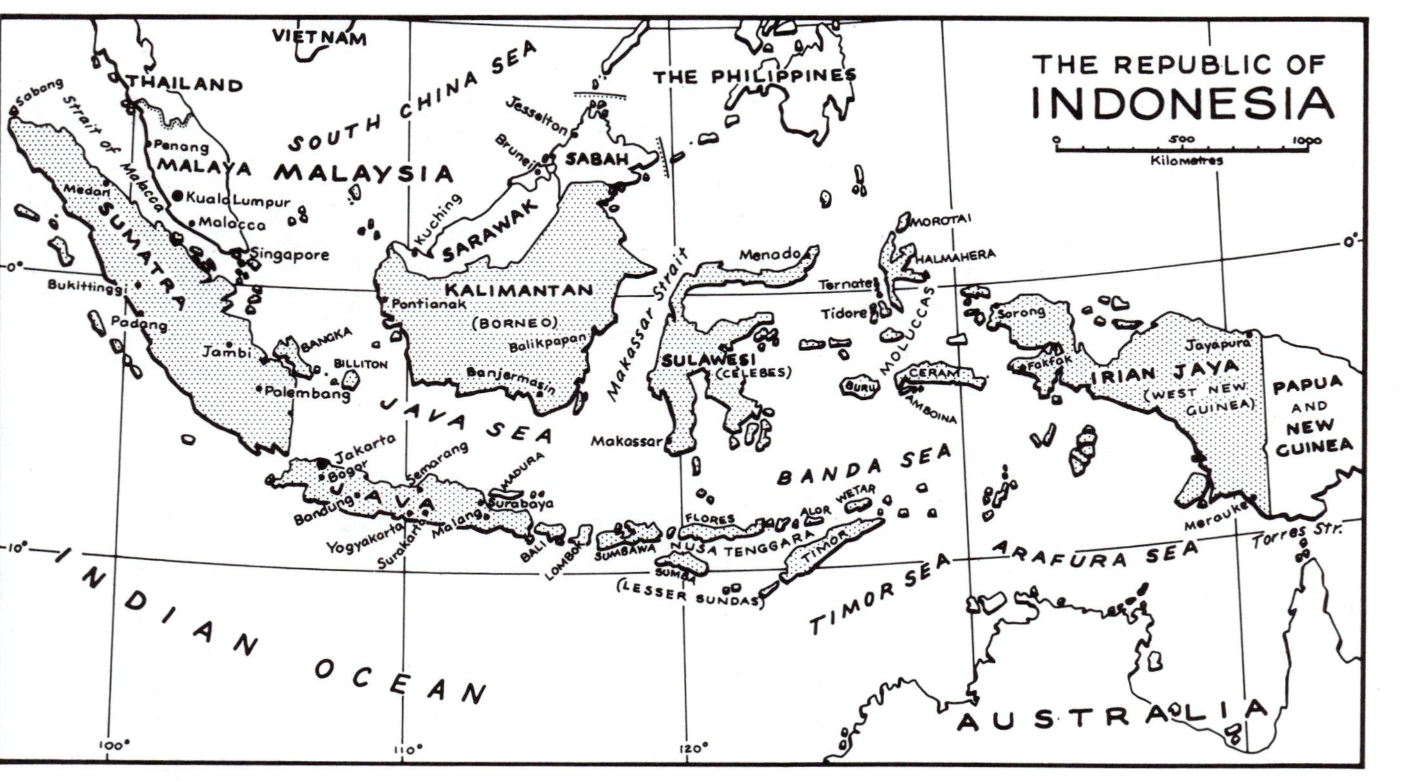

SOURCE: J. D. Legge, *Indonesia*, 2d ed. (Sidney: Prentice-Hall of Australia, 1977), ii.

256). In the early twentieth century *santri* merchants built batik and *kretek* (clove) cigarette industries in Central and East Javanese towns (Steinberg 1987, 301).

In the late nineteenth and early twentieth centuries, Dutch colonial concern for "native welfare" was expressed in the Ethical Policy. In an effort to stimulate peasant production of commercial crops (coffee, sugar, indigo), this policy emphasized irrigation, agricultural extension, and improving access to health, education, and credit (Booth 1988). M. C. Ricklefs (1981, 143) argues that there was "more promise than performance" in the Ethical Policy and that the fundamental relationship of exploitation and subjugation remained intact. During this time, emigration to the Outer Islands was encouraged as a method of dealing with increased population growth (Hart 1986b, 24).

In 1924 the Japanese invaded and occupied what would become Indonesia until 1945, a period of extreme deprivation that many still recall bitterly. Sukarno and Hatta announced Indonesia's independence on 7 August 1945, the day after the atomic bomb was dropped on Hiroshima. After the Japanese surrendered, the Dutch reoccupied Indonesia, and a war of liberation began. In 1949 Sukarno was named the president of the newly independent Republic of Indonesia.

Under Sukarno, a tumultuous time ensued as political parties competed and fought internally and the Indonesian Communist Party (PKI) grew in popularity. Many poor peasants joined the PKI because it actively improved rural conditions (e.g., by building schools and dams and organizing literacy courses) and because the PKI promised to represent their interests. Some of the leading Communists in rural areas were either large landowners or those with political authority (Hart 1986b, 26). The national elections of 1955 led to the end of parliamentary democracy in Indonesia, and the political turmoil that followed led to Sukarno's abrogation of the provisional constitution and the establishment of Guided Democracy in 1959 (Lev 1966; Steinberg 1987, 23).

The economy stumbled badly under Sukarno's leadership. There was little movement in industrial production or agricultural output, resulting in shortages, rising food prices, hyperinflation, and increasing urban political unrest (Husken and White 1989). In the meantime, the PKI continued to work for peasant interests, particularly in the area of land tenure, and tension grew between the PKI and the army.

THE NEW ORDER

Suharto's "New Order'" regime (as opposed to the "Old Order" of Sukarno) took power in 1966, when Sukarno's postindependence leadership ended in a horrific and bloody CIA-approved massacre of hundreds of thousands of PKI members, supporters, and alleged supporters in rural East and Central Java following a failed coup. This change in regimes was marked by the "entrenchment and centralisation of authoritarian rule by the military, the appropriation of the state by its officials, and the exclusion of political parties from effective participation in the decision-making process" (Robison 1986, 105). The military has strengthened its control of all levels of the state apparatus, and the state has spread its tentacles into every village and hamlet; there remains little hope for democratic processes or a strong opposition party. Rather, state leaders argue that the Indonesian form of democracy, Pancasila Democracy, has already been instituted (B. Anderson 1983, 490), but this state ideology excludes the participation of the populace. Under the New Order, Golkar (the state party) continues to win carefully orchestrated elections; opposition parties have been deprived of power, and President Suharto has not faced an opposition candidate in twenty-five years (B. Anderson 1983, 490; Crouch 1978, 245).

Suharto and his advisors quickly attempted to formulate growth-oriented development policies that would avoid the economic problems that occurred under Sukarno. Advised by Western-trained technocrats, the New Order has been redirected by the priorities of political and economic stability and a particular type of economic growth acceptable to the new political leaders (Glassburner 1971, 5; Robison 1986, 109). "Once properly established, Suharto's Indonesia has been run, rather like Singapore, as if it were a corporation rather than a nation" (Steinberg 1987, 425).

INDUSTRIAL POLICY UNDER THE NEW ORDER

Industrial policy under Suharto's New Order was devised by Berkeley-trained economists (also called the "Berkeley Mafia") who created policies "designed to win the sympathy of the Western capitalist powers and Japan" (B. Anderson 1983, 488). They encouraged large-scale industrialization and foreign investment based on the free-market ideology of Western liberal economics and favored by the International Monetary Fund (IMF), the World Bank, and the Inter-Governmental Group on Indonesia (IGGI) (Robison 1986, 110).

The current regime's friendly posture toward foreign investment distinguishes it from Sukarno's (B. Anderson 1983, 488). A new foreign investment law drafted in 1966 is much more encouraging to foreign investors than the previous regime had been (McCawley 1981, 64). Multinational corporations provide Suharto with revenues (i.e., taxes) without conflicts over power. As Benedict Anderson points out (1983, 489), foreign investors are, after all, less politically threatening to the state than an indigenous and wealthy business class would be.

Although the Indonesian government encourages foreign investment, it remains highly protectionist. A restrictive system of licensing and regulations, imposed on both foreign and domestic investors, "intrudes upon virtually every significant private sector investment decision. . . . [This system] would tend to retard growth even if it only postponed implementation of investment, as it surely does" (Gillis 1983, 25–26). The World Bank has pushed Indonesia to abandon its protectionist barriers, a strategy that international capital would also appreciate, but, as Richard Robison notes (1986, 386), state leaders remain committed to the goals of nationally integrated industrialization.

In addition to the thick web of bureaucratic procedures, widespread corruption hampers investment in Indonesia, as has been noted by several researchers, the World Bank, and other business organizations (Robison 1986, 393). Harold Crouch has documented the involvement of state bureaucrats, the military, and local officials in such corruption and the generally laissez-faire attitude toward it (1978, 273–99). This corruption is but one of the strong connections among the military, powerful state bureaucrats, and industrial investment.

According to Robison (1986), the power of the technocrats to create and push through free-market policies has been tied to Indonesia's particular need for international loans, aid, and capital investment at specific historical moments. When an increase in oil revenues (1973–81) created less need for external assistance, the technocrats conceded to more nationalistic economic policies. For example, in 1974–75 and 1981–82 the state played an active role in "financing, protecting, and subsidizing domestic capital and in direct investment" (Robison 1986, 131), countering the free-market ideologies of the World Bank and the IMF.[1] By contrast, during economic crises such as the mid-1980s decline in oil reserves and revenues, the relative strength and influence of IGGI, IMF, the World Bank, and international capital in general have increased (Robison 1986, 111).

State-owned corporate enterprises constitute the most "crucial element" of domestic capital in Indonesia (Robison 1986, 211). In the mid-1970s state-owned corporations accounted for about 20 percent of all employees in the manufacturing sector. In recent years state enterprises, which are usually large and diverse, have expanded rapidly in industries such as steel, fertilizers, cement, and paper (McCawley 1981, 74); their holdings also include oil (Pertamina), tin mining, and forestry, all major sources of foreign exchange. The exact amount of state-owned capital investment, however, is difficult to calculate.

In the mid-1970s regulation was introduced forcing foreign investors to have domestic partners with a minimum of 20 percent equity to create joint ventures that would lead eventually to equitable partnerships. Chinese Indonesians were required to share their equity with Pribumis. (*Pribumi* literally means "native" or "indigenous." In contemporary Indonesia, it is used to distinguish between indigenous Indonesians and Chinese Indonesians, although many of the latter have been in Indonesia for generations.) Because of a lack of equity coupled with a lack of management skills among the Indonesian partners, foreign investors were able to retain control of firms and of crucial decisions related to production or distribution (Robison 1986, 194).

Because of the push for joint ventures and a dearth of potential Pribumi partners, a high proportion of the "local partners" are Chinese businessmen or "indigenous front men" who can contribute political connections and political resources yet "give the impression that Indonesians share in foreign investment" (Robison 1986, 191–93).[2] Crouch points out (1978, 285) that Indonesian military officers are often involved in business in this manner. Thus, some of those who mediate for capitalists and who can benefit from capitalist growth are in the military or the state bureaucracy, where they can protect and enhance their positions while lining their pockets.

INDUSTRIAL GROWTH

Industrial growth in Indonesia has been described as both "substantial" and "patchy" (Hill 1984). From the late 1960s to the mid-1980s industrial growth was "sustained and rapid," broadly comparable to that of the Asian newly industrialized countries (NICs) although substantially smaller (Hill 1987, 71). During that period, real industrial output grew by about 10 percent per annum, and the manufacturing sector quadrupled between 1970 and 1982, ranking tenth among less developed countries. Hal Hill attributes these changes to several factors, one of which is an increase in export-oriented manufacturing (1987, 72).[3]

The percentage share of manufacturing in Indonesia's gross domestic product (GDP) is relatively low in comparison with that of other Asian countries, yet it has increased consistently over the past years (table 1). From 1973 to 1984 Indonesia's manufacturing output grew faster than that of all the Asian countries listed. In 1986 manufacturing's share of GDP was up to 14 percent (Meyer 1988, 22). By 1988 manufacturing contributed 18.4 percent to GDP (Mackie and Sjahrir 1989, 6), and in the same year the GDP growth rate of nonpetroleum manufacturing was 14 percent (Pangestu and Habir 1990, 5). Although many traditional household, cottage, and small industries still exist, most manufacturing growth has occurred in medium and large-scale "modern" firms that are usually more capital than labor intensive (G. Jones 1987, 272; McCawley 1981). In addition, many working in more traditional labor-intensive handicrafts have lost their livelihoods because their products simply cannot compete with the cheap manufactured goods, such as plastics and textiles, flooding the markets (Mather 1982, 4; Wieringa 1981).

The government's policy of import substitution has been only partially successful. Indonesia produces labor-intensive consumer goods (cigarettes, cloth, batik, garments) and some intermediate goods (paint, paper, glass products, chemicals, fertilizers), but few capital goods. Growth in production of the latter two categories has been slower, although since 1970 consumer goods declined by about one-half in their share in manufacturing value added while capital and intermediate goods rose by the same amount (Hill 1987, 72). Unskilled labor-intensive industries producing consumer goods dominate the manufacturing sector, particularly now that there has been a greater push toward export-oriented industrialization. In the mid-1980s, as the economy confronted declining oil revenues, economists urged that Indonesia either tackle more difficult aspects of import substitution or engage in more aggressive export-oriented growth (Hill 1984); in recent years the latter has occurred.

INDONESIA IN THE GLOBAL ECONOMY

Indonesia's role in the new international division of labor has increased rather dramatically. Manufacturing exports have grown in value and volume, from $12 million in 1970 to $2.6 billion in 1981 and $9.3 billion in 1988; however, the last figure is inflated because of changes in classification concerning crumb rubber and processed timber (UNCTAD 1982, 115; Mackie and Sjahrir 1989, 10). Earlier, manufacturing exports, however large, appeared as an extremely small proportion of total exports because of the large volume of petroleum exports. Since oil reserves and revenues are dwindling and investment in export-oriented industrializa-

TABLE 1

COMPARATIVE INDICATORS OF INDUSTRIALIZATION IN INDONESIA AND SELECTED ASIAN DEVELOPING COUNTRIES

Region/country	GNP per capita 1984 (U.S.$)	Manufacturing growth, annual average percentage		Manufacturing output, 1984, as percentage of		Manufacturing output		Manufactures, 1983, as percentage of merchandise		Manufactured exports, per capita, 1984 (U.S.$)
		1965–73	*1973–84*	*GDP*	*Agriculture*	*1984 (U.S.$ M)*	*1984 per capita (U.S.$)*	*Exports*	*Imports*	
Indonesia	540	9.0	14.9	13	50	11,155	70	8	63	11
Other ASEAN[a]										
Malaysia	1,980	n.a.[b]	8.7	19	90	5,756	376	22	72	236
Philippines	660	8.5	4.3	25	100	8,811	165	50	60	50
Singapore	7,260	19.5	7.6	25	2,500	3,994	1,597	57	56	5,485
Thailand	860	11.4	10.0	19	83	8,170	163	32	64	47
Other Asian										
India	260	4.0	5.9	15	43	29,219	39	52	49	7
Korea	2,110	21.1	11.5	28	200	23,691	591	91	51	664
Lower middle-income countries	740	8.5	5.9	17	77	n.a.[b]	n.a.[b]	21	63	n.a.[b]

SOURCES: Hill 1988, 10; World Bank (annual).

NOTE: Some data refer to a year earlier than that mentioned. Per capita manufactured exports were derived from 1984 total exports and population, and 1983 shares of manufactures in total exports.

[a] Association of Southeast Asian Nations.

[b] n.a. = not available.

tion has increased, manufacturing exports as a percentage of total exports jumped to close to 50 percent by the late 1980s (Mackie and Sjahrir 1989, 10).

Indeed, those who monitor the Indonesian economy seem surprised by the growth spurt in export-oriented industrial investment, output, and revenues in the late 1980s, a phenomenon few predicted. Domestic investment increased even more than foreign investment in that period, with a high proportion of production aimed at export. For example, in 1989, 780 domestic investment projects, compared with 295 foreign investment projects, were approved (though not necessarily realized), with approximately 80 percent of projects in each category aimed at export markets (table 2).

Manufactured exports typically have been narrowly based in semiskilled, labor-intensive goods such as clothing, textiles, yarn, and transistors; the production and export of rubber shoes, garments, and textiles

TABLE 2
APPROVED EXPORT-ORIENTED INVESTMENT, 1986–89

	1986	1987	1988	1989
Domestic Investment				
Total new projects				
Number	334	587	829	780
Value (Rp B)	5,689.5	11,850.7	16,320.5	21,576.6
Export-oriented projects	166	369	595	631
(% of total projects)	49.7	62.9	71.8	80.9
Planned exports (U.S.$ M)	1,756.7	3,939.5	8,680.6	9,388.0
Foreign Investment				
Total new projects				
Number	94	141	135	295
Value (U.S.$ M)	1,049.6	1,900.9	4,487.1	5,920.2
Export-oriented projects	20	44	105	242
(% of total projects)	21.3	31.2	77.8	82.0
Planned exports (U.S.$ M)	245.3	498.4	2,497.7	4,327.9

SOURCES: Pangestu and Habir 1990, 3; Indonesian Investment Coordinating Board (BKPM).
NOTE: Figures refer to "approved" investment and do not include the financial and oil sectors. Here "recapitulated" investments are used (i.e., new investment + expansion + changes + mergers + changes in status − withdrawals).

have recently increased. This spurt of investment comes from Japan and East Asian NICs (Taiwan, South Korea, Hong Kong, and Singapore) whose firms have relocated to take advantage of Indonesia's low wage rate and may well relocate again if labor makes demands on them (Mackie and Sjahrir 1989; Pangestu and Habir 1990, 8). Japan continues to be the primary recipient of nonpetroleum exports, followed by the United States, Western Europe, and Singapore (Booth 1988, 19). The Labour Working Group of the International NGO Forum on Indonesia points out that consumers may not be aware of the tremendous increase in exports of garments and rubber shoes made in Indonesia. It appears to be common practice, even with well-known brand names such as Calvin Klein, for Indonesian workers to sew in labels stating that the items were made in Japan, the United States, Canada, or Hong Kong (INGI 1991a, 5).

THE CONTROL OF INDONESIAN LABOR

Part of the attraction that Indonesia has for international capital is its large, low-wage labor force. Robison (1986, 71) points out that export-oriented industrialization requires a higher level of state involvement in disciplining labor than does import substitution industrialization; without question, the Indonesian state has sought to control the labor force, keeping wages and labor unrest down and unions inactive (Crouch 1978; Mather 1985). In an effort to lure foreign investors, the Indonesian government advertises one of the lowest average wage rates in Asia and proclaims that workers are controlled by the state, which forbids strikes (Indonesia, Consulate General 1983).

Wages in Indonesian manufacturing are among the lowest in the world (see table 3; Froebel 1981, 35). One British manufacturer compared labor costs internationally and ranked Indonesia as the lowest (*Financial Times of London*, 29 June 1981). In a recent two-page advertisement for Indonesia in the *International Herald Tribune*, a section entitled "Attractive Incentives for Foreign Investors" asserts that "Indonesians are willing to work harder and cheaper than any of their neighbors in Southeast Asia." The advertisement also points to a spurt in foreign investments encouraged by recent deregulation (3 Oct. 1988, 16).

The New Order regime has played an active role in paralyzing the unions and suppressing labor unrest. Most important for foreign investors, strikes are outlawed. In theory, the Department of Labor monitors factories' adherence to labor laws, but it ignores most violations. Unions

TABLE 3
WAGES PER HOUR FOR FEMALE WORKERS
(U.S.$)

	Wage	Wage and fringe benefits
Hong Kong	$1.15	$1.20
Singapore	.79	1.25
South Korea	.63	2.00
Taiwan	.53	.80
Malaysia	.48	.60
Philippines	.48	.50
Indonesia	.19	.35

SOURCE: *Balai: Asian Journal* 2, no. 4 (1981):11.

within factories, when they exist at all, are simply there in form only. Unions are not allowed to educate workers on their rights, and they can intervene only at the workers' request.

Strikes and lock-outs are strictly forbidden by the government because they are not "in harmony" with the state philosophy of labor relations (Indonesia, Consulate General 1983, 228). According to the state ideology of Pancasila, strikes are opposed to national development, "irreconcilable" with national goals, and "unnecessary" (Goderbauer 1987, 16).

In October 1987 members of the Asia Watch Committee testified before the U.S. trade representative concerning labor rights in Indonesia. The committee members explained that under Suharto the labor union has "acted to stifle independent factory-level workers' unions and even internal criticism. The main purpose (of Pancasila Labour Relations) has been to obfuscate the inherent conflict of interest between labour and management. . . . The inevitable dissent is thus condemned as being anti-consensus, hence anti-Pancasila and hence subversive." Those testifying concluded that "the climate of fear and intimidation is in itself an abuse of the rights of workers in Indonesia" (quoted in "Workers' Rights" 1987, 18–19).

Despite attempts by the state to control labor, in the early 1980s, "after a decade or more of quiescence, industrial disputes . . . increased significantly" in all sectors (Scherer 1982, 32). Although industrialists attempted to quell the expression of worker discontent, in some of the factories workers engaged in spontaneous labor protests without the help of the union. Indeed, the Labour Working Group of the International

NGO Forum on Indonesia (INGI 1991b, 4) reports that strikes have continued to increase; the number of strikes in 1990 grew by 200 percent from the previous year. Nonetheless, research on labor in Indonesia has been critical of the union's inactivity even within its prescribed boundaries. P. Scherer argues that, although the unions are nominally independent, "their relatively weak position" has often led "to their being coopted" (1982, 36). Those carefully watching the contemporary labor situation in Indonesia feel that the union has taken "an extremely passive stand" even in situations where it could have an impact (INDOC 1981). In many factories in Indonesia (INDOC 1983, 9) military men serve as personnel officers in direct control of workers and in direct contact with those who can enforce control. Indeed, at every Nike-licensed factory in Indonesia, "there is at least one former officer working as personnel manager" (INGI 1991c, 9).

The interconnectedness of state bureaucrats and the military with capitalists is crucial in the control of Indonesian labor. As Robison notes, "The penetration of the capitalist class into the state apparatus . . . invades and subsumes the very heart of military and politico-bureaucrat power" (1986, 396). The power holders themselves urgently feel the demands of capital as labor unrest or demands for higher wages threaten the very basis of their status and wealth (Robison 1986, 396). It is not surprising, then, that the state has been so willing to provide the political conditions for capital accumulation, which include low wages and muting the voice and will of labor (Robison 1986, 374).

EMPLOYMENT IN JAVA

Data on labor force activity from an agrarian-based country such as Indonesia are fraught with problems of measurement in addition to definitional differences between surveys.[4] Gillian Hart comments, "Intense controversy surrounds the interpretation of national survey and census data on employment trends in rural Java" (1986a, 681); those working closely with the data are the first to admit the often confusing and contradictory trends (Manning 1988; G. Jones 1987). Additionally, findings from the 1990 census have not yet been published, so these statistics do not reflect the effects on employment of the late 1980s growth spurt in export-oriented industrialization.

In absolute numbers, agriculture still employs the greatest number and proportion of women and men in Java, but the growth of agricultural employment has been minuscule and certainly has not kept up with

TABLE 4

DISTRIBUTION OF EMPLOYED PERSONS IN JAVA ACCORDING TO THE 1961, 1971 (SERIES C), AND 1980 CENSUSES

Industry	Males			Females		
	1961	*1971*	*1980*	*1961*	*1971*	*1980*
	Absolute numbers (in thousands)					
Agriculture	11,075	10,636	11,591	3,782	5,070	5,127
Mining	20	32	164	9	1	30
Manufacturing[a]	994	1,264	2,025	530	1,150	1,622
Construction	423	519	1,158	14	8	24
Trade	1,096	1,809	2,522	604	1,613	2,541
Transport	481	644	1,010	19	15	16
Services	1,485	2,106	3,546	923	890	1,650
Total	15,574	17,010	22,016	5,881	8,747	11,010
	Percentage distribution					
Agriculture	71.2	62.5	52.6	64.3	58.0	46.6
Mining	0.1	0.2	0.7	0.2	—[b]	0.3
Manufacturing[a]	6.4	7.4	9.2	9.0	13.1	14.7
Construction	2.7	3.1	5.3	0.2	0.1	0.2
Trade	7.0	10.6	11.5	10.3	18.4	23.1
Transport	3.1	3.8	4.6	0.3	0.2	0.1
Services	9.5	12.4	16.1	15.7	10.2	15.0
Total	100.0	100.0	100.0	100.0	100.0	100.0

	Intercensal change: average annual percentage			
	Males		*Females*	
	1961–71	1971–80	1961–71	1971–80
Agriculture	−0.4	1.0	3.0	0.1
Mining	4.8	19.9	—[c]	—[c]
Manufacturing[a]	2.4	5.4	8.1	3.9

Continued on next page

TABLE 4 —*Continued*

	Intercensal change: average annual percentage			
	Males		*Females*	
	1961–71	1971–80	1961–71	1971–80
Construction	2.1	9.3	—[c]	—[c]
Trade	5.1	3.8	10.3	5.2
Transport	2.9	5.1	—[c]	—[c]
Services	3.6	6.0	−0.4	7.1
Total	0.9	2.9	4.0	2.6

SOURCES: G. Jones 1987, 263; Central Bureau of Statistics (BPS) Population Censuses of 1961, 1971 (series C and E), 1980 (series S, no. 2), Jakarta, various dates; *Supas* and *Sakernas* reports.

NOTE: Data are adjusted to distribute persons with activities not adequately described and to exclude Irian Jaya and, in 1980, East Timor.

[a] Includes electricity, gas, and water.

[b] Less than 0.05.

[c] Numbers too small to be meaningful.

population growth (table 4). In 1980, 47 percent of economically active women were employed in agriculture compared with 53 percent of men, followed by trade (23 percent of females, 11.5 percent of males), services (15 percent and 16 percent), and manufacturing (15 percent and 9 percent). The employment structure for women shifted considerably from 1971 to 1980, with a smaller proportion (though slightly more in absolute terms) in agriculture and higher proportions and numbers in trade, services, and manufacturing; male employment followed a similar pattern.

For both sexes, trade and services provided more new jobs than did either agriculture or manufacturing in the 1970s (G. Jones 1987, 277). Many rural people, however, were forced into low-paying trade and service jobs in the informal sector because of shifts in the demand for agricultural labor and the exclusionary age and gender requirements of factory jobs.[5] The government's dramatic budget cuts in 1986 were expected to depress construction employment and to swell the informal sector (i.e., trade and services) even more than is demonstrated in these statistics.

In comparison with the male labor force, a higher proportion of the female labor force is in manufacturing employment, although in absolute terms males outnumber females. Females experienced a higher growth rate in manufacturing jobs in the 1960s, whereas jobs for males increased slightly in the 1970s (about 250,000 jobs). The female marginalization theory posits that women are pushed out of higher-paid sectors and pushed into lower-paid, low-status jobs as industrialization proceeds (A. Scott 1986). In terms of female marginalization, it appears that proportionately more females than males were pushed into the informal sector (trade and services), although in absolute terms almost one half million more males than females sought jobs in those areas. These data do not fully demonstrate that females are being pushed out of manufacturing, but they do indicate that they are being pushed into low-paying informal sector work. Analysis of data from the late 1980s and early 1990s will provide important information on these questions; I suspect that manufacturing employment will demonstrate growth for both sexes, although more for women because of recent growth in export-oriented manufacturing.

THE NATURE OF MANUFACTURING EMPLOYMENT

The growth in manufacturing firms in Indonesia has been concentrated in large-scale, urban-based, more "modern" units rather than traditional cottage industries, which employ far more people (Scherer 1982, 19).[6] Manufacturing employs a far smaller proportion of the labor force in Indonesia than it does in neighboring countries, and the structure of such employment differs considerably as well. In Indonesia in the mid-1980s, three-fourths of manufacturing employment was "in rural areas, most of it in cottage and small-scale industries and as self-employment or unpaid family work" (G. Jones 1987, 272). Women held almost half of all manufacturing jobs in 1980.

The Industrial Census (1974–75) documented that 80 percent of the manufacturing work force was located in cottage industries, with the majority in rural areas and with women constituting half the work force. Women tend to be unpaid family workers, while males tend to receive a wage (McCawley 1981, 69; Hart 1986b, 64). More than half of these cottage industries engage in bamboo weaving or coconut sugar production, both of which provide extremely low returns to labor; these returns are often below the agricultural wage but are steadier (Hart 1986b, 64). Small-scale household and cottage industries also produce such goods as foodstuffs (e.g., tofu, shrimp crackers), chicken coops, bricks, roof shingles, furniture, batik, and the like. In the 1974–75 Industrial Census

13 percent of the manufacturing work force was located in large and medium firms but was responsible for 80 percent of value added.

THE RURALIZATION OF INDUSTRIALIZATION

The 1980 Indonesian census shows that "almost one-third of those working in rural areas (about 13.7 million people) found their livelihood outside agriculture, mainly in trade, services, and manufacturing" (G. Jones 1987, 283). Terry McGee (1984) has termed the process of increasing rural nonagricultural employment *kodesasi* (from *kota,* "city," plus *desa,* "village"). Spatial maps of employment changes in Java from 1971 to 1980 demonstrate that agricultural employment declined in periurban areas and some rural areas, with industrial employment increasing in those same periurban and rural *kabupaten* (regencies). These latter increases occurred most often in medium- and large-scale modern factories, as opposed to small-scale traditional batik factories. These conditions suggest that, when analyzing economic change, particularly industrialization, it is more useful to think of rural-urban integration as a continuum rather than a dichotomy (G. Jones 1984, 153).

AGRARIAN CONDITIONS

Java has provided fertile ground for intensified agricultural production as well as for theory formulation and academic debates. Javanese agrarian relations and practices are the basis of J. H. Boeke's (1953) theory of dualism as well as Clifford Geertz's (1963) well-known theory of agricultural involution and highly contested concept of "shared poverty."[7] Agrarian differentiation best describes conditions in rural Java, both historically and today.

AGRARIAN CHANGE UNDER THE NEW ORDER

The New Order set out to change certain agrarian conditions and policies that had existed under Sukarno. During Sukarno's administration, crop production failed to keep up with population growth and food deficits necessitated rice imports. When the government could no longer afford food imports, severe food scarcities resulted. According to Frans Husken and Benjamin White, these scarcities were

> more important causes of the collapse of the Sukarno regime than the so-called 30 September Movement which in more favorable economic circum-

> stances might have proved a crisis no less manageable than others which Sukarno had overcome during twenty years as President. Rapidly rising urban food prices are closely linked to urban political unrest in Indonesia as in many other countries. (1989, 178–79)

After 1965 Suharto's New Order sought to impose political control in the rural areas while ensuring the availability of food in urban markets at stable prices. These goals led to a "top-down" approach to agricultural development (Husken and White 1989, 179) and the abandonment of all democratic procedures in rural areas.

In the 1970s the state promoted "Green Revolution" rice varieties and the intensification of rice production.[8] Some of the revenues from the oil boom were funneled into agricultural subsidies and public works such as roads, irrigation, and electricity projects. These subsidies included providing farmers with subsidies for fertilizer, agricultural credit, and free or subsidized irrigation; as a result, the rice harvest more than doubled (Husken and White 1989, 181–82), and Indonesia is now self-sufficient in rice. Increases in rice production, have, however, been accompanied by intensified political repression in rural areas; the state controls when farmers plant and what rice variety they plant.

During the 1970s researchers concerned with poverty and inequality produced microlevel studies of rural Java that documented an alarmingly high level of landlessness, the high degree of socioeconomic inequality and its rapid increase, and the disturbingly high proportion of the rural population living under the poverty line (Collier et al. 1973; Sayogyo 1977; Hart 1978). Longitudinal studies are continuing to analyze such trends (Manning 1988; G. Jones 1984; White and Wiradi 1989).

CHANGING RELATIONS OF AGRICULTURAL PRODUCTION

One of the most disconcerting trends researchers found in the 1970s was the increasing commercialization of patron-client relationships of agricultural production (Collier and Soentoro 1978). This increase in capitalist relations of production is associated with the introduction of the Green Revolution. For example, many investigators documented an increase in *tebasan,* a commercial process of harvesting that replaced village-level patron-client ties. In the tebasan system, the farmer sells the crop as it stands in the field to an intermediary, the *penebas.* The penebas, in turn, contracts a crew of harvesters, who are paid a fixed daily wage to go from harvest to harvest in different villages. This process excludes poor villagers, particularly poor women, for whom such harvests constituted one important form of rice income.

Kedokaan (or *ceblokan*) is another exclusionary practice that is reappearing in Java (Hart 1986a). It is a type of sharecropping arrangement in which laborers forego payment on the pre- and postharvest work they perform on the farmer's land (planting, land preparation, weeding, harvesting, threshing), instead receiving their pay in *bawon* (that is, in kind) during the harvest. For the laborers, this practice ensures that they will receive an invitation to the harvest and may lead to renewed contracts in the following years. However, this practice removes some of the risks of crop failure from the farmer (owner) and places it on the worker-tenant. Another disadvantage for tenants under this system is that they must forego income for a long period and may need to borrow money (with interest) in the interim (Hart 1986b). Benjamin White and Gunnawan Wiradi (1989, 289) found that laborers usually ask the farmer-owner, their employer, for a loan, which is deducted with interest from the laborer's share of the harvest.

Before tebasan was prevalent, those who participated in a harvest received wages in rice. In the 1970s and 1980s studies pointed to a decrease in the bawon for harvesters from one-sixth or one-seventh to as little as one-tenth (White and Wiradi 1989). Although some argue that the terms are worse for harvesters even though output per hectare has increased, others argue that yield increases have compensated the decline in bawon. Indeed, White and Wiradi (1989) found that the total paid to harvesters had increased considerably in the nine Javanese villages they resurveyed in 1981.

In the 1970s labor-saving technologies were introduced that rationalized the labor process in agriculture and displaced poor laborers, particularly poor women. Husken and White attribute a lack of resistance and political struggle against such changes to an increasingly repressive political regime that has extended its control into each and every rural hamlet and household (1989, 182).

Several technologically related changes particularly affected women's labor and the income of the poorest households. One of these changes, from the *ani-ani* to the sickle, is perhaps the most often cited example of female economic displacement in the literature on women and development (Charlton 1984; H. Papanek 1983). Traditionally, women used the *ani-ani,* a small razor, to cut rice stalk by stalk. The *ani-ani* was replaced by the sickle, which is used by men and is estimated to reduce labor requirements in harvesting by up to 60 percent (Collier et al. 1973;

Hart 1986b). Mechanized rice hullers were also introduced, replacing women who pounded the rice by hand. This change alone translated into an estimated loss of $50 million in annual income for women (H. Papanek 1983, 71). In addition, in some parts of Java rotary weeders have replaced hand weeding, another source of income for women from poor households (Husken and White 1989, 182). These technological changes affected most adversely the poor women who depended on income earned from these activities (H. Papanek 1983).

Most researchers associate the introduction of the Green Revolution with increased capitalist relations of production in rural Java and with these changes in agricultural technologies (see Hayami and Kikuchi 1982; Hart 1986b). Although tebasan and kedokaan existed before the introduction of high-yielding rice varieties, they have been used more frequently since Green Revolution varieties have proliferated.

AGRARIAN DIFFERENTIATION AND INEQUALITY

How have such changes in agricultural technology, relations of production, and differentiation affected income in Java? This is an extremely difficult question, and researchers do not agree on the answer. Some argue that "the incidence of rural poverty declined markedly" in the 1970s (Manning 1988, 49; see also Collier et al. 1982), yet others argue that despite agricultural and nonagricultural growth, there is increased disparity between the poor and the better-off, with poor people struggling even more just to earn a basic subsistence income (Hayami and Kikuchi 1982, 166; Hart 1986b; White 1979; Husken 1984).[9] In a recent summary of these debates, Chris Manning (1988, 50) shows that aspects of both arguments are true. According to Manning, although many poor villagers have benefited from employment created by the oil boom and the Green Revolution, most rural households have not participated in the recent expansion of new jobs.

Macrolevel statistics demonstrate an increase in nonagricultural employment for the rural population,[10] but it is important to understand that changes caused by the Green Revolution and the New Order have tipped the balance in favor of the rich and the landed, leaving the poor with little bargaining power. Poor households must engage in long hours of labor with low returns in order to survive. Although some poor households have benefited from nonagricultural employment, they have less of a safety net underneath them. Recent dramatic cuts in government spending on development projects (irrigation, roads, electricity) that provided some of this nonagricultural employment have left many poor households in a precarious situation.

According to a World Bank report, socioeconomic conditions in rural Java are indeed unequal. World Bank researchers found that rural Java "has a higher incidence of poverty than Indonesia as a whole, it has more than its share of the poor and less of the rich; it contains 55% of all households, but 77% of poor households and only 25% of rich households" (Chernichovsky and Meesook 1984, 2).

Agrarian class divisions have worsened over the past two decades: most rural households now own a tiny piece of land, if any. Husken and White found that "about 73% of rural households had a farm (of more than 0.1 ha) in 1963 and only about 57% in 1983, suggesting a rather dramatic increase in absolute landlessness" (1989, 183). In rural Java today, a small proportion of households—10 to 20 percent—control "70 to 80 percent of all farmland" (Husken and White 1989, 184). Changes in agricultural technology have increased output per hectare such that those few who own land and have been able to keep it have become wealthier over time. Such dramatic changes have led one researcher to write that in contemporary Java, "rural" can no longer by equated with "agrarian" (White 1989).

RURAL HOUSEHOLDS: PRODUCTION AND CONSUMPTION

What are the implications of such changes in land and labor relations for the men, women, children, and households affected by such shifts? Research on gender, households, and employment in Java add up to one critical fact: households in Java tend to be units not of production but of consumption. Most rural households still gain some income from agricultural production, yet for most, this income is insufficient for minimal reproduction.

Increasingly, rural households—approximately 80 percent of them—must seek income from nonagricultural activities in order to survive (Husken and White 1989; White and Wiradi 1989; Manning 1988). In such cases the household is an indirect unit of production and remains basically a unit of consumption—the site of most but not necessarily all consumption (White 1976). In cases where one household member migrates, the household might be a unit of income pooling (Smith, Wallerstein, Evers 1984), as suggested by Graeme J. Hugo's research (1975), but few Java researchers have made this argument. Benjamin White (1976) points out that income pooling and joint consumption may be points of contention in households with adult children who increasingly refuse to pool income; similar patterns have been noted in rural Malaysia (Wong 1984; Ong 1987).

It is important to understand that the household's function as a unit of consumption rather than production does not necessarily indicate vast socioeconomic shifts over time, particularly given the inegalitarian class relations found in rural Java historically. What appears to have changed, however, is the prevalence, not the existence, of households primarily as units of consumption.

GENDER, CLASS, AND LABOR ALLOCATION

How do such class differences translate into daily life activities for Javanese men, women, and children? Time allocation studies have documented the effects of class status on households, with particular attention to labor differences between males and females and between adults and children. Rural Javanese households are characterized by "occupational multiplicity" (White 1976), with each productive member engaging in several economic activities (both agricultural and nonagricultural), some of which change seasonally; family members often engage in several forms of production simultaneously (Friedman 1984). This phenomenon challenges the classification of labor activity because singular categories (e.g., laborer, farmer, self-employed, informal sector) oversimplify a more complex situation.

White (1976) found that children from poor households begin engaging in economic activities as early as four years old and continue to contribute substantially during their childhood and adolescence. Gillian Hart (1986b) found an inverse relationship between the class status of households (as measured by control over agricultural land) and hours of work among household members. Female children born into poor, landless households are "destined from an early age to a work pattern that changes very little" over the course of their lives (1986b, 128). Long hours of low-paying work, often at a distance from home, and labor-intensive domestic work typify the life of poor women. During the year of Hart's survey, women from landless households divided their income-earning time between trade (1,323 hours per year) and heavy physical labor (1,201 hours), often at a distance from home and particularly during low periods in the agricultural cycle; they also engaged in fishing and gathering (160 hours per year). They then returned home to do housework (800 hours per year). Despite all this labor, the income of the poorest households (measured in rice consumption equivalents) fell below the poverty line most months during the year (1986b, 138).[11]

Ann Stoler's research (1977a) also corroborates that poorer women's lack of access to productive resources is directly related to long hours of labor. According to Stoler, harvest shares are directly related to control over productive assets, with poorer women receiving a smaller share of the harvest than do women from better-off households.

TRADE AND MIGRATION

Rural women engage in agricultural production, either as landowners or as renters, sharecroppers, or wage laborers, but they are also ubiquitous as traders in the marketplace. Again, there are class differences, with poorer women peddling only a few goods and better-off women able to invest capital in more and varied goods (Dewey 1962; Alexander 1987). With few employment opportunities in agriculture and a limited number in manufacturing, more women are moving into trade in the informal sector.

Many rural Javanese women and men migrate to seek income (Hetler 1984). Hugo (1975; 1983) has documented the tremendous amount of short- and long-term migration occurring in Indonesia. The high prevalence of circular migration is facilitated by the recent revolution in inexpensive, accessible transportation in rural Java. In a village case study of temporary commuting migrants, Carol Hetler (1984) found that village women (both single and married) were just as likely to migrate as males were, whereas Hugo (1975) found more female than male migrants in Jakarta among those between the ages of fifteen and nineteen.

The migrants from the village of Hetler's study engaged in circular migration (one to three months) and specialized in what they sold. Women from this village sold herbal medicine (*jamu*) in urban neighborhoods or markets, carrying their wares on their backs, while men more often sold fish-ball soup (*bakso*) from a cart or, if they were successful, from a stand (*warung*). Male migrants made more money than female migrants did, despite the fact that males had higher costs because of higher initial investments. Whereas bakso sellers can improve their lot by expanding to a stand or supplying a restaurant, jamu sellers never make much money and can sell only what they can carry on their backs (Hetler 1984).

CONCLUSION

This brief description provides an overview of structural changes in both agriculture and industry that affect the men, women, households, and villages at the center of this study. Most Javanese live in rural areas, belong to poor households, and must work hard to survive. The majority of rural women are forced to combine a number of economic activities and to work long hours for low returns. They are undeniably affected by the ebb and flow of agrarian change and industrial growth as employment opportunities shift for them and for other family members. Women are also affected by the kinship system, which maps out certain domains of obligation and entitlement while setting boundaries for their activities and behaviors. The next chapter analyzes the position of women in the Javanese kinship system, the realm of the feminine, and state-generated images of womanhood.

CHAPTER III

Javanese Women and the Family

In comparison with women in South Asia or East Asia, women in Java, in Indonesia, and in Southeast Asia more generally are thought to have high status because of their ability to control their own movements outside the village and in the marketplace, to control their earned income, and to own property (Atkinson and Errington 1990, vii).[1] At the same time, women in Southeast Asia are conspicuously understudied, especially when compared with their counterparts in adjacent regions. As feminist scholars have discovered, strikingly little documentation on Southeast Asian women exists; Penny van Esterick comments, "What do we find? A delightfully refreshing cliché about the high status of women in this part of the world and very little else" (Esterick 1982, i; quoted in Errington 1990, 3).

In this chapter I first delineate the different arguments and approaches to women's status in Java and then examine women's position in the kinship system and in the family with regard to income, decision making, marriage, and sexuality. Finally, I explore aspects of female gender, particularly femininity, and how the state-run women's organizations at the village level reinforce particular notions of women's roles.

GENDER AND GENERATION IN STUDYING JAVANESE WOMEN

In the introduction to a collection of essays on Indonesian politics, Daniel S. Lev (1982) argues that there are distinctly different generations of

Indonesia scholars, marked by the timing of their entry into Indonesia. Different entry points into Indonesian political and social life "gave rise to divergent initial perceptions and perspectives," which then affected the researcher's "understanding, sympathies, and approaches." As a result, different theoretical issues "arose out of questions posed by the politics of each period" (Lev 1982, vi–vii). The major divide in interpretation, as Lev views it, is between Sukarno's Guided Democracy (1949–65) and Suharto's New Order (1966 to the present), corresponding to a shift in academic emphasis from culture to political economy. These shifts can also be seen in gender, family, and household studies in Java. However, I would add that conceptions of gender are shaped not only by generational paradigmatic shifts but also by the gender of the researcher, particularly since the rise of feminist scholarship.

There is clearly disagreement about Javanese women's status, autonomy, and agency. Generally, research that draws on postindependence ethnographies is more sanguine about women's position and presents a somewhat unidimensional image of high female status and autonomy. The "baseline" typically used when referring to women's position or gender relations in Java comes from *The Javanese Family* (1961), by Hildred Geertz, and *Javanese Villagers* (1969), by Robert Jay, scholars whose postindependence research has had a profound (and perhaps misleading) effect on conceptions of Javanese women and the family.[2] Their strong statements about female domination of the domestic realm and their focus on women as primary nurturers has influenced research—and as Jan Branson and Don Miller (1988) argue, state policy—for the past twenty-five years.[3]

Such research emphasizes the freedom of Javanese women, portraying them as independent, economically autonomous, and equal if not superior to their husbands (Alisjhabana 1961; Koentjaraningrat 1967; Meyer 1981; Geertz 1961; Jay 1969). A slightly different but related portrayal shows Javanese women as neither superior nor subordinate to their husbands; instead, they have hidden or different powers and exert their influence indirectly (Reid 1988; Willner 1980; Koentjaraningrat 1967a, 260; see also White and Hastuti 1980 for a discussion of different approaches to Javanese women's status). A corollary to this last argument is that women's status in Java may not be equal to men's, but it is certainly better than women's status in other less-developed countries (Koentjaraningrat 1967; Wertheim 1964).

By contrast, those influenced by feminist approaches to social science have questioned the generally accepted view of high female status and relatively egalitarian relationships within the family, challenging earlier assumptions and arguing that Javanese women are not as autonomous or powerful as was commonly accepted. Although Javanese women may enjoy some economic autonomy, they probably enjoy less than was previously thought since patriarchal controls may coexist simultaneously. Additionally, the constraints of class and poverty further limit women's lives, tainting terms used more frequently by the first two groups such as *autonomy, freedom,* and *choice* (Manderson 1983; Mather 1982; Saefullah 1979; Smyth 1986; Wieringa 1988; White and Hastuti 1980).

Male and female scholars of Geertz's and Jay's generation differ little in their analyses of Javanese women. However, contemporary female scholars tend to be influenced by feminist scholarship and thus question earlier assumptions about women's high status more than do male scholars. Female scholars today are also much less likely than male scholars are to assume household cohesion and consensus and more likely to analyze intrahousehold conflict (Guest 1989; Hart 1986b; McDonald n.d.; Williams 1990; Stoler 1977a; Wieringa 1988; Pyle 1985; Mather 1982; V. Hull 1975; D. Wolf 1990; White 1976 is an exception).

Although Hildred Geertz's useful and important book has yet to be replaced with a more comprehensive one, both she and Jay may have overemphasized somewhat the level of independence or autonomy Javanese women have. I am not arguing that Geertz and Jay were somehow "wrong"; rather, their approach ignores key points of tension in Javanese women's lives, obscuring such issues as women's lack of control over sexuality and lack of power within and beyond the household, the constraints of poverty on women's lives, the minuscule amount of financial resources they might control, and the contradictions in expectations concerning women's economic behavior and "feminine" behavior. These points of tension are taken up in this chapter.

THE JAVANESE KINSHIP SYSTEM

The predominant kinship system in Southeast Asia differs from systems in East Asia, South Asia, and other parts of the Third World, particularly with regard to bilateral inheritance, nuclear family structure, and the status accorded to women. Not only do these traits resemble Western family systems, but their uniqueness in the Third World challenges scholars who attempt to categorize family systems (Goldschmidt and Kunkel 1971; Todd 1985).[4]

Java is one of the few historical exceptions in which women maintained their precolonial position, particularly their productive activities, during colonialism (Chafetz 1980). The Dutch-imposed sugar production that existed alongside traditional paddy production (C. Geertz 1963) allowed women to continue their important role in wet rice cultivation (Stoler 1977a). Janet Chafetz (1980) points out that women usually have relatively lower status in agricultural societies, but societies based on irrigated rice production, particularly in Southeast Asia, provide the exception to this rule (Blumberg 1984; Michaelson and Goldschmidt 1971). This regional pattern is reflected in Java, where lineage and inheritance are bilateral and women can and do own land.

According to Islamic law, sons should inherit twice as much as daughters; by contrast, Javanese traditional law (*adat*) dictates that sons and daughters inherit equally. Hildred Geertz (1961) found flexible adaptations to the inheritance system, including some cases in which both laws were ignored. The system of inheritance is flexible and bilateral, yet females do not usually receive even half of the inheritance (H. Geertz 1961; Mather 1982). Women in Celia Mather's West Javanese site also complained about not receiving their full divorce entitlement (1982, 160), but this difficulty may be particular to West Java, which is ethnically Sundanese (rather than Javanese), more Islamic, and more patriarchal than are Central and East Java.

The basic unit of the Javanese family is nuclear. Approximately 60 percent of the 250 households I surveyed were nuclear, compared with 76 percent in Hildred Geertz's (1961) and Jay's (1969) earlier studies. Once children begin to marry and have children, families may remain extended for many years, particularly if they are poor and cannot afford to build a house for their children. Once children move out, elderly parents may move in, usually with a daughter, or may live alone.

When Javanese women marry, they initially live within an extended family context. Postmarital residence is predominantly matrilocal for anywhere from five to ten years, until the couple (with help from parents) can build their own house.[5] Matrilocality is beneficial for the new bride, who need not adjust to a new village or a new and sometimes hostile family. Although Javanese brides are not subject to domination by their mothers-in-law as their Indian or Chinese counterparts are, Williams (1990) found that they are still subject to pressure from their parents and parents-in-law in decision making as long as they remain in the same village, even if they have their own households.[6] Only when the couple moves to another village does parental influence subside, giving the woman greater independence in household decision making.

However, the Javanese kinship system is flexible and if the groom's parents are better off than the bride's, the couple will choose patrilocal residence (Koentjaraningrat 1985). In a third mode, *nglor-ngidul* (going north and south), each spouse stays at home with his or her parents, and the couple occasionally sleep together (Singarimbun and Manning 1974, 77). Although the nuclear family household set up by the young couple is neolocal in theory, Linda Williams (1990) found that the general practice is to set up a home near the wife's parents.

Additionally, because of poverty and death, many Javanese women live in circumstances quite different from the nuclear family that appears in billboards pushing various state campaigns aimed at the family or in the advertisements in most women's magazines in Indonesia. In 1978, 20 percent of rural Javanese households were headed by women, compared with 14 percent in urban areas (Chernichovsky and Meesook 1984, 9). In a village study, Carol Hetler (1984) found that almost 14 percent of the 915 households surveyed were headed by a female because of divorce, separation, or widowhood; women headed another 9 percent because of male migration. These figures are comparable to those of other studies in rural Java (Guest 1989, 44). In her Central Javanese study, Valerie Hull (1975, 44) also found considerable desertion and separation (*pisah kebo*). The World Bank's report on poverty in Indonesia did not find a statistically significant difference in the incidence of poverty between male- and female-headed households but that the poorest rural households are female headed (World Bank 1990, 32, 53, as cited in Smyth 1991, 3; Hart 1986b).

Hildred Geertz (1961) found that beneath the primary emphasis on the nuclear family, there exists a secondary structure, a strong network of ties among kinswomen. This network offers loyalty and mutual aid in times of distress (1961, 78), a form of support for Javanese women. My observations extend Geertz's finding beyond kinswomen to friends. I found that factory workers forged networks with each other as co-workers and as friends; these networks offered financial help and solidarity in times of need.

DAUGHTERS AND FAMILIES IN TAIWAN

The flexibility of the Javanese kinship system, the economic autonomy that it accords women, and the more egalitarian relations between men and women within it are cast in a different light when it is compared with the Chinese kinship system and other patrilineal systems. The

Chinese kinship system is patriarchal, patrilineal, and patrilocal, meaning that daughters are not included in the lineage and that women cannot own, inherit, or bequeath property. Traditionally, after marriage the bride went to live with her husband's family, where she was under the often oppressive direction of her mother-in-law and received little support from her husband. In that setting, her main duty was to produce sons for the continuation of the patriline. When she became a mother-in-law, however, she could attain some control and power within the household; ironically, such power (and sometimes oppression) was directed toward another woman—the new daughter-in-law.

In Taiwan, daughters are still taught to be filial and to pay back the debt they incur to parents for bringing them up.[7] Parents socialize daughters "to believe that they themselves [are] worthless, and that literally everything they [have]—their bodies, their upbringing, their schooling—belong[s] to their parents and [has] to be paid for" (Greenhalgh 1985, 277). Daughters can pay back their debt to parents only during their single years since they, unlike their brothers, will leave their family when they marry. Daughters are coerced to pay back this filial debt for fear of sanctions by their parents and siblings, who represent the only security daughters have ever had (M. Wolf 1972).

This juxtaposition will continue to cast different shadows over these two cases as we examine how the structure of the kinship system mediates the experience of factory employment for young women in these settings.

JAVANESE FAMILY VALUES AND FAMILY CYCLES

Javanese families strive for certain norms that may be difficult to reach but nevertheless affect how people interact with each other. Javanese families strive for *slamet* (emotional calm) so that no harm will come to family members. Upsetting or disturbing experiences make the family vulnerable to supernatural dangers which can result in illness, accidents, and death (Koentjaraningrat 1985). The likelihood of such misfortune can be diminished by observing certain rituals and taboos, including the *slametan* (a ritual feast) for various events of the life cycle events.

Families also endeavor to attain the important norm of *rukun*—social peace and harmony. Rukun, the ideal underlying social relationships, represents cooperation and minimal conflict. For example, Hildred Geertz (1961, 48) explains that the direct expression of self-interest works against rukun; seeking rukun may therefore encourage constraint, compromise, or even sacrifice, something she observed in inheritance conflicts and that Robert Jay observed in a divorce settlement (1969, 67). Despite (or, more realistically, alongside) this stated ideal of harmony, Benjamin White (1976) and I both found considerable intrafamilial conflict over money and labor. In other words, family practices diverge considerably from family ideals.

Finally, the family value of respect or *hormat* (*urmat* in Javanese) is connected with the view that all social relationships are hierarchically ordered. This hierarchy is maintained, observed, and respected through hormat, which is taught to children at a very early age (H. Geertz 1961, 147). Although the ideal of hormat encourages young women to obey their fathers and brothers, or the factory's personnel manager, in practice women sometimes disobey or negotiate.

Sociologists and demographers use life-cycle models with stages of maturity to categorize families or domestic groups, but the fluctuation and flexibility of Javanese patterns defy such linear categorizations. Again, such findings suggest that considerable distance exists between social ideals and local practices. For example, Terence and Valerie Hull (1987) argue that Hildred Geertz generalized the ideal stages of marriage among the elite—(1) legal registration, (2) religious ceremony, (3) social ceremonies, and (4) consummation—to all Javanese. The Hulls, by contrast, found tremendous variation in the timing of consummation, which could occur at any point along the continuum.

Likewise, my interviews with women in their forties concerning marriage, divorce, and childbirth, with particular attention to where the women lived and with whom, also suggest that tremendous variation exists in marital, childbearing, and family sequences. Women's movements in and out of marriages and different family forms demonstrate a highly fluid situation not easily reduced to evolutionary categories. One woman, Rini's mother, experienced approximately eight changes in her family situation during her first three marriages, including the dissolution of the marriages, the deaths of three of her eight children, and movement in and out of different living situations. Thus, the recent research on gender and family in Java suggests that Hildred Geertz may have often extrapolated from her interviews with the elite to the entire population (Martokoesoemo 1979).[8]

MARRIAGE AND SEXUALITY

In Java, marriage is almost universal; not marrying is an option only for those who are physically or mentally handicapped. Women have little choice about whether they want to marry, and only recently have they had any choice about whom they marry. Parents do not wish to have a *gadis tua* (old maid) on their hands. Fathers and brothers protect and do their best to control a young woman's sexuality until she marries; at that time, her husband becomes her guardian. A young woman must, in the end, adhere to a father's or older brother's decisions.[9]

Mather (1982; 1985) argues that, although marriage is also universal for Javanese males, they are more independent with regard to sexually related decisions. A woman who does not marry or who bears children out of wedlock may be ostracized while her male partner is not. Men can become involved with divorced or widowed women or engage in polygamy without stigma, but women have little room to maneuver. Indeed, young and middle-aged divorced or widowed women are seen as sexually seductive and are usually suspected of luring married men into affairs.

Monogamy and relatively easy divorce have constituted the main pattern in Java for the past centuries (Reid 1988). Polygamy, though not common, is still legal.[10] Masri Singarimbun and Chris Manning (1974) found a high proportion of de facto marriages and consensual unions and a small number of cohabiting couples, called *kumpul kebo* (marriage in the manner of water buffalo). Cohabitation, although taboo, may occur when a woman is separated from her husband or when a husband and wife are forced to divorce on the advice of a healer (*dukun*) to avoid misfortune but continue to cohabit; and, of course, women and men sometimes simply form unions without legal marriage (V. Hull 1975, 193).

Before the 1974 Marriage Law, it was not uncommon for parents to marry their children off at an early age (often before puberty). In 1974 the legal age of marriage was raised to sixteen, and child and forced marriages were made illegal (see Katz and Katz 1978). Still, the majority of rural parents continue to arrange marriages for their daughters, but not until after menarche. In 1980 the Asian Marriage Survey (conducted a few kilometers from my research site) found that in this rural area 58 percent of females aged fifteen to twenty-four ($n = 95$) still had marriages arranged by their parents, echoing the same high proportion of arranged marriages found by Singarimbun and Manning (1974) more than a decade earlier (Hull, Adieotomo, and Hull 1984, 6). The age at marriage throughout Indonesia has been increasing in part, it is thought, because of increased education among the general population and a slow increase in self-selection of spouse. For example, by 1976 the average age at marriage in rural Java had increased to nineteen, according to an analysis of a survey made in that year (P. Smith 1981).

One result of arranged marriages at an early age was that they remained unconsummated (Singarimbun and Manning 1974). Valerie Hull (1975) found little delay in consummation when the couple chose each other, but one-third of the couples in arranged marriages delayed consummation, with 12 percent never consummating.

Hull stresses that conceptions of marriage differ by class in Java, and these differences are basic to understanding divorce patterns. Indeed, it is important to understand that class differences *between* women in Java are at least as great as gender differences. Valerie Hull (1975, 154–58) found that the common villager (*abangan*) expects considerable separateness to exist between husband and wife, since love and companionship are not important reasons for marriage. (This conception is changing because of communication and popular culture.) By contrast, the elite (*priyayi*) assume that love will eventually develop between spouses. Both the *santri*—the religious teachers—and priyayi feel that husbands should support their wives, whereas the abangan—the focus of this research—view marriage much more as economic partnership.

Like women in matrilineal family systems, Javanese women do have high marital instability. Singarimbun and Manning (1974, 19) found that 42 percent of first marriages in the village they studied ended in divorce, as did one-third of second marriages, one-fourth of third marriages, one-third of fourth marriages, and one-fifth of fifth marriages! Abangan do not judge divorce as morally wrong; rather, they see it as the best solution to a conflictual and potentially harmful situation (V. Hull 1975, 160). Because they see marriage as a separate partnership, women are fully prepared to continue taking care of themselves after divorce. Divorce carries greater stigma among the santri and the priyayi, who perceive it as morally wrong and shameful. Additionally, elite women would seek to avoid divorce because they are economically dependent on their husbands.

Why do couples divorce? Budi S. Martokoesoemo (1979) found that most divorces occur within the first two years of marriage. "Dislike" or incompatibility (*tidak cocok*, "not fitting"), the primary reason given, is much more likely to occur in an arranged marriage. If the couple are unfamiliar with each other, they may not be attracted to each other, resulting in an unconsummated marriage (Singarimbun and Manning 1974, 82). Rural parents often are quick to marry off a daughter for the first time to control her sexuality, but they feel that there is no problem if the marriage ends because the couple doesn't fit well. Divorce is not difficult to obtain in Indonesia, and through it couples can nullify what is believed to be the inevitable danger of incompatibility, namely, a psychic imbalance causing illness or death. The second highest reason given for divorce in Singarimbun and Manning's (1974) study was infidelity, even though it is known and somewhat accepted that men play around (*jajaan,* "to snack"). Conflict over the place of residence is also a frequent reason for divorce.

Divorce is associated with an early age at marriage and arranged marriages and is inversely related to class. A high rate of divorce reflects the strains of poverty and perhaps women's ability to fend for themselves, but it also creates the necessity for female economic independence. Hannah Papanek (1975) argues that the bilateral kinship system is also related to the high rate of divorce since there are loose relationships and few pressures from in-laws and other kin members, at least among abangan, to maintain an unhappy marriage. Finally, although Javanese women share high marital instability with women in matrilineal kinship systems, they do not have the sexual freedom and power enjoyed by women in matrilineal kinship systems (Safilios-Rothschild 1982).

GENDER AND POWER

Both Hildred Geertz and Robert Jay point to the dominant if not domineering role of Javanese women in financial household decision making. Jay frequently refers to female dominance in the household and the emasculating effects on husbands: "Wives . . . expect their husbands to leave completely to them most of the domestic decisions, especially on expenditures. The result is a marked degree of female dominance in most of the everyday affairs of the family and many henpecked husbands" (1969, 87); "there is an astonishing degree of female dominance to be observed in everyday village life" (1969, 92; see also 45, 61, 124; H. Geertz 1961, 123–25).[11] Jay's analysis of Javanese gender relations, with its images of strong, domineering women who rule their husbands and the roost, may reflect American gender and family ideology during a time when patriarchal relationships were the norm as much as it reflects Javanese ideology.

Researchers have pointed to control over income as an indicator of Javanese female autonomy and high status (H. Geertz 1961; Jay 1969; Blumberg 1984). Yet, although control over money is equated with power in Western culture, Javanese forms of power emanate from other sources

(C. Geertz 1960; B. Anderson 1972; Djajadiningrat-Nieuwenhuis 1987). In fact, dealing and bargaining in the marketplace for daily necessities with the small amount of money most Javanese women have to spend is considered, within Javanese culture, to be a low-status activity. Seeking refinement, or being *halus*, is an indication of power in Java, and it is limited to males (Djajadiningrat-Nieuwenhuis 1987). A refined person seeks inner peace and harmony and does not concern himself with the earthy and earthly activity of exchanging money, an activity seen as crude and coarse (*kasar*). Indeed, as Shelly Errington points out, whereas Westerners identify power with activity, forcefulness, and effectiveness, in Southeast Asia exerting such force or engaging in such activities demonstrates the very opposite—"a lack of spiritual power and effective potency, [which] consequently diminishes prestige" (1990, 5).

Conceptions of gender in Java indicate some of these points. Males are perceived as financially incompetent, women as frugal, resourceful, clever (H. Geertz 1961, 123; Jay 1969, 92; V. Hull 1975, 113). These conceptions extend to Southeast Asia more generally: women are seen as "more calculating and instrumental than men, in control of practical matters and money" (Errington 1990, 7). As Errington emphasizes, such economic "power" may in fact represent the opposite of power in cultural terms, accruing lower rather than higher prestige.

What do we know about women's control over income or the household finances? In Central Java, Valerie Hull found that 80 percent of the wives she interviewed said that they usually keep household money, but a majority said that both husband and wife decide how to spend it, meaning that managing money does not mean deciding how to spend it. Like Hildred Geertz and Jay, Hull also observed that most household financial dealings are performed by the wife, as either she alone makes financial decisions or does so jointly with her husband (1975, 120). However, Hull also notes that in poor rural households there is little money over which the wife can make decisions.

Benjamin White and E. L. Hastuti's (1980) detailed study of household decision making in West Javanese villages did not demonstrate female control of the domestic realm and showed little female input in production-related decisions. Women influenced decisions concerning food but did not dominate decisions about clothing or household utensils (1980, 39). Thus, although husbands claim that women control the household purse, they do not necessarily do so in reality. Certainly Central Java is much less Islamic and patriarchal than West Java is, and women may be able to make more decisions that affect other household members. For example, in her Central Javanese research, Ann Stoler (1977a; 1977b) found that women in landed households were able to control part of the production process, especially decisions related to invitations to the harvest, but again, those who own sufficient land that they can hire laborers are an increasingly tiny minority in rural Java.

It is possible that religious differences between West and Central Java, which contribute to a higher degree of patriarchal control in the former, may explain some of these differences in women's control over household income. Additionally, different research methodologies may also contribute to the discrepancy in findings between West and Central Java. When respondents are asked to describe household financial arrangements in the abstract, it is much more likely that they will offer a normative account of how they think it should be, leading both men and women to state that women are "holding the purse strings" (Papanek and Schwede 1988). If, however, respondents are asked about specific financial decisions, as they were in White and Hastuti's (1980) study (e.g., "Who decided the last time you bought a pair of shoes?"), they are more likely to describe the actual workings of the household.

We still have few details about decision making within poor Central Javanese households; White and Hastuti's findings suggest that caution be exercised in fully accepting Hildred Geertz's and Jay's generalizations about high levels of female control over household income. Although Geertz's and Jay's views may reflect Javanese ideological notions of domineering women, the actual day-to-day inner workings of a household are more complex.

Mather (1985) and I both found that often a wife's income is used for day-to-day living expenses while the male's income is more sporadic and less reliable. "Men's contribution to the households, though believed primary and obligatory according to Islamic and secular law, is in practice discretionary and according to many women interviewed, not to be relied upon" (Mather 1985, 160). Unlike Hildred Geertz (1961), Mather did not find a majority of "joint purse" households; instead, she noted that many women "complain of the difficulty they experience in establishing a pattern of pooled income and fair distribution between themselves and their husbands" (1985, 160). Similarly, one mother of a factory daughter described to me the economic partnership to which she and her husband had agreed. She was to provide the income for daily needs such as food and small items, while he was to provide the income for larger expenditures such as their children's education. However, the husband had trouble providing such funds regularly, resulting in some of their children ending their education early.

Thus, popular conceptions of domineering women may be grounded in a somewhat different reality. Women may manage or budget household income, but such management needs to be distinguished from controlling decisions about household expenditures—a distinction that research needs to more fully substantiate.[12] These different financial roles may have been conflated in some research findings. Additionally, research suggests that women are forced to earn much of what they then can manage or control. Images of domineering women and henpecked husbands take a different form when compared with the more likely reality that many husbands shirk or may not be able to meet financial responsibilities, leaving the question of daily income, food, and other needs to their wives.

Notions of female dominance may mask not only men's sometimes shaky contributions but also women's heavy work loads. Javanese women carry a disproportionate burden of household concerns. Although Javanese men do engage in childcare, women are expected to perform almost all the household work in addition to earning income outside the household (Hart 1986b, 129; Mather 1985, 160). In addition, they are responsible for procuring and preparing food. White and Hastuti (1980) suggest that the ideology of female dominance is but one way to keep women controlled and to justify their enormous domestic burden.

Javanese women do make some economic decisions about their labor, their tiny earned income, and, occasionally, household consumption; however, such decision making must not be confused with Western conceptions of status or power. Rural Javanese women may be strong and self-sufficient, but these qualities do not necessarily indicate that they have power.

FEMININITY AND THE SPHERES OF WOMANHOOD

Although popular conceptions of Javanese women suggest that they rule the roost, Javanese norms of femininity demand that they be submissive to men. Javanese females are taught to feel shame and to be *malu* (shy), which, as Mather explains, "refers to both mental and physical attitudes, encouraging them to appear shy, embarrassed, and retiring, deferring to superiors and remaining at a distance from them, averting their eyes. . . . They are also encouraged to feel afraid (*takut*) of new experiences and new people" (Mather 1985, 168). These feminine traits contrast with the assertive (*berani*), more forceful behavior thought to be typical of males and judged inappropriate for females.

These characteristics of femininity imply female dependency on males, who need not be retiring. They also imply that females will follow the decisions of a male figure (husband, father, or brother) even if they disagree, for they will be too embarrassed to show their disagreement.[13] This ideology of female deference has state and legal support: the Marriage Law of 1974 (article 31) "stipulates that the husband is the head of the family and the wife is the mother of the family (*ibu rumahtangga*)" (Smyth 1991, 14). This particular conception of women, which encourages the widespread dependency on and submission to males in the family, is reproduced in worker-manager relations within the factory, as seen in Mather's research (1985, 168) and as chapter 5 demonstrates.

Although traits such as submission and shyness may help a woman keep a factory job, they would clearly be a disaster for a trader or a buyer in the market. Indeed, the traits associated with femininity are diametrically opposed to those that a woman needs when bargaining in the marketplace—as either trader or customer—or when earning income to keep her family fed. Again, ideological notions of femininity create social controls over women, who are expected to be both submissive to men and shrewd and calculating in the marketplace or in household budgeting. These contradictions between notions of femininity and women's lives are mirrored in the state's programs for women.

STATE AND GENDER: THE NEW ORDER AND THE NEW WOMAN

The development pursued by the New Order has undoubtedly reached Indonesian women and, to some extent, has improved their lives. However, Ines Smyth (1991) details how females fare consistently worse than do males in indicators of social welfare. First, as mentioned earlier, female-headed households are among the poorest in rural areas. Second, although educational attainment has increased, women still lag behind men in years of schooling, the percentage who have never attended school, and in the drop-out rate (Smyth 1991, 4). The status of health has improved generally (reflected in demographic measures such as infant mortality rate and life expectancy), but "women are not necessarily healthier" (Smyth 1991, 5), as reflected in the prevalence of nutritional anemia and maternal mortality rates. Finally, despite their active role in production, women's earnings are lower than men's. In 1982, "52.2 percent of all Indonesian women were classified in the lowest wage category, compared to 14.2 percent of men" (Smyth 1991, 5). Although general attempts to improve social welfare may be viewed as a success, they are "often not entirely effective in improving women's lives" (Smyth 1991, 6).

The government has set up several programs that focus specifically on women to improve social welfare and raise earnings. It is obvious from daily life in Java as well as from national statistics that most Javanese women work. But the Indonesian government also projects a particular image for women to emulate; according to this image, a woman may find fulfillment by being a supportive wife, a good mother, an impeccable housewife, and a worthy parent who raises good citizens for the benefit of the state. Such fulfillment, so the government propaganda goes, does not know or need remuneration. Such is the role of women in Indonesian development as portrayed by the New Order regime, a middle-class image completely divorced from the difficult realities and limited possibilities that most women in Indonesia must confront throughout their lives.

The complementarity of sex roles found in state ideologies serves state interests by keeping women quietly domestic rather than economically or politically active. Furthermore, there is a striking convergence between state ideologies of gender complementarity and the images of gender found in the 1950s social science literature, both of which emphasize women's domestic power and roles. This convergence of images is particularly striking in the state-run women's organization that reaches out to the grass-roots level.[14]

Although the Indonesian government expresses the desire to "enhance the role of women in development," European and Indonesian feminists argue that government organizations set up to reach women serve the state by subordinating them further (Wieringa 1988; Suryakusama 1988; Djajadiningrat-Nieuwenhuis 1987; Smyth 1991). The two main women's organizations—the PKK (*Pembinaan Kesejahteraan Keluarga* or Family Welfare Guidance) and P2W-KSS (*Peningkatan Peranan Wanita Menuju Keluarga Sehat dan Sejahtera* or Program for the Improvement of Women's Role in Fostering a Healthy and Prosperous Family)—both propagate an ideal that has been termed "State Ibuism," or state maternalism. (*Ibu* means "mother.") Unlike those seeking money or power, the Ibu engages in good maternal deeds for the welfare of the state-family without expecting anything in return (*tanpa pamrih*).[15] The Ibu acts with informal power, whereas the *Bapak* (father), also concerned with people's well-being, has authority, prestige, and formal power (Djajadiningrat-Nieuwenhuis 1987, 44).[16]

State policies do not address gender inequalities because the state argues that women and men are traditionally equal, with complementary roles. Women are domestics and mothers who support their husbands and, indirectly, the state. This domestic image, however, does not resemble the lives of most Indonesian women, who work long hours at lower wages (if they receive a wage) than men do. Because of state definitions of gender roles and domestic life, state policies ignore the inequalities, burdens, and needs poor women experience in their daily lives.

THE STATE AND WOMEN'S ORGANIZATIONS

The PKK is a large organization that includes all women at the village level and all women whose husbands are not civil servants; wives of civil servants belong to Dharma Wanita.[17] Both the PKK and Dharma Wanita parallel the male hierarchy: regardless of her capabilities, the wife occupies the same structural position that her husband does within the state bureaucracy. A 1988 official government pamphlet describing the PKK calls it a "grassroots development movement initiated by community volunteers. They develop projects, motivate others and help in implementing activities aimed at improving a family's well-being, economically and spiritually."

PKK concentrates on ten areas: "comprehension and practical application of Pancasila; mutual self help; food; clothing; housing and home economics; education and craft skills; health; development of cooperatives; protection and conservation of the environment; sound planning." Ideologically, the PKK promotes the Five Duties of Women (Panca Dharma Wanita): to be loyal companions of their husbands, to procreate for the nation, to educate their children, to manage their households, and to be useful members of society.[18]

All eligible women are required to participate in the PKK. Local chapters are led by the wife of the village head, "whether she has the capabilities or interest to carry out the task or not" (Wieringa 1988, 14). Village women and the wife of the village head are often stratified by class, for village heads tend not to come from the poorest strata. At the very least, village leaders receive land in lieu of salary, enhancing their wealth and position. The economic stratification between the local PKK head and the village women who are members of PKK can vitiate the effectiveness of projects and programs since a better-off village leader's wife may not understand poor women's problems or be particularly sympathetic to them. Village women, however, do not have a choice as to whether they would like to participate in PKK; they are often forced to do so.

The activities of the PKK can include income-generating activities but usually are concerned with domestic life: the women study sewing, cooking (often with expensive ingredients beyond the budgets of most rural women), and flower arranging and attend courses on national ideology (Pancasila), nutrition education, or maternal and children's health. Because official decree states that Indonesian women are already emancipated, PKK does not fight for women's rights. Rather, it accepts the current sexual division of labor and pushes middle- and upper-class values of domestication for women (Wieringa 1988, 15).

The P2W-KSS program also focuses on social welfare and income generation for poor women, with particular emphasis on four areas: (1) basic activities to promote literacy, sanitation, and the health of mothers and children; (2) follow-up activities to the family planning program; (3) educational support activities, for example, for the understanding of environmental issues or of government ideology (Pancasila); and (4) special activities, for example, for women in transmigration programs to improve skills of local artisans and traders. Its programs are often run jointly with PKK activities (Smyth 1991, 12).

These organizations clearly are not grass-roots movements from below but are apparatuses pushed down from above; during Suharto's regime their tentacles have forcibly insinuated themselves into every rural hamlet and household. According to Nani Yamin, such organizations, rather than serving women in the process of development—both national and personal—deprive women of any autonomy and increase their dependence on men (1988, 8). And as Smyth (1991, 12) points out, government policy as expressed in such programs is functionalist, asking how women can help the family or national development rather than the reverse.

The hierarchy of power within the PKK perpetuates and reinforces certain class hierarchies. Poor rural women are vulnerable to the whims, demands, and commands of better-off women (and men) in the village. If the local PKK leader must put on a good show for a district or regency-level official, she can force poor women to attend or participate, regardless of their need to be out earning income. For example, the poorest women are the first to be sought after by state family-planning agents who want to meet their quotas. Even though the fertility levels of the better-off tend to be higher than those of the poor (V. Hull 1975), the sexuality and fertility of poorer women is controlled more forcefully by the state.

Another example comes from my research site. The PKK has a national monthly baby-weighing program to monitor the growth of those under five years of age. Mothers are given growth charts, and a nourishing dish is to be served to the children at each monthly meeting. If the PKK leader is dedicated, the program may work well and may catch problems in the health of young children. In my research village, however, the head of the local PKK, the hamlet (*pedukuan*) head's wife, was completely uninterested in spending her time on PKK activities. She preferred to rest or to earn money by applying make-up for weddings or sewing clothes for others. Most village women considered her a snob, someone who was proud and put on airs. She refused to do the weighings unless an official was coming to observe because "it's too much trouble." Occasionally, when an official was going to visit, village women were ordered in advance to attend the weighing as though it was the usual monthly meeting, and the village head's wife simply filled in the growth charts as though she had weighed the children every month. This is an example not of poor people bravely resisting state intrusion and state demands but of a better-off woman who is more interested in earning income for herself than in helping needy villagers. Clearly, this kind of behavior does nothing to benefit those for whom the program was intended—the poorest children and their mothers.

Second, the activities and images of women propagated by these organizations (and the state) reinforce the shame that poor women feel about their poverty. Since the PKK focuses more on housewifery than on women as producers—the classes concentrate on cake decorating, cooking with ingredients that most can't buy, or flower arranging—they underscore the gap between poor and better-off women. Emphasizing and strengthening such inequalities is a far cry from enhancing the role of women in development.

The activities and philosophies of these women's programs emphasize that marriage and children are the only options open to women. Perhaps more important, their social welfare approach focuses on the symptoms of women's problems while depoliticizing causes such as unemployment, income inequality, poverty, and gender inequality. The top-down approach discourages any active political involvement as well as activities that might evolve in participation of poor women or the creation of self-help groups. Indeed, Smyth (1991, 14) argues that the Indonesian government's particular conception of development has greatly determined this top-down style of implementation, in which objectives and priorities have been predetermined by those other than the program's participants. Such an approach squelches women's questions about the status quo and increases rather than decreases controls over women.

CONCLUSION

Feminists studying women in Java have challenged popular conceptions about the status of Javanese females and pointed to a need for further research detailing daily practices of men and women and the relations between them. Their findings strongly suggest that a reevaluation of commonly accepted notions of female autonomy or power is necessary. The lives of Javanese women demonstrate both more room to negotiate and more ambiguity than do the lives of their counterparts in East or South Asia, yet their agency is confined by the oppression of poverty. A revised and more complex notion of women's position in Java is needed to better understand gender relations—a task made more urgent by the Indonesian government's active encouragement of a family and gender ideology based on female domesticity.

Feminist research has also questioned the assumption that women are fully and inextricably bound up with their families and has drawn attention to extrahousehold activities such as work. Through the rest of this book, I consider the effects of Javanese notions of gender and family relations on female factory workers. The role of the state has been to offer women factory workers to foreign and domestic investors as young, docile, cheap, and attractive females. While the state pushes women into the home to provide free goods and services, it also pushes young and vulnerable women to sell themselves to factories for wages on which they cannot survive. Although these two trends appear oppositionary, they both involve controlling women's behavior and eliminating any political resistance while benefiting those who reap the rewards of industrial capitalism and patriarchal power. By reminding women of their obligation to be loyal and obedient, quiet, accepting, and unprotesting, the state can control women's labor and keep their wages down. And state leaders, bureaucrats, and the military want to create and maintain a stable labor force for industrial capitalism not simply because they are dedicated to a national economic goal but also because they wish to enhance their own wealth and status.

CHAPTER IV

The Villages

Landscapes can be deceptive.
Sometimes a landscape seems to be less a setting
for the lives of its inhabitants than a curtain behind which
their struggles, achievements, and accidents take place.

For those who, with the inhabitants, are behind
the curtain, landmarks are no longer only geographic
but also biographical and personal.

John Berger, 1967

The entrance to the village in which I lived is a steep rocky path that twists down past a river and a dense thicket of trees and bamboo. I approached the path slowly and cautiously at any time, but particularly during the rainy season, when, to the giggles and great amusement of village children who gathered to watch, I often slipped on the mud on my way down.

This chapter, like the path, descends into the villages and households of the young women who constitute the focus of this research. The rural poverty, agrarian change, and limited employment opportunities delineated in chapter 2 are reflected in the everyday lives of village inhabitants in this setting. The meaning and impact of industrial growth in such a setting can be appreciated if the rocky and precipitous nature of rural poverty is understood. Before describing the district and village sites, I discuss my research methods, the tools that guided my path into the villages and factories, into the households, and into the lives of factory daughters.

RESEARCH METHODS

All too often, a description of methods is missing or glossed over in books based on field research concerning either peasant households or Third World women in global factories. Texts are presented as faits accomplis, without histories. This section is written with students of Third World research in mind, to place the realities and challenges of field methods in the prominent position they deserve and to underscore that fieldwork entails relationships, decision making, negotiations, and a myriad of processes related to adapting and attempting to comprehend the world one is in. As mentioned in the Preface, the unfolding of the research problematic and the dialectic between problem formulation and data gathering deserve discussion.

SITE SELECTION

Because I wanted to focus on village women who worked in factories, I wanted to find a village that was within commuting distance of the factories and that had agricultural land undisturbed by factory development so that young women might also work in agriculture. Thus, I hoped to find a village where factory employment was one of perhaps several economic options; such a situation would provide a comparative perspective. The local agricultural extension agents were extremely friendly and helped me find such a village.

One of the several villages they took me to was just a few kilometers up a mountain road that led to ancient Hindu temples and, at the top, a breezy town known for prostitution. The village to which they introduced me was about halfway up the mountain and had both factory workers and young women engaged in other activities. My assistant—a university-educated Javanese woman—and I lived in each of the hamlets (*pedukuan*) of that village for a few days so that we could get a sense of the environment and the work of the young women residents. After some consideration, I chose a hamlet (hereafter referred to as a village) that I call "Nuwun" (a pseudonym), selecting it partly because of the mixture of economic activities in which young women engaged but also because of the openness of the village leader and wife, in whose house we would live.[1]

The neighboring village, "Pamit," had more factory workers, but the village leader's wife restricted our movements considerably, dictating with whom we could speak and insisting that her sister accompany us on our visits. I could not have functioned easily in that environment and could not trust that she would not try to read my field notes in my absence, even if they were locked up. Although I eventually conducted a census of all the households in Pamit and interviewed factory workers there, I chose to make Nuwun my home base.

Initial fieldwork in Nuwun started in December 1981 and lasted until February 1982, when a three-month moratorium on village-based research was imposed by the government because of election campaigns. I returned in the spring of 1982 and stayed until early 1983. Until the last few months of fieldwork I was assisted by a woman who had graduated from Gadjah Mada University: a modest and warm woman whose husband was engaged as a research assistant elsewhere in Java and whose two children stayed with their grandparents. While I worked in Indonesian, she worked in Javanese. Eventually, I could understand most of the Javanese spoken during interviews, but I could engage only in "subsistence-level" conversations, much to the delight and laughter of villagers and traders in the marketplace. My assistant became an older sister to the factory workers, who took her into their confidences. Additionally, she became both a cultural translator and a friend on whom I relied. In turn, I tried to help her cope with the stresses in her life that she confided to me, although, to be sure, it was not a symmetrical exchange.

During the initial census of the 250 households in Nuwun and Pamit, I hired three additional enumerators, all graduate students from Gadjah Mada University. After the initial census, my primary assistant and I spent the following months gathering information from young women who worked in factories and elsewhere and their parents. We usually went on separate visits, usually two to three a day.

Except for the initial census and the income-expenditures survey, we did not use questionnaires and never introduced tape recorders. When we first were getting to know factory daughters, nonfactory women, and their families, we took notes in small notebooks during conversations. Later, when we began to focus more on factory daughters and their parents, we brought small notebooks with us and jotted down key phrases. During the evenings and the mornings, we wrote more extensive notes, reconstructing as much of the conversations as we remembered and including parts that seemed irrelevant at the time. I had designed a more detailed questionnaire that covered both daughters' and parents' perspectives, but we kept such questionnaires at home and filled them in after our visits. It took three to four visits per family to fill in one questionnaire.

We decided not to use the more formal equipment of questionnaires or tape recorders for fear that their presence would cause the respondents to become self-conscious and refrain from discussing personal stories. Indeed, some of the factory workers saw my assistant as an older sister, discussing personal stories with her and often asking for her advice. As we gathered Rini's and her mother's stories, however, we took more detailed notes in their presence to ensure the accuracy of longer quotations.

We also conducted a detailed daily survey of income expenditures among all the factory workers in Nuwun for one month. The income-expenditure surveys consisted of one sheet of paper per day on which all income, expenditures (in detail), purchases, and loans (extended or received) were recorded; the individual survey sheets were kept in binders. After daily visits for a few days, literate workers were visited about twice a week. Illiterate workers were visited every forty-eight hours and asked to recount their expenditures and income for the previous two days. We found that as workers became used to our questions, recall was not a problem.

Several workers in Nuwun kept diaries for me over a period of several months in which they recorded anything interesting that occurred at work. Until one major labor protest occurred (see chapter 5), the entries described certain basics in labor-management relationships, particularly the treatment of workers who fell ill during the workday. Additionally, one factory worker whose mother was a landless laborer kept daily records concerning her income and her mother's for about six months.

I also began to visit the twelve factories, always presenting the managers with my business card and official letters to convince them that I was not a government agent looking for fraud or tax evasion but simply a graduate student trying to obtain interviews with the managers. I visited each factory two to three times in order to meet with an owner or personnel manager and was given a tour of the production floor in each case. Most allowed me to take photographs on the production floor, and most were friendly but cautious, sending me on my way with a sample of whatever they produced, usually cookies or noodles, and inviting me not to come back. However, a few owners and managers were quite open to more visits and took the opportunity to discuss political issues with me, usually those related to their secondary status as Chinese Indonesians.

The Indian national who was the general manager of the spinning mill waved me on and told me to speak with whomever I liked, a rather unusual invitation. I took the opportunity to visit the factory compound several times and then gathered my courage to propose to him that I live in the workers' dormitory for some weeks to observe factory life; in return he asked that I offer suggestions on how to improve worker-manager relations. I spent almost a month living in the dormitory in conditions that were luxurious compared with the village; the dormitory had cement rather than dirt floors, running water, gas burners for cooking, and electricity. Without question, my productivity improved in such a setting, where I worked at night without the eye-strain that came from using an oil lamp and slept peacefully without worrying about rats or other little creatures that had visited me at night in my village bed.[2] During that month, I interviewed dormitory residents, other factory workers, Javanese middle-level managers, and Indian upper-level managers, examined personnel files and health clinic records, and had full access to the production floor any time of day or night.

In late 1982 my assistant quit her job and followed her husband to East Timor, where he had a job with the government family planning board. At that time I wanted to expand the first income-expenditure survey, whose results had been surprising, to add two other categories: migrant factory workers and factory workers who lived at home and did not commute to work. I hired three graduates from the regional agricultural high school. We made a census of the one hundred households (including two hundred migrants) in a village in which the factories had been built and conducted another daily income-expenditure survey for a month among women in Nuwun and two other groups of women who lived in a village by the factories. My assistants, who were extremely capable and enthusiastic young women, came from better-off families in villages or small towns; they were more familiar with the social circumstances of the villagers than my first group of university-educated enumerators from the university had been. The assistants I hired from the agricultural high school also adapted more easily to living in a village.

When I returned to Nuwun in 1986, I hired two female assistants, both university graduate students, and we reinterviewed the women who had been between the ages of nineteen and twenty-nine in 1982 and their parents, since most still lived at home. Most had married and borne children by then, and we focused on their employment, marriages, family economy, and family relations. Their stories and their mothers' stories were not difficult to obtain, especially since returning to the village seemed to confirm my connection with them.

My students and one reviewer of this book have asked about field relations: What did Javanese villagers think of me? How did they react to me? Why do I think they took my questionnaires seriously? Obviously, I cannot really answer for them; I can only discuss how I perceived their reaction to me. Certainly, I was an object of curiosity, and people from other villages all knew about the white woman (*londo*) who was actually living in a village.[3] They were very curious about life in America ("What do you eat?" "Do you eat rice with your potatoes and bread?" "What is the weather like?" "Where is America?" "How can an actor become president?") and about my adaptation to life in rural Java ("Do you eat rice? How many times a day? Can you speak Indonesian?"). They were also curious about the ways of a Westerner, and I became accustomed to drawing a crowd of children wherever I went and whatever I did, although over time their curiosity subsided some. All in all, I found villagers to be extremely hospitable despite their poverty. The longer I knew people and the better I understood their living conditions, the more depressed I felt about their poverty, in part because I was completely helpless to do anything about it.

To verify certain responses, a researcher must ask the same question several times in different contexts. During the census, husbands often answered questions asked of their wives; in such cases we revisited and asked the wife separately and directly. When enumerators asked villagers their age, they often responded by laughing, because not all rural Javanese actually know their ages. They told us how old they thought they were, and I tried to check these responses against an earlier village census, also an estimate, especially for those over thirty.

As I mentioned above, we tried to avoid bringing questionnaires along with us so that most interviews, particularly those in the village, were loosely structured and had more of the quality of a late afternoon chat. Since the villagers discussed daily expenses in an open manner, I did not have reason to suspect the information given to me, particularly because there was tremendous consistency among respondents. I do not believe that villagers took my questions or my research as seriously as I did—indeed, learning how unimportant such research was to their daily lives was a useful lesson for an earnest, well-meaning American graduate student—but methods of verification suggest that the responses were valid. Many of the young women we studied in Nuwun, particularly the factory daughters, became very attached to my first primary assistant; they told her a great deal about their lives, loves, and family conflict and sought her advice when they had problems. When she left to follow her husband to East Timor, many young women wept uncontrollably.

After verifying the validity and consistency of the data, I faced other concerns that went beyond whether people were telling me the truth. There are many contradictions and dilemmas inherent in such research, particularly for feminists wishing to diminish the inequalities often inherent in the research process. For example, although I desired honest answers about villagers' finances, I never told the entire truth about my own. Had it become public knowledge that I received a $400 monthly stipend—an enormous sum to most villagers—I would not have been able to cope with even more requests for money. Thus, the dilemma for me was related not to accurate reporting of economic data but to the structural inequalities of a situation that was made further unequal by my concealments.

While I was asking the villagers questions about income and marriage, I masked my own situation in both arenas. Although I said I was married to another researcher, we were in fact single. Our cohabitation would have been problematic for many people in Java, although villagers would have been more accepting of it than urban dwellers would have been. Thus, to be accepted, I felt compelled to lie, the one action I feared the most from my respondents. At times, I was forced into extremely uncomfortable situations—for example, when my hosts asked me to describe my wedding, an event that occurred several years *after* my research was complete. At times, this new persona simply made my loneliness worse: some evenings in the village, I desperately wanted to speak openly with my assistant, who had become a dear friend, about the uncertainty I felt about the possibility of marriage with the person everyone thought was already my husband. I feared that although she would have eventually accepted my cohabitation as "modern" and Western, her husband might have forced her to quit working for me since he was wary about the influence I might have on her.[4]

On my return home, I was temporarily relieved to read William F. Whyte's advice about honesty in the field: "A witness in court is required to swear to tell 'the truth, the whole truth, and nothing but the truth.' In general, it is advisable to adhere to the first and third of those admonitions in field work, but the second requires some modification" (1984, 65). Although this advice provided some solace, it remains an uncomfortable solution, particularly for those wishing to engage in a more feminist approach to research.

Because a feminist approach may entail sharing more of one's life with one's subjects, researchers can become more vulnerable if certain aspects of their identity are problematic in that particular region (e.g., religion, sexual preference, political affiliation, marital status). These attempts to become closer to one's respondents and to become friends do not necessarily create a less exploitative relationship than that found in a positivist approach (Stacey 1991). Indeed, what our subjects get out of our research usually does not constitute anything near a reciprocal exchange; rather, the relationship is typified by asymmetry and inequality (Patai

1991, 142). In my own case, I would complete my research for this book, which would be based on the lives and constraints of very poor people, but their poverty would remain and perhaps intensify while I would go on to support myself and make a career.

In *A Fortunate Man* (1967), John Berger describes the life of a doctor working in a poor rural community in England. Berger paints some of the painful contradictions that emerge when Dr. Sassall realizes that he can do little to change the situation. He must then confront the realization that he needs the situation as it is; *because* of his patients' poverty, he is able to practice as he does. Indeed, their poverty

> enables him to follow his cases through all their stages, grants him the power of his hegemony, encourages him to become the "consciousness" of the district, allows him unusually promising conditions for achieving a "fraternal" relationship with his patients, permits him to establish almost entirely on his own terms the local image of his profession. The position can be described more crudely. Sassall can strive towards the universal because his patients are underprivileged. (1967, 144)

Although I do not fully identify with Sassall, Berger does illustrate some of the uncomfortable and problematic contradictions and power relations that exist between researchers and their subjects. Many of us are motivated to study poverty or inequality in order to change that very situation, yet our research may reinforce the very First World–Third World, urban-rural, or rich-poor hierarchies we are challenging: poor women may feel unable to refuse participation in our research, and they have little input into our representation of them or their lives.

Despite the good intentions of feminist researchers who may wish to transform relations of subordination, the research relationship itself may reinforce and reproduce existing inequalities and perhaps create new ones. These issues and others are gaining attention as feminist scholars turn the lens on themselves, examining the power relations in which they are involved as researchers (Gluck and Patai 1991). This section ends, then, without a solution or closure, but with an acknowledgment of the difficult and ongoing process of confronting these dilemmas and contradictions.

THE DISTRICT

This case study of rural industrialization focuses on one district (*kecamatan*) with a population of 83,500, located in the regency of Semarang in Central Java, a part of Java well known for textile and batik production.[5] This district is approximately twenty-five kilometers from Semarang, the capital of Central Java—a large urban port with almost 1 million inhabitants (Indonesia, Office of Statistics for the Regency of Semarang 1981). In the site there is easy access to the highway that connects Semarang to several major cities in Central Java—Solo, Yogyakarta, Salatiga, and Magelang.

A combination of relatively cheap land, utilities, and labor, proximity to Semarang, encouragement from government officials, and the limits imposed on factory growth in Semarang by urban zoning laws drew industrialists to this rural area. Factories began to locate in the district in 1972 and continued to do so at least until the late 1980s. When I completed my research in 1983, three additional large-scale firms were under construction—manufacturers of pesticides, plastics, and pharmaceuticals. By 1986, more factories had been built and several were under construction; personal communication with those in the area indicates that factories continue to locate in this area.

The district, with its close proximity to Semarang, was also chosen for government housing projects, taking productive agricultural land out of production. Two large housing projects—one for civil servants and one public—were built in 1983. Despite these urban-oriented additions, the area remains largely rural. In fact, many of the factories sit in the middle of rice fields.

Compared with other districts in the same regency in 1980, the research site had the largest proportion of the population engaged in industrial work—8 percent, compared with 1 to 2 percent in other districts (Indonesia, Office of Statistics for the Regency of Semarang 1981). These figures include those working in medium-scale, small-scale, and household-level production of goods and foodstuffs such as palm sugar, tofu, flavored ices, rice crackers, and juices.[6] Despite more industrial activity, in 1980, 57 percent of the economically active population engaged in some type of agricultural production, either as owner-operators or agricultural wage laborers.[7]

NUWUN: AN AGRICULTURAL VILLAGE

Nuwun is located approximately five kilometers from the factories, off a secondary road with easy access to the factories via local transportation. The second agricultural village surveyed, Rumiyen, neighbors Nuwun in this semimountainous area and is under the same *kelurahan*. Both village economies are based on agriculture, particularly rice, and the production of secondary crops such as cassava, peanuts, corn, tomatoes, soybeans, vegetables, fruit, and cloves. I focus on Nuwun and refer to Rumiyen only when important differences merit discussion.

AGRICULTURE

Nuwun's farmland consists of forty-four hectares divided between *sawah* (wet riceland) and *tegal* (dry land), with an additional fifteen hectares for yards, homes, and home gardens (table 5).[8] The population density in the village is 1,280 persons per square kilometer. The sawah is fed by mountain springs through an indigenously built irrigation system. Because of the abundance of water all year long, farmers plant rice two to three times annually. At the time of my research, the village had begun to follow the government's program of intensified rice production (INSUS) and was switching to synchronized planting. Although this program decreases the risk of crop loss to pests, it also decreases agricultural labor opportunities for the landless, since the planting and harvesting opportunities are not staggered.

In this area, certain agricultural relationships of production had not changed in years. For example, the share of the harvest (*bawon*) for

TABLE 5
POPULATION AND LAND IN THE RESEARCH SITE

	District	Kelurahan[a]	Nuwun	Rumiyen
Total population	83,500	3,526	755	458
No. of households	16,967	694	151	97
Total land (farm and housing)	n.a.	373 ha.	59 ha.	45 ha.
% of households owning some farmland	n.a.	n.a.	90	76
Population density (per km^2)	n.a.[b]	945	1,280	1,017

SOURCES: District-level data from *kecamatan* (district) office; kelurahan-level data from kelurahan office. Data from Nuwun and Rumiyen were from my surveys.

[a] This kelurahan had five pedukuan, including Nuwun and Rumiyen.

[b] The population density for the regency was approximately 703 km^2 in 1980 (Indonesia, Office of Statistics 1981, 41).

agricultural laborers was one-eighth, the same that it had been years previously.[9] If, however, one worked as a contracted laborer under the *tebasan* system (in which wage laborers are brought on from outside the village), the share of the harvest was much lower: one-fourteenth. According to villagers, agricultural wages (based on the price of rice) had also remained the same in the recent past, as had opportunities for agricultural employment; I did not attempt to verify such statements. At times, the few larger landowners felt that the supply of agricultural labor was too small.[10] In the early 1980s, young men preferred to work on government-sponsored development projects such as construction, where they earned three to four times as much as they could in agriculture. However, the situation has changed since 1986, when the government stopped all such funding, and since then those men have sought employment in agriculture and petty trading, often in Semarang.

The exclusionary harvesting practices explained in chapter 2 function in this area. Both tebasan and *kedokaan* (in which laborers forego a wage during the season to be assured an invitation to the harvest) operate in this village, and villagers claimed that tebasan is increasingly utilized. A *penebas* (the entrepreneur who buys the crop on the fields and brings in a work gang for the tebasan system) working on the rice harvest of a villager felt that more people use this system than before because it is more profitable. One laborer who took part in kedokaan explained that she lost a small amount of money by doing so but was then guaranteed work during harvest time. Kedokaan places the risk, however, on the worker, not the landowner. Those who had worked on the land expecting to participate in the harvest experienced considerable losses in the mid-1980s, when rats devoured the rice crop.

Agricultural wages as reported by farmers and laborers in both the agricultural and industrialized villages are listed in table 6; in addition to the wage, each worker receives a meal. The normal work period extends from seven to eleven in the morning; although some laborers work in the afternoon, most take part in other economic activities at that time, including tending to their own gardens or small plots of agricultural land. At the time of my research, one kilogram of the cheapest rice (unhulled) cost 300 rupiah. The wage from most of these jobs, particularly men's work, was sufficient to buy one kilogram of unhulled rice per day, but that is only enough food for one adult male and a baby. It is estimated that one male adult needs the equivalent of almost two-thirds of a kilogram of hulled rice daily (Hart 1978, 102).

TABLE 6
AGRICULTURAL WORK AND WAGES BY SEX
(IN RUPIAH)

Sex	Type of work	Wage
Female	Planting	250
Male	Land preparation (*cangkul*)	300
Male	Fertilizing	300–400
Female	Weeding	250
Male/female	Harvesting	300–350

NOTE: At that time (1982), 650 rupiah equaled U.S.$1.00. These wages are daily, not hourly. Laborers usually worked about four hours a day.

NONAGRICULTURAL ENTERPRISES

In the early 1980s, an increase in urban consumption spawned the growth of commercial chicken farms owned by Chinese-Indonesian urban entrepreneurs in the district, and two of them were located in Nuwun. These ventures took advantage of cheaper factors of production (e.g., rent, water, labor) coupled with proximity to a large urban market. These two chicken farms together housed about six thousand chickens. The owners rented land for a fixed price; one had a twenty-year lease, and the other a ninety-nine-year lease.

Unfortunately, the development of commercial chicken farms was inconsequential for the village because the benefits were minimal. The rent paid for the land reached only the landowner and the *Lurah* (village head) who received a portion of the rent and a payoff directly from the investors. Originally, the chicken farm owners had a policy of not hiring villagers for fear of local networks stealing the chickens. In 1982, the small work force employed on the chicken farms consisted of males from other villages who slept on the premises. By 1986, the policy had changed so that village females and males were working for these enterprises.

AGRARIAN CLASS STRUCTURE

Economic stratification among the peasantry has long been recognized in theories of capitalist development (Chayanov 1966; Lenin 1977). Such stratification is affected by the household's control over different levels of productive resources (such as land, labor, and farm animals) and directly affects the degree of the household's integration with the labor market (Deere and de Janvry 1979).

Capturing class and class relations is no simple feat. Richard Wolff and Stephen Resnick (1986) have delineated the several different definitions and measurements of class seen in both Marxist and non-Marxist literatures, such as those based on (1) property ownership, (2) power and authority, (3) production, appropriation, and the distribution of surplus labor, or (4) combinations of the above, such as power and property.

Class status is clearly more complex than is ownership of goods or control over land since it entails asymmetrical and dynamic relationships of power among people, households, and groups. Those measuring and representing class and class differences in rural Javanese studies have found that productive resources have proven to be the most useful measure of important differences in subsistence between households; they are highly correlated with other class-related factors such as income, education, consumption, and standard of living (Husken and White 1989; Hart 1978; Chernichovsky and Meesook 1984; Husken 1984; Penny and Singarimbun 1973; White 1976) and undoubtedly, power.[11]

Access to land is "the single most important source of power" in village Java and is also a basic indicator of class status (Hart 1986b, 95; World Bank 1985, 1).[12] In research on Javanese peasant economy, *cukupan*—a Javanese conception of basic needs—has been used as a basis for differentiating strata within the peasantry:

> The Javanese peasantry, both its rich and its poor, has long had a concept of what constitutes "enough." The word they use is *cukupan*. It is applied to what they see as being the reasonable needs of the ordinary peasantry. . . . Their idea of "enough" is, however, modest indeed. A person who depends on agriculture for his livelihood is said to be *cukupan* (to have enough) if he can farm 0.7 hectares of rain-fed *sawah* and has also a small area, say, 0.3 hectares, on which he can grow coconut, fruit and other trees, and some vegetables, herbs and other household needs. With just one hectare of land, the average peasant knows that without undue labor he can produce enough to live on. . . . [He] will be *cukupan* and happy. *Some two thirds of the people in the area we have been studying are not* cukupan. (Penny and Singarimbun 1973, 2–3; my emphasis)

David Penny and Masri Singarimbun distinguish between three different measures of land distribution: (1) land owned, (2) land operated, and (3) land controlled.[13] The latter concept, which I use in this study, is the "single best measure of access to land" (Penny and Singarimbun 1973, 78).[14] It includes the entire area of land from which the family can derive its income (Hart 1978, 89).[15]

Several researchers have attempted to establish the basic minimum consumption necessary for survival, or the poverty line in rural Java (Sayogyo 1974, quoted in Hart 1978; Sayogyo 1977, quoted in White 1979; Penny and Singarimbun 1973).[16] To attain self-sufficiency for rice and nonrice needs, a household must produce 300 kilograms of milled rice per consumer—150 kilograms of rice and 150 kilograms to cover nonrice needs. To meet consumption needs and attain self-sufficiency, an average household would need to control a minimum of 0.575 hectare of land.[17]

I stratified Nuwun's households into three classes, following the tradition of peasant economy studies in Java, although, as Gillian Hart argues, these are basically "asset classes" (1986b, 102). These asset classes distinguish between groups who share both "a common position to the relations of production" and a "common status as either wielders of power or subject to the power of others" (Wolff and Resnick 1986, 99, 106). Thus, although the measure of class used here is based on property, the interrelationship between property and power in rural Java makes this a composite measure.

In this study, *class 1* consists of households that do not control sufficient land to meet basic food needs; it includes landless and near-landless households who control 0.24 hectare of land or less.[18] *Class 2* represents those families who control resources sufficient to cover basic food needs but insufficient to "achieve a minimum subsistence level of income"; they control between 0.25 and 0.574 hectare (Hart 1978, 103). *Class 3* indicates self-sufficiency in that the household can meet all its food and nonfood needs from its land; it includes those households controlling a minimum of 0.575 hectare.[19] Individual households were assigned to these categories on the basis of the amount of land controlled.[20]

Class 1 households are landless or near-landless and are typically semiproletarianized or fully proletarianized with most members engaged in some type of wage labor. Class 2 households are semiproletarianized, meaning that their land is not sufficient to fulfill subsistence needs and that some household members must seek wage labor to complement what is produced on the farm. The lower two strata share the common trait of controlling insufficient amounts of land for subsistence: they are not cukupan, a condition reflected in their integration into the labor market. Class 3 households have enough land to be, at the very least, self-sufficient producers, or cukupan. Some may engage in commercial production or may as landlords receive some surplus from tenants. In this stratum there is little need for members to engage in wage labor for subsistence needs.

Clearly, the differences between peasants "pale into insignificance" when compared with the differences between the peasantry and the urban elite who extract surplus from them (White 1989, 25). And the seemingly minute differences between tenths of hectares in Javanese peasant landholdings, with those controlling only one hectare deemed "large farmers," may raise some eyebrows about the entire notion of rural class differentiation. Researchers in other parts of the Third World may be particularly surprised; in Latin America, for instance, 2 to 3 hectares is considered a small farm and 3.5 to 10 hectares is considered middle-sized (Carmen Diana Deere, personal communication, 15 Oct. 1990). Benjamin White argues, however, that such reasoning does not mean that

> class relationships between peasants do not exist, cannot be objectively defined, are not viewed by those involved in them as class relations, or do not become the focus of political struggles. Those who own or control these "large" farms . . . command substantial surpluses, are sellers of commodities produced mainly or entirely by the labor of others, and through their relative dominance in agricultural production (although they represent a minority of farms) and local power relations have access to many of the most lucrative nonagricultural opportunities, displaying in many ways the classical features of the kulak. (1989, 25)

These class differences, apparently minute in the tenths of hectares they represent, bear important implications for the structure of opportunities that different households confront and, as seen in Gillian Hart's research (1986b), in the particular configuration of economic activities in which households engage. Although I do not assume that households necessarily act in concert to fulfill such needs, the overall picture of household economic activity does differ by class.

FAMILY AND HOUSEHOLD

A short methodological note on families and households is necessary before I begin the empirical analysis of village class structure. White points out that the household as a unit of analysis is

> an extremely problematic concept. Long used as a kind of catch-all minimal social-economic unit, it is now becoming increasingly recognized that we should really think more in terms of separately and carefully defined (and only partly overlapping) units of production, consumption, accumulation, etc.,

> sometimes to the extent of abandoning the concept of "household" altogether. (1989, 22)

In this study, I analyze the unit of the household, but I also examine hierarchies and dynamics within the household and link them to hierarchies beyond those boundaries. In defining the household, I follow previous studies of the Javanese peasant household economy (White 1976; Hart 1978).[21] Here, the household is conceptualized as a group of people sharing resources, particularly the kitchen and food, which is meant to be a proxy for general consumption. The phrase "cooking and eating together" does not refer "to those physical events (both of which are in fact rare) but rather symbolizes some degree of sharing of the budget for food and other items of expenditure" (White 1976, 217).

I found that most consumption, especially food consumption, occurs within the physical boundaries of the household.[22] No assumptions are made about income pooling or the egalitarian allocation of resources or goods for consumption; in fact, most households support an unequal distribution of labor, power, and consumption (White 1976, 128). Finally, there are no limits or boundaries concerning production; most Javanese rural households are indirect units of production. Respondents used the Javanese word *somah* (household),[23] whose meaning overlaps with the definition I use, and it was not difficult to resolve questions about unusual situations.[24]

The family constitutes the basis of Javanese household organization, and I used the terms *family* and *household* interchangeably only after my survey established the extent to which they are the same unit. In almost all cases, one coresidential family constituted a household.[25] In equating family with household, I am not making assertions about family structure, even though the nuclear family household is the predominant, but not the only, form in rural Java (H. Geertz 1961; Jay 1969; Hart 1986b; White 1976).

CLASS STATUS IN NUWUN

Circumstances in Nuwun echo those in Java more generally: agrarian conditions are such that the terms *rural* and *agricultural* are no longer interchangeable (see table 7; and chapter 2). Given their control over agricultural land, most village households cannot attain a subsistence level of living from agriculture. Eighty-nine percent of the village's households were in the lower two strata, meaning that only 11 percent of the households ($N = 17$) controlled enough land to meet subsistence needs.

TABLE 7
POPULATION BY CLASS STATUS AND LAND DISTRIBUTION IN TWO VILLAGES

	Nuwun	Rumiyen
Class 1		
No. of households	82	43
% of village households	54	44
Average area controlled	0.135 ha	0.112 ha
Total area controlled	11.097 ha	4.816 ha
% of all farmland controlled	25	13
Class 2		
No. of households	52	37
% of village households	34	38
Average area controlled	0.355 ha	0.354 ha
Total area controlled	18.46 ha	13.1 ha
% of all farmland controlled	41.6	13
Class 3		
No. of households	17	17
% of village households	11	18
Average area controlled	0.871 ha	1.12 ha
Total area controlled	14.81 ha	19.04 ha
% of all farmland controlled	33.4	51.5
Total no. of households	151	97
Total area	44.37 ha	36.96 ha

Such configurations are striking because the economy of rural Java is based on agriculture. These findings correspond with Penny and Singarimbun's research (1973), in which two-thirds of the households were not cukupan and therefore could not attain subsistence-level production from their land; similarly, almost three-fourths of White's sample were not cukupan (1976). In Hart's study (1986b), approximately half the households were in the lower two strata and thus below subsistence level.

Although I did not attempt to measure household income, researchers have noted a strong relationship between class, as defined by control over land, and household income (both source and amount).[26] Among the poorest households, Hart found that 90 percent of income came from manual labor. Wage labor, however, varies over the agricultural cycle; when household income was translated into rice equivalents for each month, Hart found that households in the middle strata on average fell below the poverty line during two months of the year. Upper-stratum households fell below the poverty line during one month, although during half of the year they were far above it. By contrast, households in the poorest class were above the poverty line only five months of the year, four of which coincided with periods of peak labor demand. Such differences in income have "severe welfare implications," particularly for the poorest classes (Hart 1978, 183–85).

In Nuwun, 16 percent of the households did not own land, yet only 6 percent did not control land. Although there was a higher percentage of landless households in Rumiyen, almost all of them controlled some land. The *Carik* (village secretary) lived in Pamit and was the wealthiest member of the kelurahan except for the Lurah. The Carik's land, both owned and *bengkok* (land temporarily given in lieu of a salary), consisted of 6.5 hectares of rice land and 1.25 hectares of dry land—almost 20 percent of the village's total farmland. Many villagers sharecropped the Carik's land; during my stay, however, he announced that he would no longer continue such traditional contractual relationships but would lease out his land to a contractor. He thus terminated a traditional relationship that had helped poorer villagers in favor of a more commercial relationship. As a result, it is likely that a new survey would demonstrate a higher percentage of landless households without control over land.

In both agricultural villages, control over land was related to ownership of other resources and goods (table 8). In Nuwun, the correlation between land controlled and possessions is $r = .33$; in Rumiyen, the relationship is stronger, $r = .632$. Poorer households also had slightly more land for home gardens (table 8), often an important source of food (Stoler 1976). Better-off households had more productive resources as well, such as farm animals and tools (Hart 1978), and had more houses built from plaster rather than bamboo.

CLASS AND LABOR MARKET INTEGRATION

A household's class status is reflected in its relationship to the labor market (Deere and de Janvry 1979). Poorer households—those with little or no land—will have more members participating in the labor market to secure income: in other words, an inverse relationship exists between class status and labor market participation (see table 9). There is less

TABLE 8
ACCESS TO RESOURCES AND HOUSE TYPES BY CLASS STATUS IN NUWUN

	Class 1	Class 2	Class 3
Average value of household possessions[a]	U.S.$229.00	U.S.$391.00	U.S.$482.00[b]
Average home and garden area	0.109 ha	0.091 ha	0.073 ha
% owning agricultural land	86	96	100
House types (%)			
Bamboo	17	4	6
Bamboo/wood	20	25	23
Wood	61	61	59
Plaster	2	10	12

[a] Possessions list included tables, guest chairs, cupboards (*lemari* and *biffet*), mattresses, pressure lamps, watches/clocks, radios, televisions, sewing machines, bicycles, motorcycles, goats, and cows.

[b] The means of the three groups were significantly different from each other, $p = .001$.

occupational diversity as class status increases.[27] The poorest, who have little or no access to land, must diversify and engage in agricultural and nonagricultural labor, trade, and other self-employment such as sewing or public transportation. Those in the upper strata working outside of agriculture are usually landlords.

A closer look at households in different strata illustrates how these class differences translate into concrete economic conditions for villagers.

A Poor Household: Class 1

Pak Samadi and Ibu Jumirah lived with their second daughter, Subiyati; her husband, Riman; and Subiyati and Riman's one-month-old daughter, Siyati. Pak Samadi, age fifty-two, had had three years of schooling, Ibu Jumirah none, Subiyati four years, and Riman only one year. Of the seven children to which Ibu Jumirah gave birth, Subiyati was her only living child; the other six died in infancy. Indeed, Subiyati's baby daughter was her second child; her first had died in infancy. The list on page 93 sets forth their occupations.

TABLE 9

PRIMARY OCCUPATION OF HOUSEHOLD HEADS BY CLASS STATUS IN AGRICULTURAL VILLAGES

	Class 1	Class 2	Class 3
Nuwun			
No. of households	81	52	17
Occupation of head (%)			
Renter/sharecropper	12	6	6
Agricultural laborer	6	—	—
Nonagricultural laborer	12	4	—
Factory worker	1	2	—
Farmer (owner-operator)	54	87	71
Trader	2	—	—
Household production worker	5	—	—
Other self-employed (tailor, driver, penebas)	6	2	12
Teacher	—[a]	—	—
Village official	—	—	12
Rumiyen			
No. of households	43	37	18
Occupation of head (%)			
Renter/sharecropper	42	5	—
Agricultural laborer	9	—	—
Nonagricultural laborer	—	3	—
Factory worker	—	3	—
Farmer (owner-operator)	33	78	82
Trader	5	—	—
Household production worker	—	5	6
Other self-employed (tailor, driver, penebas)	12	3	—
Teacher	—	—	—
Village official	—	—	11
Unemployed	—	3	—

NOTE: The question asked during the survey was, "What do you spend most of your time doing?" Respondents were asked to name their primary, secondary, and tertiary occupations. This question is to be distinguished from asking, "From what activity do you procure most of your income?"

Percentages may not total 100 because of rounding.

[a] Given that the criterion used to measure class was agricultural land, the two teachers fall into the lowest class category; however, they had better homes and more possessions than did others in class 1. For these reasons, I have left them out of the analysis.

HOUSEHOLD MEMBERS	AGE	PRIMARY WORK	SECONDARY WORK	TERTIARY WORK
Pak Samadi	52	Agricultural laborer	Sharecropper	Laborer: brickmaker
Ibu Jumirah	45	Household work	Sharecropper	—
Subiyati	24	Household work and childcare	Sharecropper	—
Riman	27	Laborer: stonecutter	Agricultural laborer	Sharecropper
Siyati	1 month			

Their household owned no land but sharecropped 0.25 hectare of riceland, which means that they received half the product, equivalent to the returns to one-eighth of a hectare. The household of Ibu Jumirah and Pak Samadi's was in class 1, meaning that they could not meet even their basic food needs from the land they controlled.

Their modest home was made from bamboo and wood, with a dirt floor and sparse furnishings; a small, dark house, it lacked either shutters or windows. The family owned two tables, two cupboards, and one pressure lamp, a total value of \$83.[28] They did not own guest chairs or a couch (*kursi tamu*), a deficiency that made them feel very embarrassed when I interviewed them. They kept apologizing for their poverty and for having me sit on a simple homemade wooden chair. "We're sorry, but this is all we have; we are poor people," they explained.

Ibu Jumirah and Pak Samadi's family took care of one villager's goat and another villager's cow in a shared animal husbandry relationship. The owners had promised that, when their animal bore two offspring, one would be given to Pak Samadi and Ibu Jumirah's family. In other words, eventually this family would have a cow and a goat of its own. As is typical in poorer people's quarters, the livestock shared part of the house with other family members.

This household exemplified the term *occupational multiplicity*, as most members were engaged in several economic activities and different systems of production simultaneously, challenging neat social scientific categorization (White, 1976). It is also important to note that all working members of this household *sold* their labor. At one time, Subiyati had worked in a factory for one month but had had to quit because her child would not drink formula from a bottle.

A Middle-Stratum Household: Class 2

Pak Jasman, age 75, and his wife, Ibu Parjiah, age 65, lived with their 27-year-old son, Budi, their fourth child; his wife, Nasri, age 20; Budi and Nasri's baby daughter, Tutik; their son and fifth child, Riyanto, age 20; and their 17-year-old factory daughter, Sarmiyati. Although they owned a small amount of land, their house was made from woven bamboo and wood and had a dirt floor. The following list sets forth their occupations:

HOUSEHOLD MEMBERS	AGE	PRIMARY WORK	SECONDARY WORK	TERTIARY WORK
Pak Jasman	75	Farmer (owner-operator)	—	—
Ibu Parjiah	65	Household work	—	—
Budi	27	Laborer: woodworker	Agricultural laborer	Builder of chicken coops
Nasri	20	Household work and childcare	—	—
Riyanto	20	Agricultural laborer	Laborer: woodworker	—
Sarmiyati	17	Factory worker		
Tutik	2			

Educational levels were also low in this household. Pak Jasman had had about four years of schooling, and Ibu Parjiah, none. Their children had little schooling, another indication of the household's poverty: the two sons had had two and four years of schooling each, and Sarmiyati had not been to school at all. She was illiterate, which was unusual among her peers.

Pak Jasman and Ibu Parjiah controlled sufficient land (0.25 hectare) to meet subsistence food needs, but not enough to generate income for nonfood needs. They owned 5 tables, 3 guest chairs, 3 cupboards, 1 mattress, 1 pressure lamp, and a radio, a total value of $215; some of these goods had been bought with Sarmiyati's savings from factory wages.

In this one household, members engaged in farming (self-employed), wage labor in both the agricultural and industrial sectors, household maintenance, household craft production, and industrial work. But because they owned more land than did Pak Samadi's household, there was slightly less occupational diversity in this household and somewhat less integration with the labor market. Although both households had a similar number of total activities, in Pak Jasman's household four (out of six) members had only one economic activity each, whereas almost all members of Pak Samadi's household engaged in two to three activities.

A Self-Sufficient Household: Class 3

Pak Sunadi, age 33, and Ibu Jumeni, age 28, lived with their two boys, Haryono, age 6, and Harsoyo, 2½. Ibu Jumeni had married at age 15 and had given birth to four children; two died in childbirth. Although their house was made from bamboo and wood with a dirt floor, it was larger than the other two described above and had shutters. They had a good-sized home garden adjoining the house. The following list sets forth their occupations:

HOUSEHOLD MEMBERS	AGE	PRIMARY WORK	SECONDARY WORK	TERTIARY WORK
Pak Sunadi	33	Village official	Farmer (owner-operator)	—
Ibu Jumeni	28	Household work and childcare	Farmer	—
Haryono	6			
Harsoyo	2½			

There are important educational differences between this family and the previous two. Compared with their village peers, both husband and wife had relatively high levels of education. Pak Sunadi had finished the second year of junior high school, and Ibu Jumeni had finished grammar school (six years). Ibu Jumeni received her education in the mid-1950s, when primary school was less available to villagers than it was in the 1970s, when Sarmiyati (Pak Jasman's daughter) was of school age. The higher educational achievements of this couple at a time when schooling was less accessible to the general population suggests that they came from better-off families.

This husband and wife owned 0.975 hectare of sawah, all of which was bengkok. They worked 0.450 hectare of the sawah themselves and sharecropped out the other 0.525 hectare, from which they received half the harvest. They controlled, therefore, 0.713 hectare of riceland, more than is needed for self-sufficiency, and derived income from sharecroppers' labor on their land as well as their own labor. In addition, they owned ten coffee trees and twenty-three clove trees and obtained income from selling these trees' products. Their possessions, worth about $500, included one cow. Although they perceived their situation as difficult (*susah*), they also said that their land was cukupan for their needs.

These examples elucidate some of the basic lived differences by class. These three families were in different stages of the family life cycle and had different needs, different demands on household labor, and different amounts of available household labor. Their economic bases affected their access to other goods and resources, their opportunities for employment, and the configurations of their economic activities.

DIFFERENT REACTIONS TO INDUSTRIALIZATION

Industrial development does not necessarily affect all parts of a region equally and similarly. Within one kelurahan there were several different village-level responses to industrial capitalism. One pedukuan in which I stayed for several days was much more religious in its orientation and considered rebellious by village officials in, for example, its voting patterns.[29] Young women there were much more observant of Islamic law; a few had formerly worked in factories, but at the time of my research none worked outside the village, in part because of parental control and religiosity. Local officials did not want me to spend time in this village of "fanatics."

Another small pedukuan neighboring Nuwun had fifty households but no female factory workers, although not for religious reasons. The village had only four hectares of riceland, and the head of the village controlled more than one-quarter of it; thus, most households owned or sharecropped land in other villages, if they did so at all. Instead, families worked on the production of chicken coops at the household level, which required that all productive members participate. Six intermediaries subcontracted work to households to produce chicken coops, providing the bamboo and nails. Households tended to specialize in one part of the chicken coop—for example, sides, door, or egg catcher (*tempat telor*). In some households, four different members (including children) divided the labor to produce a particular piece, with children working on tasks such as carving and smoothing the bamboo. Four working members could produce about one hundred pieces a day and received anywhere from 10 to 80 rupiah for each piece, depending on what they produced.

Several young women in this village had tried working in the factory but quit because they lost money. Because the wage is lower during the first three-month probationary period, commuters spent more money on lunch and transportation than they earned. Producing chicken coops was more lucrative and required the input of all available hands. Given the increase in urban chicken consumption in the early 1980s, making coops provided steady incomes for some households. Eventually, though, the glut on the chicken market was made manifest by pieces of coops and fully assembled coops piled up in front of houses for several months, waiting for buyers.

I had expected that given the very small land base in the village, many young women would seek factory work, but they had not done so. Different economic opportunities created a different need for, and configuration of, household labor.

This different response to the growth of industrial capitalism can be likened to the protoindustrial pattern that Hans Medick (1976) found in early European industrialization. Over a period of several decades, European households were displaced from agriculture and then moved into cottage-level production, which facilitated the transition to urban factories. In the Javanese case, a particular income-generating opportunity encouraged a different organization of production and thus created a different articulation with industrial capitalism. The results were similar to those provided by the factories—low-wage labor was provided to produce cheap goods for urban consumption—yet the social relations of production differed because the household was the direct unit of production.

PAMIT: AN INDUSTRIALIZED VILLAGE

Pamit, one of the two villages in the district chosen for factory development, hosted factories producing biscuits, bread, garments, furniture, and textiles. After selling twelve hectares to factories and the government electricity company, Pamit retained only six hectares of lowland rainfed riceland. These remaining six hectares were owned by ten households, or 10 percent of the village's households. Another twelve households owned farmland in a neighboring village. Because of a lack of water, rice was planted only once annually, then supplemented with secondary crops. Although I discuss Pamit in relation to Nuwun, an agricultural village, I do not mean to suggest an evolutionary schema—that before industrialization Pamit had resembled the agricultural village. Before, Pamit's land was sufficient in neither quality nor quantity to support its population.

Pamit's economy is now closely linked with the cash economy and dependent on industrial capitalism for factory jobs, migrant boarders, and sales of goods and services to workers. Those providing such services indirectly help sustain the factories by depressing the cost of living and, concomitantly, the level of wages. Thus, industrial capitalism and the highly developed informal sector of the village economy are interdependent.

FACTORY DEVELOPMENT AND VILLAGERS

When industrialists began to negotiate with the Lurah for land, some farmers wanted to sell their land. He decided first to sell bengkok. After that was sold, he then forced farmers to sell their land for bengkok and to the factories. Most farmers sold their land to the factories, with the Lurah acting as intermediary.

Of the ten farmers who sold land for factory development, seven said without hesitation that they had wanted to sell their land. Two initially said that they had wanted to sell but subsequently admitted to being forced by the Lurah. One clearly stated throughout the interview that he had not wanted to sell his land. The Lurah used various techniques to convince those who were attached to the land to detach themselves. Repeated visits to the owner and his family members were coupled with the threat that if they didn't sell the land immediately, the government would later appropriate it without remuneration. At that point, the Lurah told them, he could no longer be responsible for what the government did.

According to some villagers, the Lurah had already agreed on a selling price with factory owners before approaching the farmers. He then tried to drive the price paid to the farmers as low as possible to guarantee a greater share for himself. One farmer recounted how the Lurah and the Carik escorted him to the bank, where he signed a receipt for fifteen million rupiah. He was then forced to turn over half of this money to the Lurah. Given the relation of power between the farmer and the Lurah, he had no choice.

With the money from land sales—what was left after the Lurah and Carik took their cuts—the farmers improved their homes or built new ones. Only four bought land again, and a much smaller amount than they formerly owned. One lost all the money right after he sold his land, when his home was robbed.

An Indonesian social scientist observed that in Indonesia, "Social injustice is apparent in the way in which public figures dispose of their superfluous income" (Mubyarto 1984, 46). The Lurah of Pamit was envied by other Lurahs for his ability to amass wealth. With his "extra income," he owned two luxury homes in the village, a horse farm, a motorcycle, and a car.

No formal protests concerning industrial development occurred in Pamit, but a protest did occur in the other industrialized village within the same district. It is unclear exactly what happened, but according to one version, which I heard more than once, when a joint-venture bottling plant bought land, the farmers were promised that new land would be bought elsewhere with the money from the land sale. Yet no new land was ever bought, nor did the farmers receive payment for their land. Yet another version, recorded by a group of students at Gadjah Mada University, stated that the money for the land was tied up by the Lurah and Carik. In addition, the profits from selling bengkok to the factory were to have been used to benefit the village, particularly the local grammar school. This money also disappeared. At the time of the publication, the Lurah claimed ignorance and the farmers still hadn't received payment.

A second protest occurred in a village near Pamit that hosted a citric acid factory. The factory had dumped its waste into the local stream, killing the rice crop. After the protest, the plant was forced to operate at a low capacity and to build a water purification system. The chemical composition of the water was frequently checked by provincial civil servants.

VILLAGE LIFE IN PAMIT

Because of the migrant population, the scarcity of land, the highly developed informal economy, and the intense population density, Pamit resembled an urban village more than a rural one. With the increase in industrial activity, Pamit had attracted a large number of migrants, among them two hundred young people. Some of them had decided to settle, raise families, and become village members. The household survey shows that fifteen heads of households had migrated to Pamit within the past ten years and had become permanent village members. In addition, there were fifteen recent and very poor migrant families, usually with one to two children, renting rooms and attempting to live solely on one factory wage. Because of childcare constraints, only one parent could work in the factory.

The basic demographic statistics from Nuwun and Pamit demonstrate the urban character of the latter (table 10). Although the total population in both villages was similar, Pamit's population had been inflated by one-quarter through the recent arrival of migrants; it was a population in tremendous flux. Perhaps most striking is the contrast in available farmland—44 hectares in Nuwun compared with 6.8 in Pamit—and the resultant difference in population density ratios. In Nuwun, the area for houses and gardens for its population (755 people) consisted of 15 hectares of land (38 acres), whereas Pamit's even larger population (838 people) was settled on an area not even one-fifth as large—2.7 hectares (7 acres). In Pamit, houses were close together, with rows of shacks attached for migrant workers. These migrants crowded into tiny, unventilated rooms—two to four to a room—in which they dressed, cooked on kerosene burners, and slept enveloped by the unhealthy kerosene fumes. Garbage was strewn everywhere, and the smell of excrement pervaded the village. During the dry season, living conditions were particularly hazardous because of the low supply of water. Because of san-

TABLE 10
COMPARISON OF AGRICULTURAL AND INDUSTRIALIZED VILLAGES

	Agricultural village (Nuwun)	Industrial village (Pamit)
Total population	755	838[a]
Recent migrants	0	205
Total houses	152	101
Total farmland	44 ha	6.8 ha
Total land (farm and residential)	59 ha	9.5 ha
Population density per km^2	1,280	8,821
% of households owning some farmland	90	23

[a] Includes recent migrants.

itation and health considerations, this was the one village in which I did not stay overnight.

Although migrants stimulated the local economy, their influx also brought unwanted social effects. Villagers and village officials complained that many problems such as robbery, sexual promiscuity, and illegitimacy had increased as a direct result of such a large and fluctuating migrant population over which they had less social control.

EMPLOYMENT IN THE TWO VILLAGES

A comparison of employment patterns by sex in Nuwun and Pamit demonstrates three points. First, the factories provided a surprisingly small proportion of primary employment for residents of the industrial village. This employment was concentrated in age-specific groups. Second, there was a predominance of nonagricultural economic activities in the industrial village, the greater diversity of which is directly related to the introduction of the factories. Third, occupations that emerged as secondary effects of such industrialization created services within the informal sector, which aided local and migrant workers with low-cost goods and services.

Women in Pamit were scattered in a greater diversity of occupations than women in Nuwun were. It is also clear and somewhat surprising that factories provided employment for a relatively small proportion of females (table 11). Most of the female factory workers in both villages were daughters still dependent on their families rather than mothers or wives supporting a family. It was expected that where employment opportunities in agriculture were scarce, more married and unmarried females would be forced to seek factory employment. However, the data from Pamit do not corroborate this hypothesis. Instead, married women in Pamit, particularly those with children, were working not in factories but as petty vendors and traders. Only 11 percent of the females in Nuwun named agriculture as their primary occupation.[30] For female heads of households only, this proportion increased to 28 percent.[31] Although similar proportions of females in both villages stated that agricultural production was their main occupation, the relationships of production differ. Females in Nuwun in this category were owner-operators, whereas most in Pamit were landless laborers.

Almost 55 percent of women in Nuwun and 33 percent in Pamit stated that home production was their main occupation. In Pamit, selling food and goods as vendors or traders was more prevalent. Most women traders

TABLE 11
STRUCTURE OF OCCUPATIONS BY SEX IN AGRICULTURAL AND INDUSTRIALIZED VILLAGES
(PERCENTAGES OF ALL PERSONS AGED 15 AND OVER)

	Females		Males	
Primary occupation	*Nuwun (agricultural)*	*Pamit*[a] *(industrial)*	*Nuwun*	*Pamit*
Renter/sharecropper	1.5	1.3	6.9	7.0
Agricultural laborer	1.0	5.0	4.9	3.2
Nonagricultural laborer	7.4	0.6	11.7	11.3
Casual laborer	—	—	—	2.5
Village industry worker	—	1.1	—	8.2
Modern factory worker	9.3	13.0	2.5	19.0
Domestic servant	—	3.1	—	—
Other self-employed	—	—	—	8.2
Farmer (owner-operator)	9.3	3.8	64.7	8.2
Trader/vendor	16.5	21.3	1.2	6.0
Businessperson	—	7.0	—	4.4
Household production worker	53.0	32.5	—	1.8
Midwife	—	0.6	—	—
Nurse, teacher	1.0	2.0	1.2	1.2
Village official/civil servant	—	—	1.2	6.3
Student	1.0	7.5	2.5	9.0
Unemployed	—	—	—	3.7
Other	—	1.2	3.2	—
	100.0	100.0	100.0	100.0
Total no.	193	160	204	159

[a] Excludes the 205 recent migrants who boarded in this village.

or vendors in Nuwun sold their goods in various local markets. However, in Pamit there were many small and medium-sized stalls from which people sold basic necessities (rice, sugar, spices, vegetables) and fifteen to twenty small, makeshift stands, often just a table and bench outside a home, from which cooked food was sold. Many vendors and their stalls lined the dirt road next to the factory, where they sold clothes on credit as well as food, drinks, and ices to factory workers during their breaks. Women with children preferred the flexibility of working at home, where they could run a small food stall, rather than the rigidity of a factory job, even though the hours were shorter and the returns to labor higher in the latter. It was not entirely their choice, however, because factories also preferred not to hire mothers.

Males in Pamit differed from their counterparts in Nuwun, with almost 20 percent working in modern factories and another 8 percent in the local village industries specializing in tofu or bricks. Unlike females, the males working in factories were not concentrated in age-specific cohorts, because older males were hired by the factories as guards, janitors, and gardeners. Almost one-third of the male work force in Pamit was involved in either small-scale village industry or modern factory work. By contrast, very few young males in Nuwun obtained factory jobs, perhaps because most had fewer connections.

Farming clearly dominated the occupational structure of men in Nuwun, with 65 percent working primarily as owner-operators and another 12 percent as sharecroppers and landless agricultural laborers; by contrast, only 17 percent of the males in Pamit worked in agriculture. In both villages, almost 12 percent of the males were laborers outside of the agricultural sector.

The diversity of occupations in Pamit is again apparent in that more males were involved in nonagricultural work, either as employees or self-employed: 10 percent were vendors, traders, or businessmen in Pamit, compared with 1 percent in Nuwun. The problem of the landless unemployed was particularly apparent in Pamit because of the predominance of industrial capitalism and the lack of agricultural production. In Nuwun, although there was perhaps underemployed surplus labor in agriculture, no one was idle. In Pamit, where one generally needed a cash-generating occupation, 4 percent of the males said that they were unemployed. Six of these seven unemployed males were under thirty years of age.

The emergent service sector provided low-priced goods and services such as housing, cooked and uncooked food, household necessities, clothing, credit, haircuts, and tailoring. The low prices reflected the tremendous surplus of labor and the fact that some of the labor was unpaid family labor. These occupations can be interpreted as part of the "multiplier effect" of industrialization. An alternative interpretation is that an abundance of such cheap goods and services kept the cost of living down for workers, thereby keeping wages down in the formal sector, to the benefit of industrial capitalists.

CLASS DIFFERENCES

Most households in Pamit, as in Nuwun, were of modest means. Given that Pamit was not an agriculturally based village, the same criterion of land controlled cannot be applied to analyze class stratification. In Pamit, almost all households were landless, meaning that household members participated in the labor market. Thus, although in Nuwun poorer households had a higher degree of integration with the labor market, such integration does not sufficiently distinguish households in Pamit.

My purpose in studying Pamit was to survey resident and migrant factory workers concerning wages and the family economy and to compare employment patterns with those of Nuwun. I gathered similar data on landholdings, employment, and household possessions as in Nuwun, but I did not attempt to measure class in Pamit. To do so would have entailed a more elaborate labor survey to determine whether the members of the household sold their labor, were engaged in their own production, or hired labor; it would also have called for a more elaborate consumption survey. In general, most villagers in Pamit had modest means; there were, however, a few rich households that had greatly benefited from industrial development.

Families in this village were much more likely to educate their children longer than were families in Nuwun. Even in very poor households, most children under fifteen were in school. One reason for this high educational rate was that parents, being much more tied into a cash economy, had money to spend on schooling. Second, since they had no land to bequeath to their children, education was the key to earning a livelihood outside of agriculture.

One example of a well-off but landless household demonstrates some important differences from households in the agricultural village. Pak Jumadi's household consisted of five kin members and a maid. Pak Jumadi and Ibu Sumini lived with their 6-year-old son, Bandin; their 2-year-old daughter, Siti; Pak Jumadi's 18-year-old sister, Mundarsih; and a 16-year-old maid, Sugiarti. The following list sets forth their occupations:

HOUSEHOLD MEMBERS	AGE	PRIMARY WORK	SECONDARY WORK	TERTIARY WORK
Pak Jumadi	27	Tailor	—	—
Ibu Sumini	25	Clothing vendor	—	—
Bandin	6	—	—	—
Siti	2	—	—	—
Mundarsih	18	Student	Assistant to brother and sister-in-law	—
Sugiarti	16	Domestic servant	Childcare provider	—

This very young landless household was much better off than a landless household would have been in Nuwun. They owned three tables, twelve guest chairs, two cupboards, three mattresses, one pressure lamp, one watch, one radio, one tape recorder, one motorcycle, one sewing machine, and one television, for a total value of approximately $1,000. Their house was made out of plaster and had a cement floor. Seven years before, Ibu Sumini had worked in a factory for four months but quit because she didn't like it. She sold clothing on credit to factory workers—a lucrative business because factory workers spend a substantial proportion of their wage on clothes. Pak Jumadi made clothing for villagers and workers. Pak Jumadi's sister was not a hired laborer but an unpaid family worker. They were also able to afford a maid. By contrast, other landless families often rented out rooms to migrants to bring in additional steady cash income.

MIGRANTS IN PAMIT

Migration is one of the most important secondary effects of industrialization in this site. Its most striking features in Pamit were fluidity and a temporary quality that caused a high degree of anonymity rarely found in rural Java. During census interviews, it was apparent that many heads of households did not even know the names of migrants boarding in their houses. One month after the census, three of the fifteen recent migrant families and five of the thirty workers we were trying to locate had moved. No one knew of their whereabouts, again a rare phenomenon in rural Java. Migrant workers often moved from one house to another or one village to another if conditions did not please them. This horizontal mobility is apparent in many employment histories as well, for the same reasons.

Of the two hundred recent migrants to Pamit, two-thirds were female. This ratio corresponded exactly to the sexual composition of the manufacturing work force in the district. All the female migrants worked in modern factories except for those few with children. However, not all the male migrants were factory workers: some worked on local government projects such as utilities or construction. Almost all the migrants were from rural Central Java, with the exception of a few from East Java and the Outer Islands.

Social networks among migrants were strong, which helped attract other migrants to the area. These networks of friends and kin assisted in obtaining employment for the new migrants, sheltering them until they found jobs, setting up new homes. In a random sample of 50 of the 200 migrant workers in Pamit, almost all had heard about factory employment from current or former migrants, often relatives. On average, they knew five other people from their village who were employed in the same firm and three others from their village who also boarded in Pamit.

The average educational attainment of migrants—almost eight years—was double that of workers from Nuwun, the agricultural village. Eighty-eight percent of the migrants came from families who owned some farmland, a surprisingly high proportion; I suspect, however, that some respondents overestimated family landholdings. Most migrants came to the factories out of curiosity or boredom rather than poverty.

Sixteen percent of the migrants stated that their fathers were either village officials, civil servants, teachers, or state employees, but I could not verify these responses. This proportion is surprising if it is expected that migrant workers come from the poorest households. Although a few migrants did come from extremely poor backgrounds, they appeared to be in a minority.

The migrants did not migrate or work in a factory because it was a household-level decision or because they were trying to help their poor families. Some even left home without parental permission. Some had run away from unhappy home situations—either parents or a husband—or attempts by their parents to arrange their marriages. Tuminem was the fourth of five children, born to a farming family. When Tuminem was five years old her father died, and her mother did not take good care of her:

I've never felt love from my mother. I wasn't sent to school. My work was to gather wood, since the age of seven years old, and during that time she was always angry with me. I was so ignored that I couldn't stand it at home any longer. Finally, I left home and went to live with other people. These people also weren't well off. They weren't relatives. My work was to sell leaves in the market. After working in the market, I was sent to their neighbor's to draw drinking water. For one large pail, I received 10–15 rupiah [$0.015–$0.02]. From this money, I was told to buy snacks because the people I lived with weren't well off enough to give me money for snacks. I lived in misery with these people for two and one-half years.

Then one day I said to the woman with whom I lived, "Listen, I want to work for money." "Where?" "With people in Salatiga." She gave me her permission. I decided to go to Salatiga. I was only ten years old then. In Salatiga, I lived with people who told me to take care of the children and wash clothing. For one month I was paid 1,500 rupiah [$2.30] in addition to the food they gave me. I worked for them for one year. Then when I was eleven years old, I moved to work for people in the city of Semarang. There, my work was also to care for the children and wash clothing, but for one month I was paid 2,500 rupiah [$3.80]. From this little money, I saved and after one year I had savings of 5,000 rupiah [$7.70]. When my work was done, I went home and returned to the village, to live with my mother again. With that capital I wanted to buy and sell tempeh. But in the end, I couldn't last. I stopped selling tempeh and with that money I sold different foods such as *bubur* [porridge], onions, and so on. The money was all used up. I sold from the house for one and one-half years. But I wasn't strong enough to take my mother's criticisms.

Finally, I stopped selling and I used my money to go to Jakarta. Because my desire was to annoy my mother, I left without saying good-bye to her. Before leaving I had asked a friend for her address in Jakarta when she was visiting my village. I was very determined. Although I was afraid, I got on a bus for Jakarta, hoping to find my friend here. I was very stubborn. The important thing was that with my little money, my intention was to find my friend. In my heart I wasn't sure if I'd be able to find her. But maybe my fate would be lucky. Finally after asking and asking, I found my friend. I stayed with her only a few days and then was sent to people to look after their children. For one month I received 5,500 rupiah. After two years there, I moved to other people's house and there I cooked for 12,500 rupiah [$20.00] a month for two years. Then I moved to work for Thai people. I washed clothes and was paid 25,000 rupiah [$38.00] a month. But I had to buy my own food and cook for myself. I worked for them for two years and was able to save 75,000 rupiah [$115.00], in addition to a gold necklace of five grams [of gold], earrings of two grams, a ring of two and a half grams, furniture, a thermos, glasses, dishes, and so on. When I left the Thai people, I visited my friend and left her things, like the thermos, as a gift.

Then I went home and maybe it was my fate, but after reaching the bus terminal in Jakarta, I was held up by a robber. He asked for my money, necklace, earrings, ring; he took everything. Finally, I returned home bringing

> nothing, only the little money left from my bus fare. Luckily I had enough to reach home. I stayed at mother's house for one week and went to work sewing. [It was unclear whether she worked for one person or a factory.] After two months, I didn't like it and I moved to the biscuit factory [in the research site]. Until now, I've worked there for eight months.

Tuminem's story was the most moving of all those that came from the fifteen migrants whose life stories we recorded. She was from one of the poorest backgrounds and clearly was an unusual person, having taught herself how to read and write. On meeting her, I was immediately struck by her ability and desire to express herself. Surprisingly, she also was a very cheerful person, at least in her interactions with others. For Tuminem, factory employment offered stability and much-needed income, at least temporarily. Given her history, we cannot expect that such employment will be permanent.

CONCLUSION

Conditions in the agricultural and industrial villages described in this chapter mirror several important trends occurring more broadly in rural Java. In agrarian-based villages, the distribution of land is unequal, and most households do not control sufficient land for subsistence needs. As a result, household members engage in economic diversification, which is inversely related to class status. In this rural site, one does not need to search far to find industrial connections. Villages that have surrendered their land to the factories have experienced the secondary effects of industrialization. Their expanded informal sector provides goods and services to workers at a low cost, which increases the region's interdependence with industrial capitalism and an unpredictable global economy. Finally, this portrayal of rural poverty provides the backdrop for understanding the significance of industrial capitalist development for village men, women, and their households.

Factory daughters in the "cream" section of the biscuit factory, spreading jam on sandwich cookies.

Irrigated rice fields in Nuwun, my village base.

A late afternoon village scene: young children caring for livestock and women returning from a harvest carrying heavy loads.

The mother of a factory daughter in Nuwun, harvesting rice with the *ani-ani*.

A landowner dividing shares (*bawon*) of the rice harvest for herself and the harvesters.

Two neighbors pounding coffee for a better-off household while the grandmother of the house (*left*) watches.

Factories in the rice fields.

Workers sorting cookies and crackers in the biscuit factory.

Packing tins in the biscuit factory.

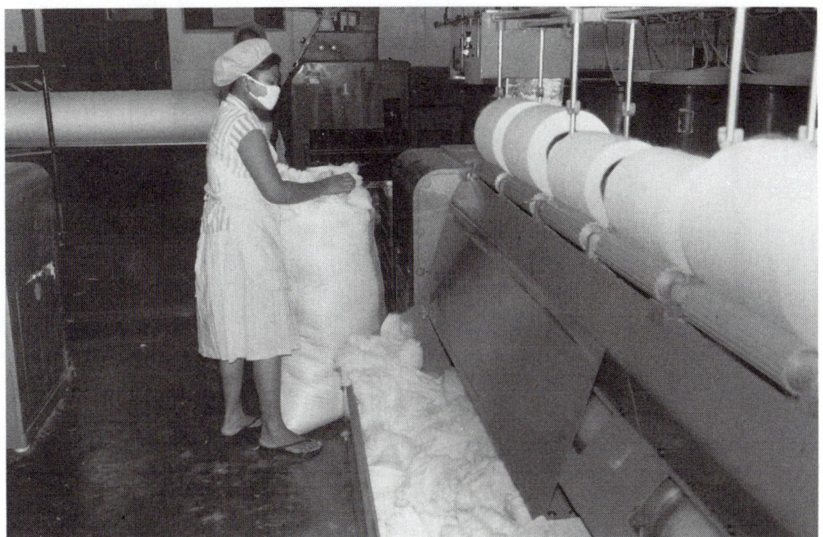

Turning cotton into thread in the spinning factory.

Attending to the machines in the spinning factory.

A worker's speed and efficiency are monitored.

At the beginning of a shift, a worker hands her supervisor a written excuse for her previous absence.

Labor-intensive work: gluing the firm's labels onto spools for thread.

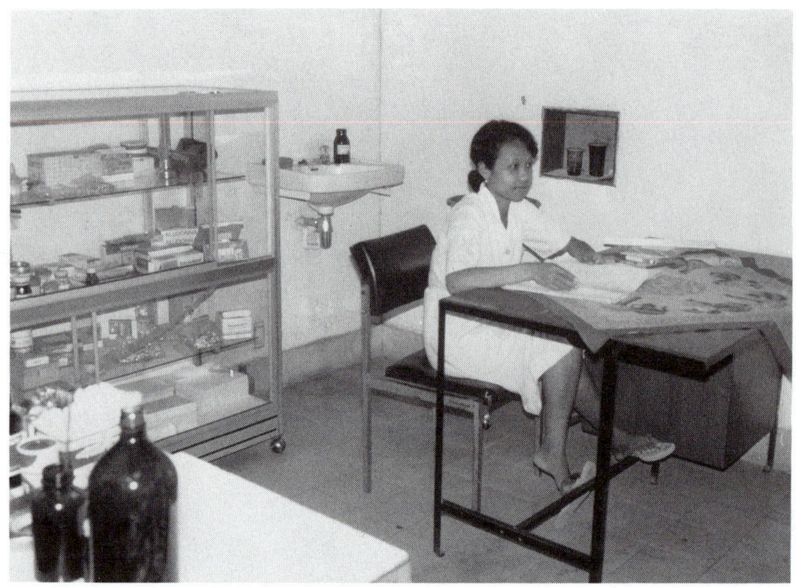

The nurse in the spinning mill's clinic.

Five of eight women who share one room in the spinning mill's dorm.

Four gas burners serve the seventy dorm residents in the spinning mill dorm.

Late-night television viewers in the spinning mill dorm.

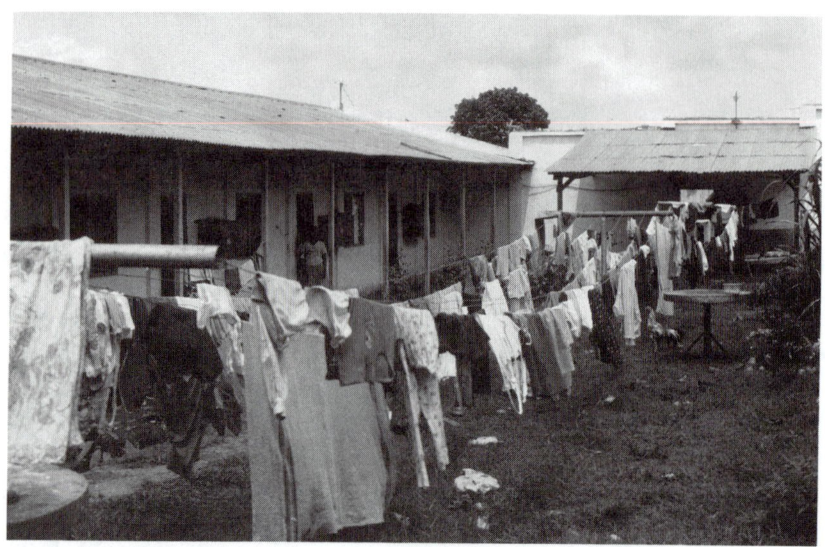

Exterior of the dorm at the textile mill. The interior was even more abysmal: several workers shared each bed, sleeping in shifts.

Migrant workers can buy cooked and uncooked food at stalls that sprang up after the factories were built.

A going-away party for my assistant with factory daughters in Nuwun.

The going-away party: my assistant is in the far corner under the light, wearing a dark patterned dress and a white sweater; Rini is sitting to her left.

The perils of rural fieldwork: a persistent hen laying an egg in my file tray, on my questionnaires. (Courtesy of Edward L. Kain.)

CHAPTER V

The Factories

Don't scornfully say
"Factory girl, factory girl."
Iwataru Kikusa is
A real factory girl.
Iwataru Kikusa is a shining
Model of a factory girl.
Let's wrench the balls
Of the hateful men!
Mr. Overseer, Mr. Supervisor,
You'd better watch out!
There is the example
Of Iwataru Kikusa.
Who dares to say that
Factory girls are weak?
Factory girls are the
Only ones who create wealth.

Popular song from the silk-producing area of Suwa, Japan, 1907 (translated by E. Patricia Tsurumi)

The contrasts in this particular area of Java are striking. Some parts look like most other rural areas in Java: villages dotted with palm, banana, and papaya trees are bordered by terraced rice fields spanning all hues of green and golden yellow; people gather at weekly markets to talk and haggle. For most rural people, their village and the market constitute the locus of their activities. However, in this site, ten large-scale "modern" factories, driven by Western machinery and technology and organized to run at a rapid, efficient pace, squat in the middle of the agricultural land of two villages that still have neither running water nor electricity and where most technology is driven by human labor or animal power. Some of these factories nest in rice fields, disrupting neat rows of rice shoots with metal fences and guards.

The transition from agrarian work, which follows the rhythm of the seasons, to industrial factories geared for time efficiency and profit was a profound event in the history of European working people. E. P. Thompson's superb analysis (1963) of the changing conception of time in village production compared with capitalist factory production still rings true in parts of the Third World today. In village life and production, people are task oriented, conceptualizing their day in terms of what needs to be done: weeding the fields, sweeping the house, drying the rice in preparation for a ritual feast, washing clothes. The sun and the mosque's call to prayer provide a sense of time and rhythm to Javanese villagers who may not even be able to read a watch or clock. In a Malay village, "when asked how long a certain activity will take, old men, drawing on their handrolled tobacco, may reply with nonchalance, 'Ah, two, three cigars' time' " (Ong 1987, 108).

When wages are set by the hour, however, the notion of completing a task changes radically to a feeling of being pressed by the clock and by the person paying the wage. Time becomes primary, towering above human consideration, because it is interchangeable with money—both profits and wages. Time is transformed metaphorically; suddenly, like money, it can be saved, spent, or wasted.

The transition to capitalist work organization imposed on workers a new, alien, and sometimes brutal system of production that required tremendous regimentation and time pressure. Predictably, the new system met with considerable resistance. Two recent ethnographies of work, capitalist discipline, and worker response from very different parts of the world (Fantasia 1988; Ong 1987) reveal the many different forms that resistance can take. The deep-seated contradictions of the capitalist system are reflected in the lives of the individuals who work in it; caught in its undertow, no longer able to acquiesce to its contradictions and constraints, they begin to resist it.

Most Javanese factory workers come from homes with dirt floors, no running water, and no electricity, homes where most technology is powered by humans or water buffalo. The only pieces of "modern technology" in their villages are treadle sewing machines, battery-powered radios, and perhaps a few televisions that run on car batteries. Workers leave their villages behind as they enter buildings filled with machinery, some of which creates a deafening noise. Anne Ruth Willner's description of workers and factories in a late 1950s rural Javanese setting is still apt today, except for the gender of most workers:

> The newcomer to the factory, especially if he is from a quiet village, is confronted with an environment that well may be alien to anything in his experience. The very building is probably higher and vaster than any in which

> he has been before. The sight of hundreds of people facing and manipulating machines may be both novel and intimidating. (1961, 165)

What is the nature of the transition to capitalist work organization in this rural Third World setting? How do the factories discipline and control a relatively inexperienced and uneducated labor force accustomed to village-based production? How do workers react to industrial capitalist work organization? What forms does resistance take in this Javanese setting?

One thread that runs throughout this chapter is that conceptions of gender have been crucial in the development of capitalist industrialization in this setting. The ways in which traditional Javanese notions of gender are reproduced and reshaped in these rural factories both create further inequalities between male and female workers and inform some of the processes through which the labor force is controlled. I also argue that the treatment of female workers is not simply an index of the relationship between factories and rural women or between the oppressive relations of capitalism and traditional patriarchal norms. Rather, the state's cozy relationship with industrial capitalism makes it very much a partner in the exploitation of women workers, in the almost total disregard for their health and safety, and in the constant effort to keep them docile and controlled.

THE LURE OF THE PERIPHERY

Factories began to locate in this Central Javanese site in the early 1970s and have continued to do so during the ensuing decades.[1] Owners and managers gave two principal reasons for their attraction to this rural area. The first, the "push" factor, derived from the state, which increasingly restricted industrial development in Semarang, a nearby port city; instead, state officials at the provincial and regency level advised investors to consider this rural area. A few owners mentioned that state officials made it clear that there would be no difficulties or bottlenecks with the necessary bureaucratic paperwork required by industrial firms. Why and how state officials had decided on these particular villages were questions to which I could not find a satisfactory answer.

The entire district had been chosen for state-directed development. In the early 1980s, more than ten hectares had been taken out of agricultural production and local farmers displaced for a housing project for civil servants. The area was desirable because of its proximity to Semarang and its relatively low prices (compared with Semarang). When asked how the two villages were chosen where factories were allowed to be built, government officials mentioned poor soil quality, high unemployment rates, and other features common to many villages. My discussions with local officials suggest that a very wealthy Lurah in one village was instrumental in bringing factories to his village.

From the industrialists' perspective, the second major reason, the "pull" factors, are clear: the low costs of land, utilities, and labor and the abundance of the latter were named as important reasons for settling in this area. Transportation costs, however, are higher for these firms because they must transport goods to and from Semarang; these costs are offset, though, by relatively inexpensive land and labor. From the perspective of multinational corporations, costs in Java, particularly labor costs, are much lower than in other nearby Asian countries such as Malaysia, Singapore, Hong Kong, or Thailand. Locating in a rural area, the "periphery of the periphery," cuts costs more, even compared with urban Java. (For details about the factories—products, ownership, and sexual composition of the work force, see table 12.)[2]

What is unusual about this site compared with a Free Trade Zone is the combination of domestic and multinationally owned firms and the firms' orientation toward *both* the global and local markets.

Only two firms are multinational.[3] These two factories—textiles and spinning—are the largest in work force and land area, with 13 hectares and 5.5 hectares respectively.[4] Both run twenty-four hours a day in three eight-hour shifts and employ 80 percent of the female, 37 percent of the male, and 66 percent of the entire manufacturing work force in the district.

Only one firm in the site—the Coca-Cola bottling company—is fully owned by Pribumis; formerly, however, it had been a multinational, owned by Australians. The remaining firms, such as the citric acid and glassware factories, are either fully owned by local Chinese Indonesians who reside in Semarang or are joint ventures between Pribumis and Chinese Indonesians.

There is no clear relationship between type of ownership and market orientation; some multinationals sell to the Indonesian market, and some locally owned firms (such as the garment factory) are oriented toward the global market.[5] Four of the firms, including the two multinationals, are export-oriented: textiles, spinning, garments, and glassware. The garment factory produces men's shirts and is the only factory that is solely export-oriented. The other three exporting firms also sell their goods

TABLE 12
THE FACTORIES: OWNERSHIP, MANAGEMENT, AND WORK FORCE

Factory	Nationality		Total workers	% by firm	
	Owners	*Managers*		*Female*	*Male*
Textiles	OC, CI	OC, CI	2,914	86	14
Spinning	I, OFI	I	950	67	33
Biscuits	CI	CI	416	76	24
Bread	CI	CI	110	50	50
Bottling	P	P	135	39	61
Citric acid	P, CI	CI	160	—	100
Glassware	P, CI	CI	380	21	79
Garments	CI	CI, P	280	84	16
Buses	CI	CI	375	—	100
Furniture	CI	CI	80	—	100
Noodles	CI	CI	60	75	25
Confectionery	CI	CI	20	50	50
Total			5,880	67	33

SOURCE: Interviews with all managers or owners of all factories in the research site.
NOTE: P = Pribumi; I = Indian; CI = Chinese-Indonesian; OC = Overseas Chinese; OFI = other foreign investors.

locally. Several younger firms had plans to develop their product for export in the future. The four export-oriented firms employed 76 percent of the area's industrial labor force. Despite the combination of multinational and local capital and the orientation toward both global and local markets, multinationals and export-oriented firms are by far the largest and most important firms in the site. In other words, this rural, industrial site is heavily tethered to foreign capital and global markets, making it vulnerable to the global economy.

LABOR AND THE WORKERS

Labor recruitment has changed over the years, as have the requirements for employment. When factories first opened, they often turned to the Lurah for aid in finding workers. The Lurah sent local villagers, and the factories paid him a commission. Indeed, in West Java, Celia Mather

(1982) found that this process constituted a convenient method of labor control. In her research site, a patron-client bond was created between the Lurah and those workers (usually female) whom he had helped obtain jobs. The Lurah exerted power and control over the lives and behavior of these workers, since their misbehavior or protests within the factory reflected badly on him.

In this rural site, during the early days of industrial growth, firms could easily work through the Lurah because they did not ask for many qualifications beyond the minimum age. One manager explained that a potential worker, male or female, only had to be (or had to look) fifteen or sixteen years old; in addition, males had to be 150 centimeters tall and weigh at least 50 kilograms.

As the educational level of the general population has increased over the years and the requirements for employment have stiffened, factories no longer fully depend on the Lurahs for labor recruitment, a source of bitterness for Lurahs in the two industrial villages. Larger firms now advertise with posters at the local movie theaters or, for skilled workers such as laboratory technicians, at various technical high schools. Since smaller firms have hired most of the labor, their demand for more workers is limited; they simply rely on word of mouth when they have openings, thus bypassing the Lurah's commission.

Age and education standards for production workers have become more stringent. In 1983, the minimum age was increased in most factories from about fifteen to seventeen or eighteen. The noodle factory, however, still employs uneducated, often illiterate females of thirteen and fourteen years, which is below the legal minimum working age. Six of the firms would still accept illiterate workers, but five firms required literacy (which is achieved with three to four years of schooling), and three firms required a primary school diploma. In 1981, the spinning factory changed its educational requirement from the completion of primary school to the completion of middle school (nine years), a requirement that disqualified most young women in my research villages. Several of the managers I interviewed felt that a better-educated work force would have more experience with regimentation and therefore would be more disciplined.

There are other, more questionable requirements for young female applicants. The spinning and textile factories administer a dexterity test that consists of quickly distributing spools in bottles and then pulling them out again. In the garment factory, potential applicants are asked to tie knots in single sewing threads. Some firms ask for a letter from a doctor certifying good health. Those with clinics in the factory usually have the prospective worker see the company doctor, who draws blood for a pregnancy test and often tests stools for worms.

Since most firms prefer hiring single females because they are cheaper to maintain than married ones, they request a letter from the village head confirming the applicant's single marital status. The justification for this preference is that the allegiance of a married woman to her husband, particularly to her children, disrupts steady work attendance. Young women seeking a job sometimes misrepresent their marital status, enlisting the help of the village leader to do so, in order to secure employment. One day as I stood by the guard's gate in front of the textile factory, a stream of young female job applicants walked by after their interviews. The guard asked one woman what happened, and she replied that once they found out she was married, they rejected her. "It's better to fib about this; next time say you're single," he advised her. In this way, village leaders and those already employed in factories aid would-be workers by resisting rules they find unreasonable and irrelevant to the worker's ability to labor.

THE WORK FORCE

Females constitute two-thirds of the industrial labor force in this site. The demographic structure of the work force is typical of those of other Third World countries: most of the female work force is young and single (table 13). Almost 40 percent of the female work force is under the age of 20, and 90 percent of the work force is under age 24. Eighty-five percent of those under 20 are single. Only 10 percent of the workers are older than 25, and all of these females are or have been married.

Researchers have pointed to the role of the state in proliferating gender

TABLE 13

AGE AND MARITAL STATUS OF FEMALE WORKERS (N = 3,935)

Age	Percentage	Percentage never married
15–19	39	85
20–24	51	51
25–29	10	0

SOURCE: Interviews with management.

stereotypes of docile, "nimble-fingered" Asian females in order to draw foreign investors to Southeast Asia (Ong 1987, 152; Grossman 1979; Froebel et al. 1980). This rural site is no exception in the way gender images are constructed to attract investment and perpetuated to keep labor unrest and costs down.

When questioned about the sexual composition of the work force, owners and managers clearly stated that they greatly preferred female workers to males. Males were described as too aggressive and assertive (*berani*) toward those above them in the firms' hierarchy, yet they were also described as lazy. Almost all those interviewed said that males are difficult to discipline and control. Females, by contrast, were thought to be easier to control (*mudah menatur*), quicker, and more diligent (*lebih teliti*); although supervisors complained that the available labor force was generally unskilled, they found female workers more cost-effective than males because they were paid less and were less likely to disrupt the production process with complaints or labor protests. Moreover, rural females were easier to control and intimidate than urban females were.

LABOR LAWS, STATE-INDUSTRIAL PRACTICE, AND THE ABANDONMENT OF WORKERS

Most female employees are unskilled or semiskilled laborers who work thirty-six to forty-eight hours a week. The majority of production workers are permanent daily laborers (*harian tetap*). This group is distinct from staff and administration, who are paid on a monthly basis (*bulanan*), and casual workers (*harian lepas*) or those paid according to piece rate (*borongan*).

At the time of my research, the basic minimum daily wage for Central Java was 425 rupiah. However, the Department of Labor sets minimum wage rates for every sector and subsector. For example, within the sector of manufacturing firms, the daily minimum wage for a production worker was 625 rupiah in textile and garment factories and 500 rupiah in food factories. Differential wages were meant to reflect differences in skill, and there were no rural-urban differences in these minimum wages. The daily wage for female production workers in the factories studied ranged from 400 to 900 rupiah.

Several of the factories I studied did not pay the already low minimum wage. The little research that has been conducted on modern firms elsewhere in Java strongly suggests that urban and periurban industrial firms do pay the minimum wage, in part because female workers there are more aware of their rights and more likely to protest illegally low wages (Mather 1985). Additionally, migrant workers who have gone to urban or periurban sites for a job often do not have their family nearby to fall back on.

Four of the largest factories had created economic incentives such as bonuses to encourage time discipline in their work forces. The systems varied, but a worker usually received an extra 100 rupiah or so if she came to work on time every day for a certain period, ranging from one week to one month.

Although the Department of Labor establishes minimum wages, there is no mechanism for enforcement (Daroesman 1981, 33). Thus, workers who wish to protest their illegally low wages or other transgressions of labor laws have little recourse. For example, the noodle factory in my site employed uneducated females below the legal minimum age. Even if they were to protest their illegally low wages—and this is highly unlikely—and even if the union or appropriate state organ were to intervene—an even more unlikely event—these young women would lose their jobs because they are too young to be employed. The factory banked on workers' shyness and legal ignorance to perpetuate such illegalities.

The FBSI (All Indonesia Labor Federation) conducts a monthly market survey to determine the cost of basic needs—food, household goods, clothing, and so on. A single worker in Jakarta in December 1982 needed 36,000 rupiah monthly for subsistence (FBSI 1982). An official working for the Department of Labor at the regency level told me that a single worker in the area I studied would need 24,250 rupiah monthly for subsistence needs. Female workers in this study averaged approximately 15,500 rupiah monthly, 36 percent below the subsistence level.

Female workers in Central Java earn much less than do their counterparts in other Asian countries (table 14), which makes Java more attractive to foreign investors. Indeed, managers in this site who had worked in other East and South Asian countries all felt that wages were lower in Java. Equally important is that, comparatively, their wages buy much less. In the research site, one bar of soap costs the equivalent of almost three hours of work at the minimum wage—and many workers do not earn minimum wage. The wage level and its buying power demonstrate that factory wages for female workers in Central Java were not sufficient for one person's subsistence.

Male factory workers were paid at least 50 percent more than female workers were, an amount sufficient for subsistence, according to union calculations. Management used two arguments to justify paying higher

TABLE 14
COMPARATIVE BUYING POWER OF ASIAN WOMEN

Item purchased	Time worked[a]					
	Sri Lanka	*Malaysia*	*Thailand*	*Philippines*	*Hong Kong*	*Indonesia*
1 kg rice	2 hrs., 41 min.	1 hr., 15 min.	55 min.	1 hr., 10 min.	55 min.	4 hrs.
1 egg	29 min.	14 min.	10 min.	20 min.	5 min.	45 min.
1 Coke	1 hr., 24 min.	45 min.	23 min.	27 min.	11 min.	4 hrs.
Cheapest meal out	2 hrs., 14 min.	1 hr., 58 min.	55 min.	2 hrs., 3 min.	56 min.	1 hr., 15 min.
	Average Daily Wage (U.S.$)					
	2.40	2.60	3.40	2.40	6.90	0.96

SOURCES: *Balai Asian Journal* 2 (Dec. 1981) for all but the Indonesian data. The Indonesian data are from my Central Javanese research site only, from my market survey and my fieldwork from 1981 to 1983.

[a] The prices calculated into time are based on a situation in which minimum wage is paid. Not all factories pay the minimum wage, and in those cases, the time spent working to buy such goods would increase.

wages to males: males did "heavier" work and thus received a higher wage, and they also needed the money to support their families. Although the division of labor in the factories separates work tasks by sex, male tasks are not necessarily more taxing, nor do they require more skill than female tasks do. The argument about male workers supporting a household is based more on normative assumptions than on the actual life-cycle position of male workers. None of the male factory workers in the agricultural villages researched was married, and only one-fifth of the twenty-five male migrant workers living in the industrialized village were married. Factories kept male workers as a minority of the work force, but it paid them more to avoid labor problems.

These fallacious assumptions about male workers—that their work is harder or more difficult and that they support families—justify a substantial income gap between male and female workers, immediately elevating all males to a superior economic position. Any such assumptions justifying male superiority are of course coupled with assumptions justifying female inferiority or subordination.

Because of the particular location of these factories, most workers lived at home; therefore, factory managers assumed that these young, rural females would turn to their families for financial support. That these workers lived at home with their parents may also have put a damper on possible worker protests while giving industrialists yet another rationale for low female wages.[6] Managers argued that young women "don't need the income to live" because they could turn to their fathers and their farm families, who produced whatever the household needed; the low pay for females was justified (by management) because it represented surplus income, "pocket money." These arguments are rooted in conceptions of gender relations in Java, particularly a daughter's dependence on her father. They also draw on class and differences between owners or managers and their employees, particularly the assumptions of the former about the lives of the latter. Chapters 7 and 8 present a more detailed analysis of this particular relationship among factories, working daughters, and the family economy.

WORKER BENEFITS, LABOR LAWS, AND STATE-INDUSTRIAL PRACTICE

Although managers all assured me that they adhered to labor laws, workers told another story. Permanent daily workers are entitled to certain paid benefits, such as two days of menstruation leave per month, three months of maternity leave, and one to two weeks' annual vacation. However, only one factory granted workers paid menstruation leave, and workers who took it were punished and lost their monthly bonus. In other factories, workers were not paid if they went home because of menstruation, again a punishment. In certain factories, workers had to prove to a female supervisor or nurse that they were indeed menstruating: only those who could no longer stand up would be willing to submit to the humiliation of such an examination. Workers' diaries indicate that at times even those suffering from menstrual cramps were not allowed to go home.[7]

Other benefits decreed by labor laws were also ignored. Most firms did not pay the three months' maternity leave. Only the textile factory paid two-thirds of the basic monthly wage if the worker had provided documentation for her file proving that she was married. Those who had failed to do so did not receive any maternity pay.

Each firm was supposed to have a collective labor agreement (*peraturan perusahaan*), but most did not. In the glass factory, owned in part by the family of President Suharto, the agreement clearly stated that workers were entitled to one and one-half months of leave at the basic pay level before and after their baby's birth. But one manager unwittingly gave me a form new female employees are asked to sign, waiving their maternity benefits. He explained that this practice was initiated when the firm started out, to save costs. The form included the following statement: "As long as I am pregnant, I agree that my rights to wages and benefits will not be granted." Most factories did not bother formalizing illegalities: they simply did not pay maternity benefits, and, because of the state's benign neglect, they did not need to justify ignoring the law.

Because the state plays an active role in suppressing the union, controlling labor, and creating minimal labor laws that are then ignored by state bureaucrats, it obstensibly hands over the issues of worker protection to industrialists, a group not generally known for creating conditions with workers' well-being in mind. As mentioned in chapter 2, under Suharto the state has prevented the union from becoming an activist or political organization. The union is not allowed to educate workers concerning their rights, nor can it intervene on workers' behalf without their prior request. According to Indonesian labor laws, a union must be formed in firms with more than fifty employees. In such firms, managers assured me that unions indeed existed. However, in interviews with nineteen workers who lived in the village where I was based, I learned that none of them knew what a union was or whether one existed in their firm.

HEALTH AND SAFETY

In keeping with their general disregard for labor laws, most factories also ignore basic safety regulations. But it must be stressed that they are able to do so with the knowledge of corrupt state officials.

Examples of factories ignoring health and safety regulations are rampant. For instance, according to labor laws, workers in textile mills should be provided with a cap, a nose and mouth cover, and glasses. The latter two pieces prevent irritation of the lungs and eyes from the excessively high fiber levels on the production floor. The cap is meant to prevent on-the-job accidents. But the textile factory in the research site endangered the health and lives of the workers by not supplying them with any of these items. Workers complained of constant eye irritations and coughing spells, and at least once a year, a worker lost her hair when it got caught in the machines. Such on-the-job accidents resulted in injuries and an occasional death, for which factories paid the worker's family a sum of money.

Another aspect of well-being and safety concerns night work. By law, factories that run on shifts or require some type of work at night must provide transportation between the factory and the workers' homes. In the research site, the only factory that provided transportation was the Indian multinational spinning mill. Since this was the only factory that refused to bribe state bureaucrats, officials from the Departments of Labor and Industry sought revenge by arguing that the vans should take the workers to their front doors, not just to the village entrance. The textile factory also operated in shifts, but it did not provide any transportation whatsoever for workers; nor did the garment factory, which sometimes required workers to stay late for overtime. As a result, female workers traveling to or from the factories alone at night were vulnerable to attack by male thieves. I heard about six such cases in which female workers were threatened near the factory by knife-wielding males who proceeded to take all their gold jewelry and money. On two occasions, young women suffered superficial knife wounds.

How do such legal transgressions become normal factory routines? The Department of Labor is responsible for visiting and evaluating each factory, checking for transgressions of labor laws and for worker safety. It became evident during interviews at the regency and district levels of the Departments of Labor and Industry that government officials were easily corrupted; indeed, they apparently expected and demanded money. In return, they were very willing to ignore workers' health, wages, and interests.

During interviews, lower-level civil servants explained that the blatant transgressions of important labor laws by factories were simply ignored because those factories paid bribes to Department of Labor bureaucrats—that is, their own superiors. After receiving a bribe, the state inspectors then wrote either a positive evaluation of the factory or simply none at all. These frustrated lower-level civil servants who explained this process to me showed me folders on which the names of the factories in the site were written. These folders should have contained records of official inspections, with evaluations and notations of any transgressions. Instead, most were empty.

The personnel manager of the spinning factory, formerly the personnel manager of the textile factory, verified that bribes were extended and received to bypass state inspections or corrections. She also explained that it was common practice for firms to do "double bookkeeping" to avoid taxes and to appear to be paying legal wages. She found it difficult at times to work for a factory that refused to extend such bribes, if only because of the constant harassment by the Department of Labor.

When I asked a Department of Labor official directly responsible for overseeing factory evaluations about the lack of night transportation for workers, he assured me that all factories provided such transportation and proceeded to focus on and criticize the spinning factory: the only factory that upheld labor laws and refused to bribe him. These bribes had facilitated his ignoring below-minimum wages, dangerous working conditions, the withholding of benefits, the practice of putting female workers on the night shift in a highly vulnerable situation, and tax evasion in the other factories.

Thus, although lower- and middle-level state officials give factories a fairly free hand in exploiting the workers and endangering workers' health and safety, upper-level state bureaucrats attempt to keep wages low and labor controlled. In this way, certain Indonesian men maintain and enhance their power and wealth and their position on top of poor female workers.

HIERARCHIES IN THE FACTORIES

The sexual division of labor among and within factories reflects notions of gender that relegate women to the most menial and worst-paid sections in the production process. In the research site, females were predominant in textiles, spinning, garments, and food processing. By contrast, males worked in jobs thought to require more physical exertion; they were predominant in the bus, furniture, and glassware factories. Within predominantly female factories, males were assigned all jobs that were in any way mechanical or technical or were perceived as heavier work.[8] For example, tasks in the bread and noodle factories were assigned in the following manner:

MALE TASKS	FEMALE TASKS
Bread Factory	
Make and knead dough	Measure ingredients for dough
Operate mixers	Weigh dough
Operate ovens	Cut dough
Maintain machinery	Take bread off trays (after baking)
	Spread cream on cookies and bread
	Pack final product

Noodle Factory	
Put dough into mixers	Sort dough after boiling
Cut dough	Carry boiled noodles outside on trays to dry
Put dough in boilers or steamers and remove	Attend to drying noodles
	Pack final product

When asked why females were the main production workers in the biscuit factory, the manager responded, "After all, who makes the bread at home?" Probably no one, given the rice-based diet of most Javanese.

Within predominantly female factories, the production process is divided into a series of highly compartmentalized tasks. In the garment factory, for example, each worker was responsible for one small part of the blouse—sleeves, buttonholes, pockets, collars—in order to hasten the production process as much as possible.

LABOR RELATIONS AND WORKER-MANAGEMENT HIERARCHIES

Notions of gender play a crucial role in the way management treats and attempts to control labor; such notions, along with class and ethnic differences, shape the ways in which managers perceive and treat workers. Most production workers are female, with little chance of vertical mobility. Their immediate supervisors are usually female in certain factories (e.g., spinning, textiles, biscuits), but not in all. These supervisors enter the firm as workers and later oversee five to twenty workers. Middle and upper-level managers are usually male and hired from outside the firm. Thus, as is common elsewhere in global factories, female workers are managed by men.

In all factories save one, regardless of the nationality of upper-level managers or owners, the personnel manager is Javanese. This circumstance is not coincidental, and it serves the factories in two ways. First, the Javanese personnel manager deals with state-level officials and bureaucrats, paving the way with bribery when necessary. Factory owners depend upon the personnel manager to deal with such bureaucratic problems as foreign managers' visas.

Second, and perhaps more important, the Javanese personnel manager helps control the labor force. The male personnel managers, by virtue of their age, sex, and power differences compared with young female workers, rely on traditional precapitalist dependencies, encouraging patron-client (*Bapak-anak buah*) ties with workers. These particular age, sex, and power differentials are also concurrent in the relationship between a daughter and her father, a relationship to which personnel managers liken their relationship to female workers. However, the Javanese father-daughter relationship is conditioned by conceptions of gender that dictate that the female role is to be subdued, shy, quiet, fearful, and submissive. Daughters are hesitant and fearful to express an opinion that may disagree with their fathers'. When fathers make decisions, daughters obey (*harus ikut Bapak*), an acquiescent behavior that personnel managers attempt to cultivate. Personnel managers assure workers that they, as their patron-fathers, are on the workers' side, doing all they can for workers; but all the while they are attempting to subdue and control the labor force in the interests of their employers, the industrialists. Disguising company self-interest in the form of benevolent paternalism and familism has and continues to be useful to capitalists everywhere in the world, from the Ford Motor Company to Japanese firms (Fantasia 1988, 28; Weix 1990).

Although personnel managers and workers are both Javanese, considerable class differences exist between the two groups. All the personnel managers live in towns, and, even if originally from village backgrounds, they look with disdain on villagers. One Javanese personnel manager said: "It is difficult to control these young villagers (*anak desa*) because they have such little education. They are too traditional. They always listen to their parents (*ikut orang tua*) and don't come to work if there is something important at home or a party. Plus, many steal." I often heard such condescending statements from managers in which a town or city dweller clearly separated himself from poor, "backwards," traditional peasants.

Ethnic differences between owners and other high-level managers (except personnel managers), on the one hand, and workers, on the other, were expressed with disdain by both workers and owners/managers, representing a long and bitter history of conflict between Pribumis and Chinese Indonesians. The Javanese manager quoted above distanced himself from the workers, for whom he expressed disdain. But a Chinese-Indonesian manager expressed deep animosity: "There is a low skill level and low motivation among both male and female workers. It's like whipping a horse. If one isn't on them and angry, they won't work. They are the most lazy people. They don't want to work, but they want to eat" (*Tidak mau kerja, tapi mau makan*). Indeed, factories whipped their worker-horses into shape by imposing various disciplinary restrictions and by hiring a horse tamer–manager whose anger workers did not wish to incur. Viewing workers with such disdain, or dismissing them as brute animals who are meant to work, reinforces management's attempts to keep workers quiet, productive, and not overfed.

Male-female differences in the worker-management relationship are not particularly new in Southeast Asia and in the Third World more generally (Ong 1987), nor are ethnic differences (Robinson 1988). In this site, however, another layer of power was superimposed on this relationship, reinforcing the control of one gender by another. In the larger factories (those with at least 100 workers), the personnel managers are almost universally former army or police officials. When asked why police and army men are chosen as personnel managers, one with some training at West Point responded, "We know how to control and manage people; we have discipline."

The increased penetration of the military into rural areas and in the daily lives of villagers has been an integral part of Suharto's attempt to maintain power and control. Militaristic (or paramilitary) group activities such as the Scouts, marching bands, and government party campaigns are encouraged among young people. Hiring men who represent state power and control as personnel managers is highly suggestive of violence and suppression; it is meant to elevate the position of personnel managers and can only instill fear among the workers. Thus, the industrialists' particular and consistent choice of army and police officers as personnel managers brings militarism, state power, and the hint of violence and oppression to the multiple hierarchies already existing in worker-management relationships.[9] The inclusion of the military in such capitalist development is apparently not peculiar to Central Java. INDOC (1983, 9) reports that evidence exists that in Kalimantan there were military placements in the union in the early 1980s.

Although gender is at the basis of hierarchical factory relations, processes controlling workers are textured with class and ethnic differences and laced with the militaristic power of the state. Female workers are at the bottom of the rung in all these hierarchies, a position that offers them little room to maneuver. Nevertheless, although Javanese female workers may be fearful and docile in some respects, they have not remained passive, accepting everything that management dictates. (In the section "Labor Protests," I examine another dimension of state power and gender hierarchies in the factories.)

WORK DISCIPLINE AND THE CONTROL OF THE LABOR FORCE

Factories have different methods of trying to instill time discipline into their labor force. As mentioned above, most of them offer economic incentives for daily attendance and promptness. Managers often complained that the work force was *kurang disiplin*, or not disciplined enough. By increasing the educational requirements for workers, industrialists hoped to capture a labor force familiar with regimentation and discipline. But they didn't want a highly educated work force, which might stage labor protests.

During my stay, two factories imposed new forms of regimentation. One factory began to demand that workers always wear uniforms, consisting of a dark skirt and white blouse or T-shirt, echoing paramilitary conformity and discipline. They forced workers to pay for the company T-shirts by deducting the costs from wages. Another factory began to demand that workers use a time card and that they bring it to work daily. Workers who arrived without the card were sent home, thus losing a day's wage and any bonus they might have earned until then; workers who lost the card were fined 100 rupiah.

Workers reported that supervisors and managers reacted harshly to workers perceived as inefficient or lazy. Worker diaries report frequent incidents of managers' subjecting workers to angry, impolite treatment, sometimes even causing female workers to cry. Two incidents were reported of a supervisor or manager acting so harshly that the worker was startled (*kaget*) and either went to the clinic or went home for the day.[10] One worker reported that in her factory, female workers often cried when the manager's assistant criticized them because he was very harsh (*keras*). He told them, "If you don't work, you won't get paid." In larger factories, about three to four workers a week were called into the manager's office and warned about inefficiency or frequent absences. One worker so enraged the foreman that she hid in the toilet for fear of being hit.

Another aspect of discipline related to maintaining a stable work force concerns worker health. The largest factories have on-site clinics, whereas smaller factories provide either basic medicine (e.g., for headaches, pain, or stomachaches) or nothing at all. The clinics are staffed by a full-time nurse and visited once a week by a doctor. In theory, the clinics could improve the health of a population with a high incidence of anemia and little access to health care; indeed, preventive health care could increase worker productivity and thereby maximize profits for factory owners. In practice, however, the clinics support and enact the short-term goals of owners and managers by testing potential workers for "illnesses" such as pregnancy that are perceived as a cost to the factory, by not treating ill workers properly, and by forcing some who are ill to continue to work. Workers complained that (1) the clinics often ran out of medicine; (2) if workers didn't have an obvious wound, the nurse did not believe they were ill; (3) the nurse was often absent; and (4) medicine was administered somewhat randomly, without proper diagnoses.

In addition, workers' accounts of maltreatment were common. Worker diaries report a small but consistent number of cases in which an ill worker was forced to continue working. For example, one worker became ill with a stomachache. Even though the clinic had run out of the appropriate medicine, the supervisor refused to allow the sick worker to go home and forced her to return to her job. Clearly, I could not verify the reputation of the worker or the severity of her illness, yet workers made it clear to me that they felt such practices to be unwarranted and unnecessarily harsh.

LABOR PROTESTS

How did workers react to factory discipline, policies, and illegally low wages? As mentioned earlier, unions should have been formed in these factories. Yet if a union existed in one of the factories, it was in form only. In the factories in my research site, the workers' representative—the person who would request union involvement in case of a problem—was either handpicked by management or, more typically, was part of management, namely, the personnel manager. These former army or police officers clearly represent the interests of industrial capitalists and the state and are essential in the control and suppression of workers and their demands.

In the few cases where the workers' representative was a worker chosen by management, she or he was either too comfortable or too intimidated to seek outside arbitration. In the garment factory, the scene of some important labor disputes, the workers' representative was fired because of her labor organizing, leaving the position unfilled. Her firing was a clear message to discontented workers and to potential workers' representatives. Using such methods, industrialists took advantage of workers' illiteracy, fear, and "feminine" traits to maintain control over workers and illegal conditions within the factory. District- and regency-level union officials did little to change these conditions. The only activity by the union in factories in the site was organizing volleyball and table tennis games.

Male workers in predominantly male factories felt freer to engage in strikes, even though it was illegal. The bus factory owner recounted at least three strikes. In 1981, workers left a half-hour early to protest a particular change in the technical system of production. In 1982, however, they conducted a three-day strike because they wanted to borrow money for Lebaran, the celebration after the fasting month of Ramadan. Most other factories gave workers a bonus at this time of year. This particular factory owner, however, would not agree to lend workers additional money. He called in a regency-level official from the Department of Labor "who made things clear to them; these people don't have common sense."

Attempts to control female workers were not entirely successful. Rather than engage in strikes, shy young factory workers used acceptable forms of Javanese resistance within the factory context. At what point, however, did female workers protest? Workers resisted when a certain line of safety and perhaps morality had been trespassed, and these protests occurred more frequently (although not exclusively) in the most tightly controlled factories. There were four different forms of female labor resistance beyond verbal complaints: walkouts, production slowdowns, stayouts, and visions of ghosts or spirits.

The walkouts—protests that most readily resemble a Western-style strike—occurred in the Indian multinational spinning firm, where the controls over workers were least severe. Indian factory managers encouraged a more open atmosphere in which labor issues were discussed, and labor protests were not particularly surprising, even to them.

When workers were angry with management in the textile factory, a highly controlled atmosphere, they slowed down production. For example, when some workers were given two pieces of cloth for the Lebaran bonus and others only one, a group of workers in the latter group slowed down their machines. Another time, one section of weavers slowed production when they heard a rumor that their supervisor was to be replaced. In the end, she was not. In the garment and spinning factories, some workers helped themselves to products, which is either stealing or an act of resistance, depending on one's perspective.

The other two forms of resistance—stayouts and spirit visions—both drew on culturally based images and forms of social interaction; they usually occurred in the most highly controlled factories.

GHOSTS AND SPIRITS

Female workers call on aspects of traditional Javanese cosmology—ghosts and spirits—to legitimize the expression of some form of protest, usually fear. In both textile factories, workers' fears of ghosts and evil spirits have slowed down or stopped production. Such episodes occur most often shortly after a worker's injury or death and are symptomatic of the fears and anxieties workers feel after such an event. These ghosts and spirits materialize in different forms.

In the textile factory in particular, workers expressed more anxiety and fear about the constant possibility of ghosts. They believed that the textile factory was haunted by village spirits angry with the construction of the factory on farmland. "When they turned the sawah into a factory, many people died and disappeared," one worker explained. This same factory also applied uncomfortably tight screws on factory workers' behavior, and managers were rude and abrupt in criticizing workers. In such conditions of control and worker anxiety, any strange or unusual behavior was automatically suspected of "outside" influence. For example, one worker was crying in the bathroom; when she did not stop after a reasonable time, other workers became uncomfortable, fearing the interference of spirits. Whenever a worker faints, which occurs with some regularity, others become fearful that evil spirits may be the cause.

Some workers may suddenly see ghosts in the factories, and such incidents temporarily arrest production. Two women told me about ghosts—old men with white beards—who appeared in the factory or dormitory. In one factory, shortly after a female worker had died from unspecified causes, a female worker was washing her face in the bathroom when she saw the head of a person who was crying. She looked, but saw no one, then began to cry herself.[11]

STAYOUTS

Workers also resist undue pressure through stayouts, or mass absenteeism. The personnel manager in the garment factory, a former army officer, was a tough, intimidating person described by one worker as sly, cunning, and slick (*licik*). Indeed, he sometimes wore his army uniform to work. I, too, felt uncomfortable with his threatening and intimidating mannerisms. I dreaded meeting him during my numerous visits to his factory when I came to see if the owner had given me permission to take photographs.[12] In this one person, several relationships were reproduced and reconstructed: male-female, father-daughter, and patron-client. He also evoked the forceful and violent power of the military and the state. The manager easily called on such traditional norms, posing as an older, empowered, fatherly male interested in protecting workers' interests. Given this manager's tough stance, the method of labor protest that workers used in this factory is not surprising.

Workers were involved in two incidents of protest against this manager, which they recorded in part in their diaries and told me directly as well. The first interaction concerned money. Management decided to create a savings-and-loan association within the factory; the workers believed that the personnel manager was behind this idea and its execution. Two hundred rupiah were withheld from workers' salaries for five consecutive paydays so that each worker eventually contributed 1,000 rupiah to the fund. However, the deductions were made without the consent of the workers themselves. In addition, 200 rupiah, about 8 percent of a weekly wage, represented a fair amount of money to those earning an already low wage. For those who lived in the agricultural village Nuwun, 200 rupiah covered transportation and lunch for one workday; it was money on which they counted.

There were stirrings of dissatisfaction among the workers because, although money had been withheld, those who asked to borrow money were told by the personnel manager that there wasn't any. He attempted to pacify the workers by promising money on a particular day; on the specified day, he didn't come to work.

During one of my visits, a group of about thirty female workers stormed into his office, with a few vocal workers asking him where the money was. This impressive show of strength and force was completely contrary to Javanese norms for female behavior with males. Individually, these workers could not and would not have confronted the manager. Collectively, they gathered their courage and encouraged each other, creating a "culture of solidarity" (Fantasia 1988) to confront this army man, who pretended to protect them and their interests while supporting the systematic theft of workers' wages.

My presence appears to have catalyzed this particular protest; workers had unhappily complained for days, and, as some later told me, they decided to challenge him when a foreigner was in his office, hoping to embarrass him. As I emphasize above, verbal and direct confrontation is avoided in Java; silent or physical withdrawal (e.g., leaving) are more frequent demonstrations of anger or dissatisfaction. This group confrontation with a Javanese manager signifies how frustrated and helpless workers felt.

His reactions ranged, but he maintained his tough and threatening stance. At first he mocked them. Then he explained that those who had initially borrowed some money had not yet returned it. However, the workers told me that none of them knew any workers in the factory who had borrowed money. The manager then promised that they could have money on the following Tuesday. Finally, he tried to embarrass them in my presence: couldn't they see that he had an important visitor from America? They were making a bad impression on me, he chided.

The strength and force with which they entered the office quickly drained as he shouted at them. They left the office meekly and quietly. As predicted by some of the workers who lived in Nuwun, he did not come to work the following Tuesday to fulfill his promise. The workers believed that he had taken the rather considerable sum of money—more than $400—for his own pleasure, as there were many stories about his relations with certain female workers. At that point, I could not interview him about wage payments and who withheld the workers' salary. The money was never returned to the workers, either through loans or through reimbursed salaries, and it appears that those in management benefited financially. The problem was never resolved, but workers' anger simmered and several months later bubbled up and spilled over.

Production fluctuated at this factory because it was geared solely to fill orders from abroad. Thus, at times workers were sent home early with no work to do, and at other times overtime was required. Wages were low—about 400 rupiah a day—and paid according to a piecework system. Wages were thus tied to the fluctuations and demands of the global market.

In 1982, during an attempt to fill a large order from abroad, the manager forced the workers to stay overtime. He first told them that they had to stay until 10:00 P.M.—seven to eight hours' overtime. The workers cried in protest because it would be difficult and dangerous to get home in the dark; furthermore, it was the rainy season, making it extremely hard for some workers to return to their villages. He relented slightly when they cried, and he finally allowed them to leave at 8:00 P.M. The following day, one entire section of workers—the ironing section—simply did not come to work, thus paralyzing the entire production process. When they returned to work the following day, the manager announced that if a worker was absent for more than three days within a two-week period, she would be fired. He then ordered the workers who had stayed out in protest not to come to work for the following three days as punishment, but he did not fire them. Three days later, all the seamstresses—the majority of the factory's work force—were told to stay late for overtime. Again they cried, and again they were forced to stay until 8:00 P.M. The following day, about thirty of the workers forced to do overtime stayed home in protest. When they returned the next day, they were ordered to stay out for two days as punishment. He then requested, rather than ordered, everyone to do one hour of overtime, but some workers chose not to do so.

Apparently, at that time the manager attempted to ask the workers why they didn't want to stay for overtime, and they gave him the same explanations: they were afraid to return home alone in the dark, and it was difficult to reach some villages late at night, particularly in the rainy season. Indeed, as mentioned above, labor laws mandate that factories requiring night work provide transportation for female employees, but this law was ignored. Traveling alone late at night was undesirable because it made female workers vulnerable to thieves and because it was difficult to find transportation to more remote villages. There were no street lamps in most villages, and workers did not carry flashlights. Even if they reached the village by local transportation, they were afraid of walking alone in the dark because of spirits.

Two days later, six workers from the packing section stayed home to protest forced overtime; they were promptly fired when they returned. In the meantime, the wage was changed from piecework to a fixed daily rate of 425 rupiah, and the manager again announced that anyone absent for more than three days in a two-week period would be fired. The switch to a set wage automatically lowered wages for some workers, who then sought employment in the nearby biscuit factory.

The first problem of involuntary deductions in wages had been confronted actively by workers who felt indignant that management had stolen from their already low wages. Although they were not able to recover their losses, they were successful in preventing such deductions from continuing. Since there was no workers' representative, the union was never involved. When crying, pleading, and complaining did not solve the second problem—forced overtime—young women felt forced into an uncomfortable, vulnerable, and dangerous position that could threaten them if they were alone on the road at night. They reacted to this threat in a typically Javanese way, adopting an acceptable form of sociocultural interaction that expresses discontent or anger—namely, withdrawal. When daughters don't wish to obey their mothers' orders to work in the rice fields, they become silent and don't go. Others simply depart, as illustrated by the life story of Rini (see the Preface): when she didn't want to marry her parents' choice, she ran away, preferring to send a message through absence rather than direct confrontation or disagreement (see Weix 1990, chap. 4). When the personnel manager refused to consider workers' direct pleas, ignoring their concerns with safety and well-being in a most unfatherly manner, they reacted in a most daughterly manner, sending him a quiet but strong message that he could not fail to understand. The one important difference is that the workers stayed out collectively, again demonstrating solidarity (Fantasia 1988), encouraging and reinforcing each other's anger, distress, fears, and indignation at the personally dangerous situation into which the manager was forcing his workers, the daughters and clients he had promised to protect.

PROTEST AND ADAPTATION: THE NATURE OF THE TRANSITION TO FACTORY WORK

Aihwa Ong, in her recent analysis of female factory workers in Malaysia and the transition to industrial capitalist work organization, argues that workers express the "trauma" of this transition by protesting "against the loss of humanity and autonomy in work" (1987, 7–8). Ong contends that workers resist capitalist work discipline—a "continuing personal and social crisis"—by drawing on precapitalist imagery: seeing ghosts (all male images), fainting, succumbing to mass hysteria, and having seizures.

My research supports Ong's contention that workers resort to noncapitalist forms of interaction and imagery to protest factory practices. However, the techniques of resistance include the passive-aggressive stay-outs described above, which occurred when workers felt personally threatened: that is, when they feared that bodily harm could come their way. In the textile factory, where workers are tightly controlled, slowing down production and seeing ghosts are the only weapons workers have to express their anger. Workers in the highly controlled garment factory did not see ghosts but used other noncapitalist forms of protest.

But in contrast to Ong's interpretations, in their daily discussions and behavior the factory daughters with whom I worked did not express anything close to what might be termed a Javanese version of trauma or alienation, or a "continuing personal and social crisis" because of factory control and discipline (Ong 1987, 8). Workers did not resist the daily mechanisms of factory organization, capitalist discipline, or low pay even though they were fully cognizant that they were not receiving a subsistence-level wage. Indeed, in light of the low level of remuneration, poor working conditions, and attempts to control the labor force, there were surprisingly few outbursts from workers. This lack of protest may be connected to the nature of the transition itself, from village production to factory work.

How and why the workers accept and sustain such exploitive conditions can be understood only by examining conditions of labor in agriculture, trade, and other village-level economic activities in which young Javanese women engage. Industries are able to take advantage of rural females more than urban ones because the former are accustomed to long hours of work at low returns. The tendency for peasants to engage in "self-exploitation"—producing beyond a point at which the return is so low that any capitalist firm would stop—has been transferred to factory production. This is what social historians have somewhat euphemistically termed the continuation of precapitalist values and practices (Hareven 1982; Tilly and Scott 1978). For centuries the Javanese peasantry has been exploited by the Javanese aristocracy, the Dutch, and the Japanese; contemporary industrial capitalism is just one more link in a long chain of extractive relations. Indeed, the low expectations of female workers accustomed to inadequate returns to their labor in the village have made for a relatively quiet recent history of industrial disputes.

Although villagers entering factory work experience tremendous shifts in technology, much of the literature on Third World industrialization assumes that factory work represents a shift from autonomous, flexible agricultural or crafts production to the hierarchies of industrial production and the "oppressive compulsion of labor discipline" (Ong 1987, 151; Robinson 1988). For these rural Javanese women, changes in labor regimes were somewhat less dramatic than such images of precapitalist work suggest. Factory daughters formerly engaged in domestic work at home, in agricultural work on their parents' land as an unpaid family worker or as a wage laborer for someone else, in domestic service, in petty trade, or in some combination thereof. Although there is less regimentation and more flexibility in some of these activities than there is in factory production, it is incorrect to assume that the workers experienced a high degree of flexibility or autonomy in production.

Although Ong found that village women were rarely monitored in their work and "enjoyed self-determination in setting the pace" (1987, 168), few factory daughters experience such autonomy in their preindustrial work lives. Household work is directed or judged by mothers and older sisters; agricultural work is guided if not controlled by parents; agricultural wage labor is often performed under the eyes of landowners; trade is usually undertaken with a more experienced trader, most often the mother; and domestic servants live and work like serfs.

It is important to understand that workers find factory employment preferable to arduous agricultural labor, to highly controlled and poorly paid positions in domestic service, and to being under the eyes and constant control of parents and other relatives in the village. The controls of factory work organization are different and more taxing, but the workers do not perceive them as vastly worse than the controls of domestic service. Former servants turned factory workers described how eight hours of factory work was much shorter than the serflike conditions of domestics who were paid even less.

I do not wish to suggest that factory work is "good," nor do I wish to obscure the intense level of exploitation that exists within factory walls. My task has been to underscore these ever-present contradictions in the lives of factory daughters even though they may not be experienced by workers as contradictions. Although it is undeniable that factory work is exploitive, it is equally undeniable that young village women prefer it to their other meager choices. Although factory work organization and discipline are strict and often brutal, female workers perceive factory employment as a progressive change in their lives, not as a gaping, unhealed wound.

CONCLUSION

Noncapitalist gender hierarchies are at the basis of relationships of power, and new ones are reproduced through processes of labor control within capitalist factories. Because of the rural locale of this site and the relatively low educational level of the residents, industrialists were better able to take advantage of female workers. These workers are preferred by managers because they can be counted on to accept illegally low wages and to forego their benefits, and the state can be counted on to ignore such transgressions of the law. Workers have little recourse to address infractions of labor laws because the state has handed over worker protection to industrial capitalists; the interests of powerful state bureaucrats, leaders, and industrial capitalists are highly complementary. The result of the comfortable, corrupt relationship between industrialists and state bureaucrats at the Departments of Labor and Industry is the abandonment of young female workers. Indeed, lower- and middle-level state bureaucrats tacitly approve of and aid in the perpetuation of labor law transgressions and in the exploitation and control of the work force; upper-level state bureaucrats, who often have a financial interest in large industrial firms, further the oppressive and exploitive programs of their colleagues.

The subjective experiences of workers demonstrate a high degree of tolerance, perhaps the legacy of centuries of highly exploitive relations between Javanese peasants and those who dominated them and appropriated their labor. Resistance, however, does occur, particularly when the workers' sensibilities are offended and their fears and anxieties activated. Young women's "preference" for factory employment and their relatively few complaints about it reveal their comparative analysis of their limited and constrained options. In light of low, exploitive wages, poor working conditions, labor hierarchies, and the level of labor control within factories, this "preference" reveals a great deal about the controls in village work and the poverty that young women experience in family and village life.

CHAPTER VI

Life in a Spinning Mill

To enter the grounds of the spinning mill, I first passed through a tall metal gate. Several guards sat in the office right inside the gate; I presented myself, and they noted my name, the purpose of my visit, and the person I was visiting. I was then escorted to the office of another guard further inside the complex. After a telephone call, I was led inside the main office and warmly greeted by the Indian general manager. He was interested in my project and allowed me to talk with whomever I wished and to look at the production floor for as long as I wanted. After several visits, I asked him, with great caution and trepidation, if I might live in the workers' dormitory for some weeks to better study his factory. He greeted my suggestion with instant approval and then asked if I would reciprocate by giving the Indian managers a seminar at the end of my stay on how to improve worker-manager relations within the factory.

In this chapter, I depict the inner workings of the Indian owned and managed multinational spinning mill, the second largest employer in the research site. I had full access to the production floor and personnel files, and for three weeks I lived in the workers' dormitory. Although this case study illustrates some of the broader issues and problems discussed in the previous chapter, the spinning mill is not representative of other firms. The style of management practiced by the Indian managers created an atmosphere distinctly different from that of other factories in the site. Indeed, that I was even allowed to conduct research in this factory seems closely tied to the nationality of the managers and their particular management style.

BACKGROUND OF THE FIRM

This factory (hereafter referred to as "LamaTex," a pseudonym) started production in 1976 and was owned by several groups. The mother company, a well-known pharmaceutical and chemical firm in India, owned 51 percent of the stock; 20 percent was owned by the International Finance Corporation, 10 percent by PIKA (Private Investments in Asia), 12.8 percent by Indovest, 5.2 percent by a private development corporation in Indonesia, and 1 percent by Indonesian Pribumis. The managing board was multinational, representing the different investors: four were Indians working in Indonesia, one was Indonesian, one was Japanese-American (PIKA), and one was Italian (Indovest).

The mother company had an interesting and somewhat unusual history. It had originated in the mid-nineteenth century in Ahmedabad, Gujarat, as a textile factory owned by a progressive Indian merchant who advocated women's education as an important part of social progress. In the early 1900s, his son worked with Gandhi to organize trade unions. In addition, he started a hospital for his employees and their families and a crèche for the children of female employees, years before these services were required by law. Since then the firm has diversified to pharmaceuticals, chemicals, and dyes, carrying on joint ventures in Malaysia, Mauritius, and Kenya; it also has training offices in New York and London.

When asked why LamaTex chose rural Java as its production site, the general manager stated that the mother company wanted to "go to underdeveloped areas and develop them." The company had ordered studies of several Third World countries for possible investments. An important incentive to invest in Indonesia was that "there are no political unions and strikes are banned"; clearly, the company has moved far beyond its early progressive history. According to the manager, this particular rural site also offered the incentives of inexpensive land, labor, electricity, and water.

The firm had a policy against engaging in bribery, which they claimed was one of many factors considered when deciding to invest in Indonesia rather than in other countries. Given that the problem of corruption in Indonesian business is well known, it is unclear how this factor affected their decision. However, the problem may be worse in other countries considered. This was the only factory in the site that refused to bribe government officials, another atypical feature underscoring the difference between this firm and the others in the area.

INVESTMENTS AND SALES

LamaTex produces yarn to be sold by the bale (one bale equals four hundred pounds), and it started to produce dyed sewing thread in the early 1980s. The initial investment of $7.1 million in 1975–76 was divided among purchasing a ninety-nine-year lease on the land, building the factory, and buying machinery and other necessities. In 1978 and 1981, additional investments were made, adding another building and more machinery for the sewing thread component.

The sources of machinery and raw materials were as international as the board of directors. Machines ranging from one to six years of age came from Belgium, France, India, Indonesia, Switzerland, and England. Raw materials for production were a mixture of local and imported goods. Ninety percent of the cotton came from the United States, and the remaining 10 percent from India, Egypt, and Africa. The polyester was from Indonesia.

LamaTex grossed approximately $1 million monthly from selling its product in Java alone. The financial manager stated that the company should have earned from $14 to $15 million in 1982 but, because of lower sales that year, would be in the red. The main product, cotton yarn, grossed $850,000 to $900,000 monthly, and sewing thread brought an additional $150,000. However, because of the glut in textiles in 1982 (*Tempo* 1982), the firm experienced lower sales and had to cut back on production.

THE WORKERS

When LamaTex first located in the site, managers consulted with the local village leader. Later, though, the Lurah was bitter and said that the factory had made promises it didn't keep: "This factory lies. Before, when they wanted to buy land, they promised lots of things, and when they looked for workers they wanted to go through me. But it turned out that they looked for workers themselves or through the newspaper." As an intermediary between the factory and potential workers, the Lurah would have received financial benefits from the factory and would have wielded some control over the workers, as Cecilia Mather observed of a Lurah in West Java.

However, the head of personnel, a Chinese Indonesian woman who had been hired recently, did not want the Lurah's help. She said that the Lurah was referring people who were "undesirable." The class and ethnic divisions between workers and managers are once again clear in her statement: "This area is full of dropouts, lazy teenagers, and gangsters. Workers from this desa are lazy; they steal and are often fired." She felt that the most industrious workers came from outside the area. In recent years, the factory had begun to seek workers by placing advertisements in newspapers and in nearby high schools.

Conditions for employment had changed over the years, which could also partially explain why the Lurah was no longer helpful as a labor recruiter. Higher skills were demanded of new workers. In 1976, management accepted applicants with a minimum age of fifteen who had graduated from grammar school (six years) and were literate and single. Shortly before my research, the requirements had changed to a minimum age of eighteen and graduation from middle school (nine years). A letter from the village leader certifying that the applicant was not married was still required. Dexterity and intelligence tests were introduced as well; the dexterity test usually included pulling spools out of or placing them into bottles, but I do not know the nature of the intelligence test. If the applicant seemed acceptable, she was checked by a doctor and given blood and stool tests to check for pregnancy and worms.

This increase in educational requirements paralleled an increase in the general education of the population. The head of security (a Javanese) felt that graduating from grammar school was not enough; workers were not "disciplin" enough. With more education, they had more "moral training, like Pancasila," the state ideology. The general manager, an Indian national, felt that more education led to a more disciplined and productive work force. He stated, however, that "intelligence is not needed for this job. . . . In fact it's better *not* to be too intelligent because then the workers are too demanding."

Workers' files typically included their original letter of application, an evaluation made during their interview, a letter of acceptance with their initial salary, annual short evaluations, and any warnings issued to them. The latter typically included reprimands for coming to work late, working inefficiently, or taking long rest periods. Ratings of workers by management during interviews followed a very British style, highly inappropriate for this Javanese context. For example, office workers in particular were rated on attitude, achievement, drive, leadership, self-image, goals (realistic or unrealistic), ability to organize workers and to command respect, responsibility, and initiative. Those applying for staff positions had to fill out very British forms, in English. Their English comprehension was tested, and typically Western questions inappropriate to this Javanese context were asked, such as, "What was your most memorable experience?"

STRUCTURE OF THE WORK FORCE

The firm is hierarchically organized (figure 1), and with the exception of the female personnel manager, all those in power at the time of my research, from the top down to shift leaders, were male. The general manager and all managers right below him, with the exception of the personnel manager, were Indian nationals. The assistant masters and su-

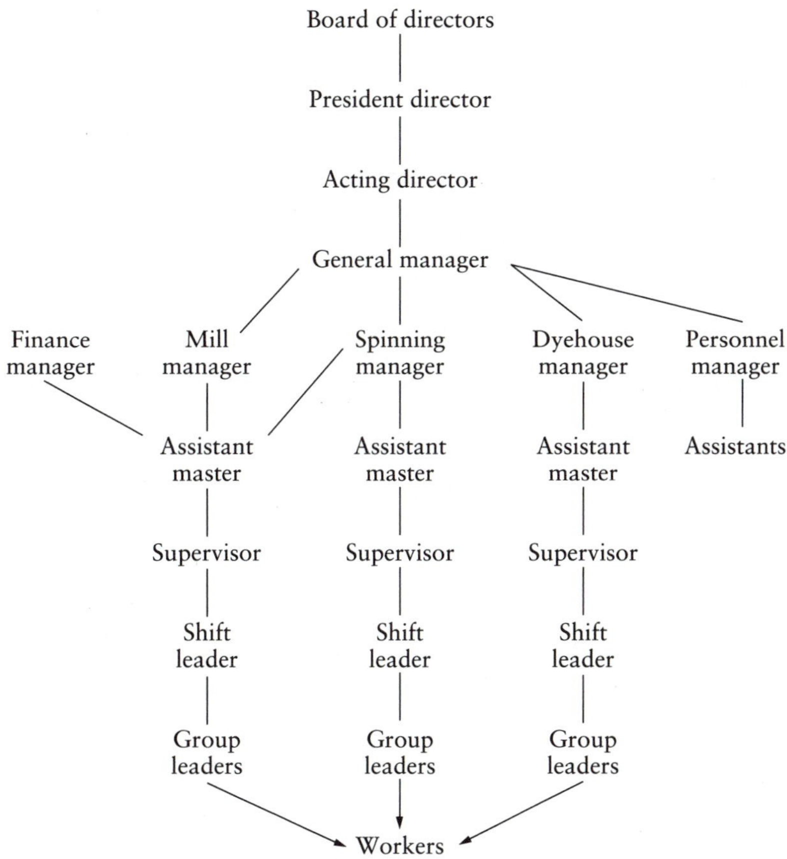

Figure 1 Hierarchical Structure of LamaTex

pervisors were all Indonesians. Supervisors, all males, were graduates from a textile academy and were hired directly from school or from a previous job. As a rule, shift leaders were also hired directly from high school and were paid on a monthly basis. Shift leaders were responsible for recording absenteeism, for maintaining the logbook, for coordinating rest time, and for assigning workers to machinery. Each was responsible for fifty to one hundred workers during one eight-hour shift. Only group leaders came up through the ranks, and they were responsible for their own work as well as supervising a group of eight to ten workers in their area. The sexual composition of the supervisors and group leaders was broken down as follows:

	MALE	FEMALE
Shift leaders	21	42
Supervisors	12	0

In this factory, women directly supervised other women as shift leaders. The male shift leaders were responsible for both males and females. However, only males were in higher supervisory positions, reproducing the male-female hierarchy found in all other factories in the area.

THE COMPOSITION OF WORKERS

The work force at LamaTex expanded along with production over the years. When the factory began production in 1976, it employed 450 workers. It added 150 more workers in 1978 and an additional 350 workers in 1980–81 as the production of yarn expanded and the sewing thread division was built. Most production operates on three eight-hour shifts. The very small dyeing section operates in two shifts and the winding section on one shift only. Currently there are 950 workers.

As in other factories, most production workers are females hired as permanent daily workers. Some males who are permanent daily workers are production workers, but most work in maintenance. Within the factory, males, being permanent monthly workers, occupy a higher proportion of better-paid, more prestigious jobs. Such workers are engaged in supervisory positions as shift leaders or in office work. Currently, the 950 workers (excluding managers) break down into the following categories:

	FEMALES	MALES	TOTAL
Permanent daily	567	172	739
Permanent monthly	69	142	211
Total	636	314	950

Although the sexual composition of various classes of employees corresponds to gender hierarchies in most factories, there was one important demographic difference in this factory. At LamaTex only a minority of female workers were less than twenty-five years old, reversing the age pattern of other factories. In addition, most female workers were married (table 15).

This striking difference in the composition of the female work force compared with that of other factories was related to several factors. From random interviews with 100 workers, I found that they had averaged 3.75 years with the firm and more than one-third had worked there from five to seven years. This high percentage of longer-term married workers was unusual for factories in the site. Many of the women came from landless households in surrounding villages, where opportunities for agricultural employment were sparse. Unlike the women in Nuwun, these women, once they had children, did not have the option of quitting work and picking up seasonal agricultural labor. Thus, LamaTex held on to a high proportion of its initial work force, in part because of a lack of other employment opportunities in the area and in part because its wages and benefits were better than those of other factories.

More important, however, was that even though only single workers were hired, once they married and had children, management allowed and even preferred them to continue working. They sought to cultivate loyalty and realized it could be developed only over time. It was clear

TABLE 15
AGE AND MARITAL STATUS OF FEMALE WORKERS AT LAMATEX

Age	Total workers (%)	Never married (%)	Ever married (%)
18–19	10	30	70
20–24	20	50	50
25–40	70	0	100

that a sense of loyalty outweighed the costs of paying maternity benefits and of risking worker absenteeism caused by children's illnesses. As discussed in the last chapter, most firms sought to cut costs by not paying reproduction costs such as maternity benefits, nor did any other managers see the importance of loyalty or commitment from their unskilled and semiskilled work force.[1]

LABOR LAWS AND LABOR PRACTICE

Permanent daily workers were divided into two groups: production workers and maintenance workers. Most production workers were female, and their daily salaries were 850 to 910 rupiah. They were entitled to benefits such as paid pregnancy and menstruation leave. Of the male permanent daily workers, those who were production workers usually received the same salary as females unless they worked in areas requiring more training. Most males in this category worked in maintenance, receiving 910 to 1,100 rupiah daily. One more highly paid area of production was the dyeing section, which was staffed mostly by males. The general manager had tried to encourage some female workers to train in dyeing, but they refused. Permanent monthly workers, supervisors, and office workers, most of whom were male, received an average salary of 24,000 rupiah monthly, about 4,000 rupiah more than production workers.

Unlike the other factories in the site, LamaTex paid above the legal minimum wage and offered menstruation leave and maternity benefits. These payments were not insignificant since most of the work force consisted of married females.

SAFETY, HEALTH, AND ILLNESS

Although government-issued safety posters were mounted on many walls in the factory, not all regulations were followed in factory production. Workers were provided with caps and nose and mouth covers. Yet safety glasses, also required by law, were not provided, nor did workers buy their own. Most accidents involved loose hair or long sleeves. Management enforced the use of nose and mouth covers and caps more strictly after one worker lost her hair in the machinery.

Accidents have occurred in the factory, often catalyzing some form of worker protest as an expression of fear and anxiety. Some workers told us that every forty days—a significant period in Javanese rituals commemorating the dead—a person died of blood cancer in the dyeing section.[2] Actually, although one worker died from cancer and another worker died from burns after accidentally and prematurely opening a dyeing vat full of boiling water, subsequent deaths did not occur in the same section. In any case, these accidents stirred up strong emotional reactions—mostly fear—which then affected production.

This factory did provide transportation for female workers who had to travel at night. Workers who finished at 10:00 P.M. were taken to their villages, and those starting work at 10:00 P.M. were picked up. Factory vans picked up and dropped off workers at the entrance to their village.

A clinic within the factory was staffed by a nurse for eight hours daily and a doctor twice a week. The records for March to August 1982 showed a total of 3,600 visits during those six months, averaging 600 visits per month for a work force of 950 people. The nurse explained that influenza and conjunctivitis were common health problems, in part because they spread quickly. Anemia, influenza, lung problems, peptic ulcers, digestion problems, kidney disorders, muscle aches, and diarrhea were the most prevalent diagnoses. Anemia was diagnosed in 17 percent of the cases; 18 percent had influenza; 10 percent had respiratory problems; 5 percent had muscle problems; and 7 percent suffered intestinal problems such as diarrhea and amoebic dysentery. There were minor occurrences of other illnesses, such as tuberculosis, scabies, parasites, ear problems, hypertension, and skin infections. Eye infections accounted for only 4 percent of the cases reported. Given the noise and air pollution on the production floor, it seems likely that hearing, respiratory, and eye problems were underdiagnosed and underreported.

As mentioned in the previous chapter, state bureaucrats from the Department of Labor and Industry sought their revenge on LamaTex for refusing to offer bribes and were arguing that LamaTex was not obeying the law. They argued—and one state official told me himself, with great anger and gusto—that LamaTex was breaking the law and should be providing door-to-door transportation for female workers. When I asked this same official about the other factory operating on three shifts—a factory that did not provide any night transportation at all but did pay off state officials—he told me that they obeyed the law and drove female workers home. State inspectors, however, did nothing about one blatant transgression of labor regulations in the factory—not providing workers with safety glasses. Despite the unhealthy, sometimes unsafe, and generally difficult conditions of production in this spinning mill, compared with other factories in the site, LamaTex seemed like an oasis of responsibility in terms of adhering to labor regulations. At the same time, these minimal regulations barely cover the basics, leaving workers poorly paid and overexposed to danger and illness.

ON THE FACTORY FLOOR

Workers are supposed to enter the factory grounds from twenty to thirty minutes before their shift begins. They must pass the security post, pick up their time cards, and then enter the factory and wait on benches until their shift begins. The production floor is extremely noisy, with a high fiber content in the air. I found it difficult to conduct research for long periods without earaches and eye irritations. I wore the same nose and mouth masks that the workers wore, but glasses, required by law, were not available.

As the shift starts, the shift leader takes the roll and any letters of absence from workers. These may be excuses from coworkers who could not come to work or letters from parents or doctors explaining why a worker was previously absent. The shift leader records production numbers from all machines in the log at the beginning of the shift. More absences occur on the night shift than on the two other shifts, with the most absenteeism occurring on Saturday nights and holidays. Whenever a certain minimum number of workers are not present, the shift leader sends a message or goes to the dormitory to recruit more workers.

Approximately two hours into the shift, workers begin to rotate their half-hour rest periods. They are given different-colored passes (pieces of wood) depending on whether they leave the production floor to go to the lavatory, the clinic, the prayer room, or the canteen for their break. The system is similar to that used in elementary schools in the United States. The canteen is a sparse room with long tables and benches where workers socialize, eat, and sometimes sleep. Canteen graffiti warns, "Beware, there are ghosts!" (*Awas, ada hantu!*)

During the two daytime shifts, workers often stroll outside the factory grounds to buy snacks such as drinks, ices, soup, and rice from vendors. By the time the night shift starts, all food stalls are closed. According to labor regulations, coffee should be served to workers during the night shift, but they are served only tea.

Approximately one-half hour before the shift is over, workers begin to slow down production; they take the cotton fibers out of their hair and off their clothes, apply make-up, and prepare to leave. Since the sounds of the machines are deafening, red lights flash to indicate that the shift is over. Outside the factory walls, a siren is activated.

About once a month, workers are required to attend an after-work training session, for which they are paid. I observed one meeting attended by fifty workers that lasted for forty-five minutes. The following matters were discussed by the shift leader:

1. Workers were illegally extending their half-hour rest time.
2. Machines were left alone for too long on bathroom or prayer breaks. Workers were allowed to leave only one by one and were exhorted to be more considerate of their friends who were left covering their machines.
3. Work tools were disappearing because workers took them home, lost them, or forgot them.
4. Workers needed to give one week's notice if they wanted time off.
5. Marital leave (*cuti kawin*) was allowed only once, and a letter from the village leader was necessary to confirm the marriage. At least one week's notice was needed.

Workers then asked questions about reimbursements for medical costs, which were given annually. The supervisor lectured briefly on increasing accuracy and efficiency. They were offered two crackers each and tea, but only five glasses were provided for the fifty workers.

MANAGEMENT AND LABOR RELATIONS

There are at least three different labor-management relationships to analyze in this factory. First, there is an important relationship between higher and lower levels of power and authority in management. This stratification between higher and lower levels of management corresponds to ethnic differences since upper-level managers are Indian and middle-level managers are Indonesian. The second relationship of interest is between Indonesian managers and Indonesian workers, and the third is between Indian managers and Indonesian workers.

The relationship between the Indian and Indonesian managers had deteriorated over time to the point of animosity. The Indian managers, particularly the general manager, were frustrated by the Indonesian managers. The general manager felt that they were "too soft," that they "couldn't control subordinates," and that they "were not capable of maintaining discipline." He mentioned that Indonesian managers were afraid of being beaten up by male workers they reprimanded. Indeed, such a beating had actually occurred once. "They are afraid of being called a stooge of the Indians." Although the Indian managers promised "full protection and security," the Indonesian managers had still not taken on a more assertive role, much to the dismay of the Indian managers.

According to Indian managers, another major and related problem was that the Indonesian managers would not make decisions or "take a responsible role. They want power but not the responsibility." The general manager complained that Indonesian managers wouldn't work overtime, wouldn't speak up, and wouldn't make "useful, practical suggestions." At a meeting called to discuss this issue, the Indian management directly asked the Indonesian managers what the problems were for them: "We asked them, what can we [Indians] do? There was no response; they [the Indonesians] said, 'We don't know our roles or authority.' " The general manager felt that the Indonesians were given room and even encouraged at meetings to make suggestions, "but if anything comes out, they are usually ridiculous suggestions which don't consider the company." He foresaw a problem in the future when by law the Indonesians would take over the firm: "They don't perceive of themselves as managers."

The general manager told me that one afternoon, an office worker was asked to send a telegram at 4:45 P.M. and refused because it was time to go home. The worker was almost fired but then apologized. "In India," the general manager explained, "one would feel grateful and would obey the boss. The boss would develop the bright ones so that they would succeed. Here, there is little initiative."

The responses of Indonesian management reflected these tensions. The Indonesian managers were not fond of their supervisors, the Indian managers. One manager had worked for Chinese, Japanese, and now Indians. He did not like working with Indians because he felt that there was "no planning." Complaints voiced from Indonesian managers centered on not feeling any common bond with most (not all) of the Indians and on resenting their cliquishness. A few embittered managers were open about these problems, but others, perhaps concerned with endangering their positions, were more evasive. One manager found the Indians' style of management difficult, as it coupled abrupt changes in plans with demands for expediency.

One decision-making process demonstrated an underlying double message from the Indian to the Indonesian managers. An Indonesian manager was asked by the surrounding village for access to the factory's water supply during a particularly long dry season. He agreed, meaning that he took the responsibility for making a decision, but he was then castigated by the general manager, who said that "only the highest can decide that." The Indonesian manager was angry because of the mixed message from Indian management; he had been told to be assertive and take responsibility, but then he was reprimanded for doing just that. This particular person was from Sumatra and more expressive of his discontent than the Javanese managers were.

Much of this conflict can be explained by two factors. First, it appears that Indonesian managers in general lack sufficient background and training in management techniques, a problem noted by those studying foreign investments in Indonesia (Clapham 1970). The second problem is based in cultural differences. Indian-style management includes certain forms of social interaction—raised voices, arguing, directness—considered unacceptable or simply rude in Javanese social relations. The Javanese are less assertive, direct, and competitive than Indian nationals are. Conflict results when Indian managers expect the Javanese managers to be like them.

Workers' attitudes toward the Indian managers were benign because there was little contact. A few office workers talked about their preferences for a particular manager because he did not openly express anger. The way in which Indian managers openly and loudly expressed their feelings contradicted Javanese norms of behavior. Workers also expressed little discontent with the Indonesian managers, except for the personnel manager, a Chinese Indonesian. Again, this attitude reveals deep bitterness over ethnic differences. Workers openly stated that this personnel manager was corrupt; they delighted in telling stories about her corruption, her extramarital liaisons, and her sordid business practices. She was truly and thoroughly disliked. In turn, she harbored no fondness for her Javanese work force. Her talks with me were sprinkled with expressions of distaste for and distrust of her workers and her Indian superior as well.

The Indian managers were well aware of the personnel manager's corruption but felt helpless because she was the link between the firm and the government bureaucracy. The Indian nationals in particular depended on her for help with immigration officers. She had formerly worked for Chinese Indonesians in the textile factory in the same district and was therefore accustomed to a more closed, tightly organized style of management. Her reaction toward the firm was that the Indians were too open with the workers about problems and procedures.

I asked two managers to compare LamaTex with their previous experience in other firms. The personnel manager felt that requirements for workers were stricter, salaries similar, turnover lower, absenteeism the same, accuracy in production better, and benefits worse at LamaTex. It must be noted, however, that she was complaining about her own benefits as a manager and may not have responded to the question of benefits from the workers' perspective. The general manager, comparing this firm with his experience in Indian factories, stated that requirements for workers were similar, salaries lower, turnover higher, absenteeism lower, accuracy in production lower, and benefits fewer. His and other foreign managers' responses about lower wages and fewer benefits in Indonesia correspond with international research findings concerning low wages in Indonesia. In addition, foreign managers also found productivity, efficiency, and accuracy levels lower.

MY SEMINAR TO MANAGEMENT

After completing my case study, I gave a talk to the Indian managers under the general rubric of improving worker-management relations, an area the Indian managers constantly stressed. Although they took some of my suggestions seriously, particularly with regard to the Indonesian production workers, their relationship to the Indonesian middle managers was under stress and they were less receptive to the changes suggested.

I reported on such issues as the workers' dislike of the personnel manager, their objections to leveling the annual bonus, their request for coffee during the night shift, and their fears of the factory going bankrupt. I discussed health problems and encouraged the managers, because of the prevalence of anemia among workers, to administer iron supplements. I also suggested that they hire a consultant from a business institute in Jakarta to study their firm, suggest changes, and hold in-house training for the Indonesian managers.

I spent a great deal of time discussing and explaining aspects of Javanese culture that directly concern interactions at work. For example, I explained that office workers found the Indian managers rude because they rarely said "Good morning" or "Good afternoon," something easy to rectify. I also explained that raised voices and shouting are unacceptable in Javanese culture and suggested that the Indian managers quell their urge to shout when speaking with Indonesians.

The general manager in particular seemed satisfied with my observations, as did most of the others, but some of my suggestions sparked noisy disagreements among the managers. They were concerned about worker morale (particularly worries about bankruptcy), and they agreed that the Lebaran bonus should offer incentives and rewards, particularly for those who had worked for many years. They discussed and argued over problems in motivating the Indonesian managers, but they seemed reluctant to take my suggestion about seeking outside help. Despite their internal disagreements, the general manager seemed to find my observations and at least some of my suggestions helpful.

LABOR PROTESTS

There was a union in the LamaTex factory, and the workers' representative was chosen by the workers, although not many voted. The union was not very active beyond organizing sports activities, but there was considerable labor activity in this factory that was not instigated or facilitated by the union. Despite union inactivity, labor in this factory was more organized and active than it was at other factories in the area.

LamaTex had a lively history of walkouts and verbal protests in reaction to several policy changes; there had also been some fainting spells and ghost visions in response to unsafe working conditions. What was unusual about this factory is that both workers and the Indian managers recounted this history to me, and managers seemed to view it as quite normal. In other factories, managers usually denied labor protests and problems in their interviews with me. The LamaTex case is interesting because the founder of the mother company worked on organizing unions in India, yet his successors sought to invest in a country without much labor activity. Despite their desire for a quiet labor force, the Indian managers seemed to accept labor protests as normal, as though they would have expected them from Indian workers at home.

One policy change that had stirred up labor protest was the leveling of the annual Lebaran bonus—at the holiday after the fasting month of Ramadan—so that older and newer workers received the same amount. Eventually, the policy was reversed, and bonuses reflected seniority. When the factory started to pay for maternity leave, some female workers who had previously taken an unpaid maternity leave protested. They did not, however, receive compensation retroactively, and the issue was dropped. Another policy change occurred when management decided to dock the wages of dormitory workers. When the dormitory residents protested, management rescinded the practice.

LamaTex also experienced other culturally based forms of labor activity. Workers generally believed that evil spirits and ghosts roamed the factory. On several occasions, the Indian managers called in local healers (dukuns) to exorcise the spirits and calm down the workers. Managers reported that fainting spells occurred every few weeks, and depending on the situation—whether one worker or a group of workers fainted—a dukun was called in. Workers reacted with anxiety and fear to accidents that occurred in the factory, one of which had resulted in death. The incidences of seeing ghosts or fainting increased after such accidents. Mass hysteria like that reported in Malaysian factories (Grossman 1979; Ong 1987) had not occurred here.

The generally higher level of labor activity in LamaTex can be attributed to two factors. One is the style of Indian management, which is more open with workers than Chinese management is. Although the Indian managers constantly stressed that they were interested in improving labor-management relations, this interest is double-edged, as exemplified by the Indians' behavior toward Indonesian managers. Their reactions toward their Indonesian workers were less ambivalent, and they were willing to listen to workers' complaints and to reverse policy decisions, which then encouraged workers to speak up about their grievances. The tighter control of the work force in other factories actively discouraged such activity.

The higher educational level required of workers in this factory, in addition to the training they received, created a higher level of consciousness about the work situation as compared with that in other factories; this circumstance also contributed to the level of labor activity. For example, although workers everywhere discuss corruption, I overheard two workers at LamaTex discussing the difference between accuracy and productivity, a conversation workers in Nuwun could not and would not have been able to have. During my first visit to the dorm, I was surprised by the statement of one dorm dweller: "Wow, far out (*assik*), in America you have capitalism, but in Indonesia we have a protected economy." This comment demonstrated an unusually high level of education. In general, the higher education of workers created a greater awareness about labor issues and labor activity, both of which were encouraged by management's willingness to change certain decisions or practices.

LIFE IN THE COMPLEX

THE INDIAN SIDE

Within the factory complex, a life is created that differs vastly from the one outside its gates. The enclave is divided by functions and by ethnicity, with the factory as its central focus. Javanese workers live in a dormitory at one end of the enclave of ten hectares, while the Indian managers and their families live in a section at the other end of the grounds, in seven two-story flats. Tennis courts and a clubhouse separate the Indian managers from the much smaller apartments provided for Indonesian managers and their families. The Indonesian managers are situated between the Indonesian workers' dormitory on one end of the complex and the Indian managers' apartments on the other, replicating in living space the hierarchy within the firm.

The life-style of the Indian managers is one of privilege and luxury. Each of their two-story flats has a large living room, dining room, and one or two bedrooms, decorated with identical imitation-leather couches and chairs. The women's world is limited to the tiny complex of apartments, the clubhouse (which contains a table tennis set, a card table, a small library, and current newspapers), and a few markets. During the day, when the men are at work, their wives visit each other and spend their time sewing, cooking, and improving their domestic skills (for example, cake decorating). The wives cook all their meals, even though all of them hire Indonesian servants to do the cleaning and the laundry. Twice a week the wives are driven in a van to do their food shopping—once to the nearby district town, and once to Semarang, to the large fruit and vegetable market and the more modern supermarket. In the late afternoon, the women might stroll together, but they walk only in front of the apartments and never venture beyond. None of these women, incidentally, has ever been in the factory.

In the afternoon, when the men come home from work, younger couples often play tennis. In the evening, several couples typically play cards or watch television together. All their televisions are hooked into a video player owned by one of the managers, and about twice a week they watch a Hindi or English film.

The Indian managers and their families are as distant as possible from Indonesians of all ranks. All children of school age are sent to India to live with grandparents. The managers and their wives never attempt to learn anything about Indonesia. Several of the couples bragged that they had never eaten in an Indonesian restaurant—partly because of their vegetarian regime and partly because of their fear of contracting diseases. Indeed, the Indian wives did not want their Indonesian servants to cook for them. That the Indian women did not even attempt to teach some Indian cooking to their servants is a strong statement of their distrust.

There is equally little interest in Indonesians: the general attitude expressed toward them was condescending and distrustful. There is little attempt to understand and adapt to Indonesian cultural forms of social relations. On one occasion, several managers and their wives questioned me about the sanitary habits of villagers as though they were animals in a zoo—Did they really wash and when?—expressing the view that Indonesians were primitive and unclean compared with Indian villagers in India. In short, the attitude toward Indonesians is one of anything but respect.

Even though the Indian nationals made little effort to socialize with the Indonesian managers and their wives, there was a formal attempt to improve social relations between the two groups by having a joint dinner every two months at the clubhouse. This social gathering formerly had occurred every month, and it showed signs of being stopped altogether.

People gathered at the clubhouse by 8:00 P.M. The Indian women sat in a line on one side, and the Indonesian women sat in two rows to the right, perpendicular to the Indian women. The Indian men sat in three rows to the left, perpendicular to the Indian women, and the Indonesian men sat in three rows next to the Indian men. The two groups of men were separated by an aisle. Thus, seating was voluntarily divided by gender and ethnicity at a gathering meant to be a "mixer."

Everyone played bingo, for which there were four prizes, after which Indian hors d'oeuvres were brought out. Two tables were set up with food—Indonesian food with plenty of meat on one, and vegetarian Indian food on the other. Few people crossed over and sampled food from the other ethnic group. After dinner, ice cream and fruit were served, and people went home. The Indonesian staff felt that these meetings were useless: "What are they for? What is there to talk about?"

Both groups felt that although they had made an effort to be friendly, there was no response. Some of these problems were culturally based since the Indians expected the Indonesians to reciprocate dinner invitations. Although dinner parties are not part of Indonesian culture, the lack of reciprocation was interpreted by the Indians as rude, ungrateful behavior. Another example given by the wives of Indonesian managers was that although they were invited by the Indian wives to join them on their shopping excursions, the Indonesians were relegated to the front seat with the driver and never spoken to by the Indian women. Feeling insulted, they stopped joining these excursions.

Given the peculiar nature of life and work in such a compound, social relationships took on a greater intensity. There is no escape for the Indonesian managers living in the complex. These tensions both reflect and intensify working relationships in the factory. And the relationships in the workplace are naturally of much greater concern to management than dinner parties are.

THE WORKERS' DORMITORY

The dormitory, a small white stucco structure surrounded by barbed wire, was a short walking distance from the factory. It had a rectangular shape with a small courtyard in the middle with a badminton net. There were thirteen rooms for workers and three rooms for staff. Each room for workers was the same. There were four bunk beds with mattresses and pillows, a small cupboard with a lock for each inhabitant, and a table with a few chairs. Each room had one large window, which looked either onto the grass courtyard or onto the enclave. Curtains were provided, and many workers had purchased plastic wardrobes for clothes.

The dorm at LamaTex had electricity and abundant lighting, a large recreation room with a large color television, living room chairs, and tables. In addition, there was a meeting and dining room with many chairs and tables, a table tennis set, and a sewing machine; workers usually ate in their rooms, however. The kitchen had four gas burners and a sink with running water. Large pots, pans, and woks were provided. Next to the kitchen was a large room with sinks where workers could wash their hands and faces, spigots for washing dishes, an ironing board, and an iron. This room led to the bathrooms and toilets. The staff (those in charge of the dormitory) had access to one particular toilet and bathroom that were kept locked to "protect" them from workers' use. A full-time maintenance man was in charge of the dormitory so that it always appeared clean and well maintained. According to workers, a ghost resided in one of the dorm rooms: several residents reported seeing a white dog and an old bearded man walking around.

Conditions in the dorm of the other textile factory in the site were completely different and, acting on management's orders, the dorm manager asked me to leave after a quick visit. The other dormitory resembled a scene from volume 1 of Marx's *Capital*. Each room housed between nine and twelve workers, who shared two to three large wooden platform beds without mattresses. This overcrowding forced the workers to sleep in shifts. Workers provided their own kerosene burners and cooked in the rooms. Water was available from a well. Sanitation was poor and the dorm dirty. Compared to such conditions, the electricity, running water, and kitchen at the LamaTex dorm seemed extraordinary.

When I show slides of the kitchen at LamaTex—four burners for almost sixty people, with white walls blackened by the gas fires from the burners—I am reminded of a *New York Times* article on a slum apartment in Harlem. I am also reminded of how luxurious the dormitory seemed after months of living without such amenities. I felt as though I was in a hotel; I found that my sleep was untroubled by rain or rats, that writing notes went more quickly under electric lights, and that I could finally cook something because of the gas burners.

There were fifty-eight residents in the LamaTex dorm during my stay, although the capacity was more than one hundred. Workers who request to live in the dorm are reviewed by the personnel manager. Only those considered diligent (*rajin*) are accepted. Dorm residents receive free rent and are given two packages of tea and one kilogram of sugar free each month.

This rent-free situation has its costs. First and most important, the purpose of the dormitory is to provide a reserve labor force when there are too many absences during a shift. Dorm residents have to be available to work overtime, including Saturday nights and holidays, the times when most absences occur. Filling in sometimes means working sixteen hours straight. Second, the residents' movements and social life are more restricted than are those of the migrants who rent rooms from villagers. Dorm residents are not allowed to have any visitors in the dorm itself. Any visitor—parent, other relative, or suitor—is required to meet with the residents in the guard's post. No relatives or friends may stay overnight. In addition, time restrictions are imposed on evening excursions with a curfew of 9:00 P.M. to prevent "immoral behavior." At the entrance to the dorm stand a blackboard for announcements and a table on which there is a logbook. Workers are supposed to sign out and in if they take off for part of a day or for vacation; this system does not, however, seem to be enforced.

LamaTex usually hires a "dorm mother," but at the time of my research no one had been hired since the last woman quit. Instead, a young shift leader was designated dormitory supervisor. The twenty-three-year-old shift leader had graduated from a high school specializing in economics and had been hired directly from school to a supervisory position. There was considerable tension between the dorm residents (workers) and the dorm supervisor (shift leader) based on the supervisor's distant and sometimes harsh behavior. There were clearly educational power differences between the supervisor and the other dorm residents, most of whom were production workers. However, rather than cultivate the friendships of those in the dormitory, the supervisor was fairly cold and distant to most, which was interpreted as snobbishness and arrogance (*sombong*). She socialized only with those few in the dorm from a similar educational background. She also wielded her power rather harshly. Dorm dwellers were not indirect when describing their intense dislike for her.

The dormitory supervisor, who was also a shift leader, was told by other shift leaders during every shift how many workers they needed in their section. It was then her responsibility to choose the dormitory residents who were to fill in for absences. One Saturday night after roll was taken in the factory for the ten o'clock shift, she came into the television room in the dormitory at about 10:15 P.M. and abruptly chose about six women, ordering them to go to work. Some of these workers had just returned from an eight-hour shift; others were scheduled to work the morning shift at 6:00 A.M. and would also have a sixteen-hour workday. Clearly, the workers had little bargaining power in such a situation, since the principal requirement for living in the dorm is to be available for overtime when needed. Nonetheless, the supervisor's unfriendly manner did not help.

Although dorm residents were terribly exhausted from working extra shifts, they felt that living in the dorm allowed them to save more money, and to do so while enjoying certain amenities—a large color television, sewing machines, and table tennis and volleyball equipment. Such luxuries are rare in the villages of Central Java. I visited one dorm resident in her home in a village in Wonosobo. The difference between the two conditions was striking, as her landless family lived in a small house with a dirt floor. Most dorm residents did not have electricity, running water, a television, or a sewing machine at home.

The atmosphere of the dormitory was like that of a college dormitory full of freshmen in the United States. It was very unlike any other Javanese environment I had observed. The residents were young, friendly, and affectionate with each other, often gossiping and giggling. Usually several roommates with similar shifts cooked cooperatively. Loud pop music was often playing, and during television programs such as "Trapper John, M.D." or "CHiPs" the women engaged in considerable sexual joking about which of the stars was most handsome and which women loved which television stars. Once a week I tried to interpret what was happening on "Laverne and Shirley," explaining that the show's 1950s setting did not reflect contemporary life in the United States.

The manner of dress that the residents adopted was perhaps their most striking characteristic. Most wore gold earrings and either gold rings or gold necklaces and pendants, which constituted their savings. Many wore long pants, and some even walked around the dorm in shorts. In Nuwun at that time, females wearing long pants symbolized Western style; it was a statement about being different, and the religious elite objected to it. A female wearing shorts seemed far more radical, and her behavior would not have been tolerated in the village or even in most urban households, where it would have been interpreted as suggestive of immorality and sexual promiscuity. Here, however, the young dorm supervisor (a shift leader) wore shorts herself.[3]

CONCLUSION

This case study of one spinning mill represented an unusual opportunity to observe Indonesian factory work and life without restrictions in a somewhat atypical factory. Upper-level management at LamaTex consisted of well-educated Indian nationals who had somewhat more progressive views of capitalism and worker-manager relationships than did managers at other firms. At the same time, LamaTex's progressiveness had definite limits: working conditions were still dangerous, and the managers basically distrusted their host population. Gender, class, and ethnic differences between Indonesian workers, Indian managers, and Indonesian middle managers created a system of stratification and frequent tension, conditions similar to those found by Kathryn Robinson in her study (1988) of INCO, another multinational firm in Indonesia.

As Chris Manning (1979) notes in his work on Indonesian firms, conditions in multinational corporations are often better than those in domestically owned firms. Management at LamaTex upheld most (but not all) labor laws, and their particular style of management gave labor more opportunity to organize. Although workers were undoubtedly better off in this firm than were workers in other firms in the area, in part because of more adherence to labor regulations, it is important to understand that such regulations only minimally protect workers and do not guarantee them a subsistence-level wage.

CHAPTER VII

Determinants of Factory Employment

In Java, as in other Third World settings, most industrialists prefer young, single females as workers. However, the demand for labor represents only part of the initial employment equation, since it is equally true that most young Third World women do *not* work in factories. In this rural site, a minority of young Javanese women were factory workers, and women from the very poorest households, those who needed the income the most, were not working in factories. In this chapter, I analyze factors complementary to the demand for labor—those affecting the supply of labor. In other words, who is and is not working in the factories?[1]

In this chapter, I examine quantified individual and household-level characteristics that shape and affect an individual's decision—or the ability to entertain the decision—to seek factory employment, following Carmen Diana Deere and Alain de Janvry's contemporary Marxist framework for the empirical analysis of peasant households (1979). The quantitative data on internal household characteristics might lead to the interpretation that factory employment is part of a strategy that provides the household with diverse sources of income. This argument falters, however, when we examine the qualitative data, in which daughters and parents recount how the decision to gain factory employment was actually made. Although factory employment does offer another source of income, the qualitative data demonstrate that more complex family dynamics are involved in a daughter's decision to seek factory employment than is suggested by the quantitative data.

This chapter, then, provides an excellent example of how different methodologies and the resultant data can produce very different perspectives on "household strategies." It also demonstrates that "the household" does not allocate labor, but that individuals in the household make decisions about labor that others may respect or contest. In this case, labor allocation is a decision involving more conflictual dynamics than is suggested by the quantitative household data or the model guiding the quantitative analysis.

THE ECONOMIC DEMOGRAPHY OF FACTORY WORKERS AND THEIR HOUSEHOLDS

Deere and de Janvry's (1979) framework incorporates a Marxist approach to the analysis of peasant households as they are integrated into the wider capitalist system. Their framework specifies both intra- and interhousehold factors such as the internal organization of the household, class differentiation, and household interrelationships to identify which households are likely to be integrated into the wider economy. I used this model to analyze both inter- and intrahousehold factors that might determine which households are likely to be connected with the industrial capitalist sector through the factory labor of young women and how these households or women differ from others in the village.

According to Deere and de Janvry's model, the household's need to seek nonagricultural sources of income varies inversely with the household's class position, as measured by control over the means of production—agricultural land. Rural landless and near-landless households are expected to be more integrated with the labor market than are households that can attain—or are close to attaining—self-sufficiency in their subsistence agricultural production. As demonstrated with the examples of households in chapter 4, poorer households engage in more economic activities, usually nonagricultural and particularly those in which they sell their labor. In this Javanese case, I expected that young women seeking factory employment would come from poorer households. Class status alone, however, does not sufficiently explain employment trajectories. If it did, all poor women would seek factory employment, but in this area, only a minority of women work in factories.

Deere and de Janvry's framework also stipulates that the internal make-up of the household interacts with class status to affect both the division of labor within the household and the type and number of activities in which a household engages. The allocation of labor within households varies over the family life cycle as internal needs change and as children age (1979, 604).[2] For example, poorer households have a greater need for members to engage in wage labor, yet having one or more young children may prevent productive members from seeking certain types of wage labor if childcare is not available. Thus, parents in a poor, young household with many dependents may be in dire need of income but are less able to engage in income-earning activities. Although I expected an inverse relationship between class status and factory employment, I also expected that family life-cycle status would intervene and modify this relationship, affecting the ability of a poor, young woman to work in a factory. The quantitative data will guide us through these household characteristics and constraints that young women confront at the household level, and the qualitative data will demonstrate how they cope with, adapt to, or resist such constraints.

SETTING AND SAMPLE

I studied two agricultural villages—Nuwun and Rumiyen—and interviewed all women between the ages of fourteen and twenty-five to compare factory workers and young women who have not worked in factories.[3] In the analysis, I compare individual and household-level characteristics of all current factory workers ($n = 39$) and all women between the ages of fourteen and twenty-five who had never worked in a factory ($n = 90$).[4] The analysis begins with individual characteristics of the women studied and then moves to their households' economic demography. Finally, both the individual and household-level characteristics are combined.

INDIVIDUAL CHARACTERISTICS

When I first started my research in Nuwun, factory workers seemed to be much more articulate and outgoing than were the young village women who did not work in factories. The workers' ease and desire to express themselves in Indonesian (rather than Javanese) led me to believe that they were more sophisticated and better educated than their peers. They dressed in skirts, blouses, and dresses rather than traditional Javanese clothing such as the *kebaya* and *sarong*. Their closest friendships were with each other rather than with village women engaged in more traditional activities. Their more outgoing manners and more Western style of dress—including make-up—set them apart from other village females. They were much more at ease with strangers, even foreigners,

TABLE 16
SOCIAL INDICATORS OF FACTORY AND NONFACTORY VILLAGE FEMALES IN NUWUN

	Factory workers	Nonfactory females
N	39	90
Average age	18.7	21
Average years of schooling	3.5	4.1
Percentage completed grammar school (6 years)	15.4	22.2
Percentage currently married	38.5	72.2
Percentage with children	15.4	67.8
Average number of children	.28	1.5

than were their peers who were not working in the factories. However, the data suggest that their outgoing behavior reflected more of the effects of factory employment rather than the cause.

Indeed, at the time of my initial research, current factory workers in general were younger, more likely to be single, and slightly *less* well educated than were nonfactory females (table 16).[5] Although average years of schooling were similarly low in both groups, a higher percentage of current workers had dropped out of grammar school, while six nonfactory females were still in middle or upper school. The most important difference is that a high proportion of nonfactory females were wives and mothers, whereas factory workers were unmarried daughters, or wives but rarely mothers, corresponding with what we know about the labor force in other parts of Southeast Asia (Mather 1982; Ong 1987). Married women and mothers were working in the factories, but not all young single females had sought factory employment.

WORKERS AND THEIR FAMILIES

I measured the internal demography and economy of households in several ways to determine the position of factory workers and nonfactory females within their households (table 17). Life-cycle differences are reflected here in that current workers were more likely to be unmarried daughters within their parents' households, whereas a significant proportion of nonfactory women were wives who comanaged the household

TABLE 17
RELATIONSHIP OF RESPONDENT TO HEAD OF HOUSEHOLD (PERCENTAGE IN EACH CATEGORY)

	Factory workers	Nonfactory females
Head of household	2.6	—
Wife and cohead of household	7.6	38.9
Daughter	71.8	45.6
Daughter-in-law	7.6	8.9
Grandchild	2.6	4.4
Younger sibling	2.6	—
Adopted child	2.6	1.1
Sister-in-law	2.6	—
Niece	—	1.1
	100.0	100.0

with their husbands. Still, in both categories some married women still lived with parents or parents-in-law. Thus, the female life-cycle variables (table 16), such as marriage and motherhood, affect women's positions in their current households.

A young woman's position in her family relative to other able-bodied female members proved important in hampering or facilitating her ability to work in a factory (table 18).[6] *Able-bodied* is defined as one who can still produce and contribute to the household; it excludes any household members who are ill, too old, or handicapped. The respondent's position in the age hierarchy of able-bodied females in her current household indicated important differences between the two groups that to some extent mirrored the life-cycle differences seen earlier. Most current workers were either the second or third able-bodied female in the family, whereas almost one-third of the nonfactory females were the oldest females in their household and thus coheads of household. Slightly more than half of the nonfactory females were the second females in their families; some of these were unmarried daughters.

Current workers' households had more able-bodied females than did the households of nonfactory females (table 18), facilitating the daily departure of one female to the factory. Seventy percent of nonfactory females' families and 90 percent of current workers' families had at least one other able-bodied female in the household. Almost half of current

TABLE 18
HOUSEHOLD CHARACTERISTICS

	Factory workers	Nonfactory females
Respondent's order among females in the family, from oldest to youngest:		
First (oldest)	11.8%	32.2%
Second	58.8	54.4
Third	27.5	10.0
Number of other able-bodied females in the family:		
0	10.3	30.0
1	43.6	45.6
2	43.6	16.7
3	2.6	7.8
Average number of able-bodied females in the family:	1.39	1.02

workers' households and about one-fourth of nonfactory households had at least two other able-bodied females. Again, this characteristic to some extent reflects family life-cycle stage in that current workers are often daughters in families at a later stage of the family life cycle, while more nonfactory women cohead their own households and are in families at an early state of the life cycle. Many of the unmarried nonfactory workers were eldest daughters and thus were responsible for childcare and other household duties. Their families still had young children to care for and required their help.

To summarize, workers are most often unmarried and married daughters living at home; most important, they are usually childless. A higher proportion of nonfactory women were already mothers, with some living in their own nuclear family households and some still living at home with parents.

FAMILY STRUCTURE AND COMPOSITION

The most obvious measures of family structure and form show that the morphology of factory and nonfactory workers' households was similar. Average household size was similar—5.6 and 5.9 for factory workers' and nonfactory families, respectively. Household age span, another measure of life-cycle differences, also was similar—43 years and 40.5 years for current workers' and nonfactory females' households, respectively. Finally, family structure differed little: in both groups, approximately 53 percent were nuclear families and 38 percent extended, with a small number of joint families.[7]

I measured the internal structure of households in two ways to reveal certain internal dynamics (table 19). The *dependency ratio* is typically used by demographers and sociologists, while the *consumer-worker ratio* is more useful for household economists.[8] These measures both indicate the relationship between daily reproductive needs (biological) and productive capabilities. The average number of dependents, the dependency ratio, and the consumer-worker ratio all indicate a higher level of internal strain within the nonfactory women's households.[9] For example, the average number of adult consumer equivalents was the same for both groups. But the consumer-worker ratios for factory workers and nonfactory females' households differed—1.27 for nonfactory households and 1.08 for factory worker households ($p < .0035$). The proportional breakdown of the consumer-worker ratios demonstrates, for example, that the proportion of current worker households with a consumer-worker ratio less than one was more than double that of nonfactory households. Fifteen percent of the nonfactory females' households, compared with 3 percent of factory workers' households, had a consumer-

TABLE 19
DEPENDENCY AND CONSUMER-WORKER RATIOS

	Factory workers	Nonfactory females
Average household size	5.6	5.9
Average number of dependents	1.9	2.4
Average dependency ratio	.205	.522
Average number of consumers	4.3	4.3
Average consumer-worker ratio	1.08	1.27
Consumer-worker ratio (percentage of households):		
Less than 1	43.5	18.9
Greater than 1	56.5	81.1
Greater than 1.5	2.6	15

worker ratio above 1.5. A higher ratio among nonfactory households typifies an early expansionary stage of the family life cycle when there are more mouths to feed than there are producers; a lower ratio is found among older families with grown children where there is somewhat less strain.

These measures echo the life-cycle differences found earlier: there are more younger children in nonfactory households. The implications for this research are that in such households, there is a greater demand on those who can labor; by contrast, factory workers' households are usually older and less in need of someone to do childcare.

This greater stress on the able-bodied members of nonfactory households appears in the reactions of parents of several thirteen- and fourteen-year-old single nonfactory females from poorer families who expressed a desire to work in a factory. Their families were in an earlier state of the domestic development cycle, and there were young children at home who needed care. In such cases, these young women were typically the oldest daughter or the oldest daughter still at home, and the mother was the only other able-bodied female in the household. Parents did not allow these daughters to work outside the home for long periods because their labor was needed at home or in the fields, in part to aid and release their mother's labor. However, the legal minimum age to work in a factory is fifteen, and that law is respected by all but one factory in the area; thus, these young daughters would have been unlikely to get a factory job even if they had sought one.

Parents of young, single, nonfactory females emphatically stated that their daughters were needed at home. One parent, when asked why her daughter was not allowed to seek factory employment, responded: "Because she's the oldest. If she works in a factory, then there won't be anyone to help in the fields or to help at home. Her siblings are still young. I can't yet expect them to fully help in the fields. Often they are told to help in the *sawah*, but they just play." In this household, the total rice harvest was not sufficient for subsistence needs. When the family needed cash, they sold part of the harvest, and when they needed more rice, they borrowed it from neighbors or sold their vegetables. They simply could not afford to let their daughter work in a factory.

The individual and household data suggest that female and family life-cycle status greatly affects who works in a factory and that the economic strain on younger families may explain why many young single women were not working in factories. Class position, however, also affects who seeks factory employment.

CLASS AND FACTORY EMPLOYMENT

The class status of rural Javanese households is largely determined by control over the most scarce productive resource—land. Following the path of previous rural studies in Java, I measured class by the amount of farmland controlled by the household. As explained in more detail in chapter 4, class 1 (0–0.24 ha.), the poorest and the largest stratum, includes the landless and near-landless households that do not control enough land to meet basic food needs. Households in class 2 (0.25 ha.–0.574 ha.) can meet basic food needs, but not their full income needs, from the land they control. Because households in these two categories cannot meet their full subsistence needs, they can be considered below the poverty line. Households in class 3 (more than 0.575 ha.) can be considered self-sufficient in that they control enough land to meet full subsistence needs.[10]

Factory workers' households were, on the whole, poorer than nonfactory households. Sixty-four percent of factory workers' households, compared with 50 percent of the nonfactory households, were in the poorest group, class 1. Close to 90 percent of factory workers' households, compared with 78 percent of nonfactory households, were in the lower two strata, below the poverty line.

An inverse relationship exists between class status and factory employment (table 20). Holding class constant, the probability of working

TABLE 20
CROSSTABULATION OF CLASS AND FACTORY EMPLOYMENT

	Class[a]			
	1	*2*	*3*	*Total*
Factory workers	36%	27%	20%	30.2%
Nonfactory females	64	73	80	69.8
Total	100%	100%	100%	100%
N	70	35	24	129

$\chi^2 = 2.466$; $p = .2914$

[a] The proportion of factory workers in classes 1, 2, and 3 are 64, 26, and 10 percent (respectively), compared with 50, 28, and 22 percent among nonfactory females.

in a factory declines as class position increases. Several young nonfactory females from the upper strata felt that factory workers weren't "good girls": "If you work in the factory you become a loose woman, joking and talking with the drivers on the road." It is also clear that factory workers are a minority in all strata, even the poorest groups. Only one-third from the poorest stratum worked in factories, compared with slightly more than one-quarter in the middle stratum. Since factory jobs were available, this difference must stem from factors related to the supply of labor, not the demand for it.

The data on class status, land tenure, and occupation (see the Appendix) reinforce the finding that the households of current factory workers were relatively poorer than nonfactory households; however, measures of household composition suggested that there was more strain within the households of the nonfactory workers because of different family life-cycle states. Thus, on the whole, factory workers' households may experience relatively more land poverty, but nonfactory women's households may experience more "labor poverty"—a shortage of able-bodied workers who can relieve some of the household's needs.

Although the data establish that factory workers usually come from the poorest households, the majority of young women from poor households do not work in factories. I now turn to the interactions between the women's life-cycle status—marital status and presence and number of children—and class position to explore this question further.

MARITAL STATUS AND CLASS

There is an inverse relationship between class status and factory employment, but there is also a high proportion of nonfactory females in poor households (see tables 16–20). Although other studies suggest that marriage is the point of labor market transition for factory workers, my data show that motherhood rather than marriage is the decisive factor in a woman's factory employment (table 21).

The strong linear relationship between class and factory employment that holds for single and married childless women does not exist among mothers. Even though most factory workers are single, marital status is much less significant than expected in affecting the decision to work; rather, childbearing, not marriage, keeps women out of the industrial work force. A large number of poor women with children have never sought factory employment because it is impossible to work in a factory without childcare.

TABLE 21
CLASS STATUS, FACTORY EMPLOYMENT, AND CHILDBEARING (ROW PERCENTAGES)

	Number of children					
	Zero			*One or more*		
Class	FW[a]	NF	Total	FW	NF	Total
1	66%	34%	100%	6%	94%	100%
2	46	54	100	14	86	100
3	29	71	100	9	91	100
Total	53%	47%	100%	9%	91%	100%
N	33	29	62	6	61	67
	$\chi^2 = 5.872$; $p = .0531$			$\chi^2 = 1.183$; $p = .5535$		

[a] FW = factory worker; NF = nonfactory female.

Some married women with children—women who had never worked in a factory and former factory workers—wanted to work in a factory but could not because they did not have a female relative in the village who could care for their children. Most of the twelve former factory workers (not included in the bivariate analysis) were married, had children, and had households in the poorest stratum. Many of these women expressed a desire to return to the factory but could not do so because they lacked childcare options. Most now worked in agricultural or household production, which allowed them to combine work with childcare. Once they had children, former factory workers turned to agricultural work and petty trade.

In 1982 only six mothers, most of them in poor households, worked in factories. A brief description of one working mother illustrates the conditions under which she had little choice but to continue factory employment despite its incompatibility with the demands of her young children.

A Working Mother

Mbak Temu was one of my neighbors. Her house had a dirt floor and was sparsely furnished with two wooden chairs; on cold nights the wind edged its way through the woven bamboo of the walls. Temu lived with her husband, children, and elderly aunt. Her husband was an agricultural laborer and a construction worker, and he picked up other jobs when he could. He also worked on the small amount of agricultural land Temu owned. In addition to the seasonality of his work, he was considered unreliable and lazy. Temu's elderly aunt took care of the young daughter, Tini. However, the aunt was feeble; she had trouble walking and could not adequately take care of household chores. When Tini was two years old, Temu gave birth to another daughter. She took two weeks of unpaid leave and then returned to the biscuit factory. With the arrival of the new baby, Tini looked increasingly neglected. She went to a relative's house (the one in which I lived) for breakfast and a bath.

Temu nursed her baby in the morning and when she returned from work. During the day, the baby was given diluted formula in an unsterilized bottle prepared by the aunt; the child drank only one bottle daily, along with a little sweetened tea. She became ill at one time and seemed to be dehydrated, but she recovered. The elderly aunt continued to have trouble walking. Every day she brought the baby to the freshwater source for a bath. She clutched the baby tightly as she hobbled through the village, bracing herself on the outer walls of houses as though she feared slipping and falling.

Temu was forced to return to work early because the factory refused to pay legally mandated maternity benefits. She was also forced to return to the factory because there was little other regular household income: "If *I* don't work, I won't have any money and my children won't eat," she said. If she had had the choice—that is, if her husband had been more reliable—she would have preferred to stay at home. The presence of her aunt allowed Temu to continue factory work; however, the situation was not easy, since Temu worried about her aunt's ability to care for the children. Had her aunt not been available, Temu would have engaged in agricultural wage labor or petty trade with an infant on her back and received lower returns to her labor. Her situation illustrates the limited, difficult choices involved in balancing the needs of a poor and young family with the production activities so desperately needed.

FACTORY EMPLOYMENT AND "HOUSEHOLD STRATEGIES"

Quantitative measures are useful in mapping the boundaries of household constraints, but they tell only a partial story about who seeks employment, under what circumstances, and why. The quantitative data correspond with Deere and de Janvry's suppositions about the interrelationships between class status, the domestic cycle, and factory employment. From the quantitative analysis alone one could conclude that if certain demographic and economic circumstances exist within a household—poverty, few small children, and available female labor—parents encourage or allow daughters to seek factory employment to fortify the family economy. If, by contrast, a poor household has small children, parents may forbid a daughter to seek factory employment, also to fortify the family economy. In both cases, one could conclude that dutiful and sensible daughters in Java are driven by the "family economy ideology": that is, they work toward the collective goal of family survival (Tilly and Scott 1978) even when the family and work are separate and work may be remunerated. In addition, one could argue—and I have argued earlier (Wolf 1984)—that factory employment is a "rational choice" for poor rural families who have few choices, constituting part of a family survival strategy. One may also argue from these data that factory *un*employment is a rational choice and a household strategy for certain households. However, the image of poor parents orchestrating the work life of daughters who put the goal of the collectivity above their own is seriously disturbed when the doors of the household are opened up and its members speak about the decision to work in a factory.

EMPLOYMENT AND FAMILY DECISION MAKING

I asked parents of factory workers in Nuwun a normative question: "In Java, who should decide where an unmarried daughter will work?" Ten out of twenty parents said the child should decide, nine felt that the parents together with the child should decide, and only one parent felt that the parents alone should decide. However, when asked, "Who in your household decided where *your* daughter should work?" all twenty parents responded that their daughter had decided alone, on her own.

Daughters had various ways of balancing parental approval with factory employment. The normatively prescribed path was to ask parental permission (*minta ijin*) first and then apply for a factory position. The more common practice, however, was to apply for a position first, receive a job, and only then ask parental permission. Although most parents agreed, not all consented to their daughter's decision. At that juncture, daughters either went along with or went against their parents' wishes.

Several of the nonfactory single females analyzed in this chapter belong to the group of thirteen- and fourteen-year-old daughters whose parents would not consent to factory employment. They lived in households where there were small children, and they were the oldest daughters living at home. Parents wanted them to stay home so that mothers could engage in other economic activities. These parents forbade their daughters' factory employment, thus controlling their labor activities. This particular group of daughters obeyed until about age fifteen. However, by that age, the legal minimum age for factory employment, those young women who wanted to work in a factory became brave enough to defy their parents' wishes and rebelled. Fourteen-year-old Maryuni, the oldest daughter in a household with two young boys, wanted to work in a factory. Her mother said: "Actually, we won't allow her to work in a factory but she kept pushing it. If she works in a factory, then there won't be anyone to help at home or in the sawah; after all, she's my only daughter."

However, not all were dutiful daughters. Surinah's widowed mother, when asked how her daughter started working in the factory, told this story:

> Actually, I didn't allow her to work in a factory, but she forced it anyway. Her older brother also forbade it. I didn't even know when she went looking for a job; I only found out after she started working. She said she wanted to have her own money. In my opinion, it's better if a daughter works at home, helping in the sawah.

As mentioned in the Preface, Rini started factory work against her father's wishes; his anger subsided after a month. Although Rini was the oldest daughter, her sister, mother, and father then traded off taking care of the youngest son. When Rini's next sister joined the factory work force, their father took over much of the childcare of his young son.

Another worker in Nuwun who had been forbidden by her parents to work in a factory secretly sought work on her own after she turned fifteen—not an atypical story: "I saw my friends work in the factories and then I wanted to work there too. Before, my parents wouldn't allow it. I didn't ask their permission and I started work right away. I went secretly because if my parents had known, they would have gotten angry with me because they had told me to go work in the sawah." Qualitative data from a sample of fifteen migrant workers (not included in the previous quantitative analysis) revealed similar, even more dramatic examples of daughters leaving home against parents' wishes. Yularikah was told by a friend about the jobs at the biscuit factory. She signed up for work and received a job immediately. When asked how her parents felt, she said, "Well, Father and Mother were forced to agree; they didn't have any choice since I decided to take the job." Yukamah told the following story:

> I sought employment at the textile factory and after two weeks I received a call from them to start work. Then I asked my parents for permission because when I had looked for work, I hadn't told them. They forbade it, but I still intended to leave. Finally, I just left, like that, without saying good-bye, and for two months I didn't go home. I took care of myself. Truthfully, I also couldn't stand it, but what could I do! Finally, I felt sorry and I went home. I gave my first monthly wage to my parents. They accepted the money and cried, maybe because they felt sorry for me. Then I told my younger sister she could also get a job in the factory, and now she likes it here.

The quantitative data suggest that a combination of household need and ability decide who works in a factory. The qualitative data suggest that more complex dynamics are occurring and that motives and goals within the household create conflict. Household need affects younger women's actions; in poor households, daughters obey their parents when they forbid factory employment. When those same daughters reach age fifteen or sixteen, they disobey their parents' directives and seek factory employment if they want a factory job.

In other words, daughters in poorer households pushed and strained at the limits of parental tolerance, viewing factory employment as a way to break out, and they sought employment without parental advice, guidance, awareness, or approval. Seeking factory employment—an important personal decision in the household economy—was not necessarily made in conjunction with parental visions of a daughter's role or as part of a household strategy. Many of these parents, rather than steering the household ship, were merely trying to keep it afloat, responding and adapting to a daughter's decision once she began factory work. This more accommodating and permissive reaction of parents is strikingly different from the control exerted over the young and the female in the Chinese family in Taiwan or in parts of Western Europe historically.

My interviews with factory workers' mothers with regard to control over labor and economic activities suggest that their daughters' fairly plucky behavior does indeed differ from the stance taken by the previous generation, in part because adolescence is a new life-cycle state in Java. Certainly, the older sisters and mothers of these young women would not have been allowed to dissent to such an extreme, but they also would have been married by a younger age.

MOTIVES FOR SEEKING FACTORY EMPLOYMENT

Most young women explained that they sought factory employment for individual social and economic reasons. To my great surprise, only one factory worker said that she had sought employment to help out her family. Instead, young women mentioned social reasons for seeking factory employment: "I wanted to be like my friends," said five workers. "Almost all of my friends here work in a factory. In the late morning it's very quiet because they've all gone to work. I wanted to work, too."

For village women, factory work was a higher-status job than agricultural labor or trade. Young women wanted to work in factories because it made their skin stay lighter, a sign of nonmanual and therefore higher-status work. "I wanted to work in a factory because it's not hot and you don't work hard," said one woman.

There are, in addition, economic rewards, and many young women desire some financial freedom from their families. Workers did not mention helping the family economy as a reason for their employment; rather, they mentioned buying soap. Most villagers purchased blocks of inexpensive, unscented soap. If the family was poor, the same soap was used for bathing and for washing clothing and dishes. Factory workers bought bars of scented (often pink) soap for bathing only, paying forty to fifty cents—more than half a day's wage—for a single bar. Buying their own bar of luxury bath soap somehow signified their independence and higher status and differentiated them from other poor villagers. Comments such as "I wanted to work in a factory so that I could buy my own soap, like Parjiah" or "It's nice to be able to buy my own soap" underscore the low level of wages and the depth of poverty in rural Java. A brief look east of Java contextualizes the response of these Indonesian factory daughters and their household decision-making processes.

TAIWANESE PARENTS AND DAUGHTERS' LABOR

Without question, Taiwanese parents have historically managed and regulated a daughter's labor—the decision to work, where to work, and her wages. In the 1920s and 1930s in Taiwan and elsewhere, parents controlled their daughter's labor and received her wage directly.[11] Fathers often signed labor contracts, turning their daughters into factory workers who were then treated as indentured servants (Kung 1983, 17–27; Salaff 1981, 40). In the 1950s, Margery Wolf found that in rural Taiwan parents still controlled the decision of where a daughter worked (1972, 98–99).

Since daughters have been socialized to feel that they must pay back their debt to parents, it is not a question of whether to work, but when and where. Although parents in the 1950s were hesitant to allow their daughters to leave home for factory work, eventually, factory employment became automatic for young women (Arrigo 1980; Diamond 1979; M. Wolf 1972, 99). Changes in the global economy make factory employment one of the few alternatives open to them and is now a common though temporary part of the female life cycle (Gates 1987; Stites 1985).

In contemporary Taiwan, parents are still involved in a daughter's work-related decisions and, according to researchers, parental opinions are heeded (Kung 1983). Indeed, Lydia Kung (1983) and Susan Greenhalgh (1985) found recently that parents decide when a daughter will stop schooling and where and when she will start working.[12] When an occupation is selected, "parents are insistent about having daughters abide by their decision" (Kung 1983, 54). Parents exert authority over which factory a daughter should work in if she is seeking employment or attempting to change factories, particularly if there is a wage differential between factories or if the job involves living away from home (Kung 1983).

From these secondary sources, it is unclear whether fathers, mothers, or both are making these decisions, because most references are to "parents" and because, given the nature of this patriarchal kinship system, we cannot assume that their interests are the same. Occasionally, there is a gendered reference to a parent, but one parent is not mentioned more than another: "Going to (company Y) was my father's idea; being just out of primary school I really didn't have many choices anyway"; "It was decided by my mother that I should go to the fish-net factory" (Kung 1983, 58).

These responses demonstrate the difference in parental involvement and deference to parental authority in Chinese families compared with the Javanese families just described.[13] Researchers contend that since a daughter's labor and returns to it are seen as economic resources that families control (Salaff 1981), parents don't demand money from daughters; there is an implicit contract, and daughters fulfill their obligation by remitting 50 to 100 percent of their wage (Arrigo 1980; Thornton et al. 1984; Kung 1983).[14]

SANCTIONS

In comparing these two groups of working daughters, it is necessary to ask what they risk in disobeying their parents: What are the sanctions that loom before them as they attempt to create new boundaries? Or what makes them adhere to old, familiar ones? Although Javanese parents are fairly tolerant of a daughter's pluckiness, they do have limits and will exert control when they perceive that things have gone too far; some examples follow in the next chapter.

Poor parents had little with which to threaten and control their grown offspring. Parents in better-off village households were able to exert control over their children's education and, to some extent, over whether they had spouses or romantic partners because they held more resources that would later be divided among these offspring. Javanese parents often divide their land among their children while they are still living; with an inheritance coming, the timing of which may not be known, children are more likely to adhere to parental wishes. Poorer parents are the least equipped to strategize because they control few resources with which to influence, intimidate, or even placate their grown children. Similar findings from rural Malaysian households indicate that young people are resisting income pooling, creating internal household conflict; these findings also suggest that parental control of grown offspring in poorer households is more difficult when the children have access to cash (Wong 1984; Ong 1987; see also White 1976).

Margery Wolf (1972) points out that for Chinese daughters, the risks involved in disobeying are high and frightening. Daughters risk being alienated from the one source of security they have known and still have—their mother and siblings. Young women work because they feel that they have a financial debt to their parents. They wish to avoid draining family resources, but they also wish to contribute monetarily. Life stories of several Taiwanese factory workers reiterate how these women would not and cannot consider making independent decisions, particularly with regard to working or controlling their own income. The price would be estrangement from family members, who, from the secondary texts I have read, appear to demand and expect hard labor and hard cash from these young women without providing much affection or support in return (Wolf 1972; Sheridan and Salaff 1984; Kung 1983). Indeed, these workers' stories are at times heartwrenching in their portrayals of harsh, cold family relations (Arrigo 1980, 125–32). There do not appear to be other outlets for these young women should they wish to disobey or rebel; their only options are solitude, alienation, and loneliness. However, the life stories I have read suggest that even some filial daughters experience these same feelings (Arrigo 1980; Sheridan and Salaff 1984).

CONCLUSION

The quantitative data fit (1) with expectations from Deere and de Janvry's model, and (2) with what we know about the demography of workers in Third World global factories from the "demand" perspective. Workers are usually young, single, and from poor households. Those in the same age group who do not work in factories are often parents or members of households with a greater need for their daily labor and constant presence. Although factory workers' households are land poor, women from the poorest families—those in poverty with a high number and ratio of dependents—do not work in factories.

Although the quantitative data support most of the expectations derived from Deere and de Janvry's model, the qualitative data demonstrate that the means to such ends are much livelier, more oppositional and more dynamic than the model had led me to expect. The result—factory employment—does diversify the household's income portfolio, but the means or process involved in reaching that end is unaccounted for by the model. Most household models—Chayanovian, Marxist, or neoclassical—do not offer tools with which to integrate the dynamic and relational aspects of intrahousehold ties into the analysis.

The stories from daughters and parents challenge certain quantitative and economistic approaches to households and the people in them. Economic and demographic characteristics were clearly important in households, but they explained factory nonemployment only until the daughter reached a certain age. At about age fifteen or sixteen, those young women who wanted to work in a factory—and not everyone did—rebelled against parental desires.

The quantitative data illuminate several problems with the household strategy approach, and these problems are further highlighted by the qualitative data. First, household strategies are inferred from factory employment rather than factory nonemployment, from activity rather than from a lack of action. This interpretation, however, inverts parents' actual role in the process. In my research the only parental pressure exerted vis-à-vis a daughter's labor is to keep them home, not to push them into factories; that is, parents pushed for nonparticipation in the labor force. Second, reading a household strategy into daughters' factory employment misses another important dynamic since one might surmise that such employment reflects a daughter's service to household needs and parental wishes. In this case, the qualitative data reveal the opposite: factory employment provides a way for daughters to oppose parents' wishes and to attend to their own. Despite the ability of a household strategies approach to explain factory employment retrospectively, such employment is the result of a contested and conflictual decision, often made secretly by determined daughters, rather than part of an overall plan implemented by parents. Parents spend more time catching up, trying to adjust their rhythm to a daughter's change of beat rather than orchestrating the household's tune and tempo.

Taiwanese parents, by contrast, appear to be able to control their daughters' labor, appropriating it for their purposes for up to a decade and thus subordinating the lives, labor, and voices of young Chinese women. The sanctions in this different kinship system suggest that young Chinese women have little choice but to engage in hard, tedious labor rather than endure alienation from their only source of security—a source that engages in deep intrahousehold exploitation of the young and female.

Finally, it is important to emphasize that the role of timing in industrialization affected Javanese and Taiwanese parents. In Taiwan, industrialization started earlier, and by the 1970s, when much of the research was conducted, factory employment was common for young women. It was a known entity, and parents understood what they could and could not gain from it. In Java, however, these factories were, at the time of my research, relatively new, and parents perceived factory employment as an unknown, foreign, and somewhat suspicious economic activity and often tried to exert control to keep their daughters out of the factories.

CHAPTER VIII

Factory Daughters and the Family Economy

In this chapter I analyze the interactions between factory daughters, their family's economy, and rural industrialization. Although factory employment eventually provides rural semiproletarian families with access to some cash, these same families help support industrial capitalism by taking care of their working daughters and keeping wages down. Thus, I examine daughters' contributions to their households in considerable detail, using parents' and daughters' explanations to amplify the quantitative data. The ways in which factories construe certain aspects of gender ideology help explain why and how factories can pay wages below subsistence level, thereby keeping daughters dependent on their families. A brief comparison with how Taiwanese factory daughters use their wages illustrates how different levels of parental controls over daughters mediate the effects of industrialization on women.

One of the main objectives of my research was to establish how much factory daughters contribute to the family economy. For theoretical reasons (see Deere and de Janvry 1979), I expected that these young women from poor families would contribute a relatively high proportion of their wages to daily household reproduction, an expectation supported by previous empirical studies across time and geographical space (Tilly and Scott 1978; Dublin 1979; Hareven 1982; Salaff 1981; Nash 1967; Arrigo 1980; Huang 1985; Kung 1983; Ong 1987; Fernández-Kelly 1982). In chapter 7, I demonstrated that, although quantitative data could lead to a household strategy interpretation, the qualitative data fatally injured this interpretation. In this chapter, the quantitative and qualitative data are more complementary. Both demonstrate that daughters are engaging more in income retention than income pooling; that is, they contribute little toward the daily working of the household. Over time, parents begin to realize the longer-term economic benefits of factory employment, particularly bonuses and savings, some of which trickle down to the household. However, the conclusion that a daughter's factory employment benefits the household does not lead to the simultaneous conclusion that it is part of a household strategy.

FACTORY DAUGHTERS AND THEIR WAGES

From an initial one-month daily survey of income and expenditures conducted among fourteen workers in Nuwun, I found that, although they contributed 28 percent of their wages to the family, in cash or in kind, they also overspent their wages by 40 percent (D. Wolf 1984). During subsequent interviews, workers and families confirmed that workers borrowed small amounts of money from parents and friends, usually for transportation and lunch. The workers were saving an average of 31 percent of their wage, suggesting that savings were almost a direct transfer from parents. For example, two workers who spent twice as much as their wages said they asked their parents for transportation money without considering it a loan. Another daughter received her biweekly wage of 5,000 rupiah and spent all but 500 rupiah immediately. Although she gave her parents 1,000 rupiah, she borrowed twice as much from them in the following two-week period for transportation and lunch costs, creating a net drain of 1,000 rupiah in cash from the family economy. Of course, this figure does not include the value of her rent or of other household goods she consumed, such as food.

These findings were extraordinarily surprising; they countered my theoretical and empirical expectations and suggested several further questions: Why do daughters continue working if parents must finance their jobs? Why work if the benefits consist of only partial daily reproduction? How can poor parents tolerate such small contributions, and why do they do so?

I next designed a more extensive survey, including questions about access to other income (other economic activities, such as money borrowed, loans repaid, debts, and savings). To determine whether the relationship between daughters and family economy was related to the place of residence or commuting, I expanded the survey to include three different groups of workers: commuters, migrants, and residents. Commuters lived with their parents in the agricultural village of Nuwun and had been the sole focus of the first income survey. Migrants were boarders who rented rooms in an industrialized village, Pamit. Residents were daughters living at home in Pamit. Although both migrants and residents walked to work and did not need to pay for commuting costs, residents also did not have to pay rent. Thus, residents in Pamit and commuters in Nuwun are both daughters living at home; the only difference is that those in Nuwun must commute to work.

The second income-expenditure survey revealed that the average salary earned by commuters, migrants, and residents was 15,600 ($24.00) per month for a forty-eight-hour work week.[1] When money from the family, loans from friends, and loans repaid to the worker were included, workers had access to an average of 18,850 rupiah per month. Migrants were often involved with other migrant workers in a complex network of borrowing and loaning money. Several residents received money from their family, with whom they lived.

How, then, did these different groups of workers allocate their wages? The proportion of wages spent on selected expenditures reveals several striking patterns (table 22). Commuters spent more than 40 percent of their salaries on two basics that only partly reproduced the ability to work daily—transportation and lunch. The 20 percent spent on food consisted of lunch and snacks. The 14 percent spent on clothing included both necessary goods and less necessary items that might be considered luxury spending, such as long pants or expensive umbrellas. The most striking feature is the juxtaposition of unexpectedly small amounts contributed to families with relatively large sums spent on luxury goods; commuters in particular contributed little directly to their family's subsistence.

Because migrants were more on their own financially, they led the most frugal lives of all three categories of workers. Although they spent less than other workers did on themselves (clothing, haircuts, jewelry, and movies), they spent more on such daily needs as food and toiletries. Migrants brought back food supplies from visits home (cooking oil, sacks of rice, cassava), so the amount they spent on food—almost 30 percent—does not represent all their food consumption.[2] Those who returned home during the month of the survey gave more to parents than did commuters.

The consumption patterns of residents suggest that they spent more on luxury goods and leisure than other workers did. Although a higher proportion of their money was given to their families, residents also

TABLE 22
SELECTED EXPENDITURES AS PROPORTIONS OF SALARY

	Commuters	Migrants	Residents
Average monthly salary (in rupiah)	15,383	16,211	15,324
Expenditures (% of salary)			
Clothing[a]	14	11	16
Food[b]	20	29	20
Transportation	25	9	10
Household goods	0.1	2	0.6
Toiletries	3	5	9
To family	2.5	6.3	17.7
Haircuts, jewelry, entertainment	6.1	2.6	10
Savings[c]	26	40	30

[a] Includes clothes bought outright and credit payments for clothing.

[b] Includes lunches, snacks, and food bought for the household. In general, commuters and residents bought little food for their households; most of their expenditures on food were for lunches and snacks.

[c] From adding these selected expenditures alone, the migrants and residents overspent their salaries (104.9 percent and 113.3 percent respectively).

received a substantial amount of money from their families, resulting in a small net flow to the family. Clothing—both necessary and luxury—consumed approximately 15 percent of salaries of all three groups. If food consumed at home were added to these figures, workers would probably be found to have spent 60 to 80 percent of their wages on food alone. Although commuters and residents spent money on prepared, cooked food, migrants cooked their own food, which cut down their food costs.

After basic fixed costs (lunch and transportation) are deducted, residents and commuters could have conceivably turned over 55 to 80 percent of their wages to their families. Instead, they spent much of their wages as they pleased, with the exception of savings.

A more detailed view of the contribution of workers' wages to the family economy is presented in table 23. The net contribution was calculated by subtracting the amount of money the worker received from her family from the total value of money or goods she gave to the family.[3] With the exclusion of two outliers, the net contribution to the family economy was extraordinarily small: 3.6 percent, 5.5 percent, and 13.6 percent for commuters, migrants, and residents, respectively.[4] These small

TABLE 23
WORKERS' NET CONTRIBUTION TO FAMILY ECONOMY

	Commuters (N = 10)	Migrants (N = 15)	Residents[a] (N = 7)
Average net contribution (in rupiah)[b]	300	900	−400 (2,011)[c]
Net contribution as % of salary	−9 (3.6)[c]	5.5	−8.6 (13.6)[c]
Range of net contributions (%)			
Negative[d]	10	7.5	28.6
Zero	20	47.5	0
1–1,000 rupiah	50	13	0
1,001–3,000 rupiah	20	13	28.6
>3,000 rupiah	0	19	42.8
	100	100	100

NOTE: For commuters and residents, net contribution was calculated as money to family plus goods and food bought for family minus money from family. For migrants, it was calculated as money to family minus money from family. Many migrants brought rice and other foodstuffs from home, but it was not possible to calculate the value of these foodstuffs for the month of the survey.

[a] Residents were daughters living at home in an industrialized village, walking to work.
[b] The average monthly wage was 15,600 rupiah (U.S.$24.00).
[c] Excludes one outlier.
[d] Ranges from −15,000 rupiah to −4,000 rupiah.

contributions indicate that daughters from poor families retained most of their income.

Thirty percent of the commuters gave nothing or actually *took* money from their families; the remaining 70 percent contributed small amounts. Fifty percent gave 1,000 rupiah or less, and 20 percent gave 1,001 rupiah or more (table 23). The average amount contributed by commuters to their families that month was *less than fifty cents from a $24.00 wage.* Their small contribution to the family economy in this survey corroborates findings from my first survey.

Partiyem, a single commuting worker who lived with her family, said, "I rarely give money to my parents; it's used for transportation alone, and then I still have to ask my parents for money." Suniwati, who lived with her parents, grandmother, and siblings and had worked in the biscuit factory for three years, said, "I give money to my parents only if there is money left over after other expenditures."

More than half of the migrants gave nothing to their families of origin during the month surveyed, but on average, those who contributed gave more than the commuters, averaging 900 rupiah. When asked about money given to parents, Siti, a worker in the textile factory, answered: "If I go home, I sometimes give money to my younger siblings, which is a good feeling because the money is from my work, but what can I do if I don't have money?" Ambarwati, another migrant worker, said, "It's already been three months that I haven't returned home even though my mother already ordered me to come home. I'll go home later when I have money; if I go home and don't bring anything, I'll feel ashamed." Alfiah's parents lived nearby, but nevertheless she boarded near the factories. She explained, "My mother sells food from our house. For my food, usually she sends things home with me, like rice. I never have enough money; there's always a shortage and I ask my mother for money."

The average net contribution of residents' wages to their families was higher than that of commuters. Suyatmini worked in the textile factory and lived with her mother and older brother in an industrialized village: "My wage is very low. I use it only for my own needs, and sometimes also I give some to my mother. Basically, the money is only enough for my own needs."[5]

Murjanah lived with her parents and worked in the garment factory. When asked about contributions to her parents, she said: "I bring home only small gifts, but my parents wouldn't ask me for money." All these contributions were surprisingly small, especially in light of the poverty of workers' families. The pattern of contributions resembled the one that Diana Wong (1984) found among grown children engaged in wage labor in Malaysia: such contributions had the quality of gifts rather than dependable flows of income.

Residence does appear to affect the contribution made. The highest amount contributed (excluding one outlier) was from residents, followed by migrants and then commuters. It must be noted that five of the seven residents had received substantial returns from the savings association (*arisan*) the month of the study; these returns may have inflated their contributions. (The arisan is discussed at length below.)

Characteristics of commuters' families were analyzed to determine whether an inverse relationship existed between the net amount contributed and the family's class position.[6] Only a slight relationship was found between the amount contributed and control over agricultural land ($r = -.35$).[7]

FLUCTUATION OF REMITTANCES

I compared the amount commuting workers reported remitting with the actual amount remitted in the two surveys. The differences between workers' responses and actual behavior toward the family economy are not consistent in either direction (table 24). The two surveys also suggest that the amount remitted to the family from workers in Nuwun varies from month to month. In the second survey, workers consistently gave a lower percentage of their wages to their families: 20 percent in January compared with less than 8 percent in December.[8] This pattern suggests that workers adjust their contributions to the family economy, particularly if the household is experiencing strain, as in the period right before the harvest when cash and food supplies are low. During months when there are sufficient rice or cash returns from farming, workers may contribute less and may receive a greater degree of subsidization from parents. The importance of this dynamic is that workers do not remit a steady, reliable flow of cash to their families.[9]

TABLE 24
CONTRIBUTION TO FAMILY INCOME BY SELECTED COMMUTERS (AS PERCENTAGE OF WAGES)

	Workers' responses[a]	Amount showed by surveys	
Worker	*December 1981*	*January 1981*	*December 1982*
Sarmiyati	33[b]	33	0
Wagini	33	25	20
Suniwati	If anything is left over, gives 4–8	10	<1
Suryani	16	26	12
Titik	Yes, unspecified	20	4
Siti	Yes, unspecified	0	10
Partiyem	Rarely contributes; instead, often asks family for money	25	0[c]

[a] The question posed was, "Do you contribute to your family from your wages, and how much?" I calculated the percentage based on each individual's wage.

[b] This percentage was calculated from the amount the worker reported giving to her family as a proportion of her reported wage that month.

[c] During December 1982, Partiyem took 4,600 rupiah—equivalent to 50 percent of her wage—*from* her parents.

PARENTAL RESPONSES

When parents were asked if their daughters' wages contributed to the family economy, most responded that their daughters contributed in one of two ways, either directly with cash and goods or, more commonly, indirectly by taking care of her own cash needs. Others were not so sure, and a few were forthright about their feelings that their daughter was concerned solely with her own pleasure. There was clearly a range of contributions, subsidization, and parental discontent.

Comments such as the following illustrate the various responses to the question of whether daughters contribute to the family economy: "Yes, a little. For example, she often leaves money underneath the tablecloth for daily [food] shopping. But if she doesn't leave it, I don't ask for it. I've never looked for money in her room." "If she's asked, yes she gives us money. But if we don't ask, she doesn't. Sometimes we ask, but she says she doesn't have any."

Although factory wages did not necessarily contribute directly to the family economy, parents generally felt that factory wages played a role that they as parents could not: "At home we can't fulfill her needs, so it's better she's working in the factory. We're happy she's working because we can't buy her anything; we can only feed her." Another ambivalent parent said:

> At home, what kind of work can she find? Anyway, we can't fulfill her needs. If it was only food she needed, we could. But I can't buy other things. Anyway, girls need a lot of things. She has three kinds of face powder, shoes and sandals. But a girl working in a factory isn't right and it shames us. But at home, we don't have money for her needs.

Many parents were not ambivalent but were simply dissatisfied. A disgruntled father complained, "She spends her salary as she pleases, for shopping; she doesn't even tell me what she earns." The worker's mother agreed: "Every day she just has fun from morning till evening. Her money is spent just for play. She never helped us; in fact, she often asks us for transportation money." Another replied, "No, she doesn't contribute to the family. Her money is spent just for her own pleasure" (*untuk senang-senang sendiri*).

All these parental responses, regardless of their content, indicate that daughters control their own wage and do not automatically give it to their families; they also control their expenditures. Again, this situation contrasts sharply with the high remittances from Taiwanese or Hong

Kong factory daughters to their parents, who then give the daughters a small allowance (Kung 1983; Salaff 1981). Lydia Kung reports that many Taiwanese mothers she interviewed said that "the minimum a daughter should give is 50 to 80 percent of her earnings, and a daughter who turns over all her wages would be considered the most filial" (1983, 116). The behavior exhibited by Javanese factory daughters would be not only unacceptable but the source of shame, even perhaps scandal and ostracism, within a Chinese family context.

Most if not all of Taiwanese factory daughters' rationale for working stems from their sense of financial obligation toward their parents (Kung 1983, 110). Kung found that even women who lived away from home in a dormitory did not change or reduce their economic remittances to their families, nor did they expect to play a larger role in family decisions because of such contributions (1983, 111). A textile worker whom Kung interviewed voiced the sentiment that Taiwanese factory daughters seem to adhere to: "After all, our parents raised us. If we don't give them money, who else should it go to?" (1983, 112). When Kung's assistant joked with this same young woman about retaining some of her earnings, she responded with a description of her complete lack of control over her wages: "That's impossible. People can read figures, and my mother would ask. I could never get away with it" (1983, 112).

Although the Javanese women whom I studied do "get away with it," their parents also expect economic returns from them, but they expect less and express their expectations less directly than Chinese parents do. Two examples are representative of parental responses to my question "Should a working daughter give her wage to her parents?" and also illustrate these cultural differences:

> No, don't! Use your money for yourself or save it. You can also give some to parents, but just enough for their needs (*secukupnya saja*). Good parents shouldn't want much money from their children.

> Parents shouldn't be like that. If they're given money, yes, they should accept it, but if they're not given money, never mind. My daughter works and I'm happy. I rarely ask for money, but she knows when I need it. Sometimes she brings a blouse for me.

The language that these Javanese parents used to discuss their daughters' work may seem vague and ambiguous, particularly when compared with that of Chinese families (M. Wolf 1972). However, Javanese parental expectations do exist, and most parents expect returns in some form from a daughter's income. The extent to which parents can control (or even attempt to control) aspects of their children's lives varies by family and kinship system, by the age of the offspring, by the class position of the family, by the resources with which parents can bargain and threaten, and by the sanctions that parents and the society at large can impose.

There is no question that access to cash wages has encouraged the consumption of goods that these young Javanese women would otherwise not ask—and in some cases dare not ask—parents to pay for, such as pants, make-up, costly cloth, and other such luxury items. By lessening their economic demands (both in cash and in goods) on their families—that is, through taking care of clothing needs and one meal at the minimum—factory workers were indirectly contributing to the family economy. The factory wage was not sufficient to relieve parents of all their daughters' needs, but it did satisfy some consumption needs. Factory employment allowed workers to move from full dependence to semiautonomy from the daughters' perspective and from full to semidependence from the parents' perspective. Although this movement constitutes an important part of their contribution, there is yet another link between wages and the family economy besides food, clothing, or cash remittances that made parents tolerant of such low remittances. For all workers, approximately one-third of their wages went to savings. Rather than daily or weekly remittances, the crucial economic link between factory daughters and their families is savings.

SAVINGS

Workers saved an average of 26 to 40 percent of their wages (table 22). Most workers surveyed participated in a rotating savings association, the *arisan*. Every payday, members of the arisan met and contributed a certain amount of cash to a pool. One or two members' names were drawn from a bottle to receive the cash. It was a fixed lottery in that each person received the cash once before someone received it twice. Depending on the size of the group, a worker might receive the arisan from one to several times a year. It was a safe way to save money without the dangers of loss or corruption, and in addition it served a social function. It is an "antihousehold" strategy to accumulate money in that it keeps cash out of circulation. Without the arisan, workers found it impossible to save because parents and siblings continually asked for small amounts of money. During the month of the survey, eight workers received an arisan, averaging 39,000 rupiah and ranging from 5,000 to 100,000 rupiah.[10] Workers felt compelled to participate in the arisan because of their low wages; as one commuting worker said, "If you don't participate in an arisan, there's nothing left over to show for your work." One-third of all the single factory workers sampled did not participate in the arisan, and they came from the poorest households.[11]

Workers used their savings first to pay off debts incurred (usually for clothing) and to buy consumer goods for the family; parents were quick to point out the much-appreciated consumer goods their daughters had bought—cupboards, radios, beds, clocks, and dishes. Some of these were high-status luxury goods—radios, tape recorders, clocks, and pressure lamps (similar to Coleman lanterns). Although daughters did not usually consult with parents about what to buy with their savings, they used most of it to buy consumer goods for the family or reinvested it in a form that families could use if necessary. Thus, some aspects of their consumption behavior benefited their households, but this behavior was not part of an overall strategy that was planned or enacted.

A substantial proportion of the arisan was spent on gold jewelry or livestock, both of which are considered savings in a peasant economy and can be resold quickly for cash. (Gold jewelry can be quickly resold to the place of purchase. Jewelry is resold according to the prevailing price of gold per gram, which may differ somewhat from the purchase price.) The gold or livestock belonged to the daughter, and most workers said these possessions would go with them when they married and moved elsewhere. However, these savings were made available to the family in times of need to pay for debts, emergencies, and life-cycle events (circumcision, ritual feasts), including the daughter's own wedding. For example, one worker sold her ten ducks at a loss at the end of the fasting month (Ramadan), a consumption-oriented time of year, when her family needed cash. Several workers gave part or all of their gold savings to family members who needed cash, but the loan was not always repaid.

One commuting worker, Suniwati, came from a family of seven members. They had sufficient rice from their 0.4 hectare of land, which they planted three times a year. Suniwati rarely gave her parents cash from her wages, but, as her mother explained: "She saved money and bought plates, glasses, clothing, and ducks, which we sold at Lebaran. She had earrings of two and one-half grams but then sold them to buy a goat. The goat didn't have kids, so we sold it."

Siti, a commuting worker, lived with her mother. One of the poorest families in the village, they owned a small amount of land that provided only four months of rice needs. They needed cash to buy rice for the remaining eight months of the year. Siti's mother worked for a penebas and traveled from harvest to harvest, often far from home. Siti and her mother lived in a tiny two-room house made of bamboo, one wall of which separated them from the neighboring family. There was no furniture in the house—not even a chair—and all interviews were conducted outside.

Siti had worked to help her family since she was small. "My first job was as a maid in Jakarta for five years, and then in Semarang for a year, and then in Salatiga. I left the job in Salatiga for a factory job here." After receiving an arisan of 100,000 rupiah, Siti had the inner walls of the house rebuilt with wood and bought living room furniture. The arisan allowed her to buy goods for family use that she and her mother could not have otherwise afforded.

In the late 1950s, Anne Ruth Willner found that the arisan was already an important aspect of factory employment. Not only did workers use savings from the arisan to pay off debts, but they were also able to use the arisan as collateral to obtain advance credit (1961, 258). This still holds true: factory workers buy clothing, furniture, and tape recorders on credit.[12]

In addition, once a year, at Idul Fitri (the feast at the end of the fasting month of Ramadan), factory workers receive an annual bonus averaging 22,000 rupiah and ranging from 8,000 to 35,000 rupiah. This is a very consumption-oriented time of year, when people buy new clothes, fix up their homes, and cook special food for guests. The low level of factory wages was quickly forgotten as villagers enviously gossiped about the size of workers' bonuses. Families without factory workers usually sold possessions for cash. Most workers bought gold jewelry and new clothes for themselves and family members, and some bought new furniture. The cash bonus at Lebaran was expected to be spent for the family's needs.

Because of the increased demand for cookies during the holiday, the biscuit factory works overtime during the entire month of Ramadan. Many of the commuters worked in that factory and hence had a high salary and bonus that month. For one worker, this sum was close to $100.00—more than four times her usual monthly wage.

For example, Siti, the very poor worker discussed earlier, earned 40,000 rupiah that month through overtime plus a bonus of 16,500 rupiah. For her two nieces, her older sister, and her mother, she bought earrings totaling five grams of gold, valued at 35,000 rupiah. These earrings could be sold back at the original purchase price to the store where they were bought if cash was needed; and indeed, some years later, they were sold.

Siti also bought clothing for herself, her sister, her mother, and her niece and nephew for 25,000 rupiah. It would have been difficult for Siti to save up this amount of money when she worked as a maid in previous years.

Factory daughters did not contribute their wages or savings to their parents' agricultural undertakings. But by using their Lebaran bonus to buy clothing and food for the holiday, they decreased their demands on parents' cash for holiday preparation and possibly freed up such cash for other needs. Willner noted that such petty accumulations of cash were important to farmers since the Lebaran bonus was given near the harvest time and the New Year's bonus was near planting time. Such bonuses provided additional cash cushions, lessening the need for farmers to budget before planting begins (1961, 160). However, in Willner's study, these male farmers were the factory workers and could directly channel their bonuses into their farms.

In short, although daughters control petty amounts of cash from their weekly wages, spending it for their own benefit, they are more family oriented with larger sums of capital. Although factory workers decided what to purchase with their savings, they relinquished control over savings (cash, gold, livestock) for family needs. Parental access to savings made a daughter's seemingly self-centered consumption behavior with her weekly wages more acceptable. Indeed, without the long-term benefit of savings, parents might have expressed more discontent than they did with a daughter's daily economic behavior.

Although parents are pleased to have access to the money or the consumer goods their daughters buy, it is important to distinguish between these commodities and productive investments. The cash accumulated was not used directly for productive investments such as fertilizer or additional land, which would have improved the family's economic condition in the long run by increasing output. Only two workers invested in livestock. One worker bought a goat, and Partiyem sold her gold jewelry to buy a calf. Her mother told me: "She didn't want to do it, but I forced her. I told her, 'A cow can increase in value, but gold cannot.' "[13]

WORKING SONS

I surveyed a very small number of male factory workers (because there were few in Nuwun) in order to compare their behavior with that of working daughters. The five males surveyed (three in Nuwun, two in Pamit, the industrialized village) earned an average of 22,000 rupiah that month, 40 percent more than female workers. On average, these male workers contributed 15 percent of their wages to their families, in cash or in kind. Of those who contributed, their contribution averaged 19 percent. These male workers remitted a higher proportion of wages and a larger amount of money to parents than did female workers, but it is not possible to discern whether such behavior is related to a higher wage or to gender differences.[14] They also did not borrow money from parents because of higher wages. In Taiwan, Chinese parents expect substantial help from their sons; however, most of their contribution comes later, when sons care for aging parents.

To summarize the economic data, savings and bonuses help the family and are used for direct and indirect investments with both short-term and long-term prospects. The prospect of future cash accumulation from the arisan and from bonuses helps parents tolerate a working daughter's frivolous consumption. Without such savings, there would probably be more daily family conflict concerning the low economic remittances of workers. Savings provide gifts to the family and emergency aid, both of which are appreciated and which signify a daughter's partial financial independence. The importance of having a family member connected with a diverse source of income became apparent over time even to those parents who were initially highly disapproving of factory employment.

EFFECTS OF INDUSTRIALIZATION ON WOMEN WORKERS AND THEIR FAMILIES

How has industrialization affected young women and their families?[15] Factory work brings young women more cash than they can earn from seasonal agricultural employment, trade, or domestic service. Perhaps because of the new life-cycle state of these young women—single, young adulthood—these earnings are subject to fewer regular familial economic obligations, and workers can freely exert more control over higher earnings. These changes in cash and control can be seen in their new consumerism and in their appearance, as well as in their exertion of increasingly assertive behavior.

Workers perceived their status to be enhanced by factory work because they were engaging in nonagricultural, steady, remunerated labor in a clean, cool environment. Their skin stayed lighter, a mark of nonmanual and therefore higher-status work. Some felt themselves to be different from fellow villagers and simply refused to help parents any longer in the fields: "I'm too lazy to work in the sawah because it's hot"; "I feel lazy when they tell me to work in the sawah. Better my brother should do it." Such reactions do not appear to be motivated by concern for familial needs, nor do they fit common conceptions of Third World women in poor families.

Factory work also allows young women to leave their parents' home, travel to work, and meet young men and women from other villages. Several romances and marriages had resulted between male and female workers or between female commuting workers and drivers of local transportation.

In comparison with their nonfactory peers, female factory workers in Nuwun exhibited an air of assertiveness. Their make-up, nail polish, and, in a few cases, long pants, were statements of their new buying power and what they viewed as a "modern style." And as mentioned in the previous chapter, many desired such financial freedom, although its small scale emphasizes their poverty and low wages. As one young woman explained, "I wanted to seek additional money to buy soap like my friend Sukemi."

THE LIMITS OF PARENTAL CONTROL

Although parents rarely exert force over decisions related to factory employment or returns from labor, patriarchal control is still exerted over issues of female propriety and movement. Parents do not simply accommodate themselves to all of their daughters' decisions; they express limits to what they will tolerate. Female factory workers in Nuwun still usually (though not always) obey their fathers (*harus ikut Bapak*), expressing dominant notions of feminine submissiveness and dependence. Fathers react strongly and more forcefully to decisions that may compromise their daughter's sexuality or thwart patriarchal control. A few examples illustrate these limits.

Several females wanted to move closer to the factories and board together to save transportation costs. Their fathers, however, would not give them permission to do so. Either fathers voice their objections more, or daughters pay more attention to their fathers' disapproval than their mothers'. Most parents (of both sexes) told me that they would not allow their daughter to board elsewhere. Rini and another worker wanted to migrate to Jakarta but were forbidden to do so by their fathers. Parents often insisted that their daughter work in sexually segregated factories, such as the garment factory, as opposed to mixed environments such as the biscuit factory. One mother explained: "I'm really strict with my daughter, but luckily she minds me. She had never brought home a boyfriend, but after working in the factory for about three years, once she brought a boyfriend home and I really got angry. After that, it never happened again."

When a father is not present, young women usually obey their older brothers, who step in when a sister's honor or sexual reputation is at stake. One factory worker was involved with a young village man against her mother's wishes. When rumors were flying that she had spent the night with him and had asked the local masseuse for an abortion, her older married brother stepped in and forced her to live with him and his family in another village.

It is curious that, although young women feel free to ignore parental input or a father's disapproval in deciding to work in a factory or in wage expenditures, they do adhere to certain of their fathers' decisions. Since I was exposed to only a limited number of decisions in their lives, it is difficult to draw out generalizations concerning when daughters adhere to and accommodate parental disapproval and when they ignore and resist it. From my observations, it appears that young women's decisions concerning their labor and the returns to it are tolerated to an extent because they can be understood within certain cultural boundaries of female activity. But when a daughter's sexuality or sexual reputation is involved—an arena that extends beyond women's control—parents step in more forcefully, and daughters then obey. Fathers whose daughters insist on working in factories in turn insist that they work in female-only factories. Some of the migrant workers had parents who still strongly disapproved of a daughter seeking factory employment far from home, for they would then be out from under their daily control; some young women simply ran away from home. The timing of marriage and choosing a spouse, two important and sexually related decisions, have long been under parental control and remain so in some households; however, this is changing as young women begin to participate in this process (see chapter 9).

This Javanese case presents a curious and contradictory situation: despite daughters' ability to control their income and their expenditures, they remain financially dependent on their families. The view from the other side—how the family affects industrialization—helps explain this paradox.

EFFECTS OF RURAL FAMILIES ON INDUSTRIALIZATION

This section focuses on factory daughters' wages from a different perspective. I contend that because of those very wages that benefit rural semiproletarian families, those same families end up contributing to the process of industrialization. Despite full-time employment in the industrial sector, factory daughters remain financially dependent on their families, who supplement factory wages. In other words, families—by providing free food, goods, services, lodging, and cash to keep their daughters afloat—help keep wages down and factory profits up.

During the second survey, twenty-two of the thirty-two single females—69 percent—overspent their wage income.[16] Of the ten who did not overspend their wages, half received arisans that month, ranging from 6,500 rupiah to 100,000 rupiah. Most workers borrowed the equivalent of 20 to 40 percent of their salary from their parents.

International comparisons demonstrate that Javanese factory workers' wages are low (see chapter 4). More important, however, their wages are insufficient even by the standards of rural Java: factory workers simply cannot pay for all of their daily needs with their salaries. The union (FSBI) estimates that a single worker needs about 24,250 rupiah a month to subsist in central Java, or 40 percent more than the average wage of these workers.[17] The wages of female workers clearly are not meant to cover full subsistence needs. Workers are fully aware of this insufficiency; one worker, when asked if she would ever consider boarding in closer to the factory to save transportation money, responded: "No, I'd lose money; my money would be spent on food alone. If I'm at home, I can eat with my parents." Factory owners in this site were well aware of local conditions and took advantage of several different factors to keep wages down: gender norms, the family context, the rural locale, and the opportunity costs of these young women.

My calculations of annual income (wages and bonuses), consumption, and expenditures suggest that savings are possible only because parents help keep daughters afloat with cash during the work week. Workers borrow 20 to 40 percent beyond their wages while saving similar proportions of their salaries. The monetary help from parents, along with their provision of free food, rent, and other goods, keeps wages down and working daughters able to return to work and to save some of their wages. Savings can in fact be viewed as a transfer from parents since the amounts borrowed from parents and the amounts saved are similar.

DAUGHTERS AND WAGES: THE VIEW FROM INDUSTRY

Industrialists justify the unequal wage structure between men and women by drawing on gendered notions of women's income as supplemental and women as economic dependents of males. The factories in the site pay higher than minimum wages to male workers because of the same gender ideology that justifies lower wages for women workers. Factory managers and owners claim that males are paid more because they have to support families, but most male factory workers are unmarried; furthermore, their factory wages are not necessarily used for household subsistence needs. The male workers surveyed earned an average monthly wage of 22,000 rupiah, or 40 percent more than the average wage earned by female workers; two of them received the amount a Labor Department official thought would match the subsistence level, and two others were quite close to that level.

A gender ideology that portrays females as economic dependents of males, working mainly to supplement family income, is further strengthened in this site and adds to industrialists' justification for low female wages because of the family context. By locating in a rural area, modern firms draw on families who provide worker-daughters with free lodging and food in the same way that any family provides for a child. In urban factory settings, a high proportion of workers are migrants, and factory owners cannot similarly justify low wages with the argument that workers are economically supported by their families.

This particular site had one more feature that, in addition to gender ideology and family presence, provided industrialists with another rationale. Most industrialists were well-off, Chinese Indonesian, urban residents who looked down on rural Javanese villagers. The Javanese managers were also urban dwellers and expressed the same scorn for farmers. They all labored under the misconception that villagers obtained sufficient livelihoods from agriculture. One manager stated, "Working doesn't affect their lives because they are from rural families and don't need the income to live. They don't consider income and the family. They don't know how to save. They just live for each day and spend what they have." The rationale is that surplus income (that beyond basic subsistence) is *unnecessary* income, an argument that managers apply to the income of others, but not to their own. Of course, workers from poorer families do depend on wages for subsistence. For those who don't, the managers' paternalistic attitude suggests that they don't deserve the money since they don't spend it "properly."

A rural environment also provides a less educated, more docile female work force than do periurban or urban areas; factories in these latter locations may confront more protests if they pay less than minimum wage because there is greater awareness among workers (Mather 1982; 1985). The worker protests occurring in Java today appear to cluster in urban and periurban areas (INGI 1991b). Although factory owners in all parts of Java capitalize on traditional Javanese female traits of shyness and fear, in this particular area, workers' low educational levels compounded female docility (see chapter 5).

Factories can rationalize paying below the minimum wage, which is itself below subsistence level, with the following interrelated arguments: according to their ideology, females are economic dependents earning supplemental income; their families provide free lodging and food for dependent daughters, thereby decreasing the need for a higher wage; and the proximity of the agricultural economy meant that factory income is not only supplemental but surplus. The family presence and the illusion of an equitable agricultural economy reinforces a particular ideology of gender and further justifies a wider gap between male and female workers, resulting in below-subsistence-level wages for women.

Willner unwittingly highlighted the economic advantages of rural industrialization, pointing out that any additional costs required to set up factories in "economically less desirable locations" would be offset by the "savings implicit in the *lack of necessity to provide benefits and services that are provided by the community*" (my emphasis). Indirect costs such as labor protests would also be avoided, as would "the need to overcome them by welfare expenditures" (1961, 341). Thus, in this setting, the transition from peasant (broadly defined) to industrial proletariat is a more dialectical one, with factory workers remaining firmly rooted in rural and agrarian production.

DAUGHTERS AND WAGES: PARENTS' VIEWS

Why do parents accept low wages for daughters? Why do parents financially support working daughters? The low opportunity costs of rural Javanese women make below-subsistence-level wages from factories not only acceptable but desirable by comparison with existing employment options.

The lack of comparable employment opportunities helps explain why parents supplement a daughter's wages. First, as discussed in chapter 2, there has been a contraction of employment opportunities for the poor, and for women in particular, in agriculture. Daughters have few options, and their mothers have even fewer. Second, there are no other economic activities for young women offering a comparable steady cash wage. Younger village nonfactory females are usually involved in household and farm production, agricultural wage labor, trade, or domestic service. One worker, who had formerly sold cooked food to schoolchildren during recess and later had tried selling vegetables at the market, made very little money. Another had worked on a coffee plantation as a wage laborer for 350 rupiah daily.

One nonfactory worker washed vegetables in the market for 400 rupiah a day, another was a petty trader, and yet another sold spinach in the market, earning 1,500–2,000 rupiah a day. Since these jobs were seasonal, there were periods during which these women worked only at home.

Several factory workers previously had worked as servants for families in the village, which entailed working long hours for only 1,000 to 2,000 rupiah monthly. They received a much lower wage for longer hours in a semibonded situation and remained in the village, under the control of villagers. Two factory workers previously had worked for families in Jakarta, receiving room, board, and 5,000 rupiah monthly. Generally, all these women found domestic service too arduous, controlled, and exploitive, especially at the low wages villagers paid. For those who had migrated to seek domestic service, factory work allowed them to earn more while living at home.

Factory workers expressed boredom with domestic activities, disdain for agricultural work, and dislike for domestic service. Regardless of tastes, no other steady jobs were available for these women. I asked workers why they continued their jobs even though the wages were so low. Factory workers continually stressed their sense of having no other options, feeling that otherwise they'd be unemployed: "If I'm at home, what kind of work will I do? I can't just plant rice." "If I were at home, I'd be unemployed and I wouldn't have my own money."

A parent of one factory worker summarized the choices and contradictions in this situation: "No, she can't save from her salary; it's used up for transportation, fun, and contributions for friends' weddings (*nyumbang*). . . . But at home, there's no work, just playing around. If she was at home, she could help gather fodder, but at the most, she'd only receive a little money." Suniwati, a commuter, explained why she continued her factory job: "I'm already used to working in a factory and

I'd feel too lazy to work in the sawah. If I stayed at home, I'd be unemployed and feel embarrassed because I'm already grown up. It's nice (*lumayan*) to be able to buy my own soap myself."

Initially, I confronted what seemed to be a contradictory situation: workers receiving wages below the subsistence level perceived themselves as privileged. Rather than dismiss their voices as "false consciousness," the task was to understand precisely what gave rise to that sense of privilege. Indeed, given the concrete socioeconomic reality of rural Java and their low opportunity costs, these women, with steady remunerated factory jobs, were in a relatively privileged situation: such is the profundity of poverty in rural Java. It is not difficult to understand why a young village woman would seek factory employment and why parents would help keep her afloat financially.

Analyzing these different strands and perspectives illustrates the interactions between poor rural households and industrial capitalism as each affects the other. However, I do not wish to romanticize the "power" that poor families have to affect industrialization, as this interrelationship is highly asymmetrical. Factories are in a much better position to impose their dictates on workers and families than the reverse. Although parents potentially could resist some aspects of factory work (such as integrated workplaces or night work) by keeping their daughters home, it is highly likely that the state would have the police or army step in to "persuade" rural parents to change their ways.

In this case, rural families affect industrialization through their support of their full-time working daughters; however, this effect does not entail any change or action on their parts. Although rural families benefit industrialization by improving factories' profits, this benefit is enacted passively through a highly normalized everyday practice—parents taking economic responsibility for daughters as they have always done.

In the next section, I explore the internal dynamics of such industrialization more closely by examining the articulation of factory work with the household economy and some of the changes and processes in family relations. The following two cases demonstrate the different roles that factory employment can play within the family economy and different degrees of parental control and subsidization.

CASE STUDIES

CASE 1: WAGIAH

I met Wagiah early in the research project because she lived next door to the Lurah at whose house I first stayed. Although she did not live in either of the two agricultural villages surveyed, I visited her frequently and she became a valued informant. She seemed immediately at ease with me and found it easy to recount factory stories to me. Eventually, she also kept a diary of events that occurred within the factory.

Wagiah, age twenty-three, lived with her mother in a small house in the hamlet neighboring the one in which I resided. They were landless and poor. When Wagiah was one month old, her father left her and her mother and married someone else who lived in the same village. Wagiah's mother recounted:

> Now, he's come back twenty-five years after leaving us. Before, when I was suffering and took care of Wagiah when she was sick, he left to marry another woman. Now after his child is big and can earn money, he comes back. When my husband left us, we didn't have anything, even our bed was borrowed from a neighbor. Now, since Wagiah works, we have our own house.

His brief return did not work out, and once again he left.

Wagiah had been briefly married when she was quite young and had moved in with her husband's family because they were better off than her mother was. But after three months, she separated from her husband. As is frequently the case in arranged marriages, she wasn't happy with him and they divorced. To divorce, they had to go see the Lurah, who tried to convince them to stay together. Wagiah didn't want to stay with her husband; she was afraid to return to his house, and said her lips would burn if she took her words back. The divorce cost the couple about ten dollars. He went back to his first wife and children in a neighboring village while Wagiah remained unmarried. She often said, rather wistfully and unconvincingly, that it's nicer to be alone.

Because of her family's poverty, Wagiah started work at an early age. She worked as a maid in Jakarta and Banten for a total of four and one-half years. With the arrival of factories in the area, she moved home and since 1979 had lived with her mother and worked in the textile mill.

When she started working in the factory, she received twenty-four rupiah an hour; in 1982, after two years, she was receiving double that amount. There were two raises annually. Wagiah always received the highest rating on the three-tiered ladder for the Lebaran bonus. She received 20,000 rupiah in 1981 and 27,000 rupiah in 1982. With her savings and bonuses in 1982, she bought gold earrings, a gold ring for her mother, a wooden cupboard, and woven grass mats. Thanks to her savings, this very poor family had furniture for guests in their tiny living room.

Since the mill operated in three eight-hour shifts, every ten days Wagiah had to change her schedule to start work either at 6:00 A.M., 2:00 P.M., or 10:00 P.M. Labor laws stated that female workers were to be picked up or brought home when night work was involved, but this factory provided no such services. When Wagiah worked in the morning, she arose at 4:30 A.M. and left the house at 5:15 A.M.; when she went to work at night or returned home at night after the second shift, she had to walk alone in the dark from the main road into the village.

Wagiah often told me about fellow workers who had accidents on the job. One day, several other village women gathered with their children to look at a picture of one of Wagiah's fellow workers, who had just died after vomiting blood. She then told me that someone else had died a few weeks before, from no apparent illness, "because the factory is haunted. There are spirits and devils in the factory which scare the workers." She explained that when the sawah was turned into a factory, many people died and disappeared because of uprooted and unhappy spirits.

One night when Wagiah was working the night shift, she fell asleep and fell down, cutting open the back of her head. A factory representative took her to a nearby hospital, where she was given stitches. The factory paid for the medical services, but, since a guest was visiting the factory, Wagiah was not driven home but left at the hospital to fend for herself. Fortunately, her friends took her home.

Wagiah was a particularly hardworking person and was rather unusual compared with most of the other factory workers I studied. She felt she had no other choice but to work hard: "If I don't work, who will feed me?" Wagiah earned extra income on the side, for instance, by ironing for neighbors during her spare time or on her one day off; she ironed for 100 rupiah an hour, with the coal for the iron provided by the client. In addition, she alone undertook all the household chores and cooking.

Because they lived next door to the Lurah, Wagiah's mother often worked in his kitchen, cooking for guests or large village events; she also worked as an agricultural laborer. Because of her relationship with the Lurah, a rather wealthy patron, she had more work and more income than the average laborer did. She said: "My daughter and I work every day from morning until evening, but why is it we can't get rich? I've even thought of asking a spirit to help us get rich."

Early on, Wagiah agreed to record the work hours and income of her mother as well as her own economic activities. It should be noted that Wagiah was much more industrious and frugal than her peers were, working a considerable amount of overtime and engaging in other eco-

TABLE 25

COMPARATIVE INCOMES OF A FACTORY WORKER AND A WAGE LABORER

	Wagiah, factory worker			Wagiah's mother, agricultural and domestic laborer			
	Wage (in rupiah)	*Extra income*	*Hours worked overtime*[a]	*Wage*[b] *(in rupiah)*	*Average hours worked*[c]	*Days worked per month*	*No. of meals*[d]
February	19,480	2,700	53	8,150	8.5	18	23
March	18,865	4,500	40	7,050	7.2	20	30
April	20,330	2,000	32	6,550	6.0	24	28
May	19,865	3,000	24	1,770	5.3	22	9

[a] Overtime is time worked in excess of eight hours a day in the factory only. Wagiah's extra income came from other economic activities, such as ironing and washing clothes for neighbors.

[b] This figure includes cash and wages in kind; e.g., if she received 4 kg of cassava, the price of the cassava was counted as wage.

[c] Average hours excluding those days she did not work.

[d] Agricultural laborers usually receive a meal as part of their wage. This woman also helped out at the Lurah's home when they were preparing for guests. She worked in the kitchen, preparing food, so she received more meals than did the average laborer in the field.

nomic activities. Four months of data demonstrate that Wagiah's wages from factory employment were considerably higher than those her mother received from agricultural and domestic wage labor (table 25). Wagiah's average monthly wage was higher than that of most workers surveyed by about 4,000 rupiah because of the large amount of overtime she worked. Even if Wagiah had earned the average amount found in the income survey, it still would have surpassed her mother's income by about half.

For this family, factory work constituted an essential part of household income; it was not surplus income by any means. The family depended on those wages for a constant cash flow. Because of Wagiah's industriousness, her wages and extra income were higher than average. However, Wagiah herself perceived little choice. It must be emphasized, though, that Wagiah was very unusual compared with her peers, who did not work much overtime, who retained their income, and who spent their wages on their own needs. Wagiah's economic behavior resembled much more that of the factory workers who were mothers since they, too, ceased to spend money on themselves.

CASE 2: RINI

When I started my research, Rini, aged eighteen, was a friendly, cheerful informant. She lived with her parents and three younger siblings. Her father farmed their small parcel of wet riceland and dry land and also worked as a sharecropper and agricultural laborer. Her mother also worked on their land in addition to doing household chores. Both parents were engaged in caring for the youngest child, age two. Rini's sister Parjiah, age sixteen, had worked in the same garment factory for a year. Although Rini had attended school for only five years, Parjiah had completed grammar school and two years of junior high school. Two other siblings—aged ten and six—attended school.

After quitting school, Rini had worked at home gathering fodder and had sold vegetables at a market. Bored, she found work in the biscuit factory, where she worked for two and one-half years. At one point workers were instructed to work overtime, which meant coming home at night. She was scared to walk from the road into the village alone in the dark because of spirits, so she quit. She then started working in the garment factory. Although the salary and Lebaran bonus were higher at the biscuit factory than at the garment factory, her father felt it was better to receive a lower wage but be safe.

Work in the garment factory fluctuated, depending on orders from abroad. Sometimes, workers were told to stay and work overtime. Once, when some workers did not want to do so, a passive-aggressive strike ensued, with several sections staying home from work for several days. Rini participated in these strikes without fear.

Rini said that she used some of her salary for herself and used the rest to help her parents buy rice and pay for her brother's education. In the first income survey, she gave her parents more than one-third of her salary; she also saved about 20 percent of her salary in the arisan. But she also consistently borrowed money from her parents for lunch and transportation and, in fact, overspent her salary by half.

She was always quite lively, energetic, and outgoing. She laughed and flirted with young men she met on public transportation and had several male visitors. For a while, she and some other workers, including her sister, had plans to rent and share a room near the factory to save transportation money. Her father tolerated Rini going against his wishes and seeking factory employment, but he would not allow this move.

After several attempts, Rini was wed in what might be termed a partly arranged marriage (described in the Preface). Although she had bought a mattress on credit for 22,000 rupiah before her wedding, she apparently did not use it much immediately after the marriage. She complained more and more bitterly about her husband and didn't want to sleep with him. Although she pointed to his laziness as the reason for her unhappiness, it was unclear at the time whether this was her real reason for rejecting him.

Thus began difficult times. The neighbor who loaned money to Rini's family for the wedding wanted his money back and went to the village head, asking that he force Rini's parents to sell their sawah. Since they had little sawah, they were not forced to sell it. Her father began to complain about her frivolous economic behavior: "She spends her salary as she pleases, shopping, and doesn't even tell me how much she earns."

In reaction to her unhappy situation, Rini began to act in ways improper for any Javanese female, but especially for a married woman, hoping her husband would leave her. She stayed out late at night, watching television at a neighbor's house. She sang and talked loudly in the village; she danced to disco music during a going-away party I gave for my research assistant. Once as we strolled in the village at dusk, she loudly imitated the male voice from the mosque calling Moslems to prayer.

She then hatched the plan to go to Jakarta with her sister to look for work because one of their former supervisors had moved there. Her father forbade this attempt to run away. When asked about leaving her husband, she said, "He can stay here; later if I have a good job, he can follow, if he wants to."

Several days later I visited her, and she recounted: "I just came home from Semarang, where I stayed for one night and didn't even say good-bye to my husband; I only said good-bye to my mother. My husband went looking for me and waited for me by the road until 11:00 P.M. A few days ago, I also went to watch a dance and a disco with some friends at the village hall in Kebonan." Rini hoped that her husband would react to this behavior by leaving her to return to his parents, but he was tenacious. At one point, he left and went home, but Rini's father convinced him to return and be patient.

For a few months, Rini's unhappiness and frustration made her truly out of control. Her postmarital turmoil provided villagers with a rich topic for gossip, during which old stories were dredged up to demonstrate her family's bad character. My other respondents were so much more interested in telling me about Rini's latest episode than in answering my questions that it was often difficult to bring them back to my more mundane questions. One story, confirmed by Rini in 1986, held that she was interested in another man. Another story, told to me more than once, was that Rini's husband had a skin problem that caused redness and a bad smell. The village head's wife, who always took pleasure in recounting the irresponsible character of Rini's family, joined in the skin disease discussion, adding that she almost couldn't stand being near him during the wedding, when she had to apply make-up, "because he stank."

The economic and psychological strains on Rini's family increased and were apparent. That year, the family needed more money than usual to buy rice because they had sold all of their harvest on the ground to a middleman. The cash from that sale was used for a ritual feast when Rini married. During the Lebaran after her marriage, Rini's bonus was only 8,750 rupiah, which was spent on food for the holiday, transportation, and having fun with a friend. Her parents were unhappy because they had debts and little else that holiday. At least when she had worked at the biscuit factory, she had received a large bonus and cookies. Her father said, "Both girls are never at home. They play all day and their money is spent just for themselves."

Rini had to drop out of the arisan because of the large debt incurred for her marriage. She became more lax about going to work. One day, when she and a friend arrived late and weren't allowed in, they went to town for the day. Amidst this financial strain and her personal problems, she bought long pants, a symbol of modernity, to wear after work. These pants were bought on credit for 10,000 rupiah—almost one month's salary. Rini didn't have the money because she wasn't working full days and receiving a regular wage.

A difficult cycle perpetuated itself. When Rini didn't go to work, her salary was lower and she had to borrow more money from her parents, who increasingly felt the strain of their debt. She felt more and more embarrassed by this situation. Finally, her parents demanded that she quit her factory job. Her mother explained:

> I really told Rini to stop working so that she could stay at home and take care of her younger siblings. If she's at home, her father can then work on felling logs, which can help us buy rice. If Rini works or doesn't work, it's the same; she never helped her parents and often asks us for transportation money.

Rini had a different version of why she quit her job: "I quit because I didn't want to see my husband every day. He worked at the poultry farm in front of the factory, and every day he waited for me after work to go home. When I decided to quit work, he quit his job, too."

A few days later, Rini didn't feel well and blamed her illness on too many bad thoughts:

> I have a husband who makes trouble for my parents because he has never given them money. My husband is still like a small child, so how can he be happy already having a wife? If he says good-bye and says he's going to the sawah, the most he does there is sleep. It's really hard to have a husband who doesn't work. Without money, it gets noisy at home with my parents because we fight.

The level of conflict in this family was far from the Javanese ideal of rukun.

This case study illustrates many of the issues discussed in this chapter. Rini's contribution to the family economy was questionable in the light of her constant borrowing of money. Her parents were able to tolerate her drain on the family economy and subsidize her only to a certain point. Their options were quite limited, but the economic strain was too great for them to remain patient with small contributions, if any, from Rini's job. During Lebaran, without access to a reasonable bonus, they were pushed to a higher degree of intolerance. Rini was relatively free to make her own decisions, but her parents exerted their authority when she sought an unacceptable amount of freedom from their control.

Rini's decision to enter the industrial labor force, her retention of wages, and her behavior as a married woman do not demonstrate family-oriented behavior. Her parents could set limits only when she reached the boundaries of respectability, economic recklessness, and their financial tolerance. Their roles as parents were fairly accommodating and basically reactive; they exerted force as family economy managers only when bankruptcy was approaching and when her sexual respectability was at stake. Indeed, although calculations and choices were made when Rini drained the family till, the general picture of economic decisions and economic behavior does not add up to much strategizing. Nor does this family strategy in any way resemble the "school of fish" or "flock of birds" analogy made about family strategies in general (Hareven 1982).

When I left the village in early 1983, Rini was still married. At that time, I felt this chapter in her life would end in pregnancy, divorce, or most likely both, and in that order. I was only partly correct. Her story will be continued in chapter 9.

CONCLUSION

In this chapter, I have analyzed the multiple interactions among young women, their poor families, and industrial capitalism and the ways in which gender ideology is conveniently called on to keep young women economically dependent and working full-time in the labor force. Industrialists are able to benefit greatly from a combination of these particular gender and family ideologies, along with the profound poverty of rural Java.

If a daughter works in a factory, there are eventual benefits for both her and her family. Working daughters are less of a financial burden on families as they become only semidependent on the family economy. Their savings provide income that may be used for nonsubsistence needs. Families gain tangible status goods that are displayed in the house, and they also have access to cash or savings for crises and cash needs. At the same time, daughters become semiautonomous: they control their income as well as what to purchase and for whom. They gain prestige as donors of thoughtful gifts to family members (a blouse, a bar of soap, a radio); these gifts also symbolize the donor's independence. Working daughters also gain prestige as providers of emergency aid. Such contributions bring them higher status than would remitting a steady and dependable flow of cash to the family economy. Compared with their mothers, they appear to have greater control over their earnings and more cash to control at an earlier age.

Industrialization is greatly benefited by rural parents and the agricultural economy; industrial firms rely on the rural family economy to keep wages down. Even though these rural families cannot do much more than react to structural change, through their subsistence production and taking care of their daughters, they are fueling industrial capitalism.

Finally, two case studies reveal the very different kinds of family dynamics that can occur around factory work. In one unusual case, factory wages became an integral part of daily household reproduction; in another, more common case, there was much more fluidity, change, and conflict related to factory wages. Factory employment eventually benefited many households with savings and goods, and parents lost their initial resistance to this foreign and suspicious form of work. They began to appreciate, look forward to, and even plan on a daughter's cash at Lebaran. This process did not, however, resemble the long-term plan or decision making involved in a "household strategy"; rather, it became acceptable through living it. Through time and experience, factory work became part of the household's normal economic routine and practice.

CHAPTER IX

Marriage

And marriage among us—miserable is too feeble an expression for it. How can it be otherwise where the laws have made everything for the man and nothing for the woman? When law and convention both are for the man; when everything is allowed to him.

Raden Adjeng Kartini, Letters of a Javanese Princess

In 1986 I returned to the village of Nuwun to seek answers that cannot be culled from cross-sectional data: What was the effect of factory employment on the role of workers in their families? Did factory employment affect young women's ability to make significant life decisions? In 1982 most factory workers in Nuwun had expressed a desire to choose their own spouse; were they in fact able to participate in this decision? Did their changing role in the family economy allow them a greater role in life decisions such as the timing of marriage or choice of spouse?

I examined intergenerational family dynamics with regard to decisions concerning marriage and to changes in the family economy—two aspects of family life that more readily reflect the social effects of economic structural change. This chapter examines such processes with regard to marriage; the following chapter returns to women's roles in the family economy as working mothers and wives. First, however, I discuss my reentry four years later.

RETURNING TO THE FIELD

Before returning to Java, I was uncertain about what I would find and could not easily prepare for research. Oil-producing countries in general had encountered lower oil prices in the 1980s, a problem compounded in Indonesia because oil reserves—the main source of government revenues and development efforts—were dwindling, promising difficult economic times ahead. Manufacturing was also experiencing problems because of a recession at home and import quotas abroad. Numerous factory shutdowns were reported in the media. The frequency of shutdowns and the number of affected employees led the government to intervene, offering minimal worker protection during layoffs. Such reports led me to anticipate the worst possible scenario when I prepared my return in 1986. I fully expected to find several empty factories sitting on land rendered unproductive from industrial development and hundreds if not thousands of unemployed young women for whom factory work, like adolescence, was a memory. Given what I read in *Tempo* (1982; 1985), I would not have been surprised to find all of the factories out of production.

But my expectations of such significant changes were not met; instead, all twelve factories were still in production, and three new factories (bottled tea, pesticides, and pharmaceuticals) had located in the site. The textile factory had shut down sewing thread production, paring down their work force by only 80 workers, but overall, the demand for labor in the new factories had increased the number of industrial workers in the district. Although factories elsewhere in Java were shutting down, lower costs of production in this area, particularly of labor, were drawing new factories to the site.[1] Nevertheless, although the general conditions of factory activity and employment had the same appearance as before, important but less obvious changes had occurred.

I began interviewing in Nuwun using a list of young women categorized by whether they had had factory work experience in 1982 (table 26).[2] As expected, most of the single women I had followed in the early 1980s had since become wives and mothers. However, I quickly found that the categories of factory worker and nonfactory worker were no

TABLE 26
CHANGES IN FACTORY WORK STATUS, 1982–86
(N = 33)

	Status in 1982	
Status in 1986	*Factory workers* (N = 18)	*Nonfactory females* (N = 15)
Factory workers	9	7
Former workers	9	—
Nonfactory females	—	8

longer as applicable as before. By 1986 most young women had had some experience working in a factory. This restudy does not cover all factory workers in Nuwun but only those who were part of my earlier research and were from ages fifteen to twenty-four in 1981.[3]

WOMEN'S WORK, INCOME, AND MARITAL DECISIONS

It is generally thought that those women with some control over their labor and particularly their income have greater control over (or at least a greater say in) significant life decisions (timing of marriage, marital partner, fertility, sexuality) compared with women who have little control over both their labor and income (Blumberg 1984; Safilios-Rothschild 1982). Indeed, the rationale behind many development projects that offer income-generating possibilities for Third World women is that access to and control over some income will improve their standing within the household and their ability to influence decisions, such as those connected with fertility.

As discussed in chapter 3, the economic autonomy Javanese women experienced in the past was not associated with control over (or even having a say in) the timing of marriage or the choice of spouse, although it may have been related to the prevalence of divorce. Factory daughters are playing an increasingly important role in the family economy; has this economic participation been matched by more participation in decisions concerning their lives and their futures? In this chapter, I describe the paths that young women are traversing as they shape their life courses. Although my primary interest in their lives focuses on the extent to which they can negotiate marriage—both when and whom they marry—the leitmotif of nonstrategic behavior resurfaces.

MARRIAGE IN JAVA

Marriage is almost universal in Java, and celibacy (lifelong nonmarriage) is rare (H. Geertz 1961; P. Smith 1981). Thus, factory employment has not led to a situation in which women can decide not to marry at all. Since remaining single is not an option, the question explored here is whether young women can decide when and whom to marry.

Traditionally, marriage typically occurred early for rural females as parents attempted to avoid having an "old maid" (*gadis tua*) on their hands (McDonald 1983; H. Geertz 1961, 70). Parents made the marital decisions for their children, usually right after menarche, as a way to control sexuality. However, young women were sometimes married off even before puberty; these marriages were not necessarily consummated until the female was more mature (H. Geertz 1961, 56; Hull, Adioetomo, and Hull 1984).

In the past, parents usually arranged marriages through a series of negotiations, some of which still occur, though in modified form. A friend or relative of an available young man would inquire whether the young woman in question was available. If so, the young male suitor came with his parents to the house of the prospective bride so that the young couple could see each other (*nonton*, "to look at"). Although the young man knew why he was calling on her parents, the young female was not necessarily told the reason for the visit. Often, she did not even know that she was to marry until right before the wedding. And even if she was aware of the circumstances, she was rarely asked her opinion. Hildred Geertz reports that daughters only infrequently reject their proposed spouses, because "very young people cannot easily oppose their parents' desires and rarely do" (1961, 63). Village women in their forties explained that if parents asked for their opinion, they were too timid to say anything and too scared to object to the match.

Once the male's family decided to pursue the marriage and serious negotiations were underway, the couple's birthdates were checked to verify that they *cocok* (fit). The engagement period was brief, from a few days to a month (H. Geertz 1961, 64). The prospective groom gave his future mate a present when the agreement was made and then later, when the wedding was to take place, gave her another. Geertz (1961, 64) points out that, although such presents may have represented a transfer from the groom's to the bride's parents, they were neither bride-price nor dowry but "tokens of the agreement reached." In Geertz's site as in mine, the engagement present consisted of clothing for the bride and possibly jewelry (usually gold). The wedding was paid for by the bride's parents.

Two examples from young village women illustrate contemporary practices in arranged marriages. Wahayu, age twenty, never worked in a factory. She lived with her parents, husband, and two-year-old son and younger sister. At the time of our interview, she took care of domestic duties and sold vegetables in the market. At age sixteen, her parents matched her up, as her mother explains: "I knew my son-in-law's parents. They had a son and I had a daughter, and it was decided. It was all right with her. Those two [the couple] were happy and now they already have a son. That's my only grandchild. They met when it was time to marry, but before then, I told her about the marriage." When asked if, when she arranged the wedding, Wahayu knew about it or knew her prospective husband, the mother replied, "She didn't know yet; usually it's like that. They meet and then marry."

Pak Sumardi, when asked if his daughter met her future husband before he asked to marry her, replied: "No, she didn't know anything about it. My son-in-law first asked for her hand right away. Because he seemed to be a good child (*anak baik-baik*), I accepted right away. We spoke and firmed things up, and before their marriage I introduced them first so that she wouldn't be frightened (*kaget*)."

Changes in marriage patterns are occurring in Java specifically as well as in Southeast Asia more generally. Recent research indicates a general trend toward delayed marriage because of changes in the economy, education, and family organization (P. Smith 1981; Adioetomo 1987). A slow but steady shift toward self-selection of mates is associated with an increase in the age at marriage, declining divorce rates, and decreasing fertility.

Hildred Geertz found that with an increase in higher education, it was becoming more typical for young couples to meet in school on their own and to marry after having a longer acquaintance (1961, 57). Although this paradigm may hold for an urban setting, it does not describe rural Java. Fifteen years after Geertz's observation, a village study found that 60 percent of women aged fifteen to twenty-four still had arranged marriages. Although this rate is rather high, it is still lower than the 77 percent of arranged marriages among women aged twenty-five to thirty-four (Singarimbun and Manning 1974, 69).

In a rural village near my site, research conducted in 1980 for the Asian Marriage Survey showed that 58 percent of females aged 15 to 24 (n = 95) had marriages arranged by their parents, echoing the high proportion found by Masri Singarimbun and Chris Manning (1974).[4] Again, more younger women had some choice in marriage; the Asian Marriage Survey found that 63 percent of females aged 25 to 34 (n = 157) and 84 percent of females aged 35 to 44 had arranged marriages (Hull, Adioetomo, and Hull 1984, 6). In 1965, the mean age at marriage for females in Indonesia was 18.6; in 1971, it was 19.2 (P. Smith 1981, 4). By 1976, the age at marriage had increased to 19.9 in Indonesia—21.8 in urban areas and 19.1 in rural areas.[5] The trend of couples arranging their own marriages based on romantic love and attraction is associated with both increased age at marriage and a declining divorce rate, caused in part by more premarital choice exerted by the couple.

MARITAL ARRANGEMENTS IN NUWUN

A majority of factory workers had chosen their own spouse, and choice is associated with a later age at marriage. Of the eighteen married women with considerable factory experience, fourteen of them had chosen their own spouse.[6] Of the seven married women without factory experience, four had had arranged marriages. The three nonfactory women who chose their own spouse included an engaged teacher from a better-off household, one woman who worked on the poultry farm, and one who worked on her family's rice fields.

Among those who had married since working in the factory, age at marriage differed little compared with those considered nonfactory workers: 18.8 and 18.7.[7] When aggregated according to how the marriage was arranged, the average age at first marriage for those who chose their own spouse was 19.1, compared with 16.2 among those whose match was arranged.[8]

One important change is that parents generally were not pushing single working daughters into marriage. One twenty-year-old woman who had been working in a factory for six years was asked if she had plans to marry: "Not yet, not for a long time. I'm only twenty years old and I still want to work and be free. I don't only work for myself; I also work to help my parents." A seventeen-year-old worker in the poultry farm had been courted by a factory worker; according to her father, "She didn't want to marry him because she still wanted to live alone and still wanted to help pay for her younger brother's schooling." Factory workers' families received economic benefits from their working daughters and did not push them into early marriage as Javanese parents might have some years before.

Research in Hong Kong and Taiwan indicates that Chinese working daughters are postponing marriage so that they might contribute longer to the family economy; however, parents play a significant role in encouraging such postponement (Salaff 1981; Sheridan and Salaff 1984). Javanese parents neither discourage factory daughters from marrying early nor encourage them to work longer while single. Although the final outcome appears to be similar, Javanese parents are more passive in this process than their Chinese counterparts are.

I sought normative responses when I asked the parents of young married village women, "In Java, who usually chooses a daughter's husband: parents, the daughter, or other people?" Twelve out of nineteen parents felt that daughters should choose their husbands. Two felt that the decision depended on the child: some daughters could choose on their own, and others would need more help from parents. Three parents believed that parents and daughters together should make the decision, and only two parents felt that daughters should be matched by parents. Parents of single women felt that parents and the daughter should make the decision together, perhaps revealing their hope for some inclusion. Indeed, there was some correspondence between parental response and the family experience during courtship, but overall the reactions of this small group mirror changes in the organization of marriage in Java.

Hildred Geertz states that in selecting a mate for a daughter or son, parents considered the prospective spouse's class status and religious orientation; villagers and urban dwellers were concerned with inequality in rank between spouses (1961, 57). However, only one respondent in my survey mentioned social rank when recounting how she broke off with a rich city boyfriend for fear he was using her—a female from a poor, rural family. When asked what qualities they looked for in a son-in-law, almost all parents said they wanted him to be a good person from a good family (*keluarga baik*), the latter of which includes some consideration of class status. Eight of the eleven parents answering this question mentioned work: he must be a diligent worker, he mustn't be lazy, and he must be able to farm. One mother described her son-in-law in the following manner, emphasizing these attributes of hard work and diligence: "He is from this village, and I've known him and his parents for a long time. When he was young, he didn't like to be idle; he often looked for work such as housecleaning for the teacher, near my house, and from that job, he often saw my daughter."

Although parents did not directly articulate concerns about social rank, there were indeed economic considerations when a daughter married. In 1982, many parents of single factory workers hoped that factory employment would help their daughters find good husbands. In 1986, I asked the same parents of married daughters if their son-in-law's family economy was the same, better, or worse than theirs. Most parents felt that their son-in-law's family economy was better than theirs, although I could not verify whether this estimate reflected modesty or concrete differences. Almost half of the factory workers' parents—eleven out of twenty-five—felt that the son-in-law's family economy was better than theirs; this status was usually judged by the amount of farmland owned. Eight parents felt that his family economy was the same, and six parents thought it was worse than theirs. Only four out of seventeen felt that their daughter married into a family worse off economically than their own, meaning that most young women at least maintained if not improved their social rank through marriage. If parents' impressions of their in-laws' socioeconomic position are valid, factory workers did well in marriage, but no better or worse than their nonfactory peers did since these proportions were similar among the eight parents of nonfactory workers.

How did these young women meet their spouses? Eight of the fourteen factory women who chose their own spouses met them through work-related events. Two met on the road to work, with the future spouse often working as a driver, four met at the factory, and three met through friends who were coworkers. The remaining four women met their husbands in the village: one man was a village resident, and the others were either working in the village temporarily (selling goods or as agricultural laborers) or visiting friends or relatives.

MEETING HUSBANDS

Choosing one's own spouse does not imply that the choice is made slowly, carefully, "rationally" (however that is judged), or with substantial knowledge of the partner. In the 1950s Hildred Geertz found that even when a couple had made their own choice, usually they were only "briefly and casually acquainted" (1961, 56). From my respondents' descriptions, it seems that marital decisions were made very quickly on the basis of sexual attraction and flirtation, without much discussion. However, this speedy choice may not cause serious problems since expectations from a marital partner in rural Java do not include deep, soul-searching communication. As Valerie Hull (1975) found, and as noted in chapter 3, most villagers view marriage as an economic partnership more than a romantic liaison, although notions of romantic love are increasingly present in popular culture in Java. A few examples of how young couples met and decided on marriage illuminate the way such decisions are made.

At age sixteen Kartiyah was working in a factory when she was courted: "From the beginning I didn't know him because he was quiet, but he liked to watch for me, especially when I was away from home or coming home from the factory. Then he inquired about me to my older brother, and my brother asked my father's opinion. Then it was all right. Only then did he court me." She was asked if she agreed right away and if she had known him already. She replied, "I never knew him before. But I agreed right away." To the question "Did you ever have your own choice—for example, a friend you knew at the factory?" she answered,

"No, even though I worked, I didn't have many male friends; I felt humble because I'm not the child of a rich person."

Rujimah, another worker, told her marital story:

> I was engaged twice. The first time, I was with someone who was a construction worker in Semarang. I had first met him in a van [public transportation] on my way to the factory. He was going to Semarang. My parents agreed to the match when he asked my parents for my hand. One month before the wedding, my older brother told my parents that my fiancé had been a thief.[9] The next morning I broke it off and returned his gold [a gift of jewelry he gave her at the engagement]. One year later I was proposed to by a man I didn't know. They say he saw me when I was bathing in the river, and then he asked my parents for permission to marry me. I was told by my parents to accept this suitor. But because I really truly wasn't happy, five days after the wedding, I fled.[10]

Although these are cases in which the parents did not seek out a partner for their daughters, the daughters were not necessarily involved in the early stages. For women, "choosing" a spouse may entail direct action, such as talking and flirting, but it may also entail accepting the marriage proposal of a stranger who approaches them without parental intervention. Females can still remain passive as before: selecting a mate does not necessarily entail looking, dating, and selecting; indeed, it may require only one response.

Choosing a spouse unknown to the family may involve more risk and vulnerability for the woman at the same time that it offers a higher degree of sexual attraction. One worker (mentioned earlier) met her husband on the way to work and was pregnant with their second child when her husband's affairs with other women became apparent. Some villagers were so angry with his behavior that they wanted to beat him up. Instead, he was brought to the village leader, and it was decided that they would divorce after the wife gave birth.[11]

Another woman (also described earlier) met her partner on her way to work because he was a driver of a small van. They never married. He lived in a nearby town and sold hot soup (*bakso*), which he carried in tin and wooden containers balanced on his back. He refused to move to Nuwun, and she did not have the heart to leave her poor, aging, and widowed mother. He returned sporadically to spend the night with her—resulting in two children—but never announced his arrivals or departures. He also rarely gave her money unless she went to visit him and brought the children. However, she felt that it wasn't worth it to visit him after she paid for transportation and snacks. Certainly her poor background may have created low expectations in terms of a husband. Because she was very poor and had only her widowed and landless mother to help her, she was particularly vulnerable in marriage.

This vulnerability may be one difficult side-effect of young women's ability to negotiate over and perhaps decide whom they will marry and when. It should not, however, cause yearning for former times, when parents made all such choices for their children within an environment more protected by kin and neighbors. The high divorce rate signals severe dissatisfaction with that particular system. Nevertheless, although more room for negotiation and choice in marriage is a positive change for young Javanese women, whether or not to marry remains a nonquestion.

PARENTS' REACTIONS TO DAUGHTERS' CHOICES

What were parental responses to daughters' marriage choices? Most went along with their daughters, but conflict or ambivalence often surfaced, as seen in the following examples.

Jumaidah had long been interested in a neighbor's son. During my first stay in Nuwun, they had run off for a few days while he was in school, taking some of her mother's money. Jumaidah became pregnant and had a local healer give her a massage that was meant to cause an abortion. The masseuse told me that she then informed Jumaidah's mother, who had Jumaidah's older brother take Jumaidah out of the village and into his home.

Eventually, however, Jumaidah moved back to the village and in 1983 married her boyfriend. Jumaidah's mother agreed to it: "Choosing a spouse depends on the child because she has to like him. My daughter is good and already works; she also takes care of her daughter. I agreed with her choice. I really like him, but his parents like to talk and they are strange. His parents believe in tradition (*adat*) too much. We are neighbors separated by a few houses, but we live west and east of each other. According to his parents, this isn't good. If people are to marry, they should live north and south of each other, not west and east, because this way, something bad may happen. But actually, I don't pay much attention to such things." The tension between the in-laws was so high that the couple lived with their respective parents although they visited each other daily (*nglor-ngidul*).

Juyatmi was an attractive divorcee who lived with her aging parents. She was illiterate but had worked in the garment factory for years. She was very flirtatious with men, and other workers told me about rumors that Juyatmi had had an affair with the factory manager. This could have been true, yet the rumors could have arisen through jealousy. At age twenty-seven, she became interested in an older man, a traveling salesman who sold kitchenwares from village to village. Eventually, the relationship became serious, and her family accepted it as a marriage although a ceremony never took place.

I asked Juyatmi's parents if they gave their permission for her to marry the salesman. Her father responded: "Yes, but initially we didn't agree. But after a while, we allowed it. If my daughter chooses her own spouse, it's all right. It's different now compared with earlier times, but you can't force people to marry. She is allowed to choose her husband herself. The match is really up to God." Juyatmi's mother said that she was at first concerned about her daughter's decision.

> Initially, I felt heavy-hearted, but now everything has worked out fine. Juyatmi is my only child; I only have one child and she's it, but I want to have many grandchildren. In the past, many men wanted to be with her—men from this village and from other villages. There was a boyfriend from work who was still very young, but she didn't want to marry him. They didn't fit (*cocok*). But I advised her of all this. My son-in-law is good and takes care of his in-laws.

The traditional practice of matching birthdates has subsided with marriages based on attraction, and many in the older generation disapprove of this blatant disregard for cosmology. Rujimah's mother had the advantage of hindsight during our interview, as Rujimah had already divorced her husband. Rujimah and her husband had met on the way to work, in a van. Did her mother agree to her daughter's decision? "You can say I agreed; you can also say that I didn't. I didn't want to disappoint my child, but I also knew that at some time, maybe they would fail because their birth dates didn't fit (*cocok*). But luckily they only divorced; if not, one of them—either the husband or wife—would have died."

These stories illuminate several points about families and household whose importance is magnified in light of the Javanese familial norm of *rukun*, or social peace. First, intergenerational conflict and ambivalence is inherent in such decision-making processes where the distribution of power has shifted. Turning over the reins to the younger generation in marriage decisions has resulted in parents voicing conflict. Second, these histories do not indicate that younger household members are sublimating their wishes to an overarching "household strategy." More young people may be seeking their own spouses, but their goal in doing so is not to help their family of origin. If, however, marriage can be considered part of a household strategy, then household strategies are anything but carefully formulated, well-thought-out plans. Rather, they combine impetuousness, risk, luck, accidents, and some hormonal reactions rather than a series of rational calculations—which are, of course, often missing from sexual attraction, love affairs, and marital decisions elsewhere in the world.

ARRANGED MARRIAGES: PASSIVITY AND CONFLICT

Some factory daughters were too shy to get involved with men and did not seem to mind if their parents arranged their marriage. In a few cases, factory workers' parents played a traditional role and exerted their will before a daughter was old enough to make her own choice. It is also interesting to examine the other side—how daughters felt about being matched by their parents and their lack of power in this process.

Sukirah was nineteen and had worked in the noodle factory for a few years but stopped after she became pregnant with her first child.[12] She was matched at age sixteen. I asked her if she had wanted to choose her own husband, and she responded: "I never thought of it. I'm just a villager. My life is simple. If they arrange my marriage, it is all right. My parents always looked for someone good. When I married, I was still very young and didn't have any ideas about it." Did she agree with her parents' choice? "I just obeyed my parents' wishes. I'm the oldest child and have to set an example for my younger siblings." The passivity Sukirah expressed is shaped by the norms of Javanese femininity. Despite their economic autonomy, Javanese females are taught to adapt and obey, and not to express their opinions.

Maryuni also exemplifies the shyness and fear instilled in females. At age thirteen, she started working in the noodle factory, which accepted workers below the legal age. At fifteen, she switched to the garment factory, and she married at eighteen. Her parents chose her spouse, another villager from Nuwun. I asked her mother what Maryuni's reaction was to the news of her upcoming marriage. " When I told her, she was just quiet, and when I asked her if she wanted to, she just laughed. That meant she agreed." I asked Maryuni if she had wanted to choose her own spouse: "No, I only obeyed my parents' wishes. Village people are like that; usually they are matched. I agreed to their choice. I obeyed my parents' advice."

Suniwati was a hardworking and shy young woman who worked in the biscuit factory for eight years and was discussed earlier in regard to her substantial savings. Her parents chose a young man who knew their relatives in Semarang. He came to visit with his parents, and one week later, he asked Suniwati's parents for permission to marry her. They accepted. I asked her how she felt when she saw her future husband for the first time: did she like him? She answered: "No, I didn't like him, but I didn't hate him either. Eventually, I liked him to the point that finally, we had a child."

Not all daughters immediately and easily agree to their parents' choices. Kotiyah, a biscuit factory worker, was matched at age fourteen and had a child at age sixteen. Initially, she was not pleased with her mother's choice, but she eventually accepted it. "At the beginning, I didn't want to marry, not because I didn't like Amin, but because I was still too young and I didn't yet want to marry. You see, I had just finished grammar school." We asked her mother why she married off Kotiyah at such a young age. "First, because he asked for her hand and she hadn't yet had any other suitors. After his proposal, I accepted it right away. To reject a proposal isn't good except if the child is already engaged. Second, besides that I'm already a widow and Kotiyah's the oldest child in this household. My two oldest children already have their own houses. If she marries, she and her husband can stay here with me and help me work the sawah."

Although arranged marriages are still occurring, the nature of arrangements differs from those of previous generations. Even if their marriages are arranged, young women today are marrying later and there is slightly more room for disagreement. Although some parents still simply inform or order a daughter about her marriage, others give daughters a chance to express strong disagreement and to negotiate for another choice. The socialization of Javanese females works against expressing disagreement in such a situation; in their mothers' generation, parents would not have even given daughters a chance to respond.

FERTILITY AND FAMILY FORMATION

It is too soon to analyze how factory work affects fertility, but there are some early indications that workers will restrict and control conception. Two current factory workers, both with two children, have been sterilized because the financial burden of two children was already quite heavy. One of the women—mentioned earlier in the description of consensual unions—is so poor that she could not even afford the five dollars for the sterilization operation; instead, the village head arranged for the procedure. Their poverty and lack of help from the family required these workers to keep their factory jobs, and factory work was not compatible with childrearing.

Family formation and family structure do, however, show more signs of change because of factory employment. The savings from factory work are facilitating the move to an independent nuclear family household. Almost all the married women (regardless of work status) interviewed still lived with parents, even if they had already had children. As demonstrated in chapter 7, factory workers come not from the poorest families but from those able to get along with little or no return from a daughter's labor. This same financial margin is affecting nuclear family formation among factory workers.

Married factory workers were actively preparing to build their future houses, piling newly bought wood, bricks, tiles, and cement in corners of their parents' houses. Each family had its own particular financial agreement, depending on what the parents owned and what they could afford. Former workers were able to put all of their savings from the arisan toward the new household. By contrast, the few married women with little or no factory experience were poorer and much more vague about future plans for their own households. Sundari worked at the poultry farm and lived with her husband and elderly grandmother, who owned less than one-quarter hectare of land. Sundari was not saving to build a new house because she felt that she had to stay and care for her grandmother. At her grandmother's death, she will probably inherit the house if not the land.

Wahayu was from a very poor and landless family, and she, too, worked at the poultry farm. She, her husband, and two children lived with her parents and younger sister in a small house with few possessions. They were too poor to live as two separate households under one roof, and money was pooled for food consumption at least. The family had three goats, and each daughter owned one.

Because of household income needs, Wahayu could not participate in the arisan at the poultry farm. She also felt that she couldn't even afford the village arisan, which required a monthly deposit of only a dollar. When asked if she planned to start her own household, she said, "From the start I had plans to build my own house, but I don't know when we'll be able to do it." Her father had given them some land behind the house, but she hadn't yet accumulated materials. She said that she wanted to sell vegetables on the side, in addition to her farm job, to earn money for building materials, but she could not do so because her child was too young to leave alone.

All young married women interviewed expressed the desire to have their own household, but women like the two mentioned above had saved little and had no tangible plans for realizing their desires. Those with factory jobs (such as Rini) estimated that it would take them four to five years from the time they were married until the house would be built. Suniwati could use factory wages and savings almost solely for her new house, and it would take her only two years to build after marriage. However, married nonfactory workers from poor families experienced the life-cycle squeeze; they could not even begin to estimate when they would have their own houses. It would take them longer than five years unless they inherited a house earlier.

Thus, factory earnings facilitate and hasten the move from an extended family household to an independent nuclear household at an early stage of a couple's life cycle. (See Freedman et al. 1982 on similar processes in Taiwan.) Economic resources from earnings also affect a factory daughter's postmarital autonomy, as she can leave her parental household earlier to set up her own.

An in-depth examination of two factory daughters illustrates more fully the interaction between structural change and the life course of those participating in such change. Their stories focus on work, family dynamics, family economy, and marital choice. These case studies continue the life histories of Wagiah and Rini begun in chapter 8.

CASE STUDIES

CASE 1: WAGIAH

When I returned in 1986, Wagiah had remarried but still continued to work in the textile factory. Her husband was quite a bit older—fifty-three—and had seven grandchildren from his previous marriage. He worked as a driver for a family in Semarang. He had wanted to remarry and, he told me, had been looking for a wife when a friend of his from Wagiah's village had shown him her photograph. He found her attractive and came to the village to meet her. He liked her very much and "asked her to marry right away. I told her that she had to tell me in a week. If she wanted to, fine, and if not, that was okay, too." They married in 1984, and this move greatly improved Wagiah's poor family, at least from the perspective of consumption. There was more furniture in the house and two large speakers attached to a radio that ran on electricity. Her new husband had also wired the house for electricity.

Wagiah's mother was happy with her new son-in-law, who made her life more secure. She had had fewer work opportunities in the past few years because the Lurah, her patron, was now retired and did not need to entertain as before. Therefore, there was less work, and she was older and couldn't work as hard.

Although Wagiah continued to work in the factory, she was able to drop her extra income-earning activities such as ironing. She complained about how tired she was from factory work and talked about quitting. Wagiah was less conscientious about work and didn't work as hard as before: if she was sick or if it was raining, she stayed home and took better care of her health. She also wanted to have a child but had not yet conceived.

Wagiah seemed to be happier and said it was nice not to be alone anymore. However, I did not have a chance to speak with her alone. Her husband answered all of the questions I asked of her and escorted us on the walks I had suggested in an attempt to speak with her privately. Wagiah was born into a poor family and had not had an easy life, but this marriage seemed to ease family economic conditions and relieve her of a difficult burden. However, her independent streak was gone.

CASE 2: RINI

Rini's story introduced this book, and it is therefore appropriate to continue her story with more details about work and marriage. Her wedding, described earlier, was one of two attempts to get her married. Initially, her parents had arranged a marriage for her. A young man chosen by her parents came with his family and asked to marry her. She agreed initially but then changed her mind. Her mother, Ngatmi, explained: "Rini is a rebellious child. Earlier, a young man courted her and the marriage agreement was made. We had set the wedding for Wednesday, but the Friday before, she ran away and went to her grandmother's in Wonogiri. The wedding was canceled because it was said that she didn't want it."

Then her uncle asked Rini if she would like to meet another young man, and she consented. Ngatmi recounted: "Rini said she wanted to see this person first. Then my son-in-law was brought here by our relative, and it turned out even Rini liked him. Then we discussed the wedding and arranged it quickly. But when it was time to marry, Rini made trouble again. Her father then told her that she had said previously that she wanted to marry him; why the sudden change? He advised her to try it first, and later, if it didn't work (*tidak cocok*), she could choose another husband." As mentioned in the Preface, when Rini married, she wouldn't pose with her husband for photographs and wouldn't sleep with him.

And so Rini ended up in a partly arranged marriage. When I left in 1983, Rini had been a drain on the family economy, which was already suffering from wedding debts, and she had been forced to quit her factory job so that she could free her father's labor to sell wood. Her mother told me, "We spent the most on her wedding. When Rini was married, I rented land to Pak Bekel for two years, but now we have it back. We had debts to some relatives, but now we've already paid back most of it. We spent a lot on food, clothes, and make-up, and we rented a tape recorder."

Rini's marriage was rocky in the beginning, and these conflicts eventually caused her mother to leave for Jakarta in protest. Ngatmi explained:

> I was so angry I wanted to leave the house. I thought of my young son and felt sorry because he's still small, but I didn't want to return because of what was happening at home. When Lebaran was almost over, I thought my son would think his mother had disappeared. Three days before Lebaran, I returned home from Jakarta. My son cried and everyone cried. I said I would leave again if things hadn't changed and were still like before. But Rini was nice to her husband; I was surprised. She's been nice to him until now, but luckily, he, too, is nice and patient.

I asked Rini about the difficult times in her marriage: "Before, when I didn't think about the long run, I wanted to still do as I liked. Before, right after marrying, I couldn't stand to look at him. I really had liked him before, but after marriage we often fought. I even slept in my grandmother's house. My grandmother was angry with me and told me to return home because I was married. He was very patient even though I left home; he stayed here with my parents. I finally went home, but I really didn't want to because I liked a man from Gentan. Every time I came home from work I met him. He was a good person and handsome. I was reckless and a lot of people talked about it." I asked about her husband's response.

> At first he didn't know that I liked someone from Gentan, but it turns out that a lot of people told him about it. He really panicked and then came looking for me. And he asked the advice of a dukun. My parents told him that if he was patient and stood up to me, then I would choose to stay with

> him. After that he began to look for me and meet me after work, but I still didn't want him to. In the end, I went home alone.
>
> . . . At home we still fought continuously even though by then I was already pregnant. I felt it was hard to feel happy with him. I was still angry with him. In the end, my mother couldn't stand it and left for Jakarta, for about five months at least. During that time my younger siblings were still small; the youngest was only four years old. I was forced to do all kinds of tasks, whereas before I had never worked at home. All the housework I did alone; even though I was seven months pregnant I cooked and cleaned and shopped. When my mother left, my brother suffered the most. Every time he was told to eat, he said he wanted to wait for mother to return. His body got very skinny.

The situation finally improved when Rini's mother returned. "Maybe we were really together, maybe because I changed jobs with my mother and I could understand and feel like a parent. Before, I really liked to do as I pleased."

In 1986, Rini returned to work in the garment factory while her mother took care of her three-year-old daughter. Ngatmi said, holding her granddaughter: "When I think of this child's mother [Rini], I feel angry. If this child's father hadn't been patient, I surely wouldn't have my granddaughter now."

Rini's mother was one of the parents who thought that factory work would improve her daughter's chances at a good marriage and thought that her son-in-law's family economy was better than hers. Although both families considered themselves farmers, Rini's family had only a little land, whereas her husband's parents had at least enough for subsistence needs.

Does factory work affect one's experience looking for a husband? Ngatmi answered, "Yes, maybe. But Rini didn't meet her husband in the factory. But I think that those who work in a factory are different compared with those who don't. Working in a factory gives you a lot of experience. Every day you meet with lots of people and you change, maybe because you meet a lot of people at work and you learn how to meet people. Also, you have a lot of friends and it's easy then to make friends."

I asked Ngatmi who usually chooses the husband: parents, the daughter, or other people? "For me, it's up to the child. Rini's younger sister chose her own husband. A daughter usually is visited by boys, and then she can choose which one she likes, that's what I mean. But for the boy, I will help choose so that he doesn't make the wrong choice, and I'll find the most suitable girl for him."

GENERATIONAL CHANGES IN MARRIAGE: RINI AND NGATMI

Certain differences between Rini and her mother, Ngatmi, exemplify broader sociodemographic changes in Java, particularly with regard to age at marriage, family structure, income earning, and family formation.

Ngatmi began her life story: "I was married when I was thirteen years old. I was still a young child, I still liked to play market, and I didn't know that I was to be married. My husband was already older. In those times, parents matched you up without telling the child first. I was married in this way and didn't know I was to marry. I hadn't menstruated yet; I only started menstruating about three years after marriage." I asked if she began having intercourse before menarche. "Yes," she replied, "but I wasn't happy about it and I was just quiet; I didn't want to say anything to anybody. I lasted about five years in that marriage, but finally I really couldn't stand it any longer and I left." She had found out that her husband had gotten a relative of hers pregnant.

Ngatmi was angry with her husband's behavior and no longer wanted to stay married to him. At about age eighteen, she went to her uncle and aunt's house, where she lived for several years.[13] She worked with them, selling cooked food. All the while she stayed with her relatives, she didn't send news home of her whereabouts. Finally, she went home to an emotional reunion because her parents had thought she was dead. These worries had made her father ill; the family had sold two cows and some land in order to look for her. Her husband was still there, and his child was already big; she immediately asked for a divorce. She met her second husband six months later and stayed married to him for a year. Another arrangement was made for her third marriage, which lasted two years. "We didn't fit and I wasn't happy. When people don't fit, rather than drag it out, it's better to split up."

Her fourth and current husband—Rini's father—met her when she was selling food at her aunt's warung. After she left for home, he came to her parents to ask her to marry. She moved to his house, where they lived with his widowed father; when he died, they inherited his house and still live there. Ngatmi had a total of eight children, three of whom died in infancy.

Ngatmi's various marriages, separations, and divorces and the deaths of her infants make her family history complex. There was no simple movement from an extended to nuclear family structures but a great deal of fluctuation from one family structure to another. Ngatmi had lived in a nuclear family of sorts about three times, complex nuclear families about three times (when she was married without children), and various extended family situations, as she did in 1986, when she lived with her children and grandchildren. Part of the complexity of her life story stems from a lack of choice in marriage partners and subsequent marital dissolution, compounded by the constraints and difficulties of poverty.

Like her mother, Rini also has a mind of her own, but she will probably have fewer husbands, fewer children, and fewer different family configurations; also, probably fewer of her children will die. Because of her earnings, she will have her own house earlier in life than did her mother, who had to wait for her father-in-law's death to have her own house.

When I left the village after my second visit, this family was calmer than it had been in 1982 and in better shape economically, with two daughters married and the two younger children in school. Rini's husband had just switched jobs to the poultry farm, where the wage was lower but the job was safer than in public transportation. The turmoil and conflict of earlier years had been resolved. Ngatmi described her own sense of satisfaction in the way things had been resolved when she stated, "In this family, there is now rukun."

MARRIAGE AND TAIWANESE FACTORY DAUGHTERS

Industrialization in Taiwan has also affected marriage practices. Research on Taiwanese factory daughters has focused more on work and the family economy than on marriage. However, Lydia Kung found that "personal autonomy increased the most for women" in dating and marital practices (1983, 127). Like their Javanese counterparts, Taiwanese factory workers have more opportunities to meet men when they work in factories. In many cases, particularly when a daughter's income constitutes an indispensable part of household income, Taiwanese parents encourage working daughters to delay their marriages and work longer for the family economy: as one parent commented, "If I let my daughters marry now, that means losing their earnings. I wouldn't let them marry so early (at twenty-one and eighteen)" (Kung 1983, 140). There is little in this literature about choice of spouse, but Kung found that women have more say in whom they will marry.

In her Hong Kong research, Janet Salaff found that, although industrialization has given young Chinese women who work in factories more room to choose their own spouses, families still expect and demand that he come from the same ethnolinguistic group and that the parents choose the year and month of marriage. As Salaff comments, "This parental concession to a love marriage does not reduce parental control," for parents may create new bonds with kin through their daughter's marriage (1981, 268–69).

What is clear, however, is that all of these years of contributing financially does not translate into influence, authority, or rights over family property. The effects of factory employment on the lives of Taiwanese women belie the image of industrialization freeing young people from patriarchal control.

CONCLUSION

This study supports the contention that Javanese women's control over economic resources may strengthen their position in other decision-making processes, particularly when their marriage, sexuality, and fertility are at stake. Industrial capitalism, through the various changes it incurs, appears to set processes in motion that encourage women to choose their own spouses. Although daughters are playing an increased role in their life decisions, choice in marriage includes behavior ranging from considerable input from the female to almost as much passivity as before, though with less parental interference. Researchers must take care not to project a Western and somewhat monolithic view of "choice" onto such variation and such a different cultural situation. These findings suggest that culturally sensitive notions of choice should be integrated into socioeconomic and demographic studies of sexuality, marriage, fertility, and family formation.

Helen I. Safa (1990) found patterns similar to those in Java in her research in Puerto Rico and the Dominican Republic, where the effects of industrialization are contradictory: women are subordinated through such employment while more traditional patriarchal patterns of family authority are challenged, giving way to more egalitarian forms. Women's decision-making roles within the family are not enhanced by their employment, however, a finding corroborated by Salaff (1981) in her detailed research in East Asia. This Javanese case suggests that industrialization may further broaden women's boundaries for negotiation within a kinship system where they already have a certain position and certain rights. In a highly patriarchal kinship system, industrial employment and wage earning does not seem to chip away at the family power structure or let women in; instead, factory employment and its wages are reasons for increasing and lengthening the period before marriage, with parents holding the reins. Thus, industrialization strengthens existing forms of family power; in Taiwan, this process permits further control of daughters, whereas in Java and perhaps Malaysia, it allows for more personal gains for the women involved.

CHAPTER X

The Family Economy Revisited: Daughters, Work, and the Life Cycle

In chapter 8 I demonstrated that young factory workers can play an important role in the family economy, but that not all necessarily do so. In this chapter I examine the economic contribution of factory daughters four years later.

WORK AND THE FAMILY ECONOMY

Both life-cycle and cohort effects are seen in the factory employment histories of village women. Some from the first generation of factory workers had left the labor force when they bore children, while younger women, who had been in the nonfactory group in 1982, had moved into the industrial labor force. Indeed, Nuwun had an entirely new generation of factory workers from younger cohorts. Late afternoon observations of young women returning home from the factories indicated that at least another twenty-five to thirty village females started factory employment after I left Nuwun in early 1983.

Of the eighteen women who had been factory workers in 1982, only half had quit their jobs. Quitting was related to life-cycle changes: either a new husband forbade factory employment, or young children required their mother's time. Two husbands demanded that their wives quit their jobs because of pride ("She doesn't need to work; I can take care of her") or a desire for control ("It's better if married women are at home"). The other seven women hoped to return to factory jobs later when their children grew up.[1]

Five years previously, motherhood had pushed working women out of the industrial work force or prevented them from attempting to enter it through a combination of childcare needs and factory policy. In 1986 the nine women who remained employed in factories were almost all married and had children.[2] Contrary to my earlier findings, motherhood had not necessarily pushed women out of the industrial labor force. Factory management did not intervene in these particular factories; when childcare was available and the mother wanted or had to continue working, factory work was not interrupted. Other Southeast Asian case studies report that "the majority of village females stop working in factories upon marriage" (Ong 1987, 98; see also Mather 1982; Mather 1985); however, most workers elsewhere are migrants. This somewhat unusual situation in rural Central Java could be attributed to the proximity of factories to villages and the availability of workers' families for childcare.

My previous category of "nonfactory workers" also demonstrated cohort effects: there were few people left in this group. Seven women who had previously been constrained by the household's need for labor and had not been allowed by parents to seek factory work were now factory workers. Only three remained single.[3]

Family structure reflected these life-cycle changes; formerly simple nuclear families were now complex nuclear families (adding a daughter's spouse) or extended families (adding her spouse and children). Most extended families would remain so for some years while the young couple saved up money to build their own house.[4] The families of those who were still single or who were married before 1982 showed no change in composition or structure.

A final category reflecting broader economic changes consists of nine women who had been nonfactory workers in 1982 and remained so in 1986. Who are the women who resist factory employment, and why? One woman from a better-off household had become a teacher in a nearby small city and was engaged to marry another teacher. Four nonfactory workers, all married, performed either agricultural or domestic work.[5] Finally, three women who remained "nonfactory workers" were employed full-time in the three chicken farms on the edge of Nuwun. These farms were owned by Chinese Indonesians from a nearby city.[6]

RURAL NONAGRARIAN PRODUCTION: VILLAGE WOMEN AND PROLETARIANIZATION

In the poultry farms, working conditions were arduous and even less protected than in the factories. Although poultry farm work was less desirable than factory work, it was one of the few choices women had for steady remunerated employment. For example, one female who worked in a chicken farm had been rejected by a factory personnel manager when she applied for work because she was below the minimum legal age (fourteen). The chicken farm, however, accepted her for employment.

Factory wages had since improved to about 900 to 1,100 rupiah a day, but wages in the chicken farm were lower by half—550 rupiah a day.[7] Transportation would have been unaffordable at such low wages. In the poultry farms, the average working day was from 7:00 A.M. to 4:00 P.M., but employees often had to work until 9:00 P.M. And they were expected to work seven days a week. If a worker missed one day, she lost her fifty-cent wage and the entire weekly bonus of 1,000 rupiah ($1.00). Therefore, she lost $1.50 for missing one day and an additional $0.50 for every day missed thereafter.

These young women, like factory workers, were rural proletarians from landless or near-landless households. Certain factors are similar in the organization of factory and poultry farm production: the inflexibility of work hours, the separation of family members during the production process, and the fact of having employers from different ethnic backgrounds. At the same time, certain features substantially distinguish the two settings of factory production and poultry production. The poultry farm is in the village, and the job consists of farm work with relatively low levels of technology. Workers are not exposed to new forms of production, nonagrarian skills, or technology or to workers from other villages. The experience and conditions of poultry farm employment are much closer to agricultural wage labor than to nonagricultural, industrial work. Because of these different conditions, I distinguish between factory workers and those without factory work experience.[8]

Both factory work and poultry farm production reflect two general trends occurring in rural Java (as discussed in chapter 2). First, there is an increase in urban capitalist ventures in rural areas. Terry McGee (1984) has argued that as urban capital draws on rural labor, materials, and rural sites for production, the former distinctions between urban and rural are blurred. Second, researchers have noted an increased proletarianization in Javanese rural households (White and Wiradi 1989; Husken and White 1989). As landholdings are increasingly consolidated, agriculture provides a smaller proportion, if any at all, of rural household incomes. Families attempt to hold on to their small parcels of land, but some family members must seek wage labor. Increased nonagricultural employment opportunities for young men and women have meant that fewer young people seek agricultural labor. Indeed, as these young women demonstrate, rural comes to refer to nonagricultural rather than agricultural. And this particular change has penetrated the consciousness of villagers.

When I arrived in 1981, factory employment was still a relatively new employment option for young women and their families; some viewed it with skepticism and apprehension. Over time, as villagers observed young workers returning home with substantial savings or cash bonuses at the end of Ramadan, the financial aspects of factory employment became more obvious, while fears of moral laxity subsided. In the early 1980s, villagers talked to me about the factories and factory work as something new, strange, and different. They often told me how these new factories pulled village youth out of agriculture, changed the desires of the young, and affected the supply of agricultural labor. A few people told me that factory girls were not nice because they mixed with men outside the village. Yet at Lebaran, the exact amounts that workers received for their cash bonuses were discussed openly among village women with excitement and envy. At that time, factory workers were a distinct group of young females within a larger population of young village females. They were among the first generation of employees in a new and different organization of production, and even their clothing and behavior were emblems of this difference.

By 1986, with the exception of a few young women from better-off families who could afford secondary education, factory employment was considered the norm for young women. This type of work was now accepted by villagers as a natural part of the female life cycle. Factory workers were no longer distinguishable from other young women; villagers had the impression that almost all young women go directly from school into the factories, just as American teenagers start high school after finishing junior high. Villagers also knew more about the factories (such as the different types of factories, which very few people knew in 1982) and about factory employment. These young women left home daily wearing Western-style clothing and earned a steady wage while mixing with young men and women from other villages; accumulating savings had become part of the natural course of a female's life and an integral part of village life. This acceptance of factory employment, which the villagers had once viewed suspiciously, reflects their adaptation to proletarianization and industrialization.

CONTRIBUTIONS TO THE FAMILY ECONOMY

When I asked parents if factory daughters were contributing to the family economy, almost all of the ambivalence and dissatisfaction freely voiced in 1982 was gone. Most parents of current workers felt that their daughters were contributing to the family economy either directly with cash or goods or indirectly by taking care of their own needs. Changes in a daughter's contributions to the family economy were directly related to the female life cycle: married women were contributing regularly and substantially to the family economy, whereas single workers were somewhat more autonomous. Although these daughters did seem more filial in their economic behavior than they had been several years ago, many still borrowed money from parents.

From parents' perspectives, daughters were acting more responsibly—meaning, in their terms, more altruistically—with their weekly wages, which now were contributing to daily subsistence needs. When asked if their daughters contributed to the family economy, several parents responded that they took care of a substantial part of the household's daily needs, ranging from small to relatively large contributions: "Of course she contributes, even if it's a little. If I don't have money, I borrow some from her"; "She contributes to this family by lowering her daily needs in the household"; "Yes, she contributes a lot to this family's economy, helping with both daily needs and things like furniture." A widowed and landless mother who lived with her daughter and grandchildren responded: "Yes, she supports every member of this family. But we can use her wage only for our daily needs because it's so low."

The behavior of daughters changed as they became wives and mothers, and their parents benefited from these female and family life-cycle changes. Those who were still single often remained less forthcoming with their wages. Wagini, a factory worker, lived with her husband, parents, and younger brother. Her mother commented on the greater comfort for parents later in the family life cycle: "Three of my children work: two in the poultry farms, and Wagini in the biscuit factory. All of them helped us financially before they were married. But now I live with Wagini and she's the one who supports me and my husband. Now I live well." That her three children could earn steady wages from nonagrarian employment while producing for urban markets without having to move from home again illustrates the increased urban-rural connections discussed earlier.

The mother of a married worker (Rujiah) employed at the garment factory did receive contributions from her daughter, but wages were low and variable: "My daughter's income is very small—only enough to buy tea and sugar." Of Maryuni, another garment factory employee who lived with her husband, parents, and four younger brothers, her mother said, "She contributes financially even if it's only to buy daily household needs. During Lebaran, she buys clothes for everyone in the family." But she also added, "She uses her wage for herself. Before, I asked her if she wanted to help me pay for her three younger brothers' schooling, and she just laughed. Now, sometimes she buys them a notebook or a pen."

Rujiah, age nineteen, married in 1985; she was seven months pregnant during my second visit. She had worked in the biscuit factory but had switched to the garment factory. When asked if her daughter contributed to the family economy, Rujiah's mother said, "Of course. She buys rice or sugar or helps pay debts." However, Rujiah's father, when asked if she gave some of her wage to her parents before she was married, dissented: "Wah, never. She took it all herself. I don't even know how much she makes, but maybe about 500 rupiah a day."

All of these parents agreed that daughters were contributing to daily household subsistence needs, even if they provided only a small amount. These comments also reveal that despite such changes, income pooling remained a conflictual issue within the family.

It is important to understand that these workers' wages had not changed over time: they still earned about $1.00 a day, which was not sufficient for subsistence needs. The difference we are observing here is in the contents of their expenditures, particularly for the married workers with children. Many of them were buying less make-up and fewer clothes; instead of going to movies or paying for haircuts and jewelry, they were contributing that money to their families. In other words, they were still dependent financially on their parents, who took care of some needs, but they were redirecting some of their other expenditures toward the household.

SINGLE WORKERS AND THE FAMILY ECONOMY

Single factory workers were somewhat more variable in their behavior than married workers were, and parents depended less on their contributions. Suryani's family had left Nuwun and moved to a nearby town. Suryani, age twenty, worked in a well-paying small garment factory in the city. She earned more than $8.00 a week plus transportation money.[9] She had been a factory daughter since she was fourteen years old and had helped her younger brother through school. Before he was employed, she gave him 1,000 to 1,500 rupiah every week. She gave her parents money every week, and if she didn't, they asked for it. "It's not much, only 2,000 to 2,500 rupiah, which is already enough (*cukup*) because our family is small. I don't work to support only myself but also my parents and my brother when he was still in school."[10]

Although Suryani's contributions were steady and she was a faithful daughter, I also inquired if she asked her parents for money. "Sometimes, but now, rarely. If I ask them for money, usually it's for transportation [to work], sometimes 100 to 200 rupiah, but only if my weekly wage is spent on contributions for weddings. They know that if I ask for money it's because I really don't have it, and anyway, I only ask for a little." She explained that every time a friend or neighbor got married, she contributed 1,000 to 1,500 rupiah, and if there was a party, she gave about 2,000 rupiah: "This month is the best Javanese month to marry or become engaged. I continuously have to contribute [to those getting married]. This week I have to contribute almost every day. My wage from last week is almost gone because of these contributions."

The mother of Jumeni, a single factory daughter, was asked if her daughter contributed to the family economy:

> Yes, a little bit. But what she does is relieve us financially because she doesn't need to ask me or her father for money any longer. Usually, before returning home, she goes to a warung or a store to buy cooking spices, sugar, coffee, or tea. Sometimes she buys presents like oranges or cooked food. But if not, she gives me money to buy tempeh.

The parents of Kusti, an unmarried eighteen-year-old worker, said, "She doesn't help our economy on a daily basis. [Since working] she has never asked us for money; she can buy her clothes and other needs by herself and also clothing for her younger sisters." Kusti confirmed that she did not take care of daily household needs but also explained another important dynamic of the family economy: her father often asked her for money on her payday, usually 500 to 1,000 rupiah. She thought that the money was probably used to buy cigarettes. Her two younger siblings also asked her for money on payday, and she gave them about 500 to 700 rupiah each, which they saved.

The mother of Tutuk, a single factory worker, said, "Yes, she contributes to the family economy, but the amount isn't set. Either I ask her and if she has money she gives me some, or if I don't ask, she gives me about 3,000 rupiah." I asked Tutuk if she still borrowed money from her parents; she replied:

> No, only sometimes, about once a month, and I ask for 1,000 rupiah at the most. It's just the opposite: my father often asks me for money. In one month, he asks one to three times, but never for more than 3,000 rupiah. My younger brothers and sister often ask for money, especially to buy pens and pencils; like the other day, they asked me to buy books and pens. Even my older brother, who doesn't study any longer, often asks for money to have fun. They ask for about 500 to 3,000 rupiah. But I give my parents more than 2,000 rupiah and of course I say that they needn't pay it back.

Single factory daughters did not automatically contribute some of their wages to their families every week, but the above descriptions indicate that not only siblings but also parents asked working daughters for cash. Daughters developed different ways of responding to and evaluating these requests. The descriptions also emphasize that without the mechanism of the arisan, such continuous demands for cash would make saving difficult, if not impossible.

NONFACTORY WORKERS AND THE FAMILY ECONOMY

Those who had never worked in a factory had more trouble contributing to the family economy unless they earned a steady wage. The parent of a nonfactory married woman said: "She doesn't work, she only helps us in the rice fields. She's never earned money, so she's never given us any." Another nonfactory worker's parent had a similar response: "She's never worked at all, only childcare, cooking, and taking care of the house." And yet another parent said: "Oh, she doesn't contribute, but she often asks us for money to go somewhere. The money is all spent on snacks." These women *do* work and contribute their labor toward the production of subsistence. Their work is undervalued by parents ("she doesn't work") because it does not produce cash or a wage.

Even if young nonfactory women worked for wages—for instance, at the poultry farms—they had access to smaller sums of cash because of lower wages. One married poultry worker still living with her parents helped pay for the education of her younger siblings by buying books and paying fees. Her mother said: "Yes, of course she helps the family economy. In terms of daily needs, I take care of them, but she helps pay for her siblings' schooling. She buys books, pays school fees, gives them snack money, or buys their school needs." Her parents did explain that she rarely borrowed from them except when she wanted to buy something special, and then she paid them back. The schoolteacher in this nonfactory group did not remit much to her parents: "She contributes a little. Sometimes she buys household goods, but for my part, she already can take care of herself and I'm pleased."

Former factory workers—those who had stopped working because of marriage or children—were no longer contributing money to the family economy, although the family often still had access to savings from factory wages. In such cases, parents referred to contributions made when their daughter was still working.

I attempted to elicit normative responses from parents about daughters, wages, and the family economy. They were asked, "In Java, unmarried daughters who receive a wage usually (a) give all their wage to their parents, (b) give some of their wage to their parents, (c) give little of their wage to parents, or (d) give most of their wage to parents." All parents, regardless of their daughter's work experience, answered that daughters usually give little to parents. Parents were also asked if single Javanese working daughters usually spend their wages on their own needs or on family/household needs. Seventeen parents responded that daughters spend wages on their own needs; four parents, all with married factory daughters living at home, answered that daughters spend wages on household needs.

Parental responses to the general question "Should a working daughter give her wages to her parents?" appear to be fairly ambiguous, but parents' very solid expectations of remittances from daughters are expressed indirectly, as seen in the following responses:

> Oh, don't, just give a little or what is necessary, but save the rest for yourself or use it to enjoy yourself.
>
> It depends, it's not fixed. If parents are poor, it's okay to help them, but if they're not, it's not necessary.
>
> I think that the one who earns money is the one who owns it; it's up to her how to use it. She can give it to her parents or use it for herself. If she gives me some, I'l! accept it, but it needn't be much, just enough for necessities.

Although parents may have accepted their daughter's decision to keep a substantial proportion of her wages for herself, they still expected some help. Perhaps these parents seemed liberal about returns from a daughter's wages because they had access to her savings. Savings through the arisan are more substantial than wages and play an increasing role in the family economy.

THE ARISAN

The importance of the arisan became more apparent during the past several years as families experienced an agricultural disaster and as young women began preparing for their new households. The advantages of the arisan were obvious, and most workers chose to join one, but not all had the choice. Workers still could participate in an arisan only if they were not constrained by daily household financial needs. In other words, the poorest workers could not afford to save money.

WORKERS WHO DON'T PARTICIPATE IN THE ARISAN

Out of the fourteen current factory workers in my sample, only four were not in an arisan. Two married women with children, both heads of households who had previously been in arisans,[11] had been forced to withdraw because their wages went toward daily household needs: "My wage isn't sufficient (*cukup*) for an arisan; I have to support everyone in this house, so I'm responsible economically." This married worker made use of savings from former arisans; she had sold four rings and three necklaces because of crop failure and then to pay to prepare the sawah for planting again. Because her husband was working in the Middle East and could not participate, she had to pay for all necessary agricultural labor.

The other married worker, Siti, was mentioned in the last chapter because she was able to remodel the inner walls of the house and buy furniture with her savings. In the intervening years, the imitation red velvet upholstery material tore and the furniture was thrown away, leaving a tiny room with only a wooden box to sit on. With two children and a mother to support, Siti said, "I can't afford to give money to the arisan; I don't even have enough for our daily needs." And indeed she didn't: she could not afford the 1,000 rupiah needed each week to buy powdered milk for her small, sickly children, who whimpered with hunger. Her mother explained that a few years before, she had sold Siti's gold jewelry, her savings from the arisan, "to improve our fate by renting land for two years. I worked on this land with two of my sons-in-law. But it turned out that this sawah didn't bring results because the harvest was eaten by rats: it failed. We lost money. We also lost our savings and didn't get back the capital from the jewelry." Because of difficult times, they also had to sell the tiny bit of sawah they had owned in 1982 (one-sixteenth hectare). This family, living on the edge of subsistence, can easily become destitute if Siti misses a few weeks of work. This is one of the few cases in which savings had been used for a productive investment (land), but unfortunately without success.

Rujiah had worked in factories on a seasonal basis, participating in arisans on occasion. Her family was very poor and needed her weekly wage. During my stay, she was pregnant and no longer part of an arisan.

Suryani, a single woman, stopped participating in an arisan because the factory she worked in did not have one organized among its workers. She found it difficult to save money on her own because there were continuous family demands on her cash. Suryani would have joined an arisan at work had one been available. Three of these four factory workers would have joined an arisan could they have afforded it, and Suryani would have joined if one had been accessible.

ARISAN PARTICIPANTS

The other ten factory workers who were in arisans included three single and seven married women. All the married women were still living with their husbands, and six couples still lived in the woman's parents' house. These married women were saving money toward their own new houses.

It is clear that without the arisan, workers found it extremely difficult to save money. As with most villagers, saving money in a bank was a foreign idea. Workers also found it difficult to save money at home in part because of *tuyul*s: what we might call "gremlins" and what Clifford Geertz refers to as "spirit children, 'children who are not human beings' " (1960, 16). Two women had saved money that was later stolen by a tuyul. It is thought that some miserly people become wealthy by sending a tuyul to enter houses and steal things for them. One factory worker who was robbed by a tuyul told me: "People in this village here have tuyuls: maybe there are two people who have them. They are only farmers like the rest of us (*tani biasa*), but then often they buy goats or land. And they don't have other work besides farming."

Suniwati was no longer brave enough to save money at home because it had once disappeared. She had had five thousand rupiah in a coin bank that she thought could not be opened without being broken. When the money disappeared and the coin bank wasn't broken, she was sure that a tuyul had robbed her. Another worker explained that her savings of 5,000 rupiah had been taken by a tuyul. I asked her if her siblings might have taken the money, and she was convinced that it was impossible because they weren't brazen enough to take that much. "They might take one or two hundred rupiah or even as much as a thousand, but they would surely tell me. But they wouldn't dare take five thousand rupiah."

Not surprisingly, most former factory workers had withdrawn from arisans because they had no source of cash income. Two of the nine former workers were still in arisans using their husbands' income. Both were saving substantial sums of cash each month through this mechanism. Of the nonfactory workers, four out of nine were in arisans. Only one of these arisan participants did not earn a wage, and she belonged to a small village-based arisan through which she saved 1,000 rupiah a month.

On average, factory workers saved 9,400 rupiah a month in the arisan, approximately one-third of their monthly wage, and came into 56,000 rupiah every six months. After receiving an arisan, factory workers often changed the number of participants or the amount contributed or else joined a different group. In this way they could readily adjust savings to their changing cash needs or the needs of the household.

The amounts saved ranged considerably—for example, from a poor married worker with children who saved only about 4,000 rupiah a month and came into 25,000 rupiah in six months, to a working mother who saved 13,000 rupiah a month, about 45 percent of her wage, and came into 52,000 rupiah in four months. The former woman was quite poor and lived with her husband and two children; therefore, much of her wage went to daily household needs. She had not bought any consumer goods with her arisan because it was used up quickly for her children's needs.

The woman who saved 13,000 rupiah a month—Suniwati—was in a family that did not need her wage. She lived with her husband, child, and family of origin. Suniwati had worked in a factory six years before she married. She had accumulated substantial sums of capital over the years because during normal times her family didn't need her wage and because she was more frugal than were most workers, who often spent money on make-up and clothing. Various relatives had borrowed some of her savings for all sorts of emergencies. She estimated that a total of about $155 plus ten grams of gold had been borrowed but not repaid before her marriage in 1984. Extended family members are able to use factory daughters' savings for emergency cash needs, but rarely do they repay the loans.

Because there was little demand on her wage for daily household needs, Suniwati saved considerable sums of money, which she used to buy jewelry and household consumer goods such as furniture, a bed, a radio, a tape recorder, and one the few televisions in the village. She was also saving up to build her new house:

> I sold all my jewelry. Before the crop failure, my father told me to sell it to build my house, with my parents' help. Little by little, I bought building materials with my savings. When the harvest failed, I had sold some of my jewelry to pay for daily needs in this family. We didn't have an income except from my work. At that time, my two younger brothers were still in school and didn't work yet like now. So I had to support everyone.

During my visit, her house was being built and she hoped to finish it by the end of the year. Her parents had given her the land and paid for the bricks and the roofing. With her last arisan of 65,000 rupiah, she bought the cement and was able to pay the workers to start building.

In an older family such as Suniwati's, with few dependents and sufficient income for subsistence needs, wages from factory work were surplus income and could be used for larger purchases and family formation. Suniwati would have her own house within two years of marriage, a time span substantially shorter than average.

Most workers—both single and married—saved less than Suniwati did because of more pressing family economic needs and demands. Five workers saved 10,000 rupiah a month and them came into 50,000 rupiah to 80,000 rupiah every four to eight months, depending on the number of participants in their arisan. Workers in poorer families saved less and used their savings for less expensive and more practical consumer goods. For example, a worker from a poor family used her arisan to buy gold jewelry and smaller, more necessary consumer goods such as dishes and glasses. Only those from better-off families could afford to buy luxury goods with savings.

One of the single workers from a poorer family had used her first arisan to buy gold jewelry, which she later sold to rent sawah. We asked if she received her jewelry back after the rice harvest: "No, because the harvest from that sawah was rice we used to eat every day [rather than sell]. My father said then that he would pay me back, but until now, he hasn't." With her second arisan, she bought wood to panel the inner walls of her parents' house. The other single worker who saved 10,000 rupiah a month had bought jewelry, and then her father used the rest of her savings to pay for one of her brothers' education.

Of the nonfactory workers, the teacher saved 6,400 rupiah a month, one poultry farm worker saved 5,200 rupiah to 10,000 rupiah a month, and the other 4,100 rupiah to 13,000 rupiah a month. This last worker lived with her husband, child, and grandmother. The financial arrangement was such that when her husband was able to find agricultural labor, his wage—850 rupiah a day—was used for daily household needs. When he was completely occupied by working their own riceland, particularly when the land was hoed and prepared for planting, they used her wage for daily needs. They used her savings from the arisan and sold her gold jewelry (one necklace, six rings, and three pairs of earrings) to pay for the initial planting needs, including preparing the land. This woman had also bought furniture and a radio, and with the money from selling one ring and two pairs of earrings, she bought a calf.

One important difference since 1982 is that in 1986 some families were using a worker's savings for productive agricultural investments that might improve their financial position in the long run—for instance, renting more land, preparing the land for planting, or buying livestock—and several were planning property investments by building a house. Most workers and their families expressed hopes of buying land or livestock but simply did not have enough money.

By 1986, after most daughters were married, yet another type of investment was made more frequently with long-term gains in mind, namely, education. Eight current or former workers contributed to the education of their siblings, ranging from buying school materials to paying school fees. More substantial sums were spent on male siblings than on female siblings with the hopes that eventually they would secure steady, paying jobs. To some extent, this situation parallels that of Taiwanese factory daughters and their support of their brothers' education, but certainly the strength of the obligation is weaker in Java. The refusal of a working daughter to support her brother's education—and there were indeed some such refusals—did not create a family or village scandal, as it would in Taiwan, but only dissatisfied parents and perhaps brothers.

EFFECTS OF INDUSTRIALIZATION ON AGRARIAN FAMILIES

The use of a daughter's savings during an agricultural disaster is significant in terms of the relationship between industrialization and rural families. When the crops failed, those who controlled land and depended on the harvest for part or all of their rice consumption suddenly needed cash to buy rice. Others who depended on wages from harvesting other villagers' ricefields had less work and less money for food. In such a situation, the choices are either to migrate temporarily to seek employment or to sell gold, livestock, land, or other possessions. Migration would physically fragment the family temporarily, and selling possessions would result in an even lower socioeconomic position for the household. Selling land would require that more income be acquired outside the household for household survival. If employment was not locally available, one or more family members might be forced to undertake temporary migration to find work.

By contrast, parents of factory daughters were grateful that they had been able to turn to their daughters' savings during an economic downturn. A few families of factory workers had sold some land, but only after using up savings from factory employment. These savings staved off land sales as long as possible and decreased the amount of possessions a family had to sell. The economic cushion provided by factory savings strengthened the family by avoiding temporary or permanent dissolution and maintaining as much as possible the household's socioeconomic status.

I gathered data on landholdings in 1986 and compared them with figures for 1981 in order to capture socioeconomic changes, some of which are related to employment. Certainly not all changes can be directly linked to factory employment. One must take into account the various exogenous factors influencing the flow of goods into and out of the household—for example, additions from a dowry or wedding gifts, or possessions sold to pay for a wedding, birth, or family emergency.[12]

One-quarter of the households with a factory worker increased their (owned) landholdings, and none of the nonfactory households added land. A majority of nonfactory households and fewer than half of factory households had maintained their 1981 landholdings. Approximately one-third of the households in each group had sold some land, while two-thirds maintained and even improved on 1981 landholdings. Daughters rarely bought land, but their savings may have freed other family money for investment. Working daughters did buy consumer goods, and most households with a wage-earning daughter gained possessions over the five-year period.

Factory savings have allowed smallholder and landless rural families to avoid downward mobility in times of disaster and to improve the family economy during normal periods. At the very least, maintaining the family's economic status quo indicates that factory employment has helped families. Although sociologists seek signs of family change in household composition or structure, I am arguing that the sheer lack of any such family change amidst disaster is equally important. Factory savings have also helped smallholding families who needed to reinvest in their land at the beginning of each season. Factory savings were sold to pay for land preparation and initial planting costs. Otherwise, without such cash, families would either sell their possessions for cash or borrow money at high interest rates.

Factory savings have also increased the amount of money available for agricultural production needs. Because a daughter's savings could be used for education, consumption, or family emergencies, there were fewer cash demands on returns from a harvest. Factory savings could be used to perpetuate and improve the household's socioeconomic standing by providing another source for household needs. Thus, industrialization benefited the family in several ways.

CHANGING BEHAVIOR OF FACTORY DAUGHTERS

One parent of a nonfactory worker, when asked if factory work affected the behavior of village females, observed insightfully: "I don't think so. Village people are different from city people. If a villager comes home from the factory, he is right back in the village again, so there isn't much change because they associate with villagers again." However, the parents of factory workers did not share her opinion; they saw their daughters change.

Before the crop failure, families expressed pleasure at the goods daughters bought with factory savings. However, during crop failure, the importance of those savings increased, and parents realized how daughters could play an essential and lifesaving role in the family economy. The role of working daughters changed temporarily during that period as they shifted from providing surplus income for gifts and luxury goods to providing subsistence income for survival, emergency aid, and insurance. In either case, their status within the family as donors remained high.

In light of the important role that factory savings play in the family economy, it is not surprising that most parents of factory workers felt that factory experience, particularly wage earning, had affected their daughters' decisions and behavior, making them more independent. Several mothers complained about their daughters' increasing independence as manifested in their decisions to do as they wished, to buy what they wanted, to go steady without parental permission, and even to go against parental advice. For example, a father told me that his daughter "wanted to buy a necklace, but her mother wanted to buy a different one she didn't want. She does whatever she wants."

Some parents observed the same changes toward independence without criticism: "She works and can stand on her own two feet; of course she wants to make her own decisions. It's up to her, as long as she's still a good girl. She can feel free, as long as her behavior is proper." And some parents did not mind turning over some responsibility to their daughters: "She's met a lot of different people and has had a lot of experience; she knows more [than us] and is more able to make decisions"; or "A working person knows more than someone who doesn't. She knows better what to buy."

The parent of a single worker explained how her daughter had changed:

> In terms of money, for example, Tutuk is more free in her purchases. The opposite situation occurred before she worked even if she had money and wanted to buy something she always asked our permission or advice. . . . She's even brave enough to go against our wishes; for example, Tutuk's father told her younger sister to do some work, but her sister ended up studying because Tutuk was brave enough to be on her sister's side.

This particular worker was not only increasingly assertive at home but was also determined to participate in deciding her marital future: "*I* will choose my spouse alone, but if it turns out that my parents choose someone and I feel it's a better match (*lebih cocok*), then I'll agree to my parents' choice."

Rini's parents had complained about their daughter's selfish behavior years earlier before she was married. But in 1986 Rini's mother told me, "She contributes a lot; she bought almost all of our household goods and sometimes she gives me shopping money." Rini once again participated in an arisan—5,000 rupiah every two weeks, which brought her about 50,000 rupiah in five months. She had thought about investing her money: "Before, I had plans to buy a goat, but it didn't happen because there always were other needs. Now I use the money to buy materials to build my house. I've already bought the wood." Rini's parents gave her the land in their yard for her house, and, as I write this, she is still buying the materials. Roofing is expensive, so she must save for some time to buy it; however, the roof is also one of the first parts of the house to be built. Roofing will cost her about 120,000 rupiah, which is somewhat more than two arisans' worth of savings.

FACTORY DAUGHTERS AND THE FAMILY ECONOMY: A FINAL VISIT WITH RINI'S FAMILY

Rini's parents had new possessions because of factory savings over the years, including two new tables, two radios, and a tape recorder. "Usually she uses her arisan to buy gold jewelry, to pay back debts, or to pay for her younger sister's and brother's schooling. Big things in the house are mostly hers: the table, lamp, cupboard, mattress and bed frame, two radios, and a tape recorder. We only own a little, but later she will probably use her arisan to build her house. The last arisan she bought seven grams of gold, but now some relatives borrowed it and didn't return the money."

Her parents now agreed with her factory work. "Children really prefer to work in a factory rather than in the sawah. Besides that, the factory isn't very far, and the returns are good." Ironically, Rini's father had not permitted her to work in the factory initially and had not spoken to her for a month after she started her job years before. I asked her mother who had decided where Rini would work. "She decided; after all, she's the one who has to do it." Her mother thought that factory work had affected Rini's behavior:

> Probably because working in a factory, she earns money to help us: it's natural if she sometimes wants to follow her own wishes. It affects her decisions about money. Now she's saving a lot for the family, but money matters are up to her. Someone who works can already support herself, like Rini; you can believe what she says, and I leave things up to her to do what's best. But, as her parent, I often give her advice and she listens. It doesn't mean that as soon as you work you can do whatever you like. But I believe she does what's best.

During the years of my research, Rini ascended in status within her household because of her age, life-cycle position, and familiarity with the capitalist economy.

Her mother felt that an unmarried working daughter should give money to parents, but "it depends on the parents. I don't ask Rini for money. If I must, it's only for a little, but I prefer she gives money to her siblings, for schooling. They are in the third year, and the other is in the last year of junior high school." Again, when Rini was younger and unmarried, she gave little to her parents.

These responses suggest that young women are feeling increased economic independence in a cash economy and are not expected by parents to submit to parental authority concerning certain kinds of decisions. Further, some parents, feeling that their daughter knows better how to manage in a "modern" cash economy, abdicate from making decisions and turn over some responsibilities to their representative in the capitalist economy. This shift of responsibility, decision making, or power, which gives more control earlier to daughters, does seem to differ from hierarchies in households where women have never worked in factories.

CONCLUSION

The mothers of factory workers have long been accustomed to involvement in economic activities. Their daughters—the factory workers—are playing a somewhat different role in the family economy as sources of cash in a cash-scarce society and as insurance in a risky environment. However, it is important to underscore the dynamic and life-cycle aspects of daughters' relationship to the family economy when there is not a crisis. Unmarried daughters, particularly the younger generations of factory workers, continue to retain their weekly income, whereas those mothers who continue factory work shift their expenditure patterns and direct more cash toward the family economy. These findings call for a more dynamic approach to conceptualizing the economic organization of poor households.

As I left Java in 1986, the government had made drastic budget cuts in all development projects, halting projects underway and freezing new ones. Until then, village males—the brothers, husbands, and future husbands of factory workers—had been earning steady and relatively good wages from working on government-sponsored road, electricity, and construction projects in the area. Those employment opportunities completely vanished in the fall of 1986, eliminating one of the few steady, remunerated nonagricultural opportunities in this rural site. Factories had already hired the few males needed, and there were few other choices for unskilled or semiskilled males. Economists predicted that the informal economy would swell in Indonesia after the government's cuts.

Such governmental decisions affect the political economy of rural Java and the families I studied. As income-earning possibilities for young males decrease, the factory job of one household member will increasingly represent the only steady cash flow into the household. Working daughters will also become the only household members able to accumulate capital for family use. Factory work, which began as a search for new experiences for adolescent females who changed factories every six months when they were bored, has now evolved into an essential part of the family economy. The role of daughters in the family economy will most likely increase in importance, as will their financial contributions; the question remains whether their increased economic role in the household will be matched with greater participation in decisions and whether it will create new tensions or conflicts with husbands unable to find sustainable employment.

Conclusion

Sometimes people are wily and foresightful and think of strategies for getting on, but much of the time they are just holding on and defending themselves as best they can. There is no global term that catches all of this complexity and promises formal solution programs.

Henry Selby et al., The Mexican Urban Household

Through the lives and struggles of factory daughters, I have traced the complexities of early industrial capitalist proletarianization on a rural area. The longitudinal perspective adopted in this research has followed factory daughters and their families through changes as their life courses are shaped and reshaped. By focusing on different levels of analysis and the relations between them, this Javanese case study uncovers the ways in which such proletarianization works within agrarian-based families. The change wrought by factories can be understood only within the context of multiple layers—the class structure, the prevalence of poverty, the lack of employment options, agrarian change, the Green Revolution, and contradictory ideologies of gender. In this chapter, I summarize my findings, discuss their implications, and specify some of the theoretical and empirical challenges that await researchers of gender, households, and socioeconomic transformations.

INDUSTRIALIZATION AND RURAL FAMILIES

The data on factory daughters' expenditures, contributions, and savings suggest that an interdependent relationship exists between family economies and industrial capitalism, albeit an asymmetric one. To a different extent, the firms and the family economies have benefited from each other.

Industrial capitalist firms depend on rural families to provide worker-daughters with economic support that keeps wages down. The rural families of factory daughters provide free goods and services to factory employees in their households; despite working full time in the capitalist economy, daughters remain economically dependent on their families. The "aid," however, is involuntary in that these families provide free rent, food, services, and other goods for their worker-daughters in the same way that any family would provide for offspring. In this manner, industrial capitalism in rural Java is partly fueled by the subsistence production of poor, near-landless households. This particular economic tie can be seen as one form of surplus extraction from agriculture to industrial capitalism (Deere and de Janvry 1979).

At the same time, factory daughters' weekly wages initially contribute little to the daily reproduction of their households. Their daily contribution is indirect in that they decrease their burden on the family economy by eating one meal less at home and taking care of some of their own cash needs. Families benefit from the consumer goods that daughters buy and eventually from access to daughters' savings. Over time, those factory daughters who marry, have children, and continue working contribute more to the daily reproduction of the household. Thus, life-cycle changes among working women alter their consumption patterns, and those alterations benefit their families on a daily basis. Despite these changes in expenditure patterns, wages are still below subsistence level; married workers with children remain economically dependent upon their parents as before.

During emergencies, such as illness or the crop failures that occurred in the mid 1980s, the savings factory daughters amass from factory wages often keep their semiproletarian families afloat. These savings provide a crucial safety net and prevent family rupture, destitution, migration, and loss of property. In this sense, industrialization stabilizes the economies of families that have a factory worker.

Rural industrialization allows semiproletarian families to maintain their tiny landholdings, preventing further deterioration of their already low socioeconomic status. Paradoxically, although factory employment is an indication of proletarianization, that same employment guards against further proletarianization of families at the borderline of subsistence. In other words, it helps semiproletarian families brake the slide to full proletarianization, at least temporarily.

This study also suggests that, although the path of proletarianization has become normalized for young women as they end their schooling, it is not necessarily a linear course. Many factory daughters, after having children, withdraw from factory employment and stay in the village.

Although some mothers continue factory work and perhaps eventually some return to it, it is doubtful that such women constitute a major constituency in the labor force. Factories can draw on the continuous flow of young women who turn fifteen or sixteen as new workers who will not disrupt their attendance because of children. Thus, proletarianization is a more fluid process and is more sporadic than the notion of "from peasant to proletarian" suggests.

Although daughters do gain income from their factory jobs and their families are able to benefit from some of this income through consumer goods and savings for emergencies, these income benefits are conditioned by cash flows from parents to working daughters and by the free goods and services parents provide for factory daughters with their subsistence labor. If such labor were valued economically and cost of food and lodging were factored in, the net income benefits from industrialization would be extraordinarily small. Seasonal fluctuations in the availability of household cash mean that during some months parents are able to give daughters more cash; in other months, parents provide less cash, and daughters buy more for the household.

Savings are possible only because of a flow of petty cash from parents to daughters to cover lunch or transportation costs and because parents take care of many of their daughters' subsistence needs. One could also argue that the money accumulated through savings represents a direct transfer of cash from parents to daughters, providing parents with a safety net in the long run. It is important to remember that the income benefits through savings are possible only if parents can afford to give daughters pocket money. The very poorest factory daughters cannot participate in the arisan because of daily household needs and the unavailability of pocket money for them.

In terms of the assumption often asserted by policymakers, factories do appear to provide employment to those who come from poor families, but women from the very poorest families with high dependency ratios cannot afford to work in factories. Clearly, this particular type of industrialization provides some women with employment; however, the restrictive age and gender requirements of factory employment exclude most women and almost all men. Furthermore, such industrialization may be pushing a larger number of rural people *out* of employment, particularly those who engage in small-scale rural manufacturing in cottage industries or in home-based work (Susilastuti 1991). Finally, it is important to remember that factory work involves a minority of eligible village women; this localized industrialization does not affect the majority of Javanese women in the region. Although it appeared during my last visit that a greater proportion of eligible young women are entering factory employment, they remain a minority of all women.

INDUSTRIALIZATION AND WOMEN WORKERS

How does such industrialization—or, more specifically, factory employment—affect women? This case study demonstrates that the effects of factory employment on women workers are contradictory. In some sense, factory employment represents a progressive change in the constricted lives of rural Javanese women. They earn a steadier stream of cash than they would in the few other employment options they have. In general, their employment, their geographical distance from home during work, and their access to cash give them more tools with which to counter certain domestic patriarchal pressures and gain some control over their own lives. Factory employment provides them with the tools with which to hack and whittle away at parental and patriarchal controls over their lives, at least for a certain period, with longer-term implications such as deciding when and whom to marry. Compared with their Taiwanese counterparts, Javanese factory workers are subjugated to fewer familial controls; they are also less constricted than are their village peers who do not work in factories.

Factory employment elevates the daughter's position in the household as one who works in a world dominated by foreigners and a foreign work regime, but also as one fully operating in the capitalist economy with access to a steady (albeit small) flow of cash. Although factory daughters usually marry later and choose their own spouses (if they wish to do so), it is difficult to know how long-lived this increased control is. On the one hand, those who remain working in factories after having children succumb to a more constricted view of how a wife and mother should behave. On the other hand, it is very possible that women's continued steady earnings may shift the domestic balance in household decision making, particularly as husbands lost their steady wage income from state-run development projects, which collapsed in 1986.

Although I do think that factory employment has strengthened factory daughters' autonomy, I am not arguing that Javanese women can do as they please. They enjoy some limited economic autonomy within certain boundaries, but such autonomy is strongly conditioned by poverty, which forces them to work at an early age and commits them to a lifetime of hard and long labor. In other words, what good is economic autonomy when there is little money to control? Furthermore, their autonomy is limited to the economic realm; although they are increasingly choosing their own spouses, they cannot choose not to marry. Although they are postponing their marriages, and factory daughters may be postponing them longer than others are, at a certain time they are propelled by social pressures to marry and to bear children soon thereafter, carrying themselves in a more subdued and circumspect manner.

At the same time, an increased field of maneuvering at home has been matched by different patriarchal controls within the factory setting that serve to dominate and control female workers. These relations keep Javanese factory women relatively acquiescent, poorly paid, and vastly unprotected in industrial jobs that are often dangerous. And these controls are more than matched by a state-supported gender ideology that encourages women to think of the domestic realm as their place and submissive housewifery as their role rather than encouraging women to think of themselves as active and productive workers who deserve a decent wage.

Factories can draw on certain Javanese traditions of women's economic autonomy to acquire their labor force. At the same time, they draw on a gender ideology of women as economically dependent on men to keep wages low and of women as passive and submissive to keep labor quiet and controlled. Factories can count on the fear and shyness of uneducated young women who are unlikely to rock the boat.

It is possible that some of the pushing that young women do at home has given some of them the courage and confidence to do the same at the factory; for example, Rini and her coworkers decided they could not passively accept any and all conditions in the garment factory and therefore registered their dissatisfaction. Just as they challenged their fathers, so, too, did they challenge the manager. Their efforts on this front were less successful, however, than they were at home. Factory managers and factory work discipline are much less flexible and much more overwhelming and all-encompassing than are parents in their rules and discipline.

Factories do not operate alone in this control of young women but follow state edicts and regulations. The state sets but does not enforce minimum wage, establishes but ignores health and safety standards, and forbids the union from taking an active role to protect workers within their legal rights. The cozy relationship between industrial capitalists and high-ranking state bureaucrats or military personnel keeps wages and labor unrest down, maintains profit, and encourages further foreign investment while oppressing and abandoning young women workers.

It is simply not possible to reduce this situation to a judgment of either "better" or "worse" for women workers. The situation is paradoxical and contradictory and must be understood as such. Javanese factory daughters do gain more room in which to maneuver, both geographically and personally, in a situation where their life chances are severely limited.

Thus, we are confronted with the contradiction that women workers receive personal and economic gains from employment that is highly exploitive. At the same time, such exploitive conditions cannot lead us to deny the socioeconomic changes in workers' lives. Clearly, a greater ability to choose one's own spouse or buy clothing does not greatly alter structural relations of oppression and exploitation: Kathryn Robinson (1988) asks the salient question, "What kind of freedom is cutting your hair?" Nevertheless, these changes in movement, friendships, consumption, family decision making, and marital choice are important to them. Here I must agree with Lourdes Benería and Martha Roldán's conclusion that "however small the changes . . . that women have accomplished may appear to the observer, these changes do not look insignificant to the women themselves" (1987, 162).

The question remains, What do those involved in such structural change think about these changes? The workers in my study are not likely to agree with previous researchers' judgments, such as Aihwa Ong's (1987), that factory work is detrimental and alienating, a constant wound and a daily crisis. This, of course, does not mean that they are not aware of their exploitation. Javanese factory workers recognize that factory employment is poorly paid, unprotected, and unfair in those senses, yet they are also certain that it has brought them both material and personal benefits that few would give up. None of them would voluntarily trade their factory jobs for noncapitalist work in the informal sector such as trade, domestic service, or agriculture; they find such work much more arduous, and it must be undertaken in situations where they would be controlled more by parents or other villagers, would have to work longer, and would earn much less.

It is important to point out that these young women in Central Java are much less circumscribed by patriarchy or Islam than are their counterparts in West Java (Mather 1985). There, local Islamic leaders recruit young women migrant workers, but they continue to watch these women while they are off work in an attempt to control their sexuality. It would be difficult to argue that factory employment, under such conditions of constant patriarchal controls, represents a progressive change.

This Javanese case reveals that the lives, choices, and movements of these young women are highly constrained by poverty, but less so by patriarchy or Islam, particularly when compared with women in East or South Asia or even neighboring Malaysia (Ong 1987). Their decisions reflect varying degrees of female agency, with somewhat more fluidity than experienced by their counterparts in West Java, where Islam is strongly enforced. In other words, patriarchy, like female agency, operates in varying degrees and should not be assumed to have a monolithic effect or force.

The Taiwanese case, by comparison, leads to different interrelationships between factory daughters and industrialization. To be sure, export-oriented industrialization in East Asia has flourished and grown by exploiting young women within an industrial system that shares interests with the state in suppressing wages and the voice of labor. In Taiwan, as elsewhere in East Asia, these interests easily fit in with the exigencies of a kinship system in which parents can demand and expect many years of labor and income from their working daughters. The literature on Taiwan points to greater and longer controls over daughters' lives because of the changes incurred by industrialization, with few benefits going to the women who labor in the factories.

The Javanese and Taiwanese cases analyzed here support the findings of previous research in the social history of industrialization (e.g., Tilly and Scott 1978)—specifically, that industrialization perpetuates and reinforces the position of women that existed before such shifts in the global economy, and that significant family change takes time to germinate. In Central Java, industrialization has given Javanese factory daughters more room to maneuver in a setting highly constrained by poverty and by notions of femininity; in Taiwan, by contrast, factory daughters appear to be even more manipulated and controlled by parents who attempt to squeeze as much capital out of them as possible. Even though the outcome for women's position in these two cases is opposite, in neither case has industrialization dramatically transformed women's position or their relations with their families of origin; instead, it has intensified existing relations between parents and daughters, between genders and generations within families. Local kinship systems and gender and family ideologies strongly affect the effects of industrialization on women's lives, even in situations where the state's interests in low wages and quiet workers are similar.

DAUGHTERS AND PARENTS; PARENTS AND DAUGHTERS

Some of the economic behavior described in this research counters certain images about the behavior of daughters in poor rural Third World families and the assumption that they automatically act and react dutifully with the family's good in mind. Unmarried factory daughters did not greatly resemble the selfless and dutiful unmarried daughters in early industrializing Europe (as described by Tilly and Scott 1978), who were willing to sacrifice their personal desires for the household collectivity. Javanese factory daughters' behavior was much more varied and complex. Their economic behavior was dynamic and depended on the issue or problem at hand and also on their life-cycle position. Their economic behavior toward their families resembles much more the looser and casual attitude that Thomas Dublin (1979, 40) argues existed between rural families and their daughters who worked in the factories of Lowell, Massachusetts, in the mid-nineteenth century.[1]

Poor Javanese parents have limited control over their daughter's labor. Until the daughter reaches about age fifteen, parents are able to prevent a daughter from seeking factory work. But by age fifteen, the age at which factories accept workers, daughters who wish to work are no longer held back by parental restrictions. Daughters defy parents and obtain factory jobs. Better-off parents are more able to control their offspring and hold more bargaining chips—future resources. Poorer parents have little to bequeath to their children and have little with which to threaten children who disobey. The sanctions against daughters in such families are weak. These weak sanctions are connected to the kinship system as much as they are to class position. Taiwanese factory daughters submit to parental wishes to avoid alienating their parents—the one piece of security they have (M. Wolf 1972).

Regardless of the outcome, it is important to emphasize that these young Javanese women initially seek factory employment to gain new experience and some cash for themselves—not for the family's economic good. Family benefits accrue only later, over time. There is considerable conflict initially over daughters' wages, particularly parents' lack of control over wages. Unmarried factory daughters retain rather than pool their weekly income. Most parents eventually are mollified when they are able to enjoy the benefits of the Lebaran bonus or of a daughter's savings. But unless there is a family emergency and parents are forced to ask for a daughter's help, daughters maintain control over their wages, bonuses, and savings.

Clearly, during emergencies such as illness, death, or crop failure, daughters are willing to help out their families economically. However, they are not willing to comply with every request from household members and differentiate between dire necessity and "extras" and among different family members. For example, they are more likely to give younger siblings some money to buy candy or pencils than to provide their fathers with cash for cigarettes. The arisan provides one mechanism to keep some of daughter's weekly cash *out* of the hands of household members. Several workers stated directly that were it not for the arisan, their money would be eaten up by the demands for petty cash from household members.[2]

ADOLESCENCE: THE NEW TERRITORY

What is striking about this case, however, is that factory employment occurred during a period when certain demographic and social relations were undergoing a dramatic change in Java, particularly in the increased age at marriage. The convergence of this new state of single adolescence and young adulthood with factory employment and all that it implies (e.g., leaving home daily, new circles of friends, access to cash, savings) created a new and unusual period where new ground rules were created. Because they were single at an age when their mothers and older sisters would have already been married, the traditional practices of wifehood and motherhood did not apply. Instead, daughters were at once caught in a web of obligations toward the corporate entity of the household while attempting to exert their own autonomy during a fairly new and unexplored life-cycle state. There was considerable social experimentation in their behavior; many factory daughters frequently negotiated their position as they tested the limits of parental boundaries and responded to differing family needs and situations. These same changes were not apparent among village daughters who did not work in factories but engaged mostly in agricultural and domestic work.

Parents of factory workers were thrust into an ambiguous situation: on the one hand, they continued their role of protecting their daughter's reputation and controlling her sexuality, but on the other hand, they did not wish to alienate their one hotline to steady cash and the capitalist economy. Thus, parents and daughters engaged in a constant redefinition and negotiation of limits and boundaries—over money, clothing, place of residence, relations with boyfriends and suitors, and daughter's time away from home—in other words, with similar issues many parents must negotiate with their teenagers.

After factory daughters marry and have children, their behavior changes as they adhere to the norms of wifehood and motherhood. Their consumption patterns change, and they direct their earnings according to "responsible" behavior—that is, toward the purchase of food, the care and education of children, and the construction of homes. In other words, life-cycle changes catapult factory daughters from a less restricted, newer, and unmarked territory in which they are creating the lines of demarcation, often attempting to push them to the furthest edge, to a much narrower space circumscribed by patriarchal norms that still bind women to their children and families. Suddenly the rebellious and testy daughters become tame and "responsible." Parents are finally pleased with their daughter's economic behavior and go on to complain about the next generation of adolescent, unmarried factory daughters who are following the same path their predecessors did—retaining their income and spending it on themselves.

RETHINKING HOUSEHOLD STRATEGIES AND HOUSEHOLD (DIS)ORGANIZATION

We have seen factory daughters' rebellious behavior, their family-oriented behavior, and their parents' reactions; the question remains, Do these Javanese households strategize?

If one reads this case retrospectively, then one may argue that household strategies do in fact exist. From what we know today, daughters' participation in factory employment benefits the household economy through savings. Daughters' interests, parents' interests, and "the household's" interests converge over time. Household strategies can be imputed retrospectively simply because, in this case, factory employment worked, and everyone survived.

If, however, we read the case forward, from beginning to end, in the way it was lived and experienced, we confront the uncertainty and newness of factory employment and of early industrial capitalist development. Most parents initially took a conservative stance toward factory employment and were angry at their daughters' disobedience. Later, they were upset with daughters' retention of income, daughters' purchasing make-up rather than cooking oil, long pants rather than rice. Then, over time, parents were pleased with daughters' bonuses, their savings, and the goods bought with savings. Finally, some years later, parents turned to daughters for basic household survival and depended on them for help. Those women who remained in the factories after having children began to use the arisan to purchase materials with which to build their new houses.

This sequence of events, the uncertainty under which parents and daughters operated, and the often haphazard nature of decisions and interactions do not add up to a coherent long-term plan or set of decisions. Initially, decisions were made in an experimental way. Through these experiments, parents and daughters groped to set and reset boundaries and to find their way. There was considerable conflict rather than rukun as daughters and parents negotiated certain decisions. Sometimes, parents resigned themselves and adapted to daughters' behavior; other times, daughters acquiesced to parents' firmness, as when some factory workers wished to move closer to the factory. Actions and reactions were varied and sometimes passive; there were multiple motives, some conflicting and some converging; parental power was often decentered, frustrated, and challenged, but in certain conditions it was strongly asserted. Basically, after a particular practice or behavior appeared to "work," it became a routine, part of daily practice; then, another challenge or change would occur, and disruption and (re)negotiation began again. Although in the end a coherent set of practices emerged (at least temporarily) that benefited most household members, given the initial high level of uncertainty about factory employment, it would have been difficult for the participants to develop a strategy.

These patterns simply do not fit models of household decision making that are based on the assumption of consensus or of an altruistic patriarch. Indeed, applying the concept of household strategies to this Javanese case homogenizes a range of relations among household members and oversimplifies the process, the power dynamics, the coercion, and the rebellion involved in household decisions. Finally, as we saw in the Javanese case, poor parents are the *least* able to control the labor or income of their grown offspring because they have few resources or sanctions with which to bargain.

Javanese parents at times exerted their will and their decisions on daughters—isn't this a household strategy? For example, Javanese parents kept their younger daughters home and out of factory employment, at least until daughters rebelled and sought it anyway. Parents wanted daughters to stay home and take care of the household and younger children while mothers sought extra household income. Such decisions imposed on daughters by parents may be considered by some to constitute a parental strategy or the strategy of one parent. However, since there was no evidence of a long-term plan marked by a series of decisions, I would argue instead that this was a tactic, a short-term mechanism, like that used when daughters sought factory employment so they could buy soap or, later, when married workers used the arisan to save up to buy bricks. These decisions or actions involve a conscious means-ends calculation or deliberation, but each calculation is not necessarily part of a broader strategy.[3] Poor people, rural people, and peasants do make calculations, but we have also seen that not all economic behaviors or decisions are calculated. Even if some peasants wish to engage in more calculation for more decisions and have a long-range plan or strategy, the high level of existing uncertainty would not allow it.

By contrast, Taiwanese parents, not households or daughters, make decisions about their daughters' education, labor, and marriages, and Taiwanese daughters, because of a lifelong socialization into their inferior position, dutifully obey. Within the accepted cultural boundaries of parent-daughter relations, one or both of the parents play the string of filial piety by lengthening and strengthening control over a daughter's time, labor, and returns to her labor. The literature portrays Chinese parents as controlling a daughter's labor and attempting to extract as much capital as possible from her before she marries, in their own interest. The literature does not, however, differentiate much between mothers and fathers, so it is difficult to know if this is a joint effort. Taiwanese mothers and fathers may have a joint parental strategy or two different but convergent strategies, but it is important to recognize that parents alone are not households and that they do not necessarily represent the interests of all of those living in their household. The satisfaction of having been filial constitutes daughters' "benefit" from years of grueling labor and sacrifice. Parents' views of the household's interests are dominated by patrilineal and patriarchal family requisites; they do not represent the daughter's view of her present or future interests.[4]

The literature portrays Taiwanese parents as consciously plotting out their daughter's course with her wedding and dowry, and their future security, in mind. If parents speak about present decisions and the future in that way, then the Taiwanese case may represent, depending on the dynamics, a parental or a patrilineal strategy or the strategy of one parent in particular. Finally, with respect to earlier arguments about how uncertainty and poverty make strategies more difficult if not impossible to create, it is important to note that industrialization presented a less uncertain and new phenomenon to Taiwanese parents than it did to Javanese parents in the early 1980s in the rural site I studied. Finally, even if we agree that a strategy of sorts exists in Taiwanese families, it is far more illuminating to understand how and why decisions are made and the mechanisms of domination and resistance involved in getting daughters to work or to pool income. How are daughters reacting to these pressures? Are there signs of change or resistance over time?

If the story told in this book about Javanese families does not describe a "household strategy," then what can we call their behaviors? Should we call them anything? In the quotation that opened this chapter, Henry Selby and his coauthors (1990, 71) contend that one term alone cannot fully capture the complex behaviors of poor people; they instead use terms such as *getting by*. Similarly, Roger Rouse uses the term *projects* to conceptualize the simultaneous existence of both collective and individual goals, which allows for concurrent complementary and conflictual aspects. The notion of projects does not privilege a collective goal over an individual one but instead investigates the existence and interactions among different projects and those pursuing them.

For those who need to place the sum of a household's economic activities under an umbrella phrase, perhaps the entire bundle of parents', daughters', and sons' activities, decisions, and interactions may be better represented by the unassuming term *household practices*. Although this remains a rather descriptive notion, it imputes fewer motives to the actors than does *household strategies*. It does not assume either coherence or conflict (see Pahl 1984). *Coping mechanisms* (Agarwal 1991) may also aptly describe the lack of power among poor households. *Household routines* is another possibility, but it may imply more consensus and coordination, and perhaps less dynamism, than does *household practices*. However, as I have argued throughout this book, rather than packing up household behaviors into a neat coherent bundle, the most compelling view of the household comes from *unbundling* these relations, interactions, and activities. We should concern ourselves not only with the results of individual or household-level action but also with the *process* involved in reaching that decision or action, a process that may involve different amounts of conflict, domination, contestation, control, cooperation, and acquiescence.

Some researchers question using the notion of the household at all. Despite considerable conflict and negotiation, in the end, factory daughters contributed to household reproduction and to its longer-term survival. Although unmarried factory daughters did not necessarily contribute to the household's daily, weekly, or monthly needs and often refused requests for money to buy certain items, they came through to help out their families when help was really needed. The results from this case study, therefore, cannot advocate an empirical or conceptual abandonment of the household, although, without question, the boundaries of investigation need to go beyond the household's walls.

The household, Lydia Morris argues, is "the theatre of many aspects of the relationship between men and women" (1990, 2). It is "both outcome and channel of broader social processes; and is the site of separable, often competing, interests, rights and responsibilities. It is as much a 'segmented' unit as are labour markets segmented by gender, age, clan, ethnicity and so on" (Guyer and Peters 1987, 210). Households are the obvious place to start—but not stop—examining the effects of external economic changes on internal hierarchies; we may in turn question whether, and to what extent, internal practices can reshape structures and processes external to the household. As Judith Carney and Michael Watts comment, "Analyses of agrarian transformation must grasp not only how larger political economic structures frame the domestic terrain of conflict but simultaneously how domestic struggles shape certain social and political processes that may challenge in limited ways the structures themselves" (1991, 681).

Households in this case study remain the unit of some income pooling and of reproduction. They also remain the site whence class affiliation and class relations stem, affecting lifelong patterns of work and access to resources. Household reproduction is not a given, however; it remains "a contingency, a process continually in flux, with multiple sources of tension and sites of struggle" (Deere 1990, 314), a process that should be studied rather than assumed.

QUESTIONS FOR FUTURE RESEARCH

This study has demonstrated that life inside rural households, although it revolves around work and the concern for survival, is more lively and complex than it is portrayed in many economically oriented studies of household work and income practices. Although poor rural household members work extraordinarily hard to survive, household interrelationships are not based solely on economics. This case encourages an approach to household studies that includes economics but expands to a more relational and interactive view.

Contemporary studies of intrahousehold dynamics have criticized one set of economic terms that have been applied to the household (e.g., joint utility function) but have replaced them with yet another set of economic terms (e.g., negotiation, competition, renegotiation, contract, bargaining), a few of which are used here. If households are not firms, neither are they unions bargaining with firms, nor are they boxing rings. Rural research could benefit from taking a serious and critical look at its terminology and opening the frame of reference beyond economics.

Rural household research is at a crossroads, as researchers attempt to interpret and reinterpret behaviors by amending existing frameworks. Gillian Hart argues that a more politicized approach to the study of households is emerging, with the emphasis shifting to how domestic consent is produced and maintained and "the conditions under which subordinate household members are likely to challenge and redefine the rules" (forthcoming, 24):

> The rules defining property rights, labor obligations, resource distribution, and so forth are culturally variable, but they are not fixed and given. Rather, they are potentially subject to contestation, and must be constantly reinforced and reiterated. Accordingly, we need not only to ask what the rules are, but how they are constructed, maintained, reinterpreted, and on occasion challenged in everyday practice. . . . [W]e have to engage directly with questions of ideology and the construction of meaning and realize how struggles over resources and labor are simultaneously struggles over meaning. (Hart forthcoming, 24, 26)

We need to work toward a more satisfactory theoretical framework guided by feminist critiques—one that analyzes the interactions among local, state, and global structures, intrahousehold dynamics and extrahousehold networks and groups.[5] Such a framework would attend to the dynamic interplay of race, class, ethnic, and gender hierarchies in these various relationships, taking into account the often complex, fluid, interactive, and nonlinear aspects of change. This approach will require engaging in extended and intensive ethnographic fieldwork to observe intra- and extrahousehold relations, to analyze the meaning of such relations for those involved, and their ideological dimensions. This agenda, in addition to a necessary focus on the agency of these social actors, will require a generous interweaving of narratives into the text. All of these suggestions cook up a full plate for further rural research.

A new approach could seek more appropriate terms with which to conceptualize intra- and extrahousehold dynamics by incorporating a methodology that supports in-depth investigations of such interactions and the local meanings, practices, and concepts attached to them. This methodology would prevent an inappropriate imposition of prepackaged, discipline-bound concepts while helping us better understand the practices of poor women and men as they attempt to get by and survive amidst change, crisis, and uncertainty.

Such research could benefit not only from bringing in the voices of rural householders but also from bringing in the voice of the researchers. Those of us who study gender, class, and power are simultaneously enmeshed in these same hierarchical relations, yet the voice of researchers about our positions, the dilemmas we may have about our position, our relations with our subjects, and the nature of the research process is largely missing from political economy texts. It is important to acknowledge these relations and dynamics in our texts and not simply to split them from our academic writings by relegating them to separate commentaries on the fieldwork process, where the first person is freely used. Such a discussion need constitute only a small part of the text, but it would demystify the research process, a fitting task for those engaged in the demystification of the household, the village, the state, and other such entities.

• • •

To conclude, this study has presented a critical view of this particular type of industrialization in Java. Industrialization in general, and rural industrialization in particular, cannot and should not be seen as a substitute for "other critically missing elements in the development process" (Saith 1991, 487) or for meaningful political and economic changes that would have long-term implications for rural poverty, inequality, and unemployment. Rural industrialization must be accompanied by higher wages, stricter health and safety standards, better protection of workers' rights, and fundamental agrarian change such as land reform or cooperatives; otherwise such rural industrialization programs will remain ineffective and irrelevant to the lives of most of the rural poor.

A recent article in my local newspaper, the *Sacramento Bee* (Loeb 1991), tells the story of an eighteen-year-old Central Javanese woman named Riyanti who makes Nike shoes in the Tangerang area near Jakarta for 15 cents an hour. She makes $1.06 a day, only a few cents more than the women in my research earned ten years ago and not nearly enough to meet subsistence needs. Overtime is compulsory, and Riyanti often works twelve-hour days. The production cost of a pair of shoes is $5.60; they are sold for $75, and tennis, basketball, hockey, and other stars such as movie producer Spike Lee rake in thousands of dollars from endorsing Nike.

Without substantial change, the benefits from such industrialization will continue to accrue to those few who control capital and those few in the state hierarchy who set the stage for the conditions of labor—in short, those whose pockets are lined by suppressing wages and controlling the behavior of women workers. As the Nike example demonstrates, in today's global economy, many feet are made fashionable and many pockets are lined by these low wages.

Appendix

This appendix continues the bivariate and multivariate analysis presented in chapter 7, examining land tenure, household possessions, and occupations. The multivariate analysis brings together the factors singled out as the most important variables in affecting a woman's factory labor force participation.

BIVARIATE ANALYSIS

Class differentials paralleled household land tenure status (table 27): compared with nonfactory households, a higher proportion of factory workers' households

TABLE 27

SELECTED LAND TENURE CATEGORIES OF FACTORY WORKERS AND NONFACTORY HOUSEHOLDS (PERCENTAGES)

	Factory workers ($N = 39$)	Nonfactory females ($N = 90$)
Landless (no land controlled)	5	3
Rent-in and/or Sharecrop-in	24	16
Own and operate plus rent/ sharecrop-in	29	18
Owner-operator only	40	48
Own and operate and rent or sharecrop-out	0	7

NOTE: Because these are selected categories, columns do not total 100.

were land poor. A smaller percentage of nonfactory females' households were landless or needed to rent or sharecrop additional land. Other measures, such as the value of possessions, corresponded with these measures of class status.[1] For example, the average value of possessions for current workers' households was 163,800 rupiah compared with 333,450 rupiah for nonfactory households, although there was a high degree of variation among the latter group. The value of household possessions is definitely affected by factory employment, since workers often buy household possessions with their savings. Had I been able to survey workers' households before factory employment, the value of their household possessions would have been much less than 163,800 rupiah.

Class status and land tenure and the resultant differences in the social organization of household labor are reflected in occupational patterns of the head of household and second head of household. The second head of household is usually a wife, but in households headed by women, it is the next working adult, usually a son, daughter, or son-in-law.

TABLE 28

PRIMARY OCCUPATIONS OF HOUSEHOLD MEMBERS BY FACTORY WORK STATUS (PERCENTAGES)

	Head of household		Second in household	
	Factory workers	*Nonfactory*	*Factory workers*	*Nonfactory*
Sharecropper or renter	25.6	12.2	13.6	7.7
Agricultural laborer	5.1	4.5	8.1	4.3
Nonagricultural laborer (wood, stone, construction)	2.6	7.8	—	—
Factory worker	2.6	—	16.2	—
Petty trader	2.6	7.8	8.1	15.4
Household production worker	5.1	3.3	16.2	30.8
Farmer (owner-operator)	56.4	61.1	37.8	32
Gatherer of fodder	—	1.1	—	6.6
Businessperson (e.g., penebas)	—	2.2	—	—
Midwife	—	—	—	1.1
Student	—	—	—	1.1
Total	100	100	100	99[a]

[a] Excludes one able-bodied person temporarily unemployed because of illness.

About 36 percent of heads of factory workers' households sold their labor (aggregating the first four categories), compared with 24 percent of heads of nonfactory females' households (table 28). The pattern was reproduced with the second member: 37 percent among current worker households sold their labor, compared with 12 percent among nonfactory households. The occupational differences between owner-operated farming households were smaller; however, it must be remembered that factory households usually owned less farmland than did nonfactory households and needed to diversify into more economic activities.

MULTIVARIATE ANALYSIS

A triangulation of different methods has been used in this research to identify patterns and irregularities. In analyzing the data, I have sought a dialogue among the voices of individuals, observations, theory, and statistical relationships. The variables that appeared most influential from observation, interviews, and the preceding bivariate analysis are now combined in multivariate analysis. Such an analysis specifies the independent strength of each variable in determining factory employment. In this case, a more sophisticated method of quantitative data analysis was selected only after general patterns were culled from bivariate analysis. Multivariate analyses can indicate the relative importance of a number of factors, such as class or household composition, and determine the strength of variables such as marital status (see figure 2).

There were two choices for the dependent variable: length of time worked in the factory, or a dichotomous variable of "never worked" and "currently working." The dichotomous variable was chosen for several reasons. First, length of time worked in a factory was highly correlated with age, an independent variable. Workers' ages varied from sixteen to twenty-five, which would also affect the length of time worked. Second, the important research question is, What affects the decision to work in a factory? Therefore, a binary dependent variable was used so that the analysis could determine the probability of working in a factory. Nonfactory females were coded as "0" and those currently working as "1."

There are several possible methods of analysis using a dichotomous dependent variable—the linear probability model estimated by ordinary least squares (OLS),

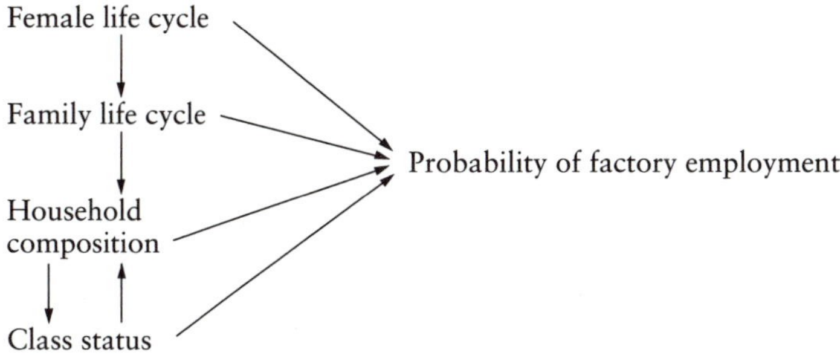

Figure 2 Variables Affecting Decision to Seek Factory Employment

the same model estimated by weighted OLS, and the logistic transformation of the dependent variable according to a specified probability density function that then estimates the transformed model. The first two techniques have weaknesses because OLS provides "inefficient estimators with imprecise predictions" (Edmonston et al. 1981, 251). In addition, OLS estimations would be statistically incorrect for the types of binary variables used. The second method also calls for continous data, which is not appropriate here. The third technique—*logit analysis*—"has developed as an algebraically simple and computationally straightforward method" (Bishop et al. 1975, 375). Simply put, logit is the natural logarithm of the odds ratio. The logit model is nonlinear and must be estimated using maximum likelihood methods.[2]

The model presented here combines five variables that were expected to be the most significant in determining factory employment. The demographic and economic variables tested were (1) control over land (used to differentiate classes); (2) number of children ever-born;[3] (3) consumer-worker ratio; (4) number of able-bodied females in the household; and (5) marital status. Although control over land was used in the previous analysis to create class categories, it is used as a continuous variable in this regression. Marital status is the only categorical variable in this model. The regression coefficients for the model are presented in

TABLE 29

PROBABILITY OF WORKING IN A FACTORY: RESULTS FROM LOGISTIC REGRESSION

Independent variables	Estimated coefficients (standard error)
Control over land	−2.60[a] (1.10)
Children ever-born	−1.16[b] (.300)
Consumer-worker ratio	−1.16[c] (.782)
Able-bodied female	.535[c] (.319)
Marital status	−.123 (.264)
Constant	1.46[c] (1.02)
N	129

NOTE: Dependent variable: 1 = currently employed in a factory; 0 = never employed in a factory. Based on χ^2 test for level of significance.

[a] $p < .05$
[b] $p < .01$
[c] $p < .10$

table 29. It is important to note that I have a full census of the eligible population, not a sample drawn from a larger population.

Several aspects of the estimated regression model offer useful information in light of the questions posed. First, the coefficients can be evaluated for the direction of their signs, which indicates the direction of their effects. The estimated regression can be used to predict the probability of the dependent variable—to seek factory employment—based on the numerical value of the independent variables. As shown below, the estimated values of (BX) for the ith individual are used to compute a predicted probability for that particular individual. Predicted values are then compared with observed choices to assess the fit of the particular model (Berman 1984, 254).

Number of children is the most significant variable, followed by class, number of able-bodied females, and consumer-worker ratio. In this model, when these variables are controlled, marital status is not significant in its effect on the decision to work. This lack of significance does not indicate that marital status is unimportant; yet, as indicated by the bivariate analysis, marital status has less of an impact on factory employment than does childbearing (table 30).

The signs of the estimated coefficients are consistent with expectations. An inverse relationship exists between factory work and marriage, class, number of children, and consumer-worker ratio. The relationship between factory work and able-bodied females is, as expected, positive.

The variables follow a slightly different order when their individual effect is examined. Control over land, a proxy for class status, has the strongest effect on the decision to seek factory employment. The consumer-worker ratio and number of children, both life-cycle indicators, have equal effects on the employment decision, but they are not as important as class. In this model, marital status and the number of able-bodied females in the household have the least effect on the employment decision.

With regard to predicted and actual probabilities for success in this model, two out of three observations fit the predictions. This result is positive, but it also suggests that the data do not support all the hypothesized relationships. The goodness-of-fit χ^2 statistic for this model is based on a calculation of the expected and actual data in ten cells. The p value was not significant. After the stepwise regression, leaving number of children and class in the model, the p value for improvement χ^2 was significant at the .077 level. This model, then, cannot be rejected; it fits the data better than does the null model, which simply predicts the means.

As mentioned above, logistic regression computes probabilities that hold variables constant while manipulating other independent variables. It allows the predicted probability to be compared with actual behavior and also offers a comparison of the relative strength of different variables.

For example, for an unmarried woman living in a landless household with a small consumer-worker ratio (0.90) and one other able-bodied female, the probability of working in a factory is .677. We can compare her with another female in a similar situation in terms of marital status, consumer-worker ratio, and number of able-bodied females but with more land. As control over land increases

TABLE 30
CORRELATION MATRIX

	Marital status	Control over land	Children ever-born	Consumer-worker ratio	Able-bodied females in household
Marital status	1.000	—	—	—	—
Control over land	−0.135	1.000	—	—	—
Children ever-born	−0.468	0.149	1.000	—	—
Consumer-worker ratio	0.189	−0.085	−0.109	1.000	—
Able-bodied females in household	0.066	−0.266	−0.028	0.021	1.000
Constant	−0.072	−0.132	−0.092	−0.851	−0.348

to 0.5 hectare, all else held constant, the probability of the second female working in a factory declines by 50 percent to .373. Thus, variation in class status dramatically affects the probability of seeking factory work, all else held constant.

The number of children born also strongly affects the probability of working in a factory. A married woman without children, living in a near-landless household (0.09 ha.) with a moderately low consumer-worker ratio (1.13) and one other able-bodied female, has a high probability of working in a factory—.637. For another married woman in similar circumstances but with one child, the probability of working decreases by more than 50 percent to .299.

Holding other variables constant, the availability of another female in the household affects the probability of factory work much less than do the variables of class or number of children. When two women in similar conditions are compared, the probability of working in a factory decreases only from .637 to .557 when there is one less able-bodied female. The relative strength of each variable's significance is evident during this manipulation. Those variables with a higher level of significance dramatically affect the probability of factory employment compared with less statistically significant variables.

To summarize, the estimated coefficients in the logistic regression model not only confirm findings from the previous analysis but also rank the importance of each of these variables when combined. Those variables with the largest coefficient most dramatically affect the probability of factory employment. Starting with the strongest, the variables are land (class), children ever-born, consumer-worker ratio, number of able-bodied females, and marital status. The model also demonstrates that each of the variables of number of children, control over land, consumer-worker ratio, and number of able-bodied females has a statistically significant relationship with the probability of factory employment.

Notes

INTRODUCTION

1. In Java, strong emotions such as anger are expressed nonverbally, through silence and withdrawal. Directly confronting conflict is thought to be highly disruptive to one's inner peace and to family peace as well.

2. Young women like Rini avoid walking home alone in the dark because they fear robbery (which sometimes occurs) and spirits (see C. Geertz 1960 for an elaboration of types of spirits). Walking in groups avoids these problems.

3. Rini often said, "Suami saya jelek, Mbak" (My husband is ugly).

4. There are rituals for greeting and leave-taking in everyday Javanese life. To leave without engaging in this custom can signify disrespect; in this instance it spoke of her anger and discomfort.

5. As reported by my research assistant, Agnes Yosephine Retno Dwidarsih, who returned to the site in 1988 to revisit certain respondents, including Rini.

6. Although I occasionally use the term *Third World* in this book, I do not do so uncritically. *Postcolonial societies* may be a more fitting and appropriate term.

1. CONCEPTUALIZING POOR WOMEN, HOUSEHOLD DYNAMICS, AND INDUSTRIALIZATION

1. Families and households may constitute two distinct entities, with the former defined by kin relations and the latter by economic factors such as co-residence or income pooling (Wilk and Netting 1984). Household economic and feminist research in the 1970s shifted the locus of attention and discussion to the household as an economic unit, often bypassing issues related to the family, for theoretical and ideological reasons. In my village research, families and households completely overlapped and I therefore use the two terms interchangeably, fully aware that such intersections may not overlap in other settings. In our

conversations, the women I studied used the terms *family* (*keluarga*) and *family economy* (*ekonomi keluarga*) in reference to parents and siblings (and later, husbands) living with them, not *household*.

2. Additionally, the worker-manager relations entailed in factory production intensify and decompose traditional forms of gender subordination as they recompose new forms of gender subordination, creating a social and psychological form of marginalization. For example, fathers and brothers may lose their authority over a young female (decomposition) while a male manager gains it (recomposition) (Elson and Pearson 1981).

3. Mohanty (1988) has made this point about the literature she reviewed on gender and Third World development more generally. For example, Elson and Pearson encourage worker associations and activities based "on an explicit recognition of gender subordination [so that] women can begin to establish elements of a social identity in their own right" (1981, 105). These suggestions, however, do not necessarily reflect what factory workers want. In Elson and Pearson's article, there is not one quotation from a factory worker in the Third World.

4. Lenin's view that capitalism was a progressive force in the formerly feudal lives of Russian peasants could apply here as well: factory work, despite its exploitive and regressive features, may still constitute a progressive force in the lives of rural women.

5. See also Tentler (1979) and Cohen (1982) for similar arguments. M. Nash's (1967) book on the effects of one textile mill on an Indian community in Guatemala demonstrates that unmarried daughters and their wages remained under a father's control and that most of a wife's factory earnings were turned over to her husband. Her increased earning power did not lead to a greater say in family decisions (1967, 68–70). However, Nash did find that when sons ended up supporting their parents, dependency and power relations were reversed. Thus, his work suggests that established cultural patterns can be subverted by new economic arrangements, even though he did not find such subversion in the case of working daughters.

6. Social historians turned to the framework of family or household survival strategies as a way of conceptualizing and linking women's work with family life, family change, and industrialization (Tilly and Scott 1978; Hareven 1982; Lamphere 1987). The term *household survival strategies* was adapted from Tilly and Scott's (1978) study of early modern Europe and applied to Third World settings (Fernández-Kelly 1982). See Selby et al. (1990) for a history of how the term has been used in Latin American research.

7. Rouse (1989, 4) points out that scholars couching their studies in frameworks as diverse as neoclassical economics, Marxist economics, world systems, and cultural ecology have utilized the concept of household strategies.

8. Conceptually, for example, it helped social historians explain how household practices were slightly modified without essentially disrupting underlying goals and values during early European industrialization (Tilly and Scott 1978).

9. This assumption is shared in Farming Systems Research and other farm household models as well (Hart forthcoming).

10. An example of this selfless individualism is seen in Hareven's description of the family in early industrializing North America: "Because the functions of

family members were defined like those of a corporate body, the timing of early and later life transitions were interconnected in a continuum of familial needs and obligations" (1982, 185). In *The Rational Peasant*, Popkin (1979) provides another excellent example of this symbiosis, as he merges two different entities and units of analysis without explanation, using the term *the peasant* to mean both the individual peasant (always a male) and the peasant family.

11. See Hart (forthcoming, 9–10) and Folbre (1988, 253) for a discussion of the "Rotten Kid theorem" and the possibility of rotten power brokers in the family—e.g., wives, husbands, and parents.

12. For example, Tilly and Scott state that in peasant, artisan, and proletarian households, the household "allocated the labor of family members. In all cases, decisions were made in the interest of the group, not the individuals" (1978, 21).

13. See Fraad, Resnick, and Wolff's (1989) recent attempt to apply a Marxist analysis to intrahousehold relations and the feminist critiques of their piece in that same volume, particularly those by Eisenstein (1989) and Folbre and Hartmann (1989).

14. It is interesting to note that Lewis's classic work, *The Children of Sanchez* (1963), documented in detail many aspects of family life that contest certain assumptions in Becker's model and in other approaches to the household with respect to consensus, decision making, altruism, and the cooperation of subordinate household members. Curiously, the implications of his book have been largely ignored in contemporary economic approaches to household studies. This lack of attention might be attributed to the increased economically oriented focus on households rather than families that occurred in the 1970s and to scholars' discomfort with Lewis's "culture of poverty" argument. In any case, his early documentation of conflict in poor families remains unique and important.

15. Agarwal's (1991) research on disaster and hardship is unusual in this account. She found not only that there is an unequal distribution of goods and an unequal allocation of labor within Indian households but also that there is an unequal distribution of hardship, with poor females suffering the most during seasonal lean times or when disasters strike.

16. Becker directly addresses this problem by stating that an economic approach does not assume that "decision units are necessarily conscious of their efforts to maximize or can verbalize or otherwise describe in an informative way reasons for the systematic patterns in their behavior" (1986, 112). Clearly, not all behavior is in the realm of consciousness; the problem herein is in imputing calculations when it is impossible to test or to refute their existence.

17. For example, Wallerstein describes the household as a "fortress . . . of resistance to patterns of labor force allocation favored by accumulators" and household decision making as "the principal everyday political weapon available to the world's labor force" (1984, 21), conjuring up an image of cohesive households as lone ships battling the capitalist sea. The only problem is that this noble image is not based on detailed household and intrahousehold data but remains the interpretation of an academic from afar.

18. For example, Rouse (1989, 36 n. 22) notes that in several Latin American household studies on which he focused, either researchers explicitly stated that they interviewed only one person in the household or such interview techniques

can be inferred from the large numbers of households interviewed. This tendency is also reflected in much of the literature on households in Southeast Asia and, I suspect, elsewhere in the world.

19. In their book on the household strategies of urban Mexican households, Selby et al. (1990, 108, 176) are among the few who acknowledge intrahousehold exploitation and domestic violence. At the same time, they fall back on the notion of household strategies (although more carefully than most other researchers do), focusing more on "the household" than probing into the gender and generational dynamics to which they allude.

20. Rouse (1989, 5) criticizes the concept of household strategies for yet another reason: the highly complex relationship between poor people and capitalism cannot be adequately represented by a framework that incorporates a set of three consecutive stages—i.e., capitalism poses a problem, household members encounter it collectively, and their actions are "treated essentially as agreed solutions which make use of any opportunities that the system simultaneously poses."

21. It is unfortunate that most of the insights gained from feminist research on households are not incorporated into household models (Deere 1991) and are incorporated into the research of only a few male scholars (Ellis 1988; Rouse 1989; White 1980; Carney and Watts 1991).

22. See Hart (forthcoming) for a more detailed summary of the domestic labor debate and the history of feminist approaches to household economics.

23. The bargaining approach was developed by neoclassical economists who based it on the principles of game theory. It was then applied to the household (Manser and Brown 1980; McElroy and Horney 1981). Most feminist applications of this approach have drawn on the concepts used in the bargaining approach but not on the assumptions of game theory. Hart points out that some of the problems involved in applying game theory to household relations stem from methodological individualism, particularly the assumption that individuals guided by self-interest enter the game arena with externally given preferences and that "the rules of the game are given and fixed" (forthcoming, 21). A full discussion of game theory is beyond the scope of this book. See Hart (forthcoming), Sen (1990), Folbre (1986; 1988), and Bruce and Dwyer (1988) for amendments to and critical discussions of game theory as applied to the household from a feminist perspective. These household models create different trajectories and imply different policy outcomes for women. The New Household Economics approach might mean endowing the household head with more opportunities or income, whereas the bargaining approach may mean endowing women so that they are more equal to men (Agarwal 1991, 227–28). Bruce and Dwyer (1988) point out that policy makers tend to prefer the former approach because it is more practical to deal with only one person.

24. Conceptually, it is problematic to apply a Western concept such as autonomy, which is "based on the hierarchal structure of our own society" (Yanagisako and Collier 1987, 37), to Third World settings where autonomy, power, or control may take very different forms or where the activities we associate with them may in fact denote something quite different (see Errington 1990; chapter 3). The feminist political theorist Di Stefano finds that feminists are questioning

the concept of autonomy "as a normative standard and empirical marker even as they continue to invoke it" (1990, 6). One important reason for such questioning in this literature is that the Third World subjects of our analyses may not seek the same goals of autonomy that First World feminists do (Ong 1988).

25. Measuring, tracking, and comparing autonomy can lead to vague unidimensional descriptions of women having a relatively high, low, or medium amount of it. In such descriptions, autonomy is more or less granted by the system, the family, or a wage, excluding women as actors. The nuances, failures, acquiescence, resistance, and successes of women's attempts to negotiate their lives are lost when researchers use a yardstick of high or low, adjectives that limit the variation between women and within women's lives. The above arguments can also be applied to analyses of "women's status," which, Errington argues, is mistakenly assumed to be easily identifiable cross-culturally (1990, 5).

26. For the most part, I reject the notion of "false consciousness"—that is, that I as a First World academic know more about my respondents' life conditions than they do. However, rejecting false consciousness does not imply that any and all of their statements must be accepted at face value. The ideological underpinnings of certain statements must be analyzed with an attempt to fully understand the subjects' rationale in making the statement.

27. In other words, women in highly patriarchal societies may express views and engage in actions that help maintain patriarchy (see Sen 1990).

28. I do not mean to imply that kinship is the only variable affecting factory women: the state obviously plays a crucial role in shaping labor laws, industrial policy, and family policy and can therefore greatly affect workers' experiences of factory employment. Generally, where Free Trade Zones and export-oriented industrialization have grown, governments in Asia have attempted to appeal to capitalists' interests by limiting or banning unions and strikes, keeping wages, benefits, and labor laws minimal, and not enforcing the laws that do exist (Phongpaichit 1988, 152).

29. I have not conducted primary research in Taiwan but draw on the abundant secondary sources.

30. Although Scott is referring specifically to the Latin American literature, this generalization holds for the Southeast Asian literature as well.

2. INDUSTRIAL AND AGRARIAN CHANGE

1. Not surprisingly, substantial growth occurred among large private business groups with military patronage (Robison 1986, 202).

2. Hal Hill has analyzed the "contentious" issue of ownership in Indonesia, using data on firm ownership. One strong argument in Indonesia among nationalists is that foreign ownership is too large and growing; others argue just as strongly that state ownership is too large and cumbersome. Both sides agree, however, that private domestic investment, especially Pribumi investment, is too small. Hill's analysis of industrial concentration does not support either side: private firms constitute the largest single ownership group, but "effective control may still reside with foreign partners or the state apparatus" (1987, 99).

3. The other factors include a shift in output such that intermediate and

capital goods increased while the share of consumer goods declined; an increase in employment and productivity; and consolidation of smaller units, resulting in ever-larger industries and firms (Hill 1987, 72).

4. See Gavin Jones (1987) and Chris Manning (1988) for thorough discussions of definitions, changes over time, problems of measurement, and so on.

5. Gavin Jones points out that service jobs also include "dynamic growth areas of banking and international trade" (1987, 280). However, those are clearly jobs for an urban, educated group. See Jones (1987) for further discussion.

6. Some of this development may in fact be periurban because of the changing definition of *urban* in the census; *urban* now includes areas that formerly may have been categorized as rural (G. Jones 1984, 23).

7. J. H. Boeke wrote about and lectured on the theory of social dualism in the late 1920s. Social dualism is the "clashing of an imported social system with an indigenous social system of another style" (Boeke 1953, 4). One social system is traditional, precapitalist, and communal, typical of "Eastern" rural societies. The other social system is modern, foreign, and imported; although it may be Socialist, Communist, or capitalist, it is usually "high capitalist" and Western (Boeke 1953, 4; Mackie 1980, 297–99). Boeke's theory includes a Durkheimian notion of organic and mechanical solidarity and reflects the traditional-modern dichotomy, seen later in modernization theory, that casts city in opposition to village, industry in opposition to agriculture, and the traits of risk taking, entrepreneurship, accuracy, individualism, and work discipline typical of the capitalist sector in opposition to the fatalism, communalism, and risk aversion typical of peasants. Although a number of criticisms can be leveled against Boeke's theory—e.g., that there are many connections between the two systems—it was influential during the colonial period. Anne Booth (1988, 253) argues that agricultural policies stemming from Boeke's notion of dualism can be found in the New Order's approach to rural development. Indeed, the conception of a dual or segmented economy remains prevalent among some academics and policymakers today (see Garnaut and McCawley 1980).

In his 1950s field research in East Java, Clifford Geertz was pessimistic about the ability of the Javanese to match agricultural output with population growth and developed a theory concerning the basis of agricultural stagnation in Java that has influenced generations of academics (Booth 1988, 4). He describes Javanese peasant agriculture and terms its methods *involutionary*. As the Javanese worked on Dutch plantations during the colonial period, rice production was intensified, and "increased institutional complexity" typified land tenure and other agrarian relations (White 1983, 21). Conceptually, *involution* denotes a system of production that is inwardly oriented and overelaborated in detail (Geertz 1963, 82); it is distinctly passive by comparison with terms such as *evolution* or *revolution*.

"Shared poverty," a notion implying socioeconomic homogeneity, is, according to Geertz, one of the results of agricultural involution. The concept of involution and shared poverty have incurred a strikingly active debate: Benjamin White (1983), in his review of the critical responses to agricultural involution, and Geertz (1984), in his response to White, cite nearly 120 references each. Many scholars have argued that Javanese society was far more stratified than

Geertz noted and that Javanese agrarian society has been "historically divided into agrarian classes" (Husken and White 1989, 171). Contemporary political economists argue that Javanese rural society has become increasingly stratified, in part because of technological changes. Although growth in agricultural output has increased in recent years, research demonstrates that rural cultivators do not share equally in the benefits of such growth (Booth 1988, 7).

8. The "Green Revolution" in Indonesia and other parts of the Third World refers to the promulgation of grain seeds, in this case rice, that necessitated the coordinated use of other agricultural technologies, such as fertilizer, pesticides, and irrigation, in order to obtain greater yields per hectare and more crops per year than with traditional rice varieties. Countries adopting Green Revolution seeds hoped to decrease food imports and achieve self-sufficiency, or at least less dependency on imported grains. Despite increased rice output in Indonesia and elsewhere in Asia, the social and economic effects of the Green Revolution have been more problematic. For example, poorer farmers could not easily afford the necessary inputs; as a result, the gap between better-off and poor villagers has often increased. Furthermore, in Indonesia, Green Revolution rice varieties led to changes in harvesting techniques that pushed poor women out of traditional employment in favor of men.

9. Jamie Mackie and Sjahrir (1989, 8) describe a speech by President Suharto in which he refers to statistics on poverty gathered by the Central Bureau of Statistics; according to Suharto, these statistics show that between 1976 and 1987, the percentage of the rural population below the poverty line (calculated by the cost of 2,100 calories per day, plus costs of basic necessities) decreased from 40 percent to 16 percent. In urban areas, the actual numbers have increased although the percentage has declined. The research methods used to gather such data are extremely important and would affect the results, but they are not discussed.

10. The most important contemporary debate on rural Java concerns the effects of the Green Revolution on agricultural employment and income. I leave the details of this argument to the economists. See Manning (1988), Hart (1986b), and Hart, Turton, and White (1989).

11. The poverty line was calculated by Sayogyo (1977) in rice equivalents. It reflects the minimum rice consumption necessary for a person or household to subsist.

3. JAVANESE WOMEN AND THE FAMILY

1. This discussion does not include the Chinese in Southeast Asia, whose kinship system is patrilineal.

2. Their research was part of a project funded by the Ford Foundation and sponsored by MIT in the early 1950s, during the time of early Indonesian nationhood. The team of researchers consisted of anthropologists and sociologists located in one town and village in Central Java, researching topics ranging from agriculture, kinship, language, family, religion, ritual, and trade (C. Geertz 1956; 1960; 1963; 1984, 512; Dewey 1962; Jay 1969). Their descriptions and analysis of social, cultural, and political life reflected their desire to know what Java and the Javanese were "really like" (C. Geertz 1984, 527) and reflected their concern

with the "cultural meanings of human action—attitudes, values, world-views and the manner in which social interactions are constellated" (White 1983, 19). These studies of Java are also fairly descriptive, although their theoretical underpinnings can be categorized as Parsonian or structural functionalist (White 1983, 19); for instance, they often use a dualistic model or worldview. They follow the argument of the modernization school of their time, with its emphasis on dualism, diffusion, and modern versus traditional attitudes, values, and behaviors (White 1983, 19).

3. For example, Paul Meyer (1981), in his study of the value of children in Sunda (West Java), wholeheartedly accepts Geertz's, Jay's, and Koentjaraningrat's views that Javanese women are very strong within the household; he "verifies" that this view is also true of the Sundanese by speaking with some colleagues who affirm that women are the "ministers of the interior" in the family in Sunda. Meyer writes, "It is quite plausible that women there [in Sunda] have a powerful voice in household matters" (1981, 100). By using this methodology—speaking with a few colleagues, probably male—he received similar ideological responses that are then taken as social facts, a method that would not be acceptable for most topics in sociology or demography without some data or critical analysis.

4. Emmanuel Todd is highly critical of the flexibility found in Southeast Asian family systems, finding it "anomic" rather than practical (1985); his critique reflects considerable confusion about Southeast Asia. He provides an excellent example of the difficulties that researchers face when attempting to fit Southeast Asia into a comparative framework. He doesn't understand how a nuclear family structure with bilateral inheritance could exist outside of the West; he thus terms the Southeast Asian system "the imperfect nuclear family," comparing it with the complete and perfect nuclear family found in his native France.

5. *Matrilocal residence* means that the husband moves into his wife's parents' house after marriage; *neolocal residence* means that the married couple can live anywhere—near one set of in-laws or far from both.

6. My older respondents said that only when they formed their own nuclear family household could they make any of their own decisions. However, they then became solely responsible for household work while jointly responsible for income-earning activities and some childcare, a pattern different from that of the extended family context.

7. Margery Wolf (1972) points out that in the 1960s some filial daughters took this burden to the extreme and became prostitutes, a decision that parents accepted; see her chapter "Filial Daughters."

8. Geertz's extrapolation is particularly apparent in the matters of age at marriage and choice in marriage. Geertz (1961) asserted that young people were meeting in school and carrying on romances, which increased both age and choice in marriage. Findings from detailed research have not corroborated such assertions, leading Budi S. Martokoesoemo (1979) to argue that Hildred Geertz may have been generalizing from the lives of the town elite, projecting a 1950s American view of dating.

9. Even the most independent women often said to me, "I must obey my Father" (*Harus ikut Bapak*).

10. According to law, in order to take a second wife, a man must appear in court and affirm that certain conditions exist: for instance, that his first wife is

physically disabled or diseased, infertile (which is usually assumed to be the woman's problem), or unable to fulfill her sexual duties (Soewondo 1977).

11. One example of contemporary research that unquestioningly and uncritically draws on Jay's and Geertz's contentions about Javanese women's status is seen in the following:

> [Javanese women] enjoy high status. . . . The Javanese wife dominates or enjoys equal status in the household decision-making process regarding production as well as consumption issues. The woman can be described as being the silent head of the household. . . . All income is turned over to the wife and she decides how it will be spent. . . . Many families, therefore, are dependent on the wives' financial capabilities. (Pyle 1985, 140)

12. Lydia Morris (1990, 106) explains that *control* involves decisions about the distribution of income and its allocation within the household. *Management* refers to the process of implementing financial decisions. *Budgeting* refers to spending within particular expenditure categories and attempting to expend as little as possible. Thus, Javanese women may be more involved in the management and budgeting of household income rather than control over it.

13. Through a close friend I met an educated young mother from Yogyakarta whose husband had physically abused her. When pregnant with their second child, she discovered that he had another wife who was also due with their second child, both within ten days of each other. All the same, she obeyed his highly patriarchal orders even when she disagreed with him, because, as she said, "*Harus ikut suami*" (I must obey my husband).

14. Women's organizations predate independence. I do not provide a history of them but only wish to point out that Indonesian women have been active in both political and religious movements (see Wieringa 1988).

15. Madelon Djajadiningrat-Nieuwenhuis asserts that Ibuism "sanctions any action provided it is taken as a mother who is looking after her family, a group, a class, a company, or the state, without demanding power or prestige in return" (1987, 44).

16. Djajadiningrat-Nieuwenhuis (1987) argues that Ibuism combines Dutch petit bourgeois and traditional priyayi values. Indeed, she argues that Ibuism goes hand-in-hand with elitism ("priyayization") because of the class position of those in power in such organizations.

17. Dharma Wanita is designed to organize and control the activities of wives of civil servants and of the civil servants themselves, since state ideology makes a wife responsible for her husband's wrongdoings (e.g., corruption), although husbands are not responsible for their wives' failings. Dharma Wanita, Dutch feminist researchers argue, is the epitome of the cultural norm of *Harus ikut suami* (I must obey my husband).

18. According to Saskia Wieringa, these tasks should be carried out according to *Kodrat Wanita* (woman's nature): "women are *lemah lembut* (soft and weak), shouldn't speak out loudly and not in their own interests, shouldn't push their own interests over their husband's and father's, but are instead docile wives and mothers and dutiful daughters" (1988, 14).

4. THE VILLAGES

1. Technically, several hamlets (*pedukuan*) are joined administratively as one village (*desa*). In this study I refer to these hamlets as villages, following the residents' perceptions of their village communities. See White (1976) for further discussion of this point.

2. In Nuwun, a woven bamboo mat had been put some feet above my bed to hold rain that poured in from the roof. A beehive hung from the ceiling, and the mat buffered me from the bees. However, rats then built a nest on the mat, and until I had the sense to buy a mosquito net, stillborn rats that the mother had pushed out of the nest or the mother rat herself fell on me in bed several times in the middle of the night. Once I awoke at about four o'clock in the morning to watch in astonishment as two rats marched up the wall to their nest, one with my toothbrush container and the other with my tube of Sensodyne toothpaste! We reclaimed them before finding out exactly how the rats planned to use them.

3. *Londo* derives from the Javanese word for "Dutch"—*Belanda*—and may be used in verbal reference to a Westerner.

4. Although my cohabitation might have raised some questions among my village hosts, divorce did not. Several years after my last visit to the village, when I was about to marry, I wrote to the village leader and his family to explain that I had divorced my so-called first husband because *tidak cocok* (we did not fit), an appropriate description that had been used by many of my respondents when explaining their divorce. They seemed to have no problem congratulating me on my "second" marriage.

5. The district consists of approximately fourteen thousand hectares of land divided into wet riceland (both irrigated and rainfed), dry land, public forest land, and plantations. The main crops are rice, peanuts, cassava, soybeans, corn, vegetables, and fruit. The district comprises 28 desa or *kelurahan* (administrative villages) and 141 pedukuan or *dukuh* (hamlets).

6. In 1982 there were approximately 100 home industries in the district, employing 168 people, 78 small industries employing 203 people, and 12 medium and large-scale industries employing 6,290. The latter were the more modern firms—the focus of this study.

7. District statistics from mid-1982 suggested that out of 54,227 people (all those age ten and over), 27 percent of those economically active were farmers (owner-operators), 30 percent were agricultural laborers, and 8 percent were industrial workers. It is unclear how *economically active* was defined. In addition, these tabulations are approximate because they are gathered by hamlet-level officials, some of whom are more conscientious than others.

8. One hectare equals 2.47 acres.

9. Farmers were interviewed in groups about changes in agricultural wages and relations. Two sets of group interviews were conducted to gather information on agricultural practices.

10. In villages bordering the factories, farmers often had to seek agricultural laborers from other villages as more young men obtained factory employment.

11. Researchers who have done rural-based studies on topics other than household economy or agrarian change have used consumption rather than pro-

duction as their measure; in particular, household possessions are often used as a measure of status differences (Berman 1984; T. Hull 1975; V. Hull 1975).

12. Although Gillian Hart and others have used land as the basis for distinguishing between "asset classes," she discusses obvious objections to using such a measure. One can argue that class structure is not simply resource differentiation. Such a "unidimensional measure" can be seen as "too narrow and might produce a distorted picture of patterns of control over resources." However, in Hart's case study and in most of rural Java, control over land is highly correlated with access to other resources such as tools, farm animals, money, and other goods, (1986b, 102). And as her study demonstrates, differential control over productive resources shapes patterns of household labor.

13. *Land owned* includes land over which the family has legal ownership and disposal rights (*tanah milik*) as well as the rice land allocated to village officials in lieu of salary or as a pension (*tanah bengkok*). Hart points out that "land owned is an important—although partial—measure of the household's physical resource base" (Hart 1978, 89).

Land operated is calculated as land owned minus land rented or sharecropped out plus land rented or sharecropped in. Benjamin White refers to this measure as "area cultivated" (1976, 124). This measure is "most useful to elucidate intensity and efficiency of resource use" (Penny and Singarimbun 1973, 78). Operators do not have access to the entire harvest of land operated; thus, this measure is "misleading if applied to questions of household welfare" (Hart 1978, 89).

14. I used the following equation to calculate land controlled, with dry land weighted (see notes 11 and 13): land owned + ½ area sharecropped in − ½ area sharecropped out + ½ area rented in − ½ area rented out. The correlation between land controlled and land owned (with tegal weighted) was significant: $r = .886$ ($p < .001$) in Nuwun and $r = .986$ ($p < .001$) in Rumiyen.

15. If a family owns and operates its land, it receives a return to both land and labor. If the land is rented out, the owner receives a return to land (50 percent of output) whereas the renter receives a return to labor (50 percent of output). Hart's analysis (1978, 89) corroborates Penny and Singarimbun's assumption of a 50–50 allocation between land and labor. In my research, land sharecropped in or out was counted as one-half, based on information from farmer interviews, even though there are some variations in costs and output covered by owners and sharecroppers. Hart's definition of land controlled is akin to Penny and Singarimbun's, whereas White counts land rented in as fully controlled (100 percent) (Hart 1978, 92). In this study, dry land (tegal) was weighted at 0.6 based on labor requirements for the secondary crops grown on this land (cassava, peanuts, corn, soybeans, and vegetables) and, more important, the potential to produce revenue per hectare of tegal given the usual mix of crops (Montgomery and Sisler 1976, 46).

16. Food and nonfood necessities were translated into kilograms of milled rice. Rice equivalents were then translated into the amount of land necessary to produce the amount of rice an average family (five people) would need to survive. Hart has further refined this measure by taking consumption differences by age and sex within the household into account, standardized by adult male equiva-

lents. The coefficients used by Hart (1978, 102) were adapted from Scarlett Epstein's research in India (1962) and are based on a study by the Food and Agricultural Organization:

SEX	AGE	COEFFICIENT
Both	1	0.10
Both	1–3	0.30
Both	4–5	0.50
Both	6–9	0.65
Females	10–15	0.75
Males	10–15	0.80
Females	16 +	0.80
Males	16 +	1.00

17. An average family of five in Hart's study had an average of 3.87 adult male equivalent consumer units per household (1978, 102). In the two agricultural villages in this study, the average household size was 4.9, with an average of 3.6 adult male equivalents per household. Given the similarities in household demographic characteristics, I used Hart's estimates of the amount of land necessary for self-sufficiency.

18. Although Benjamin White (1976) and Richard Franke (1972) used 0.2 hectare as the upper cutoff point for class 1, Gillian Hart's estimate was slightly higher, 0.24, and is used here.

19. The numeration of classes in my study is the inverse of Hart's (1978b, 1986). In her study, class 1 was the richest and class 3 the poorest.

20. In this research, each household was categorized by class according to the amount of land controlled. These categories were based on the consumption needs of an average family. As an alternative, households were categorized into class groupings based on the actual number of adult consumer units in the household per hectares of land controlled. This second class measure is based on a strong correspondence between household size, consumption, and class. When class stratification was calculated on the basis of consumer units, there was little change overall in the distribution of households in Nuwun ($n = 151$). There was only a 1 percent overall shift upward in class proportions: 88.7 percent were in the lower two strata using the average household size measure, compared with 89.8 percent calculated on the basis of consumer units per hectare. Hart used this latter measure in her study and notes that when using the per household measure, only six households changed class category (1978, 103).

21. White argues for a functional definition of the household as the group that "exercises the greatest autonomy relative to other groupings in the society with respect for the well-being of its members" (White 1980, 13).

22. Clearly, not all consumption occurs within the household, particularly when household members work away from the village, but most daily consumption and more major investments in consumption occur within the household.

23. Jeremy Evans states that *somah* is translated as "one house" in the sense of "belonging to one household." This derivation suggests that *somah* means "household" in the sense of all those who share a dwelling (1984, 156).

24. For example, several houses sheltered two related families. Since cooking

and consumption were shared, they were, according to their definition and mine, one household. In the industrialized village, many families rented out rooms to migrants who were not considered part of the family. Migrants cooked and ate on their own, sometimes sharing shopping and cooking with roommates or friends in nearby rooms on the same shift. Migrant boarders were therefore not considered part of the landlord's household; rather, they formed their own. For this study, it was neither feasible nor necessary to specify how each migrant arranged cooking and consumption.

25. In only a few instances did a non-kin member live and eat with the family in the agricultural villages.

26. For example, of the households in the upper strata, 77 percent of their income came from "own production" (farming and fishponds).

27. Another way to conceptualize the effects of class status on labor market integration is to categorize occupations by the relationships of production. For example, aggregating those engaged in wage labor (agricultural and nonagricultural, including sharecropping), there is a clear linear relationship between class status and employment. The proportion of heads of households engaged in some form of wage labor declines from 29 percent in class 1 to 6 percent in class 3 in Nuwun, whereas it is sharper in Rumiyen—from 51 percent down to zero. By contrast, the percentage of self-employed (farmer, trader, and "other") increases by class status.

28. The possessions list included tables, guest chairs (*kursi tamu*), mattresses, cupboards (*lemari* and *biffet*), radios, pressure lamps, televisions, watches, clocks, bicycles, motorcycles, goats, and cows.

29. The members of this particular village were much more assertive in local meetings, asking direct questions about matters such as money "lost" because of corruption.

30. Although the proportion of females in agriculture as a primary occupation is low in Nuwun, another 33 percent state that agricultural production is their secondary or tertiary occupation. This situation may be related to labor-intensive household production occupying most of their time. It could also be related to gender ideology, specifically, the normative role of a Javanese wife as a housewife. Even though time allocation studies demonstrate that females spend at least as much if not more time in agricultural production than males do, most of the wives in the census stated that they "help their husbands in farming" (*bantu suami*; *bantu tani sendiri*) rather than stating that they, too, are farmers.

31. *Female head of household* here refers to the woman in charge, whether she is the sole head of household or shares that position with her husband.

5. THE FACTORIES

The chapter epigraph derives from a popular song in Japan about Iwataru Kikusa, a silk worker who, in 1907, fought off an attack by a murderer who had already killed several other silk factory workers. Iwataru Kikusa "seized her assailant's testicles and pulled them so hard that he lost his stranglehold on her and revealed his face. Since she escaped not only with her life but also with the knowledge of his identity, the police, who for almost a year had been searching in vain for the perpetrator of a series of ghastly murders, swiftly captured him. As a result, Iwataru Kikusa became famous in the silk district as a courageous factory girl triumphantly resisting the powerful male" (Tsurumi 1990, 197).

1. During my visit in 1986 I found that three new factories had been built. In 1987 a large cigarette factory owned by a company normally located in East Java was being constructed there (personal correspondence, Ratna Sapthari, Aug. 1987).

2. Although I gathered data on the cost of investments, the validity of these data is questionable. Owners feared that such data would fall into the hands of the government and affect taxation. In addition, several owners/managers claimed not to know the cost of machinery. The amount invested in building the factory, renting land, and buying machinery ranged from $100,000 (the new, small confectionery factory) to $22 million (the textile factory). Many factories expanded after several years of production.

3. The raw materials and machinery needed for production were also multinational. Half of the factories are able to procure all their raw materials from Indonesia. The remainder buy some materials in Indonesia and other materials from the United States, Egypt, India, Australia, and various other African, European, and Asian countries. By contrast, none of the machinery comes from Indonesia; it is all imported from Taiwan, Japan, the United States, and Europe.

4. The spinning factory was a joint venture, meaning that eventually the Indonesians will become the majority owners; see chapter 6 for details of the ownership. The textile firm is owned by Chinese Indonesians and overseas Chinese in Hong Kong. The general manager is a Chinese Indonesian, and the assistant manager of production is Chinese and a citizen of Hong Kong. The personnel manager was, as in most factories, a Pribumi.

5. Gross returns from sales (undoubtedly understated) ranged from $1,500 to almost $2 million monthly. However, it was not possible to calculate the rate of profit. For example, at full utilization, the garment factory could produce 3,000 blouses daily at a cost of $2.30 each. However, this factory produced blouses on order only, and production fluctuated with demand.

6. One could also argue that living at home with parents who provide free lodging and food could encourage labor protests since most workers would not go hungry if they lost their job.

7. I asked five workers in different factories to keep diaries for me, noting anything interesting or unusual that happened in the factory every day.

8. In agriculture and trading, Javanese women are fully active in heavy tasks.

9. I heard of only one example in which the factory was able to use the army/police background of the personnel manager to their advantage in a different manner. During the anti-Chinese riots in 1980, the Chinese-owned garment factory shut down for a week while the Javanese personnel manager donned his army uniform and stayed in the factory office, stating that he owned the factory.

10. Being frightened or startled (*kaget*) can cause serious and perhaps fatal illness. Pregnant women or mothers with infants often talk to their fetuses or babies, telling them what is happening, to prevent the child from being startled. The firstborn child in my host family died from what was probably typhoid fever; however, his grandmother claimed that he died because he was kaget when his

mother (her daughter-in-law) frightened him by taking him on a bus ride to see her relatives.

11. This account was in a worker's diary, but I was unable to clarify whether the head of the ghost was male or female.

12. The awful irony is that after many visits and unpleasant encounters with the manager, I finally received permission to enter the factory and take photographs only to discover weeks later, at home in the United States, that my shutter had been broken and all my slides were pure black.

6. LIFE IN A SPINNING MILL

1. From interviews with a random sample of 100 female workers, I found that 61 were married and that most of them had more than one child, demonstrating how unusual this factory's policies were concerning female workers. The following list shows the percentages of the 61 workers with children:

NUMBER OF CHILDREN	PERCENTAGE OF WORKERS
0	15
1	38
2	25
3	16
4	3
5	1.5
6	1.5

2. After a death, a *slametan* (religious meal) is held three, seven, forty, and one hundred days after the death and on specific anniversaries of the death thereafter. For forty days after the death, the family puts out the kind of food that the deceased liked, near the place in the house or by the bed where she or he died. (C. Geertz 1960, 72).

3. That the atmosphere was much more free and relaxed than it was in any other situation I encountered during my research was manifested during my small thank-you party for the residents at the end of my stay. It started off in fairly typical fashion with brief speeches. The residents initiated some very funny games (reminiscent of games I played during my adolescence), and then the party erupted into a "disco" that lasted until early morning. This highly atypical behavior for rural Javanese females would be unacceptable in most other situations.

7. DETERMINANTS OF FACTORY EMPLOYMENT

1. Although I focus on the determinants of factory employment, I do not assume that factory owners and potential or actual workers were equally empowered. As demonstrated in chapter 5, managers' preferences not to employ mothers overruled efforts by village women with children to gain entry into the factories.

2. I often use the term *life-cycle stage* to describe families; however, I do not assume that all families follow a linear path of growth and change. My interviews with older women (chapter 2) revealed the incredible fluidity in their family lives,

which challenges the notion of a linear trajectory of stages. Perhaps *life-cycle state* may be a better and less ontological descriptor.

3. Nuwun and Rumiyen were hamlets (*pedukuan*) within the same administrative village (*kelurahan*). Their similar ecological and economic conditions justified the aggregation of subsample households in my analysis.

4. Two methodological caveats are necessary here. The women studied excluded twelve former factory workers, most of whom had quit the factories after childbirth. Aggregating these former workers with current workers as a group of "ever worked" would be misleading. Most former workers were in a different life-cycle state from that of current workers. Their individual and family characteristics were often quite different from when they were working in the factories, as single women or married women without children.

Second, it is desirable to measure the determinants of employment before any employment decision is made; however, it was impossible to do so in this setting. In 1981–82, I measured characteristics of factory (FW) and nonfactory (NF) females' households; I was therefore measuring characteristics after young women had decided for or against factory employment. Although factory employment could affect the very factors thought to cause it, this interaction appears to be relevant for only one measure discussed below, the value of household possessions (consumption), since consumption of certain items often increased through the buying power of factory wages.

5. Although nonfactory workers appear to be a slightly older group, the range for that particular variable was quite large.

6. The respondent's birth order was not significant because in many workers' families older siblings had already moved out, whereas many nonfactory females already lived with their husbands and children. The current composition of the families in which women lived—either the family of origin or of procreation—was more important than their birth order in their family of origin, which was not necessarily still intact.

7. Twenty percent of the households in which there was a current worker ($n = 8$) were headed by women, compared with 13 percent of nonfactory households ($n = 12$). The high proportion of female-headed households in the Third World has been an issue of concern for policymakers because of its high correlation with poverty (Youssef and Hetler 1983). Although among the current workers all the female-headed households were in the lower stratum, there was no particular relationship between the twelve nonfactory females and class status.

8. The dependency ratio is a fairly crude demographic measure of the number of dependents (ages 0–14 and 65+) per productive members (ages 15–64). This measure assumes that those less than age fourteen are full dependents, which is highly questionable given the research on child labor in Java (White 1976). The measure is perhaps more useful when applied to an entire population than to individual households.

The consumer-worker ratio is a more sensitive measure of the interaction between productive abilities and reproductive needs within the household. "Consumers" are "adult male equivalent" consumer units, measured by kilograms of rice, standardized for age and sex. Although number of consumers is measured in rice equivalents, it includes nonrice needs. I used Gillian Hart's coefficients for

Java (see chapter 4 of this book and Hart 1978, 102). Workers were counted as "1." Those over age twelve actually involved in production as a primary work activity, excluding students, the disabled, and the very old, were counted as workers. The use of age twelve as the cutoff point was based on labor activities observed in the villages. Those less than age twelve were often engaged in productive activities, but children were likely to be in grammar school until that age. The ratio used in table 19 and in other calculations refers only to the actual number of workers in the household.

9. Although the average number of dependents differed considerably, this measure was not statistically significant. The average dependency ratio was significantly different, however, with 0.205 and 0.522 for factory workers' and nonfactory females' households, respectively ($p = .0044$)

10. As pointed out in chapter 3, although household income was not measured, Hart found a strong correlation between class status and total household income in her rural Javanese study (1978).

11. Emily Honig, in historical research on women in the Shanghai cotton mills, found that in some cases, women received their wages directly, at least in the late 1930s, but most simply turned over all of their wages to their parents (1986, 170–71).

12. Honig writes that in Shanghai in the 1920s and 1930s, girls aged nine and ten were sent to work partly so that their brothers could go to school (1986, 168).

13. Although Chinese culture is on the whole patriarchal, there are important regional differences. In a few cases, women's disproportionately high contribution to the family economy gives them more bargaining power and control; for example, some women are able to resist marriage or refuse consummation of a marriage. (See Topley 1975.)

14. This particular economic relationship has been carefully studied by several researchers, because any crack in this bond, even a 5 percent increase in income retention by a factory daughter, would indicate social change (Thornton et al. 1984).

8. FACTORY DAUGHTERS AND THE FAMILY ECONOMY

1. I analyze the behavior only of single daughters, controlling for demographic position within the family. Parents have different and greater economic expectations of unmarried daughters than they have of married daughters with children.

2. Rent was not included in the table because boarders paid rent in two to three annual installments. None of these migrants paid rent during the survey. However, the average monthly rent was 1,180 rupiah, or 7.3 percent of the average monthly salary.

3. Workers typically bought food for the family or goods such as cooking oil, spices, or kerosene. Occasionally they purchased household goods such as a tray or a small tablecloth. They reported whatever they spent on goods bought expressly for household consumption.

4. If I had valued all of the workers' household consumption—food or goods produced by the household, excluding the market value of rent—it is likely that

the net contribution would be negative in all cases. Such an effort was beyond the limits of this research project.

5. *Pokoknya, uang itu cukup untuk keperluan saya sendiri.*

6. In addition, the relationships between the amount contributed and measures such as household size, the number of dependents, and the consumer-worker ratio were surprisingly weak.

7. A stronger relationship was found between contributions and the value of household possessions ($r = -.682$), suggesting that those from better-off families contributed less. However, household possessions do not reflect socioeconomic status as well as landholdings do because factory daughters buy more consumer goods.

8. This figure excludes the worker who took 50 percent from her parents, which reduces the average to a negative amount.

9. Gillian Hart analyzed monthly household income by class status for one year from a sample in a Javanese village. In December of her survey, the lower two strata (whence factory daughters come) were just barely above the poverty line. In January, however, household income in both lower two strata was below the poverty line (1978, 184). Income, particularly for those households dependent on wage labor, fluctuated in relation to the agricultural cycle; this fluctuation has dangerous implications for family welfare.

10. The entire sample consisted of thirty-nine workers.

11. Among commuting workers, there was a positive relationship between the proportion of wages saved and the family's class position ($r = .415$). Among the commuters, the four females who did not participate in an arisan came from families in the poorest stratum. Three of those four workers gave an average of 13,000 rupiah to their families during the month surveyed.

12. A well-off village woman told me, "These factory workers really take risks and ask for a lot of credit."

13. In his research on rural migrants in Java, Graeme Hugo (1983) also found that workers' remittances were not used for productive investments by families.

14. The dorm residents (all female) in the textile mill had higher wages and also reported remitting large proportions to their families; however, I was unable to verify their reports.

15. Any analysis comparing women's position in preindustrial and industrial settings must proceed with caution. Until very recently, young women in this age group (eighteen to twenty-four) would already have been married and have had children because of arranged marriages at an early age. An increase in both self-selection of spouses and age at marriage has created an unprecedented life-cycle state of single late adolescence and early adulthood still at home.

16. Seven workers—22 percent—spent more than all accessible income, ranging from 55 rupiah to 15,000 rupiah ($25.00). Twenty-five workers had some money left over from their total accessible income, ranging from a few rupiah to substantial sums, particularly for those who came into a large arisan.

17. The union conducts a monthly market survey to determine the costs of basic needs, including food, household goods, clothes, and transportation. A single worker in Jakarta during the month of the income-expenditures survey would have needed 36,000 rupiah to subsist. This figure included 10,000 rupiah

for rent. The cost of renting a room in the research site was 3,000 rupiah, and workers usually shared a room, thus reducing rent. Some of the food prices may have been higher in Jakarta than in Central Java. As mentioned in chapter 6, an official at the Department of Labor estimated that a single worker would need about 24,250 rupiah a month in Central Java to cover subsistence needs—140 percent more than the average wage of women workers. A household survey by the Union concluded that wages were not sufficient in Central Java to meet basic needs (FBSI 1982). A recent study concluded that the legal minimum wage in Jakarta is still 46 percent below the official minimum needs standard (INGI 1991a, 5). A 1989 study cited in the same article showed that 73 percent of the factories in North Jakarta, many of them textile firms, pay below the legal minimum wage. My guess is that conditions are even worse in the rural site where I conducted my research.

9. MARRIAGE

1. In 1987, one of the largest clove cigarette producers in Indonesia, with headquarters in East Java, began building a large factory in this site (personal communication, Ratna Saptari, Aug. 1987).

2. One worker and one nonfactory worker had moved and joined their husbands' families. I was able to interview one of these workers when she returned, as well as both of their families. One entire family with two working daughters had sold everything and migrated to a nearby town. I was able to interview one of these two workers when she returned to the village, but not her parents. These young women returned to the village for the annual village harvest celebration (*bersih desa*), which occurred during my stay.

3. I reinterviewed thirty-three women and their families who had constituted my previous categories of factory and nonfactory workers. I visited each family several times during a six-week period. Time constraints, coupled with my interest in following one group of women through their life course, prevented me from surveying all factory workers in Nuwun in 1986.

4. This research was coordinated by the East-West Population Institute and one institute in each of the four countries researched: Indonesia, Thailand, Pakistan, and the Philippines.

5. These figures are contradicted by a village study in the early 1970s in which Singarimbun and Manning (1974) show that there is little evidence of a trend toward later marriage. They do not, however, break down age at marriage by cohort. They do show that younger cohorts have increasingly more control over their marital decisions and that age at marriage is higher when individuals choose their own spouse.

6. Two women were involved in consensual unions, or what the Javanese call *kumpul kebo*; nevertheless, this sort of union is counted as a marriage by the Javanese and therefore by me. One was the divorcee, who was twenty-eight and childless, and the other lived with her widowed and very poor mother. Because of poverty, the latter woman's family could have ill afforded a wedding. She probably had low expectations for a partner because of her background and therefore tolerated extremely bad behavior from her partner.

7. This figure excludes the two women who married for the second time.

8. The average age at marriage in arranged marriages is exactly the average age at marriage that Peter Smith found in rural areas using the 1976 census.

9. In referring to her older brother, Rujimah used the term *kakak*, which could be an older brother or sister or any other relative, such as a cousin, in that generation.

10. Rujimah ran away without asking permission to leave, which is considered impolite. Those who leave home because of family conflict do not ask permission to leave and are making a strong statement in doing so. Conflict is not dealt with openly, but in this type of passive-aggressive manner.

11. Delaying the divorce gave the child his father's name and made him legitimate. The baby was born during a shadow-puppet performance during the village harvest celebration. As is the tradition when a birth occurs during a *wayang* performance, the newborn baby was brought outside to the *dalang* (puppeteer), who stopped the performance to bless and name the child, thereby becoming a sort of godfather to the child. In light of the circumstances—that the young mother would divorce after giving birth and would have to depend on her poor, landless parents—many villagers wept at this touching and sad moment.

12. It is not coincidental that most of the factory workers whose parents arranged their marriage worked in the noodle factory. That particular factory hired girls below the minimum legal working age and with educational levels lower than those required by other factories. They also paid a lower wage, knowing that workers would not dare protest. Some workers moved to other factories when they were old enough. As a group, workers in that factory were younger, shier, and more easily intimidated. They did not dress or act like other factory workers; for instance, they did not buy make-up or go to movies.

13. Ngatmi stated that she lived with these relatives for nine years, but that figure may well be an overestimate.

10. THE FAMILY ECONOMY REVISITED

1. One of these women, Sukirah, had continued to work after her maternity leave while her young child was at home in the care of one of Sukirah's younger siblings. The child spilled boiling water on himself and died. When Sukirah's third child was born the following year, she decided to stay home and care for the child herself.

2. One woman was single, but the remaining eight were either married or in consensual unions. Six of the nine remaining factory workers were mothers, one was pregnant, and one was unable to conceive. Four mothers had one child each, and only two had two children.

3. Of the four married workers, two had had children.

4. Hildred Geertz states that a newly married couple may live with the wife's parents for a year or two after marriage to ensure that the marriage seems relatively permanent or to give the couple time to acquire the resources to move into their own house (1961, 31). However, one of my informants, a middle-aged villager in Nuwun, thought that young couples today spend an average of about five years living with the wife's parents until they move into their own house. My

informant felt it was easier and quicker for young couples today to set up homes because of increased access to wage employment. That access shifted again in 1986, when the government cut the development budget and many rural waged jobs.

5. One married, childless, nonfactory woman said that she had never sought factory work although she wanted to because she had heard that factories required six years of education, which was double the amount of schooling she had. She remained outside the industrial labor force because of misinformation rather than choice.

6. Chicken farm owners had reversed their earlier policy (meant to prevent stealing through local networks) of not employing local residents. In 1982, the chicken farms employed several young men from other villages, but by 1984, they had begun employing young men and women from Nuwun.

7. The exchange rate in 1986 was approximately 1,100 rupiah for $1.00 U.S. The wages here are averages. Those working in the noodle factory, for example, received below minimum wage, but workers had no recourse because they were below the minimum legal age for factory employment.

8. The latter group includes (1) those who quit factory jobs during the three-month probation period and had little experience in the factories, (2) poultry farm workers, and (3) others who remained at home or worked in the rice fields. When economic data are analyzed, current workers are distinguished from former workers.

9. Employees in the factories located in the research site earned about 45 percent less than did Suryani; in addition, they had to subtract commuting costs from their salaries. Suryani had originally worked in the local garment factory, but a manager had been lured away to this smaller, urban firm, and he in turn brought some workers with him. After my departure in July 1986, Suryani wrote that the small factory had closed down; after a short period of unemployment, she went back to work in the garment factory in the site, for a much lower wage.

10. In 1982, when Suryani had earned considerably less, she gave her parents the same proportion of her salary: about one-quarter.

11. One woman was the head of the household and lived with her mother and two children in extremely poor conditions. She and her partner were in a consensual union, but he contributed little to her household. A second worker who lived with her widowed mother and her daughter was still married, but her husband was working in Saudi Arabia. He sent home considerable savings, but while he was away, she was the acting head of household and took care of daily household needs.

12. Time constraints prevented me from checking the origin or whereabouts of each individual item with the family.

CONCLUSION

1. Dublin offers several explanations for this difference: (1) the nature of the family economy in rural New England was different from that in Europe, with the former demanding less of a daughter's economic subordination; (2) New England daughters were geographically distant from their families; and (3) parents

in New England seemed not to have demanded a portion of daughters' earnings (1979, 40–41).

2. In some cases, as explained in chapter 10, family members appear to have secretly taken some cash; such thefts were attributed to tuyuls.

3. By contrast, a sociobiologically oriented former colleague of mine, Pierre van den Berghe, argues that the entire case study represents a reproductive strategy, permitting factory daughters to marry better spouses.

4. As mentioned above, the studies on Taiwan from which I drew my information do not differentiate between mothers and fathers pushing daughters into factory employment. The qualitative data quoted in various books and articles suggest that both parents engage in deciding a daughter's employment; however, it may very well be that one parent is more involved than the other.

5. As Carmen Diana Deere notes in her article on feminist contributions to peasant studies (1991), such critiques have not been integrated into household models.

Likewise, rural research has not yet adequately addressed extrahousehold "solidarity groups" that serve as important sources of economic assistance and support and can shape the nature of domestic conflict as well as extradomestic processes. For example, Gillian Hart (1991) found that poor rural women's labor gangs not only function as a unit of production but, in the process, shift certain internal household relations between poor husbands and wives; they also reflect and affect agrarian change and changes in agrarian class relations. Friendship networks constitute another unexplored arena beyond kinship or the household (Hirtz 1991) that can shape internal domestic conflicts as well as local economic processes.

APPENDIX

1. See the section "Class Status in Nuwun" in chapter 4 for an explanation of how possessions were counted and valued.

2. The logit model develops from "the assumption that the probability of the dependent variable equaling one is: $1 / (1 + \exp(-xi\ \mathrm{B}))$, where *xi* is the vector of independent variables for the *i*th observation and B denotes the vector of regression parameters (Berman 1984, 252).

3. *Children ever-born* includes all children born, regardless of whether or not they survive.

Glossary of Indonesian and Javanese Words

adat	Custom, tradition
anak, anak-anak	Child, children
ani-ani	Small, razorlike knife used by women to harvest rice
arisan	Savings association that works like a fixed lottery
baik, baik-baik	Good, nice, fine
Bapak	Father, protector; form of address to older man
bawon	Share of the harvest (Javanese)
bengkok	Land given to village civil servants in lieu of a salary
berani	Assertive, courageous
berat	Heavy
biasa	To be used to, usual, common
Carik	Village secretary
cocok	To fit, to be fitted, to be suited, to agree, to jibe, to match
cukup(an)	Enough
dukuh	Hamlet; see *pedukuan*
dukun	Healer, shaman
gadis tua	Spinster, old maid
gamelan	Javanese gong orchestra
halus	Refined, cultured, delicate
hormat	Honor, respect
Ibu	Mother, married woman; form of address to older woman or woman in higher position
Idul Fitri	Feast at the end of the fasting month of Ramadan; also called Lebaran
kaget	Startled, frightened, taken aback
kakak	Older sibling; also, form of address for older person, usually a relative such as a cousin
kasar	Coarse, rough, rude

kebaya	Woman's blouse
kedokaan	Practice in which people work on someone else's plot of land and postpone their pay until the harvest to ensure an invitation to the harvest
keluarga	Family
kelurahan	Village; administrative region that includes several *pedukuan*
kumpul kebo	Consensual union; literally, "marriage between water buffaloes"
kurang	Less, not enough, lack
kursi tamu	Guest chairs
Lebaran	Day ending the fasting period of Ramadan; also called Idul Fitri
Lurah	Village leader, head of the *kelurahan*
malu	Shy, retiring
Mbak	Older sister; form of address to older sister and older woman (Javanese)
minta ijin	To ask permission
nglor-ngidul	Going north and south; used to describe a situation in which a young couple live separately at their respective parents' houses and occasionally sleep together (Javanese)
pabrik	Factory
pedukuan	Hamlet; part of a *kelurahan*
penebas	A contractor who purchases a crop still in the fields for *tebasan*
petani	Farmer
Pribumi	Native, indigenous; applied to native Indonesians to distinguish them from Chinese Indonesians
rajin	Diligent
Ramadan	Islamic fasting month; ninth month of the Arabic calendar
roti	Bread
rugi	Loss
rukun	In harmony
rumah tangga	Household
sarong	Piece of cloth that is wrapped around the lower part of the body, much like a long skirt; traditional dress of Javanese women
sawah	Wet rice field
somah	Household (Javanese)
susah	Difficult, hard
takut	Afraid
tani	Farmer
tebasan	A practice in which a contractor buys up the rice wholesale, on the fields, before harvest and then hires labor gangs to harvest it
tegal	Dry, unirrigated land
tuyul	A childlike spirit, much like the Western European gremlin, that steals money for wealthy people
warung	Small stall where food or other goods are sold

Bibliography

Abdullah, Tahrunnessa, and Sondra A. Zeidenstein. 1982. *Village Women of Bangladesh*. Oxford: Pergamon.

Abelson, Elaine, David Abraham, and Marjory Murphy. 1989. "Interview with Joan Scott." *Radical History Review* 45:41–59.

Adioetomo, Sri Moertiningsih. 1987. "Determinants of Marriage Timing." Paper presented to the International Union for the Scientific Study of Population (IUSSP) and East-West Population Institute Conference, East-West Center, Honolulu.

Adiwinata, Nen. 1988. "Family Planning Program and Nutrition Improvement Efforts among Workers' Families in PT Perkebunan XII: Experiences of a Director's Wife: 1964–1980." Paper presented at Women as Mediators in Indonesia. International Workshop on Indonesian Studies No. 3, Royal Institute of Linguistics and Anthropology, Leiden, The Netherlands.

Agarwal, Bina. 1991. "Social Security and the Family: Coping with the Seasonality and Calamity in Rural India." In *Social Security in Developing Countries*, edited by E. Ahmad, J. Drèze, J. Hills, and A. Sen, 171–244. Oxford: Clarendon.

———, ed. 1988. *Structures of Patriarchy: The State, the Community, and the Household*. London: Zed.

Alexander, Jennifer. 1987. *Trade, Traders, and Trading in Rural Java*. Singapore: Oxford University Press.

Alisjahbana, S. Takdir. 1961. *Indonesia in the Modern World*. Bombay: Congress for Cultural Freedom.

Amsden, Alice. 1989. *Asia's Next Giant: South Korea and Late Industrialization*. New York: Oxford University Press.

Anderson, Benedict R. 1983. "Old State, New Society: Indonesia's New Order in Comparative Historical Perspective." *Journal of Asian Studies* 42, no. 3: 477–96.

———. 1972. "The Idea of Power in Javanese Culture." In *Culture and Politics in Indonesia,* edited by C. Holt, 1–69. Ithaca: Cornell University Press.

Anderson, K., Susan Armitage, Dana Jack, and Judith Wittner. 1990. "Beginning Where We Are: Feminist Methods in Oral History." In *Feminist Research Methods,* edited by J. McCarl Nielson, 94–114. Boulder: Westview.

Arizpe, Lourdes. 1982. "Relay Migration and the Survival of the Peasant Household." In *Towards a Political Economy of Urbanization in Third World Countries,* edited by Helen I. Safa, 19–46. Delhi: Oxford University Press.

Arrigo, Linda Gail. 1980. "The Industrial Work Force of Young Women in Taiwan." *Bulletin of Concerned Asian Scholars* 12, no. 2:25–38.

Atkinson, Jane Monnig, and Shelley Errington, eds. 1990. *Power and Difference: Gender in Island Southeast Asia.* Stanford: Stanford University Press.

Balai Asian Journal. 1981. "Women in Asia." 2, no. 4 (special issue).

Bartlett, Peggy. 1989. "Industrial Agriculture." In *Economic Anthropology,* edited by S. Plattner, 253–91. Stanford: Stanford University Press.

Becker, Gary. 1986. "The Economic Approach to Human Behavior." In *Rational Choice,* edited by J. Elster, 108–22. New York: New York University Press.

———. 1981. *A Treatise on the Family.* Cambridge: Harvard University Press.

Behar, Ruth. 1990. "Rage and Redemption: The Life Story of a Mexican Marketing Woman." *Feminist Studies* 16, no. 2:223–58.

Benería, Lourdes. 1982. "Accounting for Women's Work." In *Women and Development: The Sexual Division of Labor in Rural Societies,* edited by Lourdes Benería, 119–42. New York: Praeger.

Benería, Lourdes, and Martha Roldán. 1987. *The Crossroads of Class and Gender.* Chicago: University of Chicago Press.

Benería, Lourdes, and Gita Sen. 1981. "Accumulation, Reproduction, and Women's Role in Economic Development: Boserup Revisited." *SIGNS* 7, no. 2:279–98.

Ben-Porath, Yoram. 1982. "Economics and the Family—Match or Mismatch." *Journal of Economic Literature* 20:52–64.

Berger, John. 1987. *Once in Europa.* New York: Pantheon Books, Random.

———. 1967. *A Fortunate Man.* New York: Pantheon Books, Random.

Berk, Sarah F. 1985. *The Gender Factory.* New York: Plenum Press.

Berkner, Lutz, and Franklin Mendels. 1978. "Inheritance Systems, Family Structure, and Demographic Patterns in Western Europe, 1700–1900." In *Historical Studies in Changing Fertility,* edited by C. Tilly, 209–23. Princeton: Princeton University Press.

Berman, Peter. 1984. "Equity and Cost in the Organization of Primary Health Care in Java, Indonesia." Ph.D. diss., Cornell University.

Bishop, Y., S. Fienberg, and P. Holland. 1975. *Discrete Multivariate Analysis: Theory and Practice.* Cambridge: MIT Press.

Blumberg, R. 1984. "A General Theory of Gender Stratification." In *Sociological Theory,* edited by Randall Collins, 83–101. San Francisco: Jossey-Bass.

Boeke, J. H. 1953. *Economics and Economic Policy of Dual Societies as Exemplified by Indonesia.* Haarlem: H. D. Tjeenk Willink and Zoon N.V.

Booth, Anne. 1988. *Agricultural Development in Indonesia.* Sydney: Allen and Unwin.

Branson, Jan, and Don Miller. 1988. "The Changing Fortunes of Balinese Market Women." In *Development and Displacement: Women in Southeast Asia*, edited by G. Chandler, N. Sullivan, and J. Branson, 1–15. Monash, Australia: Monash University.

Braverman, Harry. 1974. *Labor and Monopoly Capital.* New York: Monthly Review Press.

Bruce, Judith, and Daisy Dwyer. 1988. "Introduction." In *A Home Divided: Women and Income in the Third World*, edited by Daisy Dwyer and Judith Bruce, 1–19. Stanford: Stanford University Press.

Burawoy, Michael. 1979. *Manufacturing Consent.* Chicago: University of Chicago Press.

Cain, Mead. 1984. *Women's Status and Fertility in Developing Countries: Son Preference and Economic Security.* World Bank Staff Working Papers No. 682. Washington D.C.: World Bank.

Caldwell, John C. 1982. *The Theory of Fertility Decline.* London: Academic Press.

Carney, Judith, and Michael Watts. 1991. "Disciplining Women? Rice, Modernization, and the Evolution of Mandinka Gender Relations in Senegambia." *SIGNS* 16, no. 4:651–81.

———. 1990. "Manufacturing Dissent: Work, Gender, and the Politics of Meaning in a Peasant Society." *Africa* 60, no. 2:208–41.

Chafetz, J. 1980. "Toward a Macrolevel Theory of Sexual Stratification and Gender Differentiation." In *Current Perspectives in Social Theory I*, edited by S. McNall and G. Howe, 103–25. Greenwich, Conn.: JAI.

Chapkis, Wendy, and Cynthia Enloe, eds. 1983. *Of Common Cloth: Women in the Global Textile Industry.* Washington D.C.: Transnational Institute.

Charlton, Sue Ellen. 1984. *Women in Third World Development.* Boulder: Westview.

Chayanov, A. [1923] 1966. *The Theory of Peasant Economy.* Edited by D. Thorner, B. Kerblay, and R. Smith. Homewood, Ill.: American Economic Association.

Cheal, David. 1989. "Strategies of Resource Management in Household Economies: Moral Economy or Political Economy?" In *The Household Economy*, edited by Richard Wilk, 11–22. Boulder: Westview.

Chernichovsky, Dov, and Oey Astra Meesook. 1984. *Poverty in Indonesia.* World Bank Staff Working Papers No. 671. Washington, D.C.: World Bank.

Christopherson, Susan M. 1982. "Family and Class in the New Industrial City." Ph.D. diss., University of California, Berkeley.

Clapham, M. 1970. "Some Difficulties of Foreign Investors in Indonesia." *Bulletin of Indonesian Economic Studies* 6, no. 1:73–80.

Clay, Daniel, and Harry Schwarzweller. 1991. "Introduction: Researching Household Strategies." In *Household Survival Strategies, Research in Rural Sociology and Development*, vol. 5, edited by Clay and Schwarzweller, 1–10. Greenwich, Conn.: JAI.

Cohen, Miriam. 1982. "Changing Educational Strategies among Immigrant Generations: New York Italians in Comparative Perspective." *Journal of Social History* 15:443–46.

Collier, W., et al. 1982. "Acceleration of Rural Development in Java." *Bulletin of Indonesian Economic Studies* 28, no. 3:84–101.

Collier, W., and Soentoro. 1978. "Rural Development and the Decline of Traditional Village Welfare Institutions in Java." Paper presented at the Western Economics Association Conference, Honolulu.

Collier, W., Gunawan Wiradi, and Soentoro. 1973. "Recent Changes in Rice Harvesting Methods." *Bulletin of Indonesian Economic Studies* 9, no. 2: 36–45.

Critchfield, Richard. 1983. *Villages.* Garden City, N.Y.: Anchor Press, Doubleday.

Crouch, Harold. 1978. *The Army and Politics in Indonesia.* Ithaca: Cornell University Press.

Daroesman, R. 1981. "Survey of Recent Developments." *Bulletin of Indonesian Economic Studies* 17, no. 2:1–41.

Davidson, Andrew. 1991. "Rethinking Household Livelihood Strategies." In *Household Survival Strategies, Research in Rural Sociology and Development,* vol. 5, edited by D. Clay and H. Schwarzweller, 11–28. Greenwich, Conn.: JAI.

Deere, Carmen Diana. Forthcoming. "What Difference Does Gender Make? Feminist Contributions to Peasant Studies." In *Women and Third World Agriculture,* edited by S. Afonja. London: Macmillan.

———. 1990. *Household and Class Relations: Peasants and Landlords in Northern Peru.* Berkeley and Los Angeles: University of California Press.

Deere, Carmen Diana, and Alain de Janvry. 1979. "A Conceptual Framework for the Empirical Analysis of Peasants." *American Journal of Agricultural Economics* 61, no. 4:601–11.

de Janvry, Alain. 1987. "Peasants, Capitalism, and the State in Latin American Culture." In *Peasants and Peasant Societies,* edited by T. Shamin, 319–404. London: Basil Blackwell.

Dewey, A. 1962. *Peasant Marketing in Java.* New York: Free Press of Glencoe.

Diamond, Norma. 1979. "Women and Industry in Taiwan." *Modern China* 5:317–40.

Di Stefano, Christine. 1990. "Rethinking Autonomy." Paper presented at the annual meeting of the American Political Science Association, San Francisco.

Djajadiningrat-Nieuwenhuis, Madelon. 1987. "Ibuism and Priyayization: Path to Power?" In *Indonesian Women in Focus,* edited by E. Locher-Scholten and A. Niehof, 43–51. Dordrecht, Holland: Foris.

Dublin, Thomas. 1979. *Women at Work.* New York: Columbia University Press.

Edmonston, Barry, William Greene, and Ken Smith. 1981. "Multivariate Analysis of Survival Data: An Appraisal Using Bangladeshi Mortality Data." In *Proceedings of the American Statistical Association,* 251–55. Washington, D.C.: American Statistical Association.

Eisenstein, Zillah. 1989. "Rejecting 'Precise' Marxism for Feminism." *Rethinking Marxism* 2, no. 4:79–81.

Ellis, Frank. 1988. *Peasant Economics.* Cambridge: Cambridge University Press.

Elson, Diane, ed. 1991. *Male Bias in the Development Process.* Manchester: Manchester University Press.

Elson, Diane, and Ruth Pearson. 1981. "Nimble Fingers Make Cheap Workers: An Analysis of Women's Employment in Third World Export Manufacturing." *Feminist Review* 4:87–107.

Errington, Shelly. 1990. "Recasting Sex, Gender, and Power: A Theoretical and Regional Overview." In *Power and Difference,* edited by J. Atkinson and S. Errington, 1–58. Stanford: Stanford University Press.

Etzioni, Amitai. 1988. *The Moral Dimension: Towards a New Economics.* New York: Free Press.

Evans, Jeremy. 1984. "Definition and Structure of the Household in Urban Java: Findings of a Household Census in Suburban Surakarta." *Urban Anthropology* 13, nos. 2–3:145–96.

Evers, Hans-Dieter, Wolfgang Clauss, and Diana Wong. 1984. "Subsistence Reproduction: A Framework for Analysis." In *Households and the World Economy,* edited by Joan Smith, Immanuel Wallerstein, and Hans-Dieter Evers. 23–36. Beverly Hills: Sage.

Fantasia, Rick. 1988. *Cultures of Solidarity: Consciousness, Action, and Contemporary American Workers.* Berkeley and Los Angeles: University of California Press.

Fapohunda, Eleanor. 1988. "The Nonpooling Household: A Challenge to Theory." In *A Home Divided: Women and Income in the Third World,* edited by Daisy Dwyer and Judith Bruce, 143–54. Stanford: Stanford University Press.

FBSI (Federasi Buruh Seluruh Indonesia). 1982. *Bulletin LITBANG* No. 13.

Fernández-Kelly, Maria Patricia. 1983. "Mexican Border Industrialization, Female Labor Force Participation, and Migration." In *Women, Men, and the International Division of Labor,* edited by June Nash and Maria Patricia Fernández-Kelly, 205–23. Albany: SUNY Press.

———. 1982. *For We Are Sold, I and My People: Women and Industry in Mexico's Frontier.* Albany: SUNY Press.

Findley, Sally. 1987. *Rural Development and Migration: A Study of Family Choices in the Philippines.* Boulder: Westview.

Folbre, Nancy. 1988. "Hearts and Spades: Paradigms of Household Economics." In *A Home Divided: Women and Income in the Third World,* edited by Daisy Dwyer and Judith Bruce, 248–62. Stanford: Stanford University Press.

———. 1986. "Cleaning House: New Perspectives on Households and Economic Development." *Journal of Development Economics* 22:5–40.

Folbre, Nancy, and Heidi Hartmann. 1989. "The Persistence of Patriarchal Capitalism." *Rethinking Marxism* 2, no. 4:90–96.

Fraad, Harriet, Stephen Resnick, and Richard Wolff. 1989. "For Every Knight in Shining Armor, There's a Castle to Be Cleaned: A Marxist-Feminist Analysis of the Household." *Rethinking Marxism* 2, no. 4:10–69.

Franke, R. 1972. "The Green Revolution in a Javanese Village." Ph.D. diss., Harvard University.

Freedman, Ronald, Ming-cheng Chang, and Te-hsiung Sun. 1982. "Household Composition, Extended Kinship, and Reproduction in Taiwan: 1973–1980." *Population Studies* 36:395–411.

Friedman, Kathie. 1984. "Households as Income-Pooling Units." In *Households and the World Economy,* edited by Joan Smith, Immanuel Wallerstein, and Hans-Dieter Evers, 37–55. Beverly Hills: Sage.

Froebel, Folker, Jürgen Heinrichs, and Otto Kreye. 1981. *The New International Division of Labour.* Cambridge: Cambridge University Press.

Fuentes, Annette, and Barbara Ehrenreich. 1983. *Women in the Global Factory.* Institute for New Communications Pamphlet no. 2. Boston: South End.

Gadjah Mada University, Christian Student's Organization. 1976. "Lead Us Not to Imitation; Lead Us Not to Temptation." Yogyakarta, Indonesia. Mimeo.

Garnaut, R. G., and P. T. McCawley. 1980. *Indonesia: Dualism, Growth, and Poverty.* Canberra: Australian National University.

Gates, Hill. 1987. *Chinese Working Class Lives: Getting By in Taiwan.* Ithaca: Cornell University Press.

Geertz, Clifford. 1984. "Culture and Social Change: The Indonesian Case." *Man* 19:511–32.

———. 1963. *Agricultural Involution: The Processes of Ecological Change in Indonesia.* Berkeley and Los Angeles: University of California Press.

———. 1960. *The Religion of Java.* New York: Free Press of Glencoe.

———. 1956. *The Development of the Javanese Economy: A Socio-Cultural Approach.* Cambridge: Center for International Studies.

Geertz, Hildred. 1961. *The Javanese Family.* New York: Free Press of Glencoe.

Giddens, Anthony. 1984. *The Constitution of Society.* Berkeley and Los Angeles: University of California Press.

———. 1979. *Central Problems in Social Theory.* Berkeley and Los Angeles: University of California Press.

Gillis, Malcolm. 1983. "Episodes in Indonesian Economic Growth." Paper presented at the Conference on World Economic Growth, Mexico.

Gladwin, Christina. 1989. "On the Division of Labor Between Economists and Economic Anthropology." In *Economic Anthropology,* edited by S. Plattner, 397–425. Stanford: Stanford University Press.

Glassburner, B., ed. 1971. *The Economy of Indonesia.* Ithaca: Cornell University Press.

Gluck, Sherna Berger, and Daphne Patai, eds. 1991. *Women's Words: The Feminist Practice of Oral History.* New York: Routledge, Chapman and Hall.

Goderbauer, Hans. 1987. "New Order Industrial Relations: Managing the Workers." *Inside Indonesia* 13:15–16.

Goldschmidt, W. and E. Kunkel. 1971. "The Structure of the Peasant Family." *American Anthropologist* 3, no. 5:1058–76.

Goode, William J. 1963. *World Revolution and Family Patterns.* New York: Free Press.

Greenhalgh, Susan. 1985. "Sexual Stratification: The Other Side of 'Growth with Equity' in East Asia." *Population and Development Review* 11, no. 2:265–314.

Grossman, Rachel. 1979. "Women's Place in the Integrated Circuit." *Southeast Asia Chronicle* 66:2–17.

Guest, Philip. 1989. *Labor Allocation and Rural Development: Migration in Four Javanese Villages.* Boulder: Westview.

Gupta, Akhil. 1987. "The Choice of Technique and Theories of Practice." Jackson School of International Studies, University of Washington. Typescript.

Guyer, Jane. 1988. "Dynamic Approaches to Domestic Budgeting: Cases and Methods from Africa." In *A Home Divided: Women and Income in the Third World,* edited by Daisy Dwyer and Judith Bruce, 155–72. Stanford: Stanford University Press.

Guyer, Jane, and Pauline Peters, eds. 1987. "Special Issue: Conceptualizing the Household." *Development and Change* 18, no. 2.

Hareven, Tamara. 1982. *Family Time and Industrial Time.* New York: Cambridge University Press.

Hart, Gillian. Forthcoming. "Imagined Unities: Constructions of 'The Household' in Economic Theory." In *Understanding Economic Process,* edited by S. Ortiz. Lanham, Md.: University Press of America.

———. 1991. "Engendering Everyday Resistance: Gender Patronage and Production Politics in Rural Malaysia." *Journal of Peasant Studies* 19, no. 1:93–121.

———. 1986a. "Exclusionary Labour Arrangements: Interpreting Evidence on Employment Trends in Rural Java." *Journal of Development Studies* 22, no. 4:681–96.

———. 1986b. *Power, Labor, and Livelihood: Processes of Change in Rural Java.* Berkeley and Los Angeles: University of California Press.

———. 1978. "Labor Allocation Strategies in Rural Javanese Households." Ph.D. diss., Cornell University.

Hart, Gillian, Andrew Turton, and Benjamin White, eds. 1989. *Agrarian Transformations: Local Processes and the State in Southeast Asia.* Berkeley and Los Angeles: University of California Press.

Hartmann, Heidi. 1981. "The Family as the Locus of Gender, Class, and Political Struggle." *SIGNS* 6, no. 3:366–94.

Hayami, Y., and M. Kikuchi. 1982. *Asian Village Economy at the Crossroads: An Economic Approach to Institutional Change.* Baltimore: Johns Hopkins University Press.

Hetler, Carol. 1984. "Female-Headed Households in Indonesia." Paper presented at the IUSSP Seminar on Micro-Approaches to Demographic Research, Australian National University, Canberra.

Hill, Hal. 1988. *Foreign Investment and Industrialization in Indonesia.* Singapore: Oxford University Press.

———. 1987. "Concentration in Indonesian Manufacturing." *BIES* 23, no. 2: 71–110.

———. 1984. "Survey of Recent Developments." *Bulletin of Indonesian Economic Studies* 20, no. 2:1–37.

Hirtz, Frank. 1991. "State, Family, and Social Welfare: Some Notes on the Philippine Experience." *Social Development Issues* 4, in press.

Honig, Emily. 1986. *Sisters and Strangers: Women in the Shanghai Cotton Mills, 1919–1949.* Stanford: Stanford University Press.

Hsiung, Ping-chun. 1988. "Family Structure and Fertility in Taiwan." *Journal of Population Studies* 11:103–28.

Huang, P. 1985. *The Peasant Economy and Social Change in North China.* Stanford: Stanford University Press.

Hugo, Graeme J. 1983. "Population Mobility and Wealth Transfers in Indonesia and Other Third World Societies." East-West Population Institute Paper No. 87. East-West Center, Honolulu.

———. 1975. "Population Mobility in West Java, Indonesia." Ph.D. diss., Australian National University, Canberra.

Hugo, Graeme J., Terence Hull, Valerie Hull, and Gavin Jones, eds. 1987. *The Demographic Dimension in Indonesian Development.* Singapore: Oxford University Press.

Hull, Terence. 1975. "Each Child Brings Its Own Fortune." Ph.D. diss., Australian National University.

Hull, Terence, S. Adioetomo, and Valerie Hull. 1984. "Ages at Marriage and Cohabitation in Java." Research Note No. 32, International Population Dynamics Program, Australian National University, Canberra.

Hull, Terence, and Valerie Hull. 1987. "Changing Marriage Behavior in Java: The Role of Timing and Consummation." *Southeast Asian Journal of Social Science* 15, no. 1:104–19.

Hull, Valerie. 1975. "Fertility, Socioeconomic Status, and the Position of Women in a Javanese Village." Ph.D. diss., Australian National University, Canberra.

Husken, Frans. 1984. "Capitalism and Agrarian Differentiation in a Javanese Village." *Masyarakat Indonesia* 11:121–36.

Husken, Frans, and Benjamin White. 1989. "Java: Social Differentiation, Food Production, and Agrarian Control." In *Agrarian Transformations, Local Processes and the State in Southeast Asia,* edited by Gillian Hart, Andrew Turton, and Benjamin White, 235–68. Berkeley and Los Angeles: University of California Press.

INDOC. 1983. *Indonesian Workers and Their Right to Organize: Update.* Leiden, The Netherlands: Indonesian Documentation Center.

———. 1981. *Indonesian Workers and Their Right to Organize.* Leiden, The Netherlands: Indonesian Documentation Center.

Indonesia, Central Bureau of Statistics for the Province of Central Java. 1981. *Central Java in Figures, 1981* (Jawa Tengah Dalam Angka, 1981). Semarang: Central Bureau of Statistics.

Indonesia, Consulate General. 1983. *Business Prospects in Indonesia Today.* Vol. 13. Hong Kong: Indonesian Consulate General.

Indonesia, Office of Statistics for the Regency of Semarang. 1981. *The Regency of Semarang in Figures, 1980.* Semarang: Office of Statistics.

INGI (International NGO [Nongovernmental Organization] Forum on Indonesia Labour Working Group). 1991a. "Button Up, Button Down!" *Inside Indonesia,* no. 27:5–6.

———. 1991b. "Labour Rights and Wrongs: The Right to Organise." *Inside Indonesia,* no. 27:2–4.

———. 1991c. "Unjust But Doing It! Nike Operations in Indonesia." *Inside Indonesia,* no. 27:7–9.

Jay, Robert. 1969. *Javanese Villagers.* Cambridge: MIT Press.

Jones, Christine. 1986. "Intra-household Bargaining in Response to the Introduction of New Crops: A Case Study from North Cameroon." In *Understanding Africa's Rural Households and Farming Systems,* edited by J. Moock, 105–23. Boulder: Westview.

Jones, Gavin. 1987. "Labour Force and Labour Utilization." In *The Demographic Dimension in Indonesian Development,* edited by Graeme Hugo, Terence Hull, Valerie Hull, and Gavin Jones, 244–97. Singapore: Oxford University Press.

———. 1984. "Links Between Urbanization and Sectoral Shifts in Employment in Java." *Bulletin of Indonesian Economic Studies* 20, no. 3:120–37.

Kandiyoti, Deniz. 1988. "Bargaining with Patriarchy." *Gender and Society* 2, no. 3:274–90.

Kartini, Raden Adjeng. 1964. *Letters of a Javanese Princess.* Trans. Agnes Louise Symmers. New York: Norton.

Katz, June S., and Ronald S. Katz. 1978. "Legislating Social Change in a Developing Country: The New Indonesian Marriage Law Revisited." *American Journal of Comparative Law* 26, no. 2:309–20.

Kim, Myung-hye. 1991. "Patriarchy, Family Structure, and Late Industrialization in Korea." Department of Anthropology, Ohio State University. Typescript.

Koentjaraningrat. 1985. *Javanese Culture.* Singapore: Oxford University Press.

———. 1967a. "A Survey of Social Studies of Rural Indonesia." In *Villages in Indonesia,* edited by Koentjaraningrat, 1–29. Ithaca: Cornell University Press.

———. 1967b. "Tjelapar: A Village in South Central Java." In *Villages in Indonesia,* edited by Koentjaraningrat, 244–80. Ithaca: Cornell University Press.

Kondo, Dorinne K. 1990. *Crafting Selves: Power, Gender, and Discourses of Identity in a Japanese Workplace.* Chicago: University of Chicago Press.

Kung, Lydia. 1983. *Factory Women in Taiwan.* Ann Arbor: University of Michigan Press.

———. 1981. "Perceptions of Work among Factory Women." In *The Anthropology of Taiwanese Society,* edited by E. M. Ahern and H. Gates, 184–211. Stanford: Stanford University Press.

Lamphere, Louise. 1987. *From Working Daughters to Working Mothers.* Ithaca: Cornell University Press.

Laslett, Peter. 1981. "The Family as a Knot of Individual Interests." In *Households,* edited by Robert McC. Netting, Richard Wilk, and Eric Arnould, 353–79. Berkeley and Los Angeles: University of California Press.

Legge, J. D. 1977. *Indonesia.* 2d ed. Sidney: Prentice-Hall of Australia.

Lenin, V. I. 1977. *The Development of Capitalism in Russia.* Vol. 3 of *Collected Works.* Moscow: Progress Publishers.

Lev, Daniel S. 1982. "Introduction." In *Interpreting Indonesian Politics: Thirteen Contributions to the Debate,* edited by B. Anderson and A. Kahin, v–viii. Cornell Modern Indonesia Project No. 62. Ithaca: Cornell University Press.

———. 1966. *The Transition to Guided Democracy: Indonesian Politics, 1957–59.* Ithaca: Cornell University, Southeast Asia Program, Modern Indonesia Project.

Lewis, Oscar. 1963. *The Children of Sanchez.* New York: Vintage Books, Random.

Lim, Linda. 1990. "Women's Work in Export Factories: The Politics of a Cause." In *Persistent Inequalities,* edited by I. Tinker, 101–22. New York: Oxford University Press.

———. 1983a. "Capitalism, Imperialism, and Patriarchy: The Dilemma of Third World Women Workers in Multinational Factories." In *Women, Men, and the International Division of Labor,* edited by June Nash and Maria Patricia Fernández-Kelly, 70–91. Albany: SUNY Press.

———. 1983b. "Multinational Export Factories and Women Workers in the

Third World: A Review of Theory and Evidence." In *Women and Work in the Third World: The Impact of Industrialization and Global Economic Interdependence,* compiled by Nagat M. El-Sanabary, 75–90. Berkeley: Center for the Study, Education, and Advancement of Women, University of California.

Lockwood, Victoria. 1989. "Tubuai Women Potato Planters and the Political Economy of Intra-Household Gender Relations." In *The Household Economy,* edited by Richard Wilk, 197–220. Boulder: Westview.

Loeb, Vernon. 1991. "Cheap Labor Draws Nike to Indonesia." *Sacramento Bee,* 29 Dec., H-1.

McCawley, Peter. 1984. "A Slowdown in Industrial Growth?" *Bulletin of Indonesian Studies* 20, no. 3:158–74.

———. 1981. "Growth of the Industrial Sector." In *The Indonesian Economy During the Soeharto Era,* edited by A. Booth and P. McCawley, 62–101. Kuala Lumpur: Oxford University Press.

———. 1979. *Industrialization in Indonesia: Developments and Prospects.* Development Studies Centre Occasional Paper No. 13. Canberra: Australian National University.

McDonald, Peter. n.d. "Issues in the Analysis of Javanese Marriage Patterns." Department of Demography, Australian National University. Mimeo.

———. 1983. "Social Change and Marriage Behavior in Indonesia." Paper presented at the Conference on Marriage Determinants and Consequences, Pattaya, Thailand.

McElroy, M., and M. Horney. 1981. "Nash Bargained Household Decisions: Toward a Generalization of the Theory of Demand." *International Economic Review* 22:333–50.

McGee, Terry. 1984. "Urban Growth in Indonesia: Its Challenge to Environmental Policy." Paper presented at the Indonesia-Canada Environment Conference, Mont Saint-Marie, Quebec.

Mackie, Jamie. 1980. "The Concept of Dualism and Its Application to Indonesian Agriculture." In *Indonesia: Dualism, Growth and Poverty,* edited by R. G. Garnaut and P. T. McCawley, 295–306. Canberra: Australian National University.

Mackie, Jamie, and Sjahrir. 1989. "Survey of Recent Developments." *BIES* 25, no. 3:3–35.

Manderson, Lenore, ed. 1983. *Women's Work and Women's Roles: Economics and Everyday Life in Indonesia, Malaysia, and Singapore.* Development Studies Monograph 32. Canberra: Australian National University.

Mani, Lata. 1989. "Contentious Traditions: The Debate on *Sati* in Colonial India, 1780–1833." Ph.D. diss., University of California, Santa Cruz.

Manning, Chris. 1988. "Rural Employment Creation in Java." *Population and Development Review* 14, no. 1:47–80.

———. 1979. "Wage Differentials and Labour Market Segmentation in Indonesian Manufacturing." Ph.D. diss., Australian National University, Canberra.

Manser, M., and M. Brown. 1980. "Marriage and Household Decision-Making: A Bargaining Analysis." *International Economic Review* 21:31–44.

Martokoesoemo, Budi S. 1979. "Marriage and Divorce in Indonesia." Ph.D. diss., University of Chicago.

Mason, Karen Oppenheim. 1984. *The Status of Women: A Review of Its Relationship to Fertility and Mortality.* New York: Rockefeller Foundation.

Mather, Celia. 1985. "Rather Than Make Trouble, It's Better Just to Leave." In *Women, Work, and Ideology in the Third World,* edited by H. Afshar, 153–77. New York: Tavistock.

———. 1982. *Industrialization in the Tangerang Regency of West Java: Women Workers and the Islamic Patriarchy.* Working Paper No. 17. Amsterdam: Center for Sociology and Anthropology, University of Amsterdam.

Medick, Hans. 1976. "The Proto-Industrial Family Economy: The Structure and Function of Household and Family During the Transition from Peasant Society to Industrial Capitalism." *Social History* 3:291–315.

Meyer, Paul. 1988. "Economic Change in Southeast Asia: The Shifts from the Agricultural Sector to the Industrial Sectors." Paper presented at the conference of the Northwest Regional Consortium for Southeast Asian Studies, Eugene, Ore.

———. 1981. "The Value of Children in the Context of the Family in Java." Ph.D. diss., Australian National University.

Michaelson, E. J., and Walter Goldschmidt. 1971. "Female Roles and Male Dominance among Peasants." *Southwestern Journal of Anthropology* 27, no. 4:330–52.

Mohanty, Chandra. 1988. "Under Western Eyes: Feminist Scholarship and Colonial Discourses." *Feminist Review* 30:61–88.

Montgomery, R. D., and D. G. Sisler. 1976. *Labor Absorption in Jogyakarta, Indonesia: An Input-Output Study.* Agricultural Economics Staff Paper No. 75-10. Ithaca: Cornell University.

Moore, Henrietta L. 1988. *Feminism and Anthropology.* Minneapolis: University of Minnesota Press.

Morris, Lydia. 1990. *The Workings of the Household.* Cambridge: Polity Press.

Mubyarto. 1984. "Social and Economic Justice." *Bulletin of Indonesian Economic Studies* 20, no. 3:36–54.

Nash, June, and Maria Patricia Fernández-Kelly, eds. 1983. *Women, Men, and the International Division of Labor.* Albany: SUNY Press.

Nash, Manning. 1967. *Machine Age Maya: The Industrialization of a Guatemalan Community.* Chicago: University of Chicago Press.

Netting, Robert McC., Richard Wilk, and Eric Arnould. 1984. "Introduction." In *Households,* edited by Netting, Wilk, and Arnould, xiii–xxxviii. Berkeley and Los Angeles: University of California Press.

Niehoff, Justin. 1987. "The Villagers as Industrialists: Ideologies of Household Factories in Rural Taiwan." *Modern China* 13, no. 3:286–307.

Nielsen, Joyce McCarl, ed. 1990. *Feminist Research Methods: Exemplary Readings in the Social Sciences.* Boulder: Westview.

Ong, Aihwa. 1991. "The Gender and Labor Politics of Postmodernity." *Annual Review of Anthropology* 20:279–309.

———. 1988. "Colonialism and Modernity: Feminist Re-Presentations of Women in Non-Western Societies." *Inscriptions* 3, no. 4:79–93.

———. 1987. *Spirits of Resistance and Capitalist Discipline: Factory Women in Malaysia.* Albany: SUNY Press.

Pahl, R. E. 1984. *Divisions of Labour.* Oxford: Basil Blackwell.
Palmer, Ingrid. 1977. *The New Rice in Indonesia.* Geneva: United Nations Research Institute for Social Development.
Pangestu, Mari, and Manggi Habir. 1990. "Survey of Recent Developments." *BIES* 26, no. 1:3–40.
Papanek, Gus, ed. 1980. *The Indonesian Economy.* New York: Praeger.
Papanek, Hannah. 1990. "To Each Less Than She Needs, From Each More Than She Can Do." In *Persistent Inequalities,* edited by I. Tinker, 162–81. New York: Oxford University Press.
———. 1983. "Implications of Development for Women in Indonesia: Research and Policy Issues." In *Women in Developing Countries: A Policy Focus,* edited by K. Staudt and J. Jaquette, 66–87. New York: Haworth.
———. 1975. "Marriage, Divorce, and Marriage Law Reform in Indonesia." Paper presented at the Workshop on the Role and Status of Women in Contemporary Muslim Societies, Harvard University.
Papanek, Hannah, and Laurel Schwede. 1988. "Women Are Good with Money: Earnings and Managing in an Indonesian City." In *A Home Divided: Women and Income in the Third World,* edited by Daisy Dwyer and Judith Bruce, 71–98. Stanford: Stanford University Press.
Patai, Daphne. 1991. "U.S. Academics and Third World Women: Is Ethical Research Possible?" In *Women's Words: The Feminist Practice of Oral History,* edited by Sherna Berger Gluck and Daphne Patai, 137–53. New York: Routledge, Chapman and Hall.
———. 1988. "Constructing a Self: A Brazilian Life Story." *Feminist Studies* 14:143–66.
Penny, D., and Masri Singarimbun. 1973. *Population and Poverty in Rural Java: Some Economic Arithmetic from Sriharjo.* Cornell International Agricultural Development Monograph No. 41. Ithaca: Cornell University.
Phongpaichit, Pasuk. 1988. "Two Roads to the Factory: Industrialization Strategies and Women's Employment in Southeast Asia." In *Structures of Patriarchy,* edited by Bina Agarwal, 151–63. London: Zed.
Popkin, Samuel. 1979. *The Rational Peasant.* Berkeley and Los Angeles: University of California Press.
Poston, Dudley. 1988. "Childlessness Patterns in Taiwan." *Journal of Population Studies* 11:55–78.
Pyle, David. 1985. "East Java Family Planning, Nutrition, and Income Generation Project." In *Gender Roles in Development Projects,* edited by Catherine Overholt, Mary Anderson, Kathleen Cloud, and James Austin, 135–62. West Hartford, Conn.: Kumarian.
Reid, Anthony. 1988. "Female Roles in Pre-Colonial Southeast Asia." *Modern Asia Studies* 22, no. 3:629–45.
Ricklefs, M. C. 1981. *A History of Modern Indonesia: Circa 1300 to the Present.* Bloomington: Indiana University Press.
Robinson, Kathy. 1988. "What Kind of Freedom Is Cutting Your Hair?" In *Development and Displacement: Women in Southeast Asia,* edited by G. Chandler, N. Sullivan, and J. Branson, 63–77. Victoria, Australia: Morphet Press.
———. 1988. *Stepchildren of Progress: The Political Economy of Development in an Indonesian Mining Town.* Albany: SUNY Press.

Robison, Richard. 1986. *Indonesia: The Rise of Capital.* Sydney: Allen and Unwin.

Roldán, Martha. 1984. "Industrial Homework, Reproduction of Working Class Families, and Gender Subordination." In *Beyond Employment: Household, Gender, and Subsistence,* edited by N. Redclift and E. Mingione, 248–85. Oxford: Basil Blackwell.

Rosenzweig, M., and R. P. Schultz. 1982. "Market Opportunities, Genetic Endowments, and Intrafamily Resource Distribution." *American Economic Review* 72:803–15.

Rouse, Roger. 1989. "Migration and the Politics of Family Life: Divergent Projects and Rhetorical Strategies in a Mexican Transnational Migrant Community." Department of Anthropology, University of Michigan. Typescript.

Rutz, Henry. 1989. "Fijian Household Practices and the Reproduction of Class." In *The Household Economy,* edited by Richard Wilk, 119–48. Boulder: Westview.

Saefullah, Asep Djadja. 1979. "The Value of Children among Tea Estate Workers' Families: A Case Study in a Village of West Java, Indonesia." Master's thesis, Australian National University, Canberra.

Safa, Helen I. 1990. "Women and Industrialization in the Caribbean." In *Women, Employment, and the Family in the International Division of Labor,* edited by Sharon Stichter and Jane L. Parpart, 72–97. Philadelphia: Temple University Press.

———. 1983. "Women, Production, and Reproduction in Industrial Capitalism: A Comparison of Brazilian and U.S. Factory Workers." In *Women, Men, and the International Division of Labor,* edited by June Nash and Maria Patricia Fernández-Kelly, 95–116. Albany: SUNY Press.

Safilios-Rothschild, Constantina. 1982. "Female Power, Autonomy, and Demographic Change in the Third World." In *Women's Roles and Population Trends in the Third World,* edited by R. Anker, M. Buvinic, and N. Youssef, 117–32. London: Croom Helm.

Saith, Ashwani. 1991. "Asian Rural Industrialization: Context, Features, Strategies." In *Rural Transformation in Asia,* edited by J. Breman and S. Mundle, 458–89. Delhi: Oxford University Press.

Salaff, Janet. 1990. "Women, the Family, and the State: Hong Kong, Taiwan, and Singapore—Newly Industrialized Countries in Asia." In *Women, Employment, and the Family in the International Division of Labor,* edited by Sharon Stichter and Jane L. Parpart, 98–136. Philadelphia: Temple University Press.

———. 1981. *Working Daughters of Hong Kong.* New York: Cambridge University Press.

Sayogyo. 1977. "Garis Kemiskinan dan Kebutuhan Minimum Pangan" (The poverty line and minimum food needs). Bogor Agricultural University, Bogor, Indonesia. Mimeo.

———. 1974. "Usaha Perbaikan Gizi Keluarga" (Family nutrition improvement program). Bogor Agricultural University, Bogor, Indonesia. Mimeo.

Scherer, P. 1982. "Survey of Recent Developments." *Bulletin of Indonesian Economic Studies* 17, no. 2:1–35.

Schlegel, Alice, ed. 1977. *Sexual Stratification: A Cross-Cultural View.* New York: Columbia University Press.

Schroeder, Richard, and Michael Watts. 1991. "Struggling over Strategies, Fighting over Food: Adjusting to Food Commercialization among Mandinka Peasants." In *Household Survival Strategies, Research in Rural Sociology and Development,* vol. 5, edited by D. Clay and H. Schwarzweller, 45–72. Greenwich, Conn.: JAI.

Scott, Alison MacEwen. 1990. "Patterns of Patriarchy in the Peruvian Working Class." In *Women, Employment, and the Family in the International Division of Labor,* edited by Sharon Stichter and Jane L. Parpart, 198–220. Philadelphia: Temple University Press.

———. 1986. "Women and Industrialization: Examining the 'Female Marginalisation' Thesis." *Journal of Development Studies* 22, no. 3:649–80.

Scott, James. 1985. *Weapons of the Weak.* New Haven: Yale University Press.

Scott, Joan. 1988. *Gender and the Politics of History.* New York: Columbia University Press.

Selby, Henry, and Arthur Murphy. 1982. *The Mexican Urban Household and the Decision to Migrate to the United States.* Philadelphia: Institute for the Study of Human Issues.

Selby, Henry, Arthur Murphy, and Stephen Lorenzen, with Ignacio Cabrera, Aida Castenada, and Ignacio Ruiz-Love. 1990. *The Mexican Urban Household.* Austin: University of Texas Press.

Sen, Amartya. 1990. "Gender and Cooperative Conflicts." In *Persistent Inequalities,* edited by I. Tinker, 123–49. New York: Oxford University Press.

Sendauer, Benjamin. 1990. "The Impact of the Value of Women's Time on Food and Nutrition." In *Persistent Inequalities,* edited by I. Tinker, 150–61. New York: Oxford University Press.

Shaver, Frances, and Bill Reimer. 1991. "Economy and Household: The Gender Based Division of Labor on Quebec Farms." In *Household Survival Strategies, Research in Rural Sociology and Development,* vol. 5, edited by D. Clay and H. Schwarzweller, 131–47. Greenwich, Conn.: JAI.

Sheridan, Mary, and Janet Salaff. 1984. *Lives: Chinese Working Women.* Bloomington: Indiana University Press.

Shorter, Edward. 1977. *The Making of the Modern Family.* New York: Basic.

Singarimbun, Masri, and Chris Manning. 1974. "Marriage and Divorce in Mojolama." *Indonesia* 17:67–82.

Smith, Joan. 1984. "Nonwage Labor and Subsistence." In *Households and the World Economy,* edited by Joan Smith, Immanuel Wallerstein, and Hans-Dieter Evers, 64–89. Beverly Hills: Sage.

Smith, Joan, Immanuel Wallerstein, and Hans-Dieter Evers, eds. 1984. *Households and the World Economy.* Beverly Hills: Sage.

Smith, Peter. 1981. "Contrasting Marriage Patterns and Fertility in Southeast Asia." East-West Population Institute Working Paper No. 8, East-West Center, Honolulu.

Smyth, Ines. 1991. "A Critical Look at the Indonesian Government's Policies for Women." Paper presented at the symposium Poverty and Development in Indonesia, The Netherlands Foreign Ministry, The Hague.

———. 1986. "Ideology and Practice of Marriage in West Java." Institute of Social Studies, The Hague. Typescript.

Soewondo, Nani. 1977. "Law and the Status of Women in Indonesia." In *Law and the Status of Women*, edited by the Columbia Human Rights Law Review, 123–40. New York: United Nations.

Sorensen, Clark. 1988. *Over the Mountains Are Mountains: Korean Peasant Households and Their Adaptations to Rural Industrialization.* Seattle: University of Washington Press.

Spencer, Robert F. 1988. *Yogong: Factory Girl.* Seoul: Royal Asiatic Society, Korea Branch.

Stacey, Judith. 1991. "Can There Be a Feminist Ethnography?" In *Women's Words: The Feminist Practice of Oral History,* edited by S. B. Gluck and D. Patai, 111–19. New York: Routledge, Chapman and Hall.

———. 1990. *Brave New Families: Stories of Domestic Upheaval in Late Twentieth Century America.* New York: Basic.

Steinberg, David Joel, ed. 1987. *In Search of Southeast Asia: A Modern History.* Honolulu: University of Hawaii Press.

Stern, Mark J. 1987. *Society and Family Strategy.* Albany: SUNY Press.

Stichter, Sharon, and Jane L. Parpart, eds. 1990. *Women, Employment, and the Family in the International Division of Labor.* Philadelphia: Temple University Press.

Stites, Richard. 1985. "Industrial Work as an Entrepreneurial Strategy." *Modern China* 11, no. 2:227–46.

Stoler, Ann. 1978. "Garden Use and Household Economy in Rural Java." *Bulletin of Indonesian Economic Studies* 14, no. 2:85–101.

———. 1977a. "Class Structure and Female Autonomy in Rural Java." In *Women and National Development,* edited by the Wellesley Editorial Committee, 74–89. Chicago: University of Chicago Press.

———. 1977b. "Rice Harvesting in Kali Loro." *American Ethnologist* 4, no. 4: 678–98.

Sundrum, R. M. 1975. "Manufacturing Employment 1961–1971." *Bulletin of Indonesian Economic Studies* 11, no. 1:58–65.

Suryakusama, Julia. 1988. "PKK: The Formalization of the Informal Power of Women." Paper presented at Women as Mediators in Indonesia. International Workshop on Indonesian Studies No. 3, Royal Institute of Linguistics and Anthropology, Leiden, The Netherlands.

Susilastuti, Dewi Haryani. 1991. "Home-Based Workers in a Garment Industry: Evidence from a Central Javanese Village, Indonesia." Master's thesis, Florida State University, Tallahassee.

Sutoro, Ann. n.d. "The Effects of Industrialization on Women Workers in Indonesia." Ford Foundation, Jakarta, Indonesia. Mimeo.

Tempo. 1985. "Yang Sedih, Yang Cerah Setelah PHK." No. 30, 15:12–17.

———. 1982. "Mereka Tidur di Atas Tekstil." No. 42, 12:82–86.

Tentler, Leslie Woodcock. 1975. *Wage-Earning Women: Industrial Work and Family Life in the United States, 1900–1930.* New York: Oxford University Press.

Thompson, E. P. 1963. *The Making of the English Working Class.* New York: Vintage Books, Random.

Thorne, Barrie, and Marilyn Yalom. 1982. *Rethinking the Family.* New York: Longman.

Thornton, Arland, Ming-cheng Chang, and Te-hsiung Sun. 1984. "Social and Economic Change, Intergenerational Relationships, and the Transition to Adulthood in Taiwan." *Demography* 21, no. 4:475–99.

Tilly, Louise A. 1979. "Individual Lives and Family Strategies in the French Proletariat." *Journal of Family History* 4:137–52.

———. 1978. *Women and Family Strategies in French Proletarian Families.* Department of History, Michigan Occasional Paper No. 4. Ann Arbor: University of Michigan.

Tilly, Louise A., and Joan W. Scott. 1978. *Women, Work, and Family.* New York: Holt, Rinehart and Winston.

Todd, Emmanuel. 1985. *The Explanation of Ideology: Family Structures and Social Systems.* New York: Basil Blackwell.

Topley, Marjorie. 1975. "Marriage Resistance in Rural Kwangtung." In *Women in Chinese Society,* edited by Margery Wolf and Roxane Witke, 67–88. Stanford: Stanford University Press.

Trager, Lillian. 1981. "Rural-Urban Linkages and Migration: A Philippines Case Study." In *Southeast Asia: Women, Changing Social Structure and Cultural Continuity,* edited by G. Hainsworth, 84–119. Ottawa: University of Ottawa Press.

Tsurumi, E. Patricia. 1990. *Factory Girls: Women in the Thread Mills of Meiji Japan.* Princeton: Princeton University Press.

UNCTAD (United Nations Conference on Trade and Development). 1982. *Handbook of International Trade and Development Statistics, Supplement 1981.* New York: United Nations.

UNIDO (United Nations Industrial Development Organization). 1980. *Women in the Redeployment of Manufacturing Industry to Developing Countries.* Working Papers on Structural Change No. 18. New York: UNIDO.

Wallerstein, Immanuel. 1984. "Household Structures and Labor Force Formation in the Capitalist World Economy." In *Households and the World Economy,* edited by Joan Smith, Immanuel Wallerstein, and Hans-Dieter Evers, 7–22. Beverly Hills: Sage.

Weismantle, M. J. 1989. "Making Breakfast and Raising Babies: The Zumbagua Household as Constituted Process" In *The Household Economy,* edited by Richard Wilk, 55–72. Boulder: Westview.

Weix, Gretchen G. 1990. "Following the Family/Firm: Patronage and Piecework in a Kudus Cigarette Factory." Ph.D. diss., Cornell University.

Wertheim, W. F. 1964. *Indonesian Society in Transition: A Study of Social Change.* The Hague: W. van Hoeve.

White, Benjamin. 1989. "Problems in the Analysis of Agrarian Differentiation." In *Agrarian Transformations, Local Processes, and the State in Southeast Asia,* edited by Gillian Hart, Andrew Turton, and Benjamin White, 15–30. Berkeley and Los Angeles: University of California Press.

———. 1983. " 'Agricultural Involution' and Its Critics: Twenty Years After." *Bulletin of Concerned Asian Scholars* 15, no. 2:18–31.

———. 1980. "Rural Household Studies in Anthropological Perspective." In *Rural Household Studies in Asia,* edited by H. P. Binswanger, R. E. Evenson, C. A. Florencio, and B. N. F. White, 1–25. Singapore: Singapore University Press.

———. 1979. "Political Aspects of Poverty, Income Distribution, and Their Measurement: Some Examples from Rural Java." *Development and Change* 10, no. 1:91–114.

———. 1976. "Production and Reproduction in a Javanese Village." Ph.D. diss., Columbia University.

White, Benjamin, and E. L. Hastuti. 1980. *Different and Unequal: Male and Female Influence in Household and Community Affairs in Two West Javanese Villages.* AgroEconomic Survey and Bogor Agricultural University, Bogor, Indonesia.

White, Benjamin, and Gunawan Wiradi. 1989. "Agrarian and Non-Agrarian Bases of Inequality in Nine Javanese Villages." In *Agrarian Transformations, Local Processes, and the State in Southeast Asia,* edited by Gillian Hart, Andrew Turton, and Benjamin White, 266–302. Berkeley and Los Angeles: University of California Press.

Whitehead, Ann. 1981. " 'I'm Hungry Mum': The Politics of Domestic Budgeting." In *Marriage and the Market,* edited by K. Young, C. Wolkowitz, and R. McCullagh, 88–111. London: Methuen.

Whyte, William F. 1984. *Learning from the Field.* Beverly Hills: Sage.

Wieringa, Saskia. 1988. "GERWANI and the PKK: Brokers on Behalf of Whom?" Paper presented at Women as Mediators in Indonesia. International Workshop on Indonesian Studies No. 3, Royal Institute of Linguistics and Anthropology, Leiden, The Netherlands.

———. 1981. "And Everywhere She Leaves Traces of Blood Behind: The Ideology of Batik Labour in Central Java." Mimeo. Translation of "En overal laat zij bloedsporen achter. Macht, sekse en klasse in die batikindustrie in Midden Java." *Socialisties-Feministiese Teksten* (Amsterdam), vol. 5.

Wilk, Richard. 1989. "Decision Making and Resource Flows Within the Household: Beyond the Black Box." In *The Household Economy,* edited by Richard Wilk, 23–52. Boulder: Westview.

Wilk, Richard, and Robert McC. Netting. 1984. "Households: Changing Forms and Functions." In *Households: Comparative and Historical Studies of the Domestic Group,* edited by Robert McC. Netting, Richard Wilk, and Eric Arnould, 1–28. Berkeley and Los Angeles: University of California Press.

Williams, Linda. 1990. *Development, Demography, and Family Decision-Making.* Boulder: Westview.

Willner, Anne Ruth. 1961. "From Rice Field to Factory: The Industrialization of a Rural Labour Force in Java." Ph.D. diss., University of Chicago.

Wolf, Diane L. 1990. "Daughters, Decisions, and Domination: An Empirical and Conceptual Critique of Household Strategies." *Development and Change* 21:43–74.

———. 1988. "Female Autonomy, the Family, and Industrialization in Java." *Journal of Family Issues* 9, no. 1:85–107.

———. 1984. "Making the Bread and Bringing It Home: Female Factory Workers and the Family Economy in Rural Java." In *Women in the Urban and Industrial Workforce,* edited by Gavin Jones, 215–31. Development Studies Center Monograph No. 33. Canberra: Australian National University Press.

Wolf, Margery. 1972. *Women and the Family in Rural Taiwan.* Stanford: Stanford University Press.

Wolff, R., and S. Resnick. 1986. "Power, Property, and Class." *Socialist Review* 16, no. 2:97–124.

Wong, Diana. 1984. "The Limits of Using the Household as a Unit of Analysis." In *Households and the World Economy,* edited by Joan Smith, Immanuel Wallerstein, and Hans-Dieter Evers, 56–63. Beverly Hills: Sage.

"Workers' Rights: Getting the Worst of the Deal." 1987. *Inside Indonesia,* no. 13:18–19.

World Bank. 1985. *Indonesia: Policies for Growth and Employment.* Report No. 5597-IND. Washington, D.C.: World Bank.

Yamin, Nani. 1988. "Indonesian Women as Mediators." Paper presented at Women as Mediators in Indonesia. International Workshop on Indonesian Studies No. 3, Royal Institute of Linguistics and Anthropology, Leiden, The Netherlands.

Yanagisako, Sylvia J., and Jane F. Collier. 1987. *Gender and Kinship: Essays Toward a Unified Analysis.* Stanford: Stanford University Press.

Youssef, Nadia. 1982. "The Interrelationship Between the Division of Labor in the Household, Women's Roles, and Their Impact on Fertility." In *Women's Roles and Population Trends in the Third World,* edited by R. Anker, Mayra Buvinic, and Nadia Youssef, 173–201. London: Croom Helm.

Youssef, Nadia, and C. Hetler. 1983. "Establishing the Economic Condition of Woman-Headed Households in the Third World: A New Approach." In *Women and Poverty in the Third World,* edited by M. Buvinic, M. Lycette, and William Greevey, 216–44. Baltimore: Johns Hopkins University Press.

Index

Compositor: Impressions
Text: 10/13 Sabon
Display: Sabon
Printer: Edwards Brothers, Inc.
Binder: Edwards Brothers, Inc.